"This volume serves as an excellent introduction to the old earth/young earth debate. Dr. Van Dam argues for a plain reading of Genesis 1–2 and exposes the folly of rationalizing the creation miracle. The relevant portions of the original text are examined with the precision of an Old Testament scholar but at a level of detail that remains accessible to the layperson. The work of other scholars who have opined on the Genesis account of creation is reviewed, and the author's bias is duly acknowledged. The analysis is crisp, frank, and, most importantly, pastoral. Highly recommended."

—Peter Buist, professor emeritus, Department of Chemistry, Carleton University

"This book on the proper interpretation of Genesis 1 and 2, as it relates to modern theories of Scripture interpretation and theories of evolution, is a very valuable resource for those who want to maintain a scriptural understanding of the origin of the universe and the creation of man. Dr. Van Dam rightly affirms that the Bible is not a science textbook and that the limits of science must be recognized. As Nobel Laureate Peter Medawar stated, 'It is simply beyond the competence of science to answer the question "How did everything begin?"' In this book, faith seeks understanding with a close reading of Genesis 1 and 2. Highly recommended."

—Richard Buist, retired research scientist, University of Manitoba

"Dr. Van Dam gives an excellent defense of the traditional reading of Genesis1 and 2. He tries to read the text on its own terms, informed by its use in the rest of Scripture, letting the exegetical chips fall where they may. It is a refreshing contrast to many Reformed commentators who have been unduly influenced by ancient Near Eastern literature or evolutionary science.

"This book gives well-grounded responses to various objections raised against the traditional view, good critiques of contrary interpretations, and many up-to-date references. I find it very readable, informative, and biblically sound. A worthwhile contribution to the current debate, also within Reformed churches, on origins. Heartily recommended."

—John Byl, professor emeritus, mathematical sciences, Trinity Western University

"If you want to get to the heart of the message of this book, you could say, 'In the beginning, there is truth.' In this in-depth investigation, Dr. C. Van Dam shows us that Holy Scripture opens with the revelation of facts. The first pages of Holy Scripture are in no way an oriental campfire fantasy or a human tale. In fact, the author convincingly argues that in Genesis 1 and 2 we have received the reliable account of how God brought the universe into being within a period of six days (qualified by evening and morning). It is no exaggeration that such an exposition about the origin of the world and about the historical Adam and Eve has probably ever been as necessary as it is today. This book definitely meets a big need!"

—Jürgen-Burkhard Klautke, dean, Academy of Reformed Theology (ART), Giessen, Germany

"The first chapters of the book of Genesis form the foundation of God's message for mankind. The last few years have witnessed more and more new interpretations of these chapters, with huge consequences for the church and its theology. Dr. Cornelis Van Dam has served the discussion well by thoroughly investigating these different visions and showing how they are in part based on current scientific notions of the origin of the cosmos and the human race. Those who want to honor the self-testimony of Genesis, however, have many good reasons to remain with the classic Christian understanding."

—Mart-Jan Paul, professor of Old Testament, Evangelical Theological Faculty, Leuven, Belgium

"This is an important book. Not only on Genesis 1 and 2 but also on the inevitable and crucial implications of the interpretation of these chapters for understanding the truth of Scripture as a whole, Van Dam succeeds admirably in meeting, in his own words, the 'need to listen very carefully to God's Word and conclude neither more nor less than what Scripture explicitly teaches.' Clearly written, carefully and thoroughly researched, fair in dealing with views he disagrees with, and balanced in his own conclusions on issues, a commendable strength as well is the pastoral tone present throughout. Particularly helpful are the treatment of the place of extrabiblical evidence in interpreting Scripture and numerous comments at various points on the relationship between Scripture and science. One need not agree with Van Dam at every point to be both instructed and edified, as I have been, by this valuable work."

—Richard B. Gaffin Jr., professor of biblical and systematic theology, emeritus, Westminster Theological Seminary

"With *In the Beginning* Cornelis Van Dam offers a thorough examination of recent developments among scholars who are desperately attempting to reconcile the account of creation in Genesis 1 and 2 with modern neo-Darwinist theory. Studiously avoiding technical jargon, Van Dam's treatment is thorough and readable. His critique aptly highlights the awkward interpretive biblical contortions attempted by those who wish to weld an uncomfortable and untenable bond between Christian belief in a biblical Creator and faith in biological evolutionary hypotheses. Though Van Dam focuses much of his attention on developments within Reformed churches, his book is worthwhile reading for any Christian who wishes to remain faithful to God's Word and avoid modern secularism and its unbiblical ethics as they attempt to creep into the church."

—Andrew E. Steinmann, distinguished professor of theology and
Hebrew, Concordia University Chicago

"A most welcome work! Van Dam's defense of the historicity of Genesis 1 and 2 is most of all humbly obedient to God and His Word—biblical in its hermeneutics, sound in its exegesis, up-to-date in its scholarship, and effective in its rebuttal of theistic evolution. Whether one seeks depth and relevance in the exegesis or a sophisticated yet accessible interaction with the multitude of nonliteral and nonhistorical theories around the biblical creation account, the work at hand provides this. In addition, Van Dam ably accounts for the ancient Near Eastern context of Israel while rightly arguing that such material is not normative for our interpretation of divine revelation. I found the emphasis on worldview and the chapter 'The Work of Creation and the Gospel' particularly helpful. I recommend this book heartily as a challenge for all to educate themselves in Scripture—some to rethink their positions and others to be bolstered in the confidence of faith."

—Theodore G. Van Raalte, professor of ecclesiology, Canadian
Reformed Theological Seminary

"The first two chapters of Genesis form the creation account as transmitted to us through the people of Israel. Nowadays it is customary to place this account side by side with creation myths of other nations and on that basis to speculate about the origin of heaven and earth, life, and humankind. It was a great relief for me that this particular book does justice to the biblical notion that God entrusted His Word to the people of Israel and to no other nation."

—Cornelis (Kees) Roos, emeritus professor of mathematics,
Delft University of Technology, Netherlands

"Do we need yet another book on the question of Bible and creation? Some will doubt it—but do not close the door too quickly! Professor Van Dam's dealing with many of the difficult issues around the Bible and creation is very much worth reading. His book offers a large number of illuminating, sober, and clear exegetical insights into Genesis 1 and 2 as well as many other related biblical passages. He relates these texts to scientific theories, especially the theory of evolution, in helpful ways, addressing also general methodological issues and reminding us of the limits of scientific knowledge in these matters.

His arguments for the historicity of Genesis 1 and 2 deserve serious attention. From an Old Testament perspective, Van Dam's remarks against an uncritical reading of extrabiblical ancient Near Eastern views into Genesis 1 and 2 are particularly important. I highly recommend this book, both for laypersons and scholars, including as a textbook for seminary courses."

—Markus Zehnder, professor of Old Testament and Semitic languages, Talbot School of Theology, California

"In this clearly written volume, Cornelis Van Dam defends a historical interpretation of Genesis 1 and 2 as an accurate account of the origin of the earth and the human race, using the language of normal human experience. He points out why the divine revelation found in these chapters cannot be reconciled with the theory of evolution. I recommend his book especially to all those who ponder such reconciliation, for it presents all the counterarguments on which they should reflect."

—Gert Kwakkel, professor of Old Testament, Theologische Universiteit Kampen, Netherlands; and Faculté Jean Calvin, Aix-en-Provence, France

"*In the Beginning* by Cornelis Van Dam is a brilliant defense of six-day creation. It is by far the most comprehensive work on this subject I have read. Van Dam carefully exegetes Genesis 1 and 2. Along the way he answers objections to the six-day view. He interacts gently but thoroughly with the various nonliteral approaches to these chapters and destroys the attempts to interpret Genesis 1 and 2 by Near Eastern cosmologies. He carefully interacts with theologians who assert theistic evolution, showing the futility and dangers of their approach. Moreover, the book is a treasure trove of bibliographic material (over sixty pages of bibliography). On top of all these things, Dr. Van Dam writes in a clear way so that readers, regardless of their theological or scientific background, may read it with profit."

—Joseph A. Pipa Jr., president emeritus, Greenville Presbyterian Theological Seminary

In the
BEGINNING

In the
BEGINNING
Listening to Genesis 1 and 2

Cornelis Van Dam

Reformation Heritage Books
Grand Rapids, Michigan

Reformation Heritage Books
3070 29th St. SE, Grand Rapids, MI 49512
616-977-0889 / orders@heritagebooks.org / www.heritagebooks.org

Printed in the United States of America
21 22 23 24 25 26/10 9 8 7 6 5 4 3 2 1

Library of Congress Cataloging-in-Publication Data

Names: Van Dam, Cornelis, 1946- author.
Title: In the beginning : listening to Genesis 1 and 2 / Cornelis Van Dam.
Description: Grand Rapids, Michigan : Reformation Heritage Books, [2020] | Includes bibliographical references and index.
Identifiers: LCCN 2020047624 (print) | LCCN 2020047625 (ebook) | ISBN 9781601788054 (cloth) | ISBN 9781601788061 (epub)
Subjects: LCSH: Creationism—Biblical teaching. | Creation—Biblical teaching. | Bible. Genesis, I-II—Criticism, interpretation, etc. | Bible and science. | History—Religious aspects—Christianity.
Classification: LCC BS651 .V27 2020 (print) | LCC BS651 (ebook) | DDC 231.7/65—dc23
LC record available at https://lccn.loc.gov/2020047624
LC ebook record available at https://lccn.loc.gov/2020047625

For additional Reformed literature, request a free book list from Reformation Heritage Books at the above regular or email address.

For Niek and Dinie Gootjes

Contents

Analytical Outline

Preface

This study was motivated in part by words allegedly spoken by Martin Luther:

> If I profess with the loudest voice and the clearest exposition every portion of the truth of God except precisely that little point that the world and the devil are at that moment attacking, I am not confessing Christ, however boldly I may be professing Christianity. Where the battle rages, the loyalty of the soldier is proved. To be steady on all the battlefield is mere flight and disgrace to him if he flinches at that one point.[1]

The meaning of the opening chapters of Scripture are very much a flash-point of contention within conservative Protestantism in North America as the theory of evolution is more and more promoted under the pressures of mainline science and its views of the origin of our world and its inhabitants. The topic of Genesis 1 and 2 is therefore very relevant, and I would like to join the conversation by carefully listening to the biblical text and interacting with the current discussion. The amount of published material on Genesis is enormous and not everything can be said within the confines of a single book. However, the footnotes often refer to related material, and thus this work can serve as a source for further study on the first chapters of Genesis.

To make the material as accessible as possible, the original languages of Scripture are used as little as possible. Transliterations and abbreviations are done according to *The SBL Handbook of Style*, 2nd ed. (Atlanta: SBL Press,

---

1. As associated with Luther in Elizabeth Rundle Charles, *Chronicles of the Schönberg-cotta Family* (New York: T. Nelson; Philadelphia: Lippincott, 1864), ii, 276; and, e.g., cited as a direct quote of Luther in Francis A. Schaeffer, *The Great Evangelical Disaster* (Wheaton, Ill.: Crossway, 1984), 50–51. This often repeated quote cannot be found in these exact words in the official edition of Luther's works, but something comparable is found in his letter to Albrecht, Count of Mansfeld, dated June 3, 1523, in *D. Martin Luthers Werke: Kritische Gesamtausgabe: Briefwechsel*, vol. 3, ed. Ulrich Köpf (1933; repr., Weimar: Böhlau, 2002), 81–82.

2014). Unless noted otherwise, Scripture quotations are from the New King James Version.

* * *

I am very grateful to the LORD God, the Creator and the Sustainer of everything, that this book on His revelation of heaven and earth's beginnings can see the light of day.

Friends in both theology and the sciences have been of help in reading over parts of the manuscript or its entirety and providing feedback. My thanks go to Peter Buist, Professor of Chemistry Emeritus, Carleton University; Richard Buist, former researcher in the Department of Radiology at the University of Manitoba; John Byl, Professor Emeritus of Mathematics at Trinity Western University; John Helder, former Director of the Muttart Conservatory and Principal of Horticulture for the City of Edmonton, Alberta; Margaret Helder, scientist and President of the Creation Science Association of Alberta; our son, S. Carl Van Dam, minister of the Word, Canadian Reformed Church of Carman East in Carman, Manitoba; and my colleague Theodore G. Van Raalte, Professor of Ecclesiology at the Canadian Reformed Theological Seminary. I would also like to express my gratitude to Margaret VanderVelde, Librarian at the seminary, for the help that she was always ready to give. And last but certainly not least, I record my great thankfulness for all the support my dear wife, Joanne, continues to give me.

A book on the early chapters of Genesis had originally been conceived as a joint project with Nicolaas (Niek) Gootjes, Professor of Dogmatology, at the Canadian Reformed Theological Seminary. But the Lord in His wisdom decided otherwise when my colleague became incapacitated with Alzheimer's disease, now already many years ago. He is still being cared for in a nursing home where his dear wife, Dinie, faithfully visits him. As a token of my great appreciation for my colleague and his wife I have dedicated this book to them.

Finally, I want to thank Reformation Heritage Books for their willingness to publish this study. It has been a great pleasure working with Jay Collier, Director of Publishing, and Andrew McGinnis, who copyedited this book. It has greatly benefited from his expertise.

May this publication be of service in promoting the glory of the Creator.

Abbreviations

Bible Translations

ASV	American Standard Version
CSB	Christian Standard Bible
DSV	Dutch Statenvertaling
ESV	English Standard Version
JB	Jerusalem Bible
JPS 1917	*Tanakh: The Holy Scriptures according to the Masoretic Text* (The Jewish Publication Society, 1917)
KJV	King James Version
LXX	Septuagint
NAB	New American Bible
NASB	New American Standard Bible (1995)
NEB	New English Bible
NET	New English Translation (The NET Bible)
NETS	*New English Translation of the Septuagint.* Edited by Albert Pietersma and Benjamin G. Wright. New York: Oxford University Press, 2007.
NIV	New International Version (both 1984 and 2011)
NIV (1984)	New International Version 1984
NIV (2011)	New International Version 2011
NJB	New Jerusalem Bible
NJPS	*Tanakh: The Holy Scriptures: The New JPS Translation according to the Traditional Hebrew Text.* 1985. Reprint, Philadelphia: The Jewish Publication Society, 1988.
NKJV	New King James Version
NRSV	New Revised Standard Version
REB	Revised English Bible
RSV	Revised Standard Version

TEV   Today's English Version (= Good News Bible)

Grammars and Dictionaries

BDAG   Frederik W. Danker, Walter Bauer, William F. Arndt, and F. Wilbur
           Gingrich. *Greek-English Lexicon of the New Testament and Other
           Early Christian Literature.* 3rd ed. Chicago: University of Chicago
           Press, 2000.

BDB   Francis Brown, S. R. Driver, and Charles A. Briggs. *A Hebrew and
           English Lexicon of the Old Testament.* Oxford: Clarendon, 1907.

DCH   *Dictionary of Classical Hebrew.* Edited by David J. A. Clines. 9 vols.
           Sheffield, U.K.: Sheffield Phoenix Press, 1993–2014.

GE   Franco Montanari. *The Brill Dictionary of Ancient Greek.* Edited by
           Madeleine Goh and Chad Schroeder. Leiden: Brill, 2015.

GKC   *Gensenius' Hebrew Grammar.* Edited by Emil Kautzsch. Translated
           by Archer E. Cowley. 2nd ed. Oxford: Clarendon, 1910.

HALOT   Ludwig Koehler, Walter Baumgartner, and Johann Stamm. *The
           Hebrew and Aramaic Lexicon of the Old Testament.* Translated and
           edited under the supervision of Mervyn E. J. Richardson. 2 vols.
           Leiden: Brill, 2001.

IBHS   Bruce K. Waltke and Michael O'Connor. *An Introduction to Biblical
           Hebrew Syntax.* Winona Lake, Ind.: Eisenbrauns, 1990.

Joüon   P. Joüon. *A Grammar of Biblical Hebrew.* Translated and revised
           by T. Muraoka. 2 vols. Subsidia biblica 14/1–2. Rome: Pontifical
           Biblical Institute, 1991.

LSJM   Henry George Liddell, Robert Scott, Henry Stuart Jones, and
           Roderick McKenzie. *A Greek-English Lexicon.* Oxford: Clarendon
           Press, 1996.

NIDOTTE   *New International Dictionary of Old Testament Theology and
           Exegesis.* Edited by Willem A. VanGemeren. 5 vols. Grand Rapids:
           Zondervan, 1997.

TDOT   *Theological Dictionary of the Old Testament.* Edited by G. Johannes
           Botterweck and Helmer Ringgren. Translated by John T. Willis et
           al. 15 vols. Grand Rapids: Eerdmans, 1974–2006.

TLOT   *Theological Lexicon of the Old Testament.* Edited by Ernst Jenni,
           with assistance from Claus Westermann. Translated by Mark E.
           Biddle. 3 vols. Peabody, Mass.: Hendrickson, 1997.

Other Abbreviations

ABD	*Anchor Bible Dictionary.* Edited by David Noel Freedman. 6 vols. New York: Doubleday, 1992.
ACCS	Ancient Christian Commentary on Scripture
AUSS	*Andrews University Seminary Studies*
BAR	*Biblical Archaeology Review*
BSac	*Bibliotheca Sacra*
BT	*The Bible Translator*
CBQ	*Catholic Biblical Quarterly*
CO	J. Calvin. *Joannis Calvini Opera quae supersunt omnia.* Edited by G. Baum, E. Cunitz, and E. Reuss. Corpus Reformatorum, vol. 29–87. Braunschweig: Schwetschke, 1863–1900.
COS	*The Context of Scripture.* Edited by William W. Hallo. 4 vols. Leiden: Brill, 1997–2017.
CRSQ	*Creation Research Society Quarterly*
CTA	*Corpus des tablettes en cunéiforms alphabétiques découvertes à Ras Shamra-Ugarit de 1929 à 1939.* Edited by Andrée Herdner. Paris: Geuthner, 1963.
CTJ	*Calvin Theological Journal*
DCS	*Dictionary of Christianity and Science.* Edited by Paul Copan, Tremper Longman III, Christopher L. Reese, and Michael G. Strauss. Grand Rapids: Zondervan, 2017.
EvQ	*Evangelical Quarterly*
ExAud	*Ex Auditu*
GTT	*Gereformeerd Theologisch Tijdschrift*
Int	*Interpretation*
JANES	*Journal of the Ancient Near Eastern Society of Columbia University*
JAOS	*Journal of the American Oriental Society*
JBL	*Journal of Biblical Literature*
JESOT	*Journal for the Evangelical Study of the Old Testament*
JETS	Journal of the Evangelical Theological Society
JHebS	*Journal of Hebrew Scriptures*
JR	*Journal of Religion*
JSOT	*Journal for the Study of the Old Testament*
JTS	*Journal of Theological Studies*
MT	Masoretic Text (of the Hebrew Bible)
OTA	*Old Testament Abstracts*
PhRef	*Philosophia Reformata*
Presb	*Presbyterion*

PSCF	*Perspectives on Science and Christian Faith*
PTR	*Princeton Theological Review*
RTR	*Reformed Theological Review*
S&CB	*Science and Christian Belief*
Targum	All references to the Targum, unless otherwise noted are to Alexander Sperber, *The Bible in Aramaic.* 5 vols. Leiden: Brill, 1992.
TJ	*Trinity Journal*
TynBul	*Tyndale Bulletin*
VT	*Vetus Testamentum*
WTJ	*Westminster Theological Journal*
ZAW	*Zeitschrift für die alttestamentliche Wissenschaft*

1

Introduction

Do the opening chapters of Genesis constitute real history or not? The prevailing academic consensus is that Genesis 1 and 2 are not recounting actual historical events. Yet, on the face of it, these chapters do appear to give an account of what happened when God created the world. What do we make of this conundrum?

Closely related to the issue of whether Genesis recounts actual history is the uncertainty and confusion about the origin of the human race that many Christians experience today. How did we get here? Does science or Scripture provide the true account of the beginning of the world in which we live? Or is this a false dilemma? Can Scripture be honored and understood to agree with current scientific hypotheses of human origins?

These are momentous questions and there appears to be a growing consensus among conservative interpreters of Scripture that we can accommodate our understanding of Scripture to the view of origins as given by current mainstream science, particularly in astronomy, geology, and evolutionary biology. Secular science excludes any intervention by God and attributes all development to the laws of nature and very long periods of time, but Christians who embrace today's regnant scientific theories speak of theistic evolution to indicate God's involvement in bringing creation to its present form.[1] Due to

---

1. It is difficult to give a brief definition of the theory of evolution. E.g., biologist Keith Stewart Thomson has shown that the word *evolution* is "used in at least three quite separate senses," namely, "the general sense of *change over time*," as a process ("*organisms are related by descent through common ancestry*"), and as "a particular *explanatory mechanism* for the pattern and process described in the first and second meanings" (italics in the original). Keith Stewart Thomson, "Marginalia: The Meanings of Evolution," *American Scientist* 70 (1982): 529–30. Also see Dennis R. Venema, "Evolution, Biological," in *DCS*, 226–28. For an analysis and critique following Thomson's article, see Stephen C. Meyer, "Scientific and Philosophical Introduction: Defining Theistic Evolution," in *Theistic Evolution: A Scientific, Philosophical, and Theological Critique*, ed. J. P. Moreland et al. (Wheaton, Ill.: Crossway, 2017), 33–49.

the pressures of the dominant scientific evolutionary hypotheses, influential evangelical, Reformed, and Presbyterian scholars who testify that they want to honor the authority of God's Word are no longer certain that they can accept the biblical account of Genesis 1 and 2 at face value. Consequently, different proposals for understanding these chapters have been made so that current mainstream science and the opening chapters of Scripture can somehow be harmonized, but the common result is that Genesis 1 and 2 cannot be accepted at face value as narrating historical events. What are we to think of this? How should we interpret the opening chapters of Scripture? How does science relate to explaining or understanding the biblical record of creation? These issues need to be addressed.

This introductory chapter will briefly illustrate the changing attitudes to Genesis 1 and 2, note the purpose of this study, outline its basic presuppositions, and touch on some current mainstream assumptions that have a profound influence on how the Bible is understood today.

Changing Attitudes to Genesis 1 and 2

Fueling much of the downplaying or denial of the literal historicity of the events reported in Genesis 1 and 2 is the enormous prestige enjoyed by science and its championing the theory of evolution as the most attractive explanation of how this present world and its inhabitants came to be. As a result the previous several decades have seen a remarkable momentum toward the acceptance of theistic evolution in theologically conservative circles. Several fairly recent high-profile cases illustrate how distinguished evangelical Old Testament scholars who were or still are respected for their generally conservative approach to Scripture have embraced theistic evolution and adjusted their understanding of Genesis accordingly.

Peter Enns, who taught at Westminster Theological Seminary from 1994 to 2008, accepted that it has been shown beyond reasonable scientific doubt that humans share common ancestry with primates. He consequently argued that "one can no longer accept, in any true sense of the word 'historical,' the instantaneous and special creation of humanity as described in Genesis."[2] The

---

2. Peter Enns, *The Evolution of Adam: What the Bible Does and Doesn't Say About Human Origins* (Grand Rapids: Brazos, 2012), xiv. Earlier, Enns had set out his views on Scripture in Peter Enns, *Inspiration and Incarnation: Evangelicals and the Problem of the Old Testament* (Grand Rapids: Baker Academic, 2005), which elicited considerable controversy. See, e.g., G. K. Beale, *The Erosion of Inerrancy in Evangelicalism: Responding to New Challenges to Biblical Authority* (Wheaton, Ill.: Crossway, 2008).

controversy surrounding his views eventually led to his departure from Westminster.[3] He now teaches at Eastern University in Pennsylvania.

During his long and illustrious career, Bruce Waltke served as professor at various conservative and Reformed seminaries, but he became controversial when he openly endorsed theistic evolution in a 2010 video in which he stated that "if the data is overwhelmingly in favor of evolution, to deny that reality will make us a cult." During the ensuing dispute, Waltke submitted his resignation from Reformed Theological Seminary at Orlando, a resignation which according to a news report was accepted because of Waltke's "mainline evolutionary views."[4] Waltke himself clarified that "I am incompetent to endorse evolution. My point is that the scientific consensus endorses it.... The Bible does not prescribe how God created the cosmos."[5] In Waltke's view there is room for the theory of theistic evolution because Genesis 1 is an ancient cosmology. How closely such a cosmology "coincides with the material reality cannot be known" since that genre "does not attempt to answer that question."[6]

The previous year, the same seminary had disinvited Tremper Longman III from further adjunct teaching due to his "questioning in a video whether Adam was a historical person." Longman, a prolific and popular author who has taught at Westminster Theological Seminary (1980–1998) and Westmont College, continues to defend theistic evolution. In his view, as articulated in a 2014 blog post, "there is a good case, especially based on the genetic evidence, that God used evolution. So I find myself affirming an evolutionary creationist perspective."[7] He is able to make such an affirmation since he considers Genesis 1–11 to be theological history that recounts real events through the use of figurative language for theological purposes.[8]

---

3. For the official "Joint Statement by WTS and Professor Enns" (July 22, 2008), as well as links to all related documents, see the Westminster Theological Seminary website at https://students.wts.edu/stayinformed/view.html?id=187; see also, Peter A. Lillback, "'The Infallible Rule of Interpretation of Scripture': The Hermeneutical Crisis and the Westminster Standards," in *Resurrection and Eschatology: Theology in Service of the Church. Essays in Honor of Richard B. Gaffin Jr.*, ed. Lane G. Tipton and Jeffrey C. Waddington (Phillipsburg, N.J.: P&R, 2008), 283–339.

4. Charles Honey, "Adamant on Adam," *Christianity Today* 54, no. 6 (June 2010): 14; also see, e.g., Bruce K. Waltke with Charles Yu, *An Old Testament Theology: An Exegetical, Canonical, and Thematic Approach* (Grand Rapids: Zondervan, 2007), 202–3.

5. In a letter to the editor, *Christianity Today* 54, no. 8 (August 2010): 43.

6. Waltke, *Old Testament Theology*, 202–3.

7. Tremper Longman III, "Tremper Longman Responds to Justin Taylor on the Historicity of Adam," *The Logos Academic Blog*, March 25, 2014, https://academic.logos.com/tremper-longman-responds-to-justin-taylor-on-the-historicity-of-adam/.

8. Tremper Longman III, "What Genesis 1–2 Teaches (and What It Doesn't)," in *Reading Genesis 1–2: An Evangelical Conversation*, ed. J. Daryl Charles (Peabody, Mass.: Hendrickson,

A final example is John H. Walton, who teaches at Wheaton College and is well known for his work on the first chapters of Genesis. In these books he stresses that Genesis 1 is an ancient cosmological text that can only be rightly understood through the lens of the ancient culture that generated this literature. Since he considers ancient cosmology to be function oriented, Genesis 1 is not about material origins. "To create something (cause it to exist) in the ancient world means to give it a function, not material properties."[9] Consequently, Genesis does not tell us how the world came to be and "therefore whatever explanation scientists may offer in their attempts to explain origins, we could theoretically adopt it as a description of God's handiwork." So, Walton is willing to go along with whatever mainstream science espouses about origins and at the moment that is the theory of evolution. "Whatever evolutionary processes may have taken place, we believe that God was intimately involved in them."[10]

Other prominent theologians have joined in supporting theistic evolution. A controversial but very influential British New Testament scholar, N. T. Wright, who is sometimes theologically very conservative, lent his support to Walton's work by contributing to the latter's book, *The Lost World of Adam and Eve*.[11] Another well-known figure, Timothy Keller, founding minister of Redeemer Presbyterian Church in New York City, sees little difficulty in accepting theistic evolution and has supported the work of BioLogos.[12]

The work of the BioLogos Foundation, an evangelical organization founded in 2007, is most noteworthy in this context. It aggressively promotes what it calls evolutionary creationism and enjoys the backing of prominent Old Testament scholars.[13] As part of its effort to convince people to accept the notion of evolutionary origins, it has published a book with the telling title,

---

2013), 103–12, 122; Tremper Longman III and John H. Walton, *The Lost World of the Flood: Mythology, Theology, and the Deluge Debate* (Downers Grove, Ill.: IVP Academic, 2018), 15–29, 91, 111.

9. John H. Walton, *The Lost World of Genesis One: Ancient Cosmology and the Origins Debate* (Downers Grove, Ill.: IVP Academic, 2009), 35.

10. Walton, *Lost World of Genesis One*, 132, 137. For an incisive critique of John Walton's approach, see Noel K. Weeks, "The Bible and the 'Universal' Ancient World: A Critique of John Walton," *WTJ* 78 (2016): 1–28.

11. John H. Walton, *The Lost World of Adam and Eve: Genesis 2–3 and the Human Origins Debate*, with a contribution by N. T. Wright (Downers Grove, Ill.: IVP Academic, 2015), 170–80.

12. Timothy Keller, *The Reason for God: Belief in an Age of Skepticism* (New York: Riverhead Books, 2008), 95–98; Tim Keller, "Creation, Evolution and Christian Laypeople" (The BioLogos Foundation, 2009), https://biologos.org/uploads/projects/Keller_white_paper.pdf.

13. See the BioLogos website for more details: https://biologos.org/.

How I Changed My Mind About Evolution.[14] In it, scientists, pastors, biblical scholars, and theologians tell how they have come to accept the theory of evolution and in their view still honor the authority of Scripture.

The current momentum among many conservative evangelical believers against taking the Genesis narrative at face value[15] is a dramatic change from the centuries-old general acceptance of the historical truthfulness and plain reading of this part of Scripture that prevailed in the early and medieval church as well as in the Reformation and post-Reformation eras. The Enlightenment challenged the literal reading of the biblical text, the repercussions of which are felt up to the present time.[16] An important indicator of the ongoing effects of the Enlightenment and developments in the natural sciences is the fact that popular annotated evangelical study Bibles are now ambivalent about whether Genesis presents a straightforward historical account of God's creative deeds. Instead, this subject is treated as one that is open to discussion and divergent views.

For example, both the *New Geneva Study Bible* and its successor, *The Reformation Study Bible*,[17] while mentioning the option of understanding the days of creation as real days, in their notes on Genesis 1:5 elaborate on other views, as can be expected in a study Bible, but without endorsing the plain reading of the text. The *ESV Study Bible* also mentions several options on how to understand the days of creation: as ordinary days, as geological ages, as analogous days, or as a literary device without a concern for temporal sequence.[18] Again, the reader is left without clear direction.

The inability of these study Bibles, which are aimed at a conservative market, simply to accept the obvious literal meaning of the text stands in sharp contrast to what we could call the Reformed study Bibles of the sixteenth and seventeenth centuries. Very important and influential were the English Geneva

---

14. Kathryn Applegate and J. B. Stump, eds., *How I Changed My Mind About Evolution: Evangelicals Reflect on Faith and Science* (Downers Grove, Ill.: IVP Academic, 2016).

15. For more examples, see Terry Mortenson, "Adam, Morality, the Gospel, and the Authority of Scripture," in *Searching for Adam: Genesis and the Truth about Man's Origin*, ed. Terry Mortenson (Green Forest, Ariz.: Master, 2016), 466–71.

16. For a comprehensive study of the shift from the dominance of a literal understanding of Genesis 1 and 2 from the early church until today, see William VanDoodewaard, *The Quest for the Historical Adam: Genesis, Hermeneutics, and Human Origins* (Grand Rapids: Reformation Heritage Books, 2015).

17. R. C. Sproul, ed., *New Geneva Study Bible: Bringing the Light of the Reformation to Scripture* (Nashville: Thomas Nelson, 1995); R. C. Sproul, ed., *The Reformation Study Bible: English Standard Version* (Orlando, Fla.: Reformation Trust, 2015).

18. Lane T. Dennis and Wayne Grudem et al., eds., *The ESV Study Bible, English Standard Version* (Wheaton, Ill.: Crossway, 2007), 43.

Bible (1560) and the Dutch States-General Bible (1636–1637), both of which had brief explanatory glosses in the margins of the biblical text. The Geneva Bible was officially endorsed by an act of the Scots Parliament in 1579, and the States-General Bible with its notes had been mandated by the Synod of Dort (1618–1619).[19]

It is striking that the notes of these two translations repeatedly accept the literal meaning of the text as a reliable historical record of what happened at the very beginning. For example, the Geneva Bible duly notes the days as sequential and the comment on Genesis 1:3 acknowledges that "the light was made before ether sunne or moone was created." Similarly, the States-General Bible in a note on Genesis 1:5 affirms that day and night make a natural day, specifically understanding it as a twenty-four-hour period. The days are understood sequentially and what is stated as created on each day is accepted as such.

With respect to the creation of man, while *The Reformation Study Bible* clearly underlines the uniqueness of man,[20] another conservative resource, *The NIV Study Bible*,[21] stresses what man and animals have in common. In its note on Genesis 2:7 it observes that the same verbs "are used to describe God's creation of both man and animals.... Humans and animals alike have the breath of life in them." That same note observes that the phrase translated as "living being" is also used of animals (Gen. 1:20, 24) and that "the words of [Genesis] 2:7 therefore imply that people, at least physically, have affinity with animals. The great difference is that man is made 'in the image of God' (1:27)." Although

---

19. *The Bible and Holy Scriptures Conteyned in the Olde and Newe Testament. Translated According to the Ebrue and Greke, and Conferred with the Best Translations in Divers Langages with Moste Profitable Annotations...* (Geneva: Rovland Hall, 1560). The Geneva Bible was probably the most important early English translation of Scripture and was widely accessible as the first mass-produced Bible. For the Scots Parliament endorsement, see Maurice S. Betteridge, "The Bitter Notes: The Geneva Bible and Its Annotations," *Sixteenth Century Journal* 14 (1983): 44. *Bijbel, dat is de gansche heilige Schrift, bevattende al de canonieke boeken des Ouden en Nieuwen Testaments, door last van de hoog-mog. heeren Staten-Generaal der Vereenigde Nederlanden [= de Staten-vertaling]* (Kampen: Kok, 1913). The Synod of Dort gave the translators the mandate to include brief explanations to the biblical text where necessary with difficult passages. This annotated translation was also enormously influential and widely used in the Netherlands for centuries. For the Dort decision, see Victor E. d'Assonville, "'Monumentum aere perennius' – Discussions and Decisions by the Synod of Dort on the Translation of the Bible," *KOERS – Bulletin for Christian Scholarship* 84 (2019): 8.

20. E.g., in notes on Gen. 2:7, *The Reformation Study Bible* states that "the Hebrew here does not say 'a living being became man'—man is not formed from preexistent life" and reference is also made to man bearing God's image and having authority over the animals.

21. Kenneth Barker, ed., *The NIV Study Bible. New International Version* (Grand Rapids: Zondervan, 1985).

the note is true to fact, it omits mentioning that only in the case of man did the breath of life come directly from God. It is difficult not to wonder whether the emphasis in the note on what is common to both man and beast could be a nod to evolutionary theory. The *ESV Study Bible* note on Genesis 2:7 makes similar comments, although man's special status is also noted.

Again a few centuries ago, there was a decidedly different emphasis. The States-General Bible specifically notes (on Gen. 2:7) the difference between man and beast. The fact that God breathed into man's nostrils the breath of life shows that "the soul of man is not created from any preexisting material, like the soul of the beasts."[22]

Happily, when it comes to annotated Scripture, mention can also be made of *The Reformation Heritage KJV Study Bible*, which clearly affirms in its introduction to Genesis a plain, straightforward reading of the text as a real, historical, and authoritative narrative of the origins of the universe, biological life, and the human race.[23] Furthermore, in its note on Genesis 2:7 it unequivocally states, "The first man was not formed of creatures already made—no evolutionary process. God made Adam from dust—the literal dust to which he must return since the fall." This approach honors the long-standing tradition as articulated by Herman Bavinck that "Christian theology, with only a few exceptions, continued to hold onto the literal historical view of the creation story."[24]

On the scientific front, it is good to note that there is significant opposition to the evolutionary theory of origins, and important critiques of it have been published.[25] Creationist societies like Answers in Genesis and Creation Research Institute enjoy considerable public support that enables them to thrive.[26] As can be expected, mainstream science tends to deride creationist efforts as unscholarly, and it not infrequently opposes their work vehemently. While any academic enterprise, including creationism, can and should be critically considered and, where necessary, criticized, the abuse the creationist movement sometimes takes is uncalled for.

---

22. My translation of "wijst ons aan dat de ziel des menschen niet is geschapen uit eenige voorgaande materie, gelijk de ziel der beesten."

23. Joel R. Beeke, ed., *The Reformation Heritage KJV Study Bible* (Grand Rapids: Reformation Heritage Books, 2014), 3.

24. Herman Bavinck, *Reformed Dogmatics*, ed. John Bolt, trans. John Vriend, 4 vols. (Grand Rapids: Baker Academic, 2003–2008), 2:495.

25. Most recently, Moreland et al., *Theistic Evolution*.

26. Their websites can be found at https://answersingenesis.org/ and https://creationresearch .org/.

It is unfortunate, for example, that a prominent evangelical historian of the stature of Mark Noll would not only give his support to evolutionary science but go on to highlight the scientific work of creationists as an example of work unworthy of academic stature, since in his view creationists are mired in obscurantism. As he makes clear in his book *The Scandal of the Evangelical Mind*, which was "meant more to incite than to inform," he gives this negative evaluation of creationist work because they do not accept the scientific theory of evolution. He writes that, "if the consensus of modern scientists, who devote their lives to looking at the data of the physical world, is that humans have existed on the planet for a very long time, it is foolish for biblical interpreters to say that 'the Bible teaches' the recent creation of human beings."[27] Some years later when reflecting on this book, he wrote that he was encouraged by the boldness and courage that some evangelicals showed in spelling out "why they are evolutionists and why they hold evolutionary theory to be compatible with traditional Christian orthodoxy."[28] In other words, current scientific *theory* on origins has more authority than the biblical text of God's revelation of the origin of mankind. Not surprisingly, Mark Noll also supports the work of BioLogos.

In the midst of the ongoing polemic about the meaning of Genesis 1 and 2, the question naturally and repeatedly arises whether it is justified to stick to an interpretation that is centuries old and continue to accept Genesis 1 and 2 as recounting real history. To answer that question, we will need to listen carefully to Scripture. After all, God was the only one present at the creation of all things and He has revealed to us what we need to know about those events at the beginning of time. So, the critical question is, what does Scripture teach, both in Genesis and elsewhere?

Compared to past generations of interpreters of Scripture, we are arguably even better equipped in terms of scholarship to tackle such a question. Modern scholarship has given us more insight into the cultural world of those who first received the revelation found in Genesis and we have greater knowledge about some of the vocabulary used. However, any interpretation of Genesis 1 and 2 needs to be weighed and tested against the claims that Scripture itself makes. It is therefore to Scripture that we must turn for direction on the issues at hand.

---

27. Mark A. Noll, *The Scandal of the Evangelical Mind* (Grand Rapids: Eerdmans, 1995), ix, 207.

28. Mark Noll, "The Evangelical Mind Today," *First Things*, no. 146 (October 2004): 37.

The Purpose of This Book

We are in the happy situation that Scripture is accepted as authoritative by Christians generally considered conservative whether they accept a literal reading of Genesis or not. This common commitment to the authority of the Word of God should make a fruitful discussion about the issues at hand possible. The purpose of this book is to contribute to that discussion.

The focus of this work is therefore not to give an all-round commentary and explanation of every verse in Genesis 1 and 2, but to listen to Scripture in order to find out what God is revealing to us about the historicity of the beginning chapters of Genesis. Concentrating on listening to what Scripture actually says brings with it the realization that the reader of the Word has a relatively modest place. The one who listens to Scripture acknowledges that the Word, not the reader, determines the meaning of the text.

A key question addressed in this book is whether the widespread departure from the historic Reformed and Presbyterian understanding of how to interpret Genesis 1 and 2 is justified. While no book can pretend to be comprehensive, this study does attempt to cover the most important elements concerning the historicity of Genesis 1 and 2. In doing so I will especially engage with and discuss approaches to Genesis by fellow conservative Christians who wish to honor the claims of Scripture but do not accept the plain sense of this part of Scripture as an accurate recounting of real historical events.

The topic of the historical value of Genesis 1 and 2 is a contentious one, and how one evaluates the evidence and what conclusions one comes to has enormous implications and consequences. After considering the evidence, this book comes to the determination that we should accept the plain, straightforward reading of the Genesis text as a reliable account of the historical events resulting in the creation of the world we now live in. This study will also try to convince fellow Christians that such a conclusion is justified.

Although the historical value of the opening chapters of Scripture is the primary focus of this study, the closely related discussion of the creation account and the theory of evolution cannot be ignored. A secondary purpose is therefore to ascertain the place of science in the study of Genesis 1 and 2 and the implications that the historicity of Genesis has for the credibility of the theory of evolution for explaining the origin of creation. Just as many theologians who have embraced the theory of evolution are not scientists, I am also not one, but I will share something of how qualified scientists who affirm the historicity of Genesis understand the scientific implications of what God's Word teaches in the first two chapters of Genesis.

To keep this study at a modest and manageable size, further discussion is sometimes relegated to a footnote or reference is made to a more detailed study that can be consulted.

Before continuing, it is proper to set forth the presuppositions that inform this work.

Basic Presuppositions

For the present purpose, one could simply define history writing as the accurate communication of events that have taken place in the past. Such a relaying of past events need not be exhaustive and include all the details we today would like to know about. But it communicates what really happened.

To properly appreciate historical information in the Old Testament, one must however realize that the Hebrew Bible is not simply an ancient history book or a collection of historical documents from the past. It is a record of historical events that was and remains unique. It emphasizes God's activity and plan in its narrating of His people's past. This history does not recount events for the sake of antiquarian interest or to provide all sorts of colorful detail for its own sake. Rather, the historical accounts are given within the context of the grand narrative of God's redemptive promises and His dealings with His people. For that reason what we generally call Historical Books, because they largely describe historical events, can better be designated as Prophetic Books. That is the way Joshua, Judges, Samuel, and Kings are identified in the Hebrew canon. The Lord Jesus could therefore refer to the Old Testament as the Law and the Prophets (Luke 16:31; 24:44). As prophetic books narrating historical events, their primary underlying purpose is to show how the LORD as covenant God was faithful to His promises and worked salvation for His people as He guided history to the goal of the coming Messiah. That basic purpose also holds for the Pentateuch, or the Five Books of Moses, of which Genesis is a part. One implication of this purpose is that Scripture does not always inform us of details that would satisfy our curiosity.

Furthermore, what also makes the account of the history narrated in Scripture unique is that through this same prophetic Word God worked faith in His people by His Holy Spirit (cf. Rom. 10:17). Indeed, it is also only through faith that God's unfolding plan of salvation can be discerned (cf. Acts 7:51–53). This necessity of faith to properly appreciate the history recounted in Scripture brings us to the first presupposition that informs our understanding and interpretation of the first chapters of Genesis.[29]

The Need for Faith

We need to read and study the biblical text in faith, receiving it as fully authoritative and trustworthy. This conviction is based on the fact that "all Scripture is given by inspiration of God, and is profitable for doctrine, for reproof, for correction, for instruction in righteousness" (2 Tim. 3:16). In his comments on this passage Calvin noted that "we owe to the Scripture the same reverence as we owe to God."[30] And God does not deceive or lie (Num. 23:19; Titus 1:2). The sixteenth-century Protestant Belgic Confession speaks of the authority of Scripture in article 5: "We believe without any doubt all things contained in them [i.e., the books of Scripture], not so much because the church receives and approves them as such, but especially because the Holy Spirit witnesses in our hearts that they are from God."[31] In other words, the Bible is self-sufficient and self-attesting. It does not need our arguments and proofs to show that it is reliable.

Such an affirmation of the trustworthiness of Scripture has been the historic position of the Christian church throughout its history. Indeed, God's Word teaches that without the activity of the Holy Spirit, who works faith, one cannot rightly interpret Scripture (1 Cor. 2:13–14; 2 Cor. 3:14–15; Heb. 4:2). We need to approach the text in faith. Also for the task of exegesis, "the fear of the LORD is the beginning of knowledge" (Prov. 1:7).[32] Faith seeks understanding. As Anselm of Canterbury put it, "I do not seek to understand that I may believe; but I believe in order to understand. For this also I believe,—that unless I believed, I should not understand."[33] It goes without saying that such

29. For what follows, see in greater detail Cornelis Van Dam, "Interpreting Historical Narrative: Truth Claim, Truth Value, and Historicity," in *Correctly Handling the Word of Truth: Reformed Hermeneutics Today*, ed. Mees te Velde and Gerhard H. Visscher (Eugene, Ore.: Wipf & Stock, 2014), 99–106.

30. John Calvin, *The Second Epistle of Paul the Apostle to the Corinthians and the Epistles to Timothy, Titus and Philemon*, ed. D. W. Torrance and T. F. Torrance, trans. T. A. Smail (Grand Rapids: Eerdmans, 1964), 330.

31. Belgic Confession, art. 5, in Canadian Reformed Churches, *Book of Praise: Anglo-Genevan Psalter* (Winnipeg: Premier, 2014), 500.

32. Also see Fred H. Klooster, "The Role of the Holy Spirit in the Hermeneutic Process: The Relationship of the Spirit's Illumination to Biblical Interpretation," in *Hermeneutics, Inerrancy, and the Bible*, ed. Earl D. Radmacher and Robert D. Preus (Grand Rapids: Zondervan, 1984), 451–72.

33. Anselm, *Proslogium; Monologium; an Appendix in Behalf of the Fool by Gaunilon; and Cur Deus Homo*, trans. Sidney Norton Deane (Chicago: Open Court, 1903), 7 (= Anselm, *Proslogium*, I); cf. John M. Frame, *A History of Western Philosophy and Theology* (Phillipsburg, N.J.: P&R, 2015), 129–34.

an approach needs to be accompanied with much prayer that the meaning and message of God's Word may be clear.

The Clarity of Scripture

Another fundamental assumption is that when God speaks to us in Scripture, His Word is clear. One must therefore accept the natural or obvious meaning of the text and not demand of it what it does not say. Calvin commented on Galatians 4:22 that "the true meaning of Scripture is the natural and obvious meaning; and let us embrace and abide by it resolutely. Let us not only neglect as doubtful, but boldly set aside as deadly corruptions, those pretended expositions, which lead us away from the natural meaning."[34] Once again, faith seeks understanding.

Put another way, the clarity of Scripture presupposes that God accurately transmits exactly what He wants to convey using the medium of human language. Against those who would deny such clarity, Benedict Pictet, a successor of Calvin at the Genevan Academy, correctly posed the dilemma: "Either God *could not* reveal himself more plainly to men, or he *would not*. No one will assert the former, and the latter is most absurd; for who could believe that God our heavenly Father has been unwilling to reveal his will to his children...?"[35] Indeed, contrary to the notions of postmodernism, there is meaning in the written text. Scripture's perspicuity means that believers reading the Bible are not dependent on specialists, be they in theology or science, in order to understand its basic message. When believers read and study Scripture, humbly submitting themselves to the Word and asking for the guidance of the Holy Spirit, then the Word is a lamp before their feet, a light on their path (Ps. 119:105).

The notion of the clarity of Scripture assumes that God speaks to us in language human beings can understand; in other words, God uses the language of normal everyday experience so that the natural or plain meaning of the text is clear to all who read it.

Affirming the clarity of Scripture does not mean that there are no difficult passages that require scholarly study and about which disagreement may remain. It does mean that the reader of Scripture is not dependent on scholars to understand the basic import and significance of the passage before them.

---

34. John Calvin, *The Epistles of Paul the Apostle to the Galatians, Ephesians, Philippians and Colossians*, ed. D. W. Torrance and T. F. Torrance, trans. T. H. L. Parker (Grand Rapids: Eerdmans, 1965), 85; see further on Calvin's understanding of Gal. 4:22, T. H. L. Parker, *Calvin's New Testament Commentaries* (Grand Rapids: Eerdmans, 1971), 63–68.

35. Quoted by Mark D. Thompson, "The Generous Gift of a Gracious Father: Toward a Theological Account of the Clarity of Scripture," in *The Enduring Authority of the Christian Scriptures*, ed. D. A. Carson (Grand Rapids: Eerdmans, 2016), 617 (italics in the original).

As a matter of fact believers should be able to discern and judge any scholarly interpretations of Scripture that are suspect (cf. 1 Cor. 2:15; 1 John 2:20).[36]

Finally, in the context of the clarity of Scripture, a brief general comment about the use of the term *literal* in this study is appropriate. The use of this term simply means understanding the biblical passage in accordance with the obvious, plain meaning of the text while taking into consideration its context. The exegetical chapters of this study will make clear what this approach entails. It does not suggest that we can fully comprehend what Scripture says when we accept the text at face value. Indeed, one often has to settle for what could be paradoxically called a precise ambiguity latent in much of what Genesis 1 and 2 tell us. God communicates what we need to know in plain and simple terms. But at the same time, the clear straightforward language can raise many questions for the inquiring reader. But such a situation is a good reminder of our limited capacities as created beings. There are clear limits to our understanding that need to be respected when we deal with the Creator's revelation of His awesome work of bringing the world and indeed the entire universe into existence. There is no shame in recognizing our limitations in not fully understanding what transpired, and such a respectful attitude is honoring to God in taking Him at His word when He graciously condescends to us and tells in clear language of His work of creation.

The Importance of Genre

Most often we can readily recognize or identify the genre of the text we are seeking to comprehend when we keep in mind its biblical context. Taking into account the genre is critical for correctly understanding the text. It would not do, for example, to read a parable and then interpret it as a true historical account to be accepted in the plain and ordinary sense of the word. It is, therefore, very important that we discern the genre of Genesis 1 and 2 correctly. We must be aware of the danger of imposing a genre on a passage in order to make it fit our preconceived notion of what it means or was meant to say. If the genre is determined to be historical narrative, then we must accept as historically true whatever Scripture affirms to be so.

---

36. Helpful recent articles on the clarity of Scripture include D. A. Carson, "Is the Doctrine of *Claritas Scripturae* Still Relevant Today?," in D. A. Carson, *Collected Writings on Scripture* (Wheaton, Ill.: Crossway, 2010), 179–93; and Thompson, "The Generous Gift," 615–43.

The Bible Does Not Contradict Itself

Since the entire Bible is the Word of God, who does not contradict Himself, the meaning of the opening chapters of Genesis should also be read in the light of subsequent biblical passages that deal with the same subject matter. Indeed, an important principle is that Scripture interprets itself so that less clear passages are interpreted in the light of those that are more clear. This basic hermeneutical rule was also clearly stated in early Reformed confessions.[37] And so a New Testament passage may, for example, throw light on a difficult Old Testament text. We will see many examples of this in the course of this study. Scripture must shape the understanding of the interpreter also for the first chapters of Holy Writ.

Use the Text God Has Given His Church

Finally, one further basic presupposition is that the text of Genesis to be used for exegesis is the canonical text God in His providence has entrusted to the church (cf. Rom. 3:2). We cannot, for example, build our understanding of Genesis 1 and 2 on the basis of a hypothetical literary reconstruction that attempts to detail the supposed process of the origin of these chapters from different traditions and documents. We must confine ourselves to the received canonical Hebrew text. We do not need to attempt to go behind the text in order to get at the so-called real account of creation.[38]

Current Mainstream Assumptions

Mainstream (post)modern scholarship however does not hold to the presuppositions that honor the Bible as the trustworthy and infallible Word of God. Its radically different presuppositions in approaching Scripture have had enormous consequences for how the Bible has been interpreted. Under the

---

37. Westminster Confession of Faith 1.9, in *The Confession of Faith and Catechisms* (Willow Grove, Pa.: The Committee on Christian Education of the Orthodox Presbyterian Church, 2005). Second Helvetic Confession 2, in Arthur C. Cochrane, ed., *Reformed Confessions of the 16th Century* (Philadelphia: Westminster, 1966). See further, e.g., J. V. Fesko, *The Theology of the Westminster Standards: Historical Context and Theological Insights* (Wheaton, Ill.: Crossway, 2014), 83–85; Mark D. Thompson, "Biblical Interpretation in the Works of Martin Luther," in *A History of Biblical Interpretation*, vol. 2, *The Medieval through the Reformation Periods*, ed. Alan J. Hauser and Duane F. Watson (Grand Rapids: Eerdmans, 2009), 303–4.

38. In this connection, also see the helpful discussion in Vern S. Poythress, *Interpreting Eden: A Guide to Faithfully Reading and Understanding Genesis 1–3* (Wheaton, Ill.: Crossway, 2019), 112–15, earlier published as Vern S. Poythress, "Dealing with the Genre of Genesis and Its Opening Chapters," *WTJ* 78 (2016): 220–22, where he concludes that "source criticism has very limited value when it comes to actually interpreting the texts that we have."

pressures of Enlightenment rationalism, many reject the divine inspiration of Genesis and consider it to be only a human book. Purely human literary works are of course fallible and need to be carefully examined to establish whether they are credible. Consistent critical scholars can only accept as historically reliable and true what is verifiable. If that is not the case, then such an event recorded in Scripture cannot be accepted as real history.[39] Since Genesis 1 and 2 give a record of events that cannot be verified as having actually happened as recorded, that fact alone will mean that critical scholars cannot accept these chapters as a reliable historical account.

In order to salvage a meaningful understanding of those first chapters of the Bible in such a skeptical intellectual environment, many scholars now suggest that the purpose of these chapters is to pass on theological truths such as that God is the creator of all things. Others affirm that the intent of Genesis 1 and 2 is to give an explanation for the origin of the present world and, for example, institutions such as the day of rest and marriage. According to them the account was not meant to convey the actual history of the beginning of creation. A related view holds that the beginning of Scripture consists of myths with no historical value. Furthermore, under the influence of the evolutionary paradigm, these chapters have been made to yield meanings compatible with the current scientific understanding of the origin of the world and the human race even if such interpretations appear to contradict the clear testimony of Scripture.[40]

In contrast to mainstream thinking, the basic presuppositional foundation of this study is to take seriously the integrity of the text of Genesis as part of God's Word. As such, it needs to be accepted and understood in faith, and its historical intent and meaning need to be judged on the basis of its own testimony.

The Structure of This Book

Before we embark on a study of Scripture, we need to be clear about the role that data from outside Scripture should play in our understanding of the Bible. The next chapter therefore deals with two important areas in this regard: the place of ancient Near Eastern accounts of earth's beginnings in interpreting Genesis and the role that scientific theories on the origin of our planet should play in seeking to understand what Scripture tells us.

---

39. See, e.g., the discussion in Iain Provan, V. Philips Long, and Tremper Longman III, *A Biblical History of Israel* (Louisville, Ky.: Westminster John Knox, 2003), 3–50.

40. For an overview of different approaches to Genesis 1 and 2, see A. H. W. Curtis, "Genesis," in *A Dictionary of Biblical Interpretation*, ed. R. J. Coggins and J. L. Houlden (London: SCM, 1990), 253–54.

Subsequent chapters deal with the necessary exegetical details of the opening chapter of Genesis, such as the genre and historicity of Genesis 1, the meaning of the phrase "in the beginning," the days of creation, and what the specific meaning of each passage is. Current popular interpretations that downplay, compromise, or deny the historicity of what the text relates will be dealt with. A similar detailed approach will be taken with Genesis 2. Overall, in discussing the text, the focus will be on those scholars who have a high view of Scripture but who have questioned the plain meaning of what is narrated. The issue of what Scripture says and teaches in Genesis 1 and 2 is of great importance and has consequences far beyond these opening chapters. This study therefore seeks to address all the main issues and to convince fellow believers that we should accept the plain meaning of the text as the LORD has given it to us. A concluding section will focus on the implications of the historicity of the creation account for the gospel and how the challenge of defending the truth of Genesis 1 and 2 can be met.

The Place of Extrabiblical Evidence in Interpreting Scripture

There has been a veritable explosion of knowledge in the last century that impacts how we read the Bible. But how should we use this newfound learning? This is no mere academic question since much is at stake. There is no doubt that we benefit greatly from linguistic and archaeological discoveries that in many cases help us to get a better understanding of the culture and milieu in which the ancient Israelites lived. But what if new discoveries seem to say something different from what Scripture appears to state quite clearly? Should our understanding of Scripture in such cases change and adapt to our new insights?

There are of course many factors that need to be considered in answering such questions. Two areas especially demand our attention in dealing with these thorny issues, namely, the place and use of ancient Near Eastern literature in interpreting the text and the question of what role, if any, modern science should play in understanding these chapters. This section is a preliminary overview, and we will be returning to both these areas as necessary in the course of listening to Genesis 1 and 2 and trying to understand their meaning.

Ancient Near Eastern Literature

The study of Genesis has been enriched with the discovery of much ancient Near Eastern literature, some of which includes myths containing information on how the origin of the world was understood. These resources go back to about 2500–1600 BC.[1] How should this material be used in listening to and trying to understand Genesis 1 and 2?

---

1. See the overview in David Toshio Tsumura, "Genesis and Ancient Near Eastern Stories of Creation and Flood: An Introduction," in *"I Studied Inscriptions from before the Flood": Ancient Near Eastern, Literary, and Linguistic Approaches to Genesis 1–11*, ed. Richard S. Hess and David Toshio Tsumura (Winona Lake, Ind.: Eisenbrauns, 1994), 27–57. For the early dating

Its Secondary Place

As a general principle, such material must always take a secondary place in the interpretation process. One should not say, as Old Testament scholar John Walton has asserted, that the key to understanding Scripture "is to be found in the literature from the rest of the ancient world."[2] The Genesis account, and what Scripture elsewhere says of creation, must have priority and is normative. Affirming this normative biblical priority makes it necessary to consider briefly: (1) the way speech act theory is used to give undue weight to ancient Near Eastern culture and (2) the nature of Scripture as divine revelation.

The use of speech act theory. Speech act theory has become an important hermeneutical tool in trying to understand the meaning of Genesis 1 and 2. It therefore merits mention especially since its application can lead and has led scholars to do injustice to the plain meaning of the biblical text.[3]

In speech act theory the process of communication is understood as proceeding from locution to illocution to perlocution. An influential proponent of applying speech act theory to a biblical context is John Walton. He identifies the locution as the text of Scripture, which he acknowledges to be the inspired Word of God; the illocution is the intention of the author, which is where authority and infallibility are located; the perlocution is the desired effect or result of the Word. What are the implications of this approach for interpreting Scripture?

Walton affirms that the text of Scripture (locution), although inspired, is culturally determined. We therefore have to "differentiate between what the communicator [the human author] can be inferred to believe [from the text of Scripture] and his illocutionary focus [the intent of what is written]."[4] In

---

of all the main Mesopotamian "creation" sources, see K. A. Kitchen, *On the Reliability of the Old Testament* (Grand Rapids: Eerdmans, 2003), 423–24; Alexander Heidel, *The Gilgamesh Epic and Old Testament Parallels*, 2nd ed. (Chicago: University of Chicago Press, 1963), 13–14; cf. Richard J. Clifford, *Creation Accounts in the Ancient Near East and in the Bible* (Washington, D.C.: Catholic Biblical Association of America, 1994), 83–84. For Egyptian dates, see Clifford, *Creation Accounts*, 100.

2. Walton, *Lost World of Genesis One*, 12.

3. For an introduction to and discussion of speech act theory, see Richard S. Briggs, "Speech-Act Theory," in *Dictionary for the Theological Interpretation of the Bible*, ed. Kevin J. Vanhoozer (Grand Rapids: Baker Academic, 2005), 763–66; Vern S. Poythress, "Canon and Speech Act: Limitations in Speech-Act Theory, with Implications for a Putative Theory of Canonical Speech Acts," *WTJ* 70 (2008): 337–54. Also helpful is Henri A. G. Blocher, "God and the Scripture Writers: The Question of Double Authorship," in *The Enduring Authority of the Christian Scriptures*, ed. D. A. Carson (Grand Rapids: Eerdmans, 2016), 497–541.

4. John H. Walton and D. Brent Sandy, *The Lost World of Scripture* (Downers Grove, Ill.: IVP Academic, 2013), 46, also see 41–48 (Walton wrote the Old Testament portion of this book).

other words, the author's intention needs to be separated from the actual words used in the text. This is necessary because in Walton's view the text of Scripture reflects the beliefs and worldview of the time in which it was written. Consequently, we cannot simply read the text and be sure we understand its meaning correctly. The text is not that clear because the author's intentions may have been different from the apparent message of the text as we read it today.

For example, in the case of Genesis 1, because of the different cultural background in which the biblical text originated, the Hebrew word *rāqî'a*, typically translated as "expanse" (of the sky) or "firmament,"[5] in its original cultural context is said to have meant a solid entity, a type of firm dome. So that is how the ancients must have thought of the sky. Because God accommodated his locution (the text of Scripture) to that cultural understanding of the time in which Genesis was composed, Walton does not accept the biblical text as authoritative because we no longer consider the sky to be a dome. Rather, he suggests that since the author's intent, the illocution, "is not to assert the true shape of cosmic geography, we can safely set those details [of the locution, the biblical text] aside as incidental…it is not the content of their illocutions."[6] Indeed he goes on to say that the beliefs articulated in the text (the locutions) may often be irrelevant or immaterial to the illocution or intent of the author. The important point to note is that separating the written text from the author's intent denies the biblical text the primary place it should hold. The authority that the text should have is moved to the intention or implied message of the author as that is reconstructed by today's reader according to his knowledge of the culture at the time of the text's origin.

This application of speech act theory is misguided and refuses to acknowledge the clarity of the plain sense of the text. In the example given, Walton assumes that the text in its ancient cultural context speaks of a firm dome, reflecting ancient cosmology. But as we will explain in chapter 7, Genesis 1 does not picture the firmament or sky as a solid mass and does not give a cosmology. God did not use language that accommodated to a pagan culture, but, as noted earlier, He used the language of human observation. The Genesis text means what it says. The text is authoritative, not the supposed meaning intended by the human communicator as determined by the contemporary scholar.[7] In other words, we are not dependent on the latest cultural studies of antiquity to discern the true and authoritative meaning of the Genesis text. Scripture

---

5. E.g., KJV; NKJV; NIV; *DCH* 7:552; *HALOT*, 1290 (also includes "the firm vault of heaven").
6. Walton and Sandy, *Lost World of Scripture*, 46.
7. Cf. Walton and Sandy, *Lost World of Scripture*, 47.

needs to be read and interpreted on its own terms. In this particular case it is also noteworthy that Genesis 1:8 identifies *rāqîʿa* as "heaven" (NKJV) or "sky" (NIV). Scripture interprets itself.

It is essential to maintain that the authority is located in the text of Scripture and not in the perceived intention of the human author according to his cultural context. There is one divine author working through the human writer. What God says and intends, Scripture says and intends. There are far-reaching consequences if we do not accept divine authority as resting in the biblical text. To give one example, according to Walton, if we follow the sense of ancient Near Eastern literature and its ideas of creation, "we find that people in the ancient Near East did not think of creation in terms of making material things—instead, everything is function oriented.... Consequently, to create something (cause it to exist) in the ancient world means to give it a function, not material properties."[8] Because Walton holds that the authority of the biblical narrative does not lie in the text of Scripture (locution) but in the intent of the human, culturally conditioned author (illocution), he reads the Genesis narrative not as describing the creation of the material world and cosmos, but as a description of how God set up the cosmos to function for human beings.[9] This view has been rightly challenged, as we shall see in chapter 6. But more importantly, not only the text of Genesis but also other texts of Scripture testify against this interpretation. God made the heavens (Ps. 33:6), and "things which are seen were not made of things which are visible" (Heb. 11:3). We need to maintain that the text of Scripture, not the human intention, is authoritative.

On a more general note, as the above example from Genesis illustrates, if we assign the authority and infallibility of a biblical passage to the human author's intent, rather than to the biblical text, then cultural arguments can be used to make Scripture say what contradicts the plain teachings of the Word.[10]

In sum, it is important to maintain not only the clarity but also the authority and infallibility of the biblical text and to accept its plain sense, keeping in mind the genre of the text and other places in the Bible that deal with the same or similar issues, since God's Word does not contradict itself.

---

8. Walton, *Lost World of Genesis One*, 35. Greater detail for his argument is found in John H. Walton, *Genesis 1 as Ancient Cosmology* (Winona Lake, Ind.: Eisenbrauns, 2011).

9. Walton, *Lost World of Genesis One*, 35–45; Walton, *Genesis 1 as Ancient Cosmology*, 139.

10. This reality was dramatically exemplified by the decision of the Reformed Churches (Liberated) in the Netherlands to move very quickly from a position against women in ecclesiastical office to the ordination of women in all church offices. A hermeneutic consistent with speech act theory helped make this turnabout possible. Henk van den Belt, "Lessons from the Reformation for Hermeneutics Today," *Unio Cum Christo* 4, no. 2 (2018): 97–100.

Genesis as divine revelation. For us to take the divine inspiration of Scripture seriously means that we treat Genesis 1 and 2 as trustworthy revelation. This material did not arise from the human mind and the surrounding culture, but it ultimately came from God Himself who ensured that what has been written is true. Genesis 1 and 2 do not contain the opinions of the ancient world as to how the world began. They are revelation from God. We are, therefore, not dependent on the latest ancient Near Eastern discoveries to finally find out in the twenty-first century what God had really intended to say in the opening chapters of Scripture. Although the distance between our current culture and that of the ancient Israelites should not be underestimated, at the same time we can be certain that the Almighty was able to ensure that what was written in the Genesis creation account would be understandable for His people in all times, places, cultures, and circumstances. This clarity of divine revelation does not belittle the benefit that we can derive from new discoveries, but it underlines the preeminent place that Scripture must have in determining its meaning. One needs to compare Scripture with Scripture first in trying to understand Genesis before one turns to possible clues from new discoveries from antiquity.

Our acceptance of the veracity of God's Word also entails that we acknowledge that the true religion of worshiping one God preceded paganism with its many gods, since this is what Genesis tells us. Although we do not know the exact manner in which Genesis 1 and 2 have come down to us, there is no warrant for suggesting that the Genesis creation account is the result of borrowing from pagan sources stripped of their polytheistic elements. Such a perception is also fallacious on methodological grounds. As eminent Near Eastern scholar Kenneth Kitchen put it, "In the ancient Near East, the rule is that simple accounts or traditions may give rise (by accretion and embellishment) to elaborate legends, but not vice versa."[11] Most Assyriologists have dismissed the idea of a direct link between the opening chapters of Genesis and the most important so-called Babylonian Creation Epic, Enuma Elish.[12] The background of the

---

11. K. A. Kitchen, *Ancient Orient and Old Testament* (London: Tyndale, 1966), 89. In a footnote, Kitchen gives examples. Also see John D. Currid, *Against the Gods: The Polemical Theology of the Old Testament* (Wheaton, Ill.: Crossway, 2013), 33–46; Murray R. Adamthwaite, "Is Genesis 1 Just Reworked Babylonian Myth?" *Journal of Creation* 27 (2013): 99–104.

12. Kitchen, *Reliability*, 424–25, 591n7; also, e.g., Wolfram von Soden, *The Ancient Orient: An Introduction to the Study of the Ancient Near East*, trans. Donald G. Schley (Grand Rapids: Eerdmans, 1994), 213. For perceptive observations on the issue of borrowing, see Noel K. Weeks, "The Ambiguity of Biblical 'Background,'" *WTJ* 72 (2010): 229–30. This borrowing is sometimes seen as a possibility: Bernard F. Batto, *In the Beginning: Essays on Creation Motifs in the Ancient Near East and the Bible* (Winona Lake, Ind.: Eisenbrauns, 2013), 52–53. Waltke goes further. He speculates that God inspired Moses to write the account of creation "that bore the garb of the

biblical creation account has also been sought in Ugaritic and Egyptian literature. However, considering the many differences between these accounts and
the biblical one, as well as the existence of various accounts of origins within
the different cultures, compelling evidence for a meaningful relationship to the
biblical account is lacking in Ugaritic and Egyptian literature as well.[13]

Challenges in Using Ancient Near Eastern Literature
Needless to say, ancient Near Eastern texts that deal with the origin of the
world must be dealt with carefully and judiciously when used in conjunction
with Genesis 1 and 2. One must consider the provenance of the text and its
relevance. For example, most texts used for interpreting Genesis come from
Mesopotamia and Egypt. Their usage for understanding Genesis, which as part
of the Pentateuch is attributed to Moses, needs to be carefully justified. One
needs to answer questions such as why might a particular ancient Near Eastern
text from a particular country and date be relevant for understanding Genesis
1 and 2.[14]

Furthermore, one needs to consider the character and purpose of the
ancient Near Eastern writings that mention creation. For example, the so-called
Babylonian Epic of Creation (Enuma Elish) actually has as its main goal not to
give an account of origins but to demonstrate the hegemony of Marduk, the
god of Babylon. Such an intention of the text impacts how the topic of origins
is approached. With respect to both Mesopotamia and Egypt there are various
myths reflecting different views on origins in both cultures and so one has to
be very careful how and what one uses to compare those creation accounts to
the biblical one.[15] Also, any possible elucidation of the meaning or vocabulary

---

Mesopotamian cosmogony." Later he concludes that "the Holy Spirit inspired the biblical narra-
tor to transform pagan myths to recount *historia* in accord with God's values." Bruce K. Waltke,
"Myth, History, and the Bible," in *The Enduring Authority of the Christian Scriptures*, ed. D. A.
Carson (Grand Rapids: Eerdmans, 2016), 569, 576.

13. Weeks, "Ambiguity of Biblical 'Background,'" 229–30, and his references to further
literature.

14. On the Mosaic authorship of Genesis, see Edward J. Young, *An Introduction to the Old
Testament*, rev. ed. (Grand Rapids: Eerdmans, 1964), 42–46; K. A. Kitchen, "The Old Testament
in Its Context: 1 from the Origins to the Eve of the Exodus," *Theological Students' Fellowship
Bulletin* 59 (1971): 9; and Duane A. Garrett, *Rethinking Genesis: The Sources and Authorship of
the First Book of the Pentateuch* (Grand Rapids: Baker, 1991), esp. ch. 3. For a critique of the
assumption that ancient Near Eastern culture was uniform, see Noel K. Weeks, "The Bible and
the 'Universal' Ancient World," 1–8.

15. On the character of the Creation Epic, see Alexander Heidel, *The Babylonian Genesis:
The Story of Creation*, 2nd ed. (Chicago: University of Chicago Press, 1963), 10–11. On various
myths and the need for caution in using Egyptian and Mesopotamian sources, see John D.

of Genesis from the literature of the ancient world needs to be evaluated on a case-by-case basis.

When utilizing ancient Near Eastern literature for understanding Scripture, it is also important to be aware of the differences between the biblical worldview and the ancient pagan one, including the difference between history and myth. Understanding these distinctions will enable one to appreciate what Genesis is saying within the context of the ancient mythic mindset. As will be shown in the next chapter, Genesis 1 and 2 demand to be read as real historical accounts. The narratives inform us of real events that actually took place in the past at the very beginning of this world. God sovereignly called creation into being. There is an absolute distinction between God and what He made. History started with God's creative activity. God issued His commands and called the heavens and the earth into existence. The almighty Creator seems to have done it all effortlessly. Since His work of creation, God has guided history according to His plan. History is linear, and all is under God's control as history moves on to the final day.

Over against this biblical testimony, ancient Near Eastern myths from all the different regions exhibit clear differences. With respect to the creation of the world, mythical thinking speculated that "the contemporary order of being was derived from a timeless event conceived of as occurring in the past." In other words, this timeless event is actually outside of time as we experience it.[16] No transcendent creator God was involved in this ahistorical event of beginnings. There were many gods who were all closely associated with different parts of creation, such as the sun, moon, and thunder. No distinction was made between the deities and the world of nature. Creation was identified with the divine. In view of these characteristics of myth, it therefore can be argued that continuity is the basis for mythical thinking. No fundamental distinctions existed between humanity, nature, and the divine. There was a community of essence; only the roles were different.[17] This mythic continuity is reflected in

---

Currid, *Ancient Egypt and the Old Testament* (Grand Rapids: Baker, 1997), 55; and K. A. Kitchen, *The Bible in Its World: The Bible & Archaeology Today* (Downers Grove, Ill.: InterVarsity, 1978), 26–27. For a study contrasting Gen. 1–3 with Egyptian creation myths, see Ángel M. Rodríguez, "Biblical Creationism and Ancient Near Eastern Evolutionary Ideas," in *The Genesis Creation Account and Its Reverberations in the Old Testament*, ed. Gerald A. Klingbeil (Berrien Springs, Mich.: Andrews University Press, 2015), 293–328; also see James K. Hoffmeier, "Some Thoughts on Genesis 1 & 2 and Egyptian Cosmology," *JANES* 15 (1983): 39–49.

16. The quotation is from Brevard S. Childs, *Myth and Reality in the Old Testament*, 2nd ed. (London: SCM, 1962), 27–28. See also John N. Oswalt, *The Bible among the Myths* (Grand Rapids: Zondervan, 2009), 50–51.

17. Oswalt, *The Bible among the Myths*, 43–49.

how the ancients viewed the origin of the world. Matter is the fundamental element and it has always existed. From it came the gods, the natural world, and ultimately humans. The creative process meant conflict. Only after enormous strife involving the gods did the creation of the natural world and humans become a reality. In the mythic understanding of reality, a cyclical concept of life predominates rather than a linear history. After all, one day follows another, one season gives way to the next, and the process repeats itself.[18]

In order to maintain this reality and the existing world order, the original cosmic events of creation had to be actualized in pagan cultic practices. In this way the timeless event of beginnings enters into the present moment. Notice once again that the origin of all things is outside time. The present is all that exists and so reality only relates to the now, the present. Time is static and does not go anywhere. The task of humans is to ensure that things remain as they are and do not go off track.[19] To maintain the current world order, myth had to be dramatized and actualized so that, for example, on each New Year festival the Babylonians would reenact the victory of Marduk over the powers of chaos as related in their Creation Epic. It is clear that a one-time creation of all things as a real historical event as found in Genesis is not the concern of the ancients. The gods were experienced by people in nature and not in history.[20]

Similarities with the Biblical Account

Although there are vast differences between the mythical accounts of earth's beginnings and the Genesis account, and although there is no evidence for a meaningful relationship between Genesis and ancient Near Eastern myths, yet

---

18. Oswalt, *The Bible among the Myths*, 58–62. All the mythic elements Oswalt mentioned in his study, Bruce Waltke has summarized in this way: "The Ancient Near Eastern cosmogony has five essential characteristics: (1) pantheism, (2) magic, (3) *Chaoskampf* (so most, not all), (4) eternal return, and (5) marginalization of *historia*." Waltke, "Myth, History, and the Bible," 552. For Egypt, see Joanna Töyräänvuori, "The Northwest Semitic Conflict Myth and Egyptian Sources from the Middle and New Kingdoms," in *Creation and Chaos: A Reconsideration of Hermann Gunkel's* Chaoskampf *Hypothesis*, ed. John Scurlock and Richard H. Beal (Winona Lake, Ind.: Eisenbrauns, 2013), 112–26.

19. Childs, *Myth and Reality*, 17–30; G. Ernest Wright, *The Old Testament against Its Environment* (London: SCM Press, 1950), 26–28; Oswalt, *The Bible among the Myths*, 50–51, 61–62; cf. 111–23; John D. Currid, "The Hebrew World-and-Life View," in *Revolutions in Worldview*, ed. W. Andrew Hoffecker (Phillipsburg, N.J.: P&R, 2007), 62–63.

20. Nahum M. Sarna, *Understanding Genesis* (New York: Schocken, 1966), 7; Wright, *Old Testament against Its Environment*, 28; cf. J. R. Porter, "Old Testament Historiography," in *Tradition and Interpretation: Essays by Members of the Society for Old Testament Study*, ed. G. W. Anderson (Oxford: Clarendon, 1979), 126–27.

it is interesting to note some hints of a common background.[21] It is especially in the order of the events recounted that we find striking similarities.

For example, Alexander Heidel has pointed out some apparent similarities between Genesis and Enuma Elish. In both, we have what appears to be a similar sequence of creation: the mythical "creation" of "primeval chaos" in darkness (analogous to "without form and void" in Gen. 1:2), light, the firmament, dry land, the luminaries, and human beings, followed by the gods resting. He nevertheless concluded that "we have a number of differences between *Enûma Elish* and Gen. 1:1–2:3 that make all apparent similarities shrink into utter insignificance."[22]

Similar comments can be made about Egyptian mythic accounts of creation. Gordon H. Johnston has detailed how Egypt's four major myths of creation, represented by rival sanctuaries, all followed the same basic story line with some variations: a lifeless, chaotic, and watery deep; a divine wind moves over the waters; creation of light; emergence of a primordial hill in primeval waters (analogous to creation of firmament in the midst of the waters); procreation of the sky with water over the earth; formation of a heavenly ocean when waters were separated; formation of dry land by separation; creation of humanity; and creation of the sun.[23] The last two obviously do not conform to the biblical order, but the overall correlation is telling.

But how can one explain these types of similarities between Genesis and ancient myths? It seems probable that where there are notable resemblances, the myths are drawing on corrupted memories of the original divine revelation

---

21. Such data can be found, e.g., in general, Walton, *Genesis 1 as Ancient Cosmology*; more specifically, on Mesopotamia, Heidel, *Gilgamesh Epic*, 82–140; on Egypt, Gordon H. Johnston, "Genesis 1 and Ancient Egyptian Creation Myths," *BSac* 165 (2008): 178–94; Hoffmeier, "Some Thoughts"; on Canaan (Ugarit), John Day, *God's Conflict with the Dragon and the Sea: Echoes of a Canaanite Myth in the Old Testament* (Cambridge: Cambridge University Press, 1985), 1–61.

22. Heidel, *Babylonian Genesis*, 140, and 128–30 for the similarities. Also see Currid, *Against the Gods*, 37–38; Kitchen, *Reliability*, 424–25. For the denial that there was a primeval chaos to be conquered in "creation" in both the myth and Gen. 1, see Alan Millard, "From Weal to Woe: Completing a Pattern in the Bible and the Ancient Near East," in *Let Us Go up to Zion: Essays in Honour of H. G. M. Williamson on the Occasion of His Sixty-Fifth Birthday*, ed. Iain Provan and Mark J. Boda (Leiden: Brill, 2012), 195–99; also see the important critique in Rebecca S. Watson, *Chaos Uncreated: A Reassessment of the Theme of "Chaos" in the Hebrew Bible* (Berlin: De Gruyter, 2005).

23. Johnston, "Ancient Egyptian Myths." Also see James E. Atwell, "An Egyptian Source for Genesis 1," *JTS* 51 (2000): 441–77; Currid, *Against the Gods*, 38–39; Clifford, *Creation Accounts*, 99–116.

about earth's and humanity's beginnings as found in Genesis.[24] As Merrill F. Unger put it: "The Genesis account is not only the purest, but everywhere bears the unmistakable impress of divine inspiration when compared with the extravagances and corruptions of the other accounts. The Biblical narrative, we may conclude, represents the *original form* these traditions must have assumed."[25]

Conclusion

The Genesis account of creation is far removed from the concepts one meets in ancient Near Eastern myths. These profound differences need to be taken into consideration in any study of Genesis 1 and 2 that utilizes ancient Near Eastern resources. Consequently, the value of comparing the creation account of Genesis with these pagan myths is quite limited.[26] These limitations are also reflected in the sparse use made of ancient Near Eastern myths for understanding the biblical account in the pages that follow. Where appropriate in giving possible further insight into the text of Genesis, account will be taken of ancient Near Eastern data, but the focus of this book is on listening to the first two chapters of Scripture as the Creator's authoritative revelation to us of His work.

Science and General Revelation

A second major extrabiblical factor that can influence our understanding of Scripture is science. Mainstream evolutionary science is having a tremendous impact on the interpretation of Genesis 1 and 2 today. We therefore need to consider briefly the character and limitations of the scientific enterprise. Since scientists study and investigate the natural world we must also reflect on what is called general revelation, which God gives through His creation. Since God reveals Himself both through His creation as well as through His written Word, we need to consider what these two sources of revelation reveal and how they relate to each other.[27]

---

24. For variations of this basic position, see, e.g., Bruce K. Waltke, "The Creation Account in Genesis 1:1–3. Part IV: The Theology of Genesis 1," *BSac* 132 (1975): 331; Merrill F. Unger, *Archaeology and the Old Testament* (Grand Rapids: Zondervan, 1954), 37; Heidel, *Babylonian Genesis*, 139; C. F. Keil and F. Delitzsch, *Commentary on the Old Testament* (repr., Peabody, Mass.: Hendrickson, 1996), 1:27–28; Ira Maurice Price, *The Monuments and the Old Testament* (Philadelphia: American Baptist Publication Society, 1909), 94–96.

25. Unger, *Archaeology*, 37 (italics in the original).

26. For issues relating to biblical and ancient Near Eastern cosmologies, see chapter 7.

27. This is obviously not a new problem. For a nuanced and detailed account of how perceived conflicts between the Bible and science were dealt with in the fifteenth and sixteenth centuries, see Kenneth J. Howell, *God's Two Books: Copernican Cosmology and Biblical*

Let us first consider the nature and limitations of biblical revelation as it relates to science, and then look at what general revelation reveals. Next we will consider the character and limitations of science, and finally how Scripture and science can interact in a profitable way.

The Bible Is Not a Scientific Textbook

With the heavy hand of scientism influencing the interpretation of the opening chapters of Scripture, nontraditional interpretations of Genesis 1 and 2 are often justified by saying that the Bible is not a scientific textbook, and so science should show us the way to a proper understanding of these chapters. It is certainly true that Scripture is not a science text. It would be misusing Scripture to utilize it as though it were, for instance, a modern handbook on biology, geology, or physics. The Bible was not written with the purpose of informing us of scientific facts now being discovered about the world in which we live. The emphasis in the creation account in Genesis 1 is not on the precise manner and processes by which God called everything into being but on the fact that He is the creator who did it. In this connection it is worth noting what Oswald T. Allis pointed out: in a chapter of thirty-one verses, God is mentioned repeatedly for a total of thirty-two times. So, he concluded, the great central thought of Genesis 1 is that "God is the author of the universe and all that it contains. That is the great outstanding fact. Not *how* it was made, but *who* made it."[28] Scripture, beginning at Genesis 1, is about God revealing Himself. Indeed, the overriding purpose of the Bible is to reveal God's grace and mercy, the good news of God's salvation in Jesus Christ. To that end, God revealed to us the origin of the world and its perfect state, the fall into sin, and the history of redemption through the ages until the coming of the Savior and the outpouring of the Spirit.

One obvious consequence of this purpose of God's written revelation is that Genesis 1 does not speak in a scientific way, nor does Scripture anywhere else. It uses language anyone can understand, the language of everyday experience. Such usage means, for instance, that when phenomena in space are spoken of, geocentric language is used, that is, the language of our everyday orientation as

---

Interpretation in Early Modern Science (Notre Dame: University of Notre Dame Press, 2002). For a general historical introduction to the complex relationship of science and faith, see John Hedley Brooke, *Science and Religion: Some Historical Perspectives* (Cambridge: Cambridge University Press, 1991).

28. Oswald T. Allis, "Old Testament Emphases and Modern Thought," *PTR* 23 (1925): 443 (italics in the original).

those living on this planet. For example, to say that Joshua's words, "Sun, stand still" (Josh. 10:12) prove that the sun rotates around the earth is to claim too much. Joshua used everyday language, which should not be pressed. We today who believe that the sun is stationary still speak of sunrise and sunset.[29] And so when there is a beautiful sunset, we do not say, "What a beautiful rotation of the earth!" We speak geocentrically, in the language of our daily experience. Similarly we cannot prove that the world is round on the basis of Isaiah 40:22, which reads in part: "It is He who sits above the circle of the earth." The circle probably refers to the horizon. Scripture speaks according to our geocentric orientation. A final example: we cannot say that the modern notion of the earth circling the sun is disproved by Psalm 93:1, which says that, "the world is established, so that it cannot be moved." Here too the poet is using the language of human observation. We need to be very careful not to impose a technical reading on the use of such language. As Calvin famously put it when discussing Genesis 1:6, "Nothing is here treated of but the visible form of the world. He who would learn astronomy, and other recondite arts, let him go elsewhere." Or, as Calvin commented on Psalm 136:7 ("to Him who made great lights"), "The Holy Spirit had no intention to teach astronomy; and, in proposing instruction meant to be common to the simplest and most uneducated persons, he made use by Moses and the other Prophets of popular language."[30]

God's use of the language of human experience is part of His accommodating revelation to the limited capacities of those receiving it. This sort of accommodation explains why Scripture describes celestial phenomena in the way that humans experience and speak of them and not with a view to technical scientific accuracy. Thus Scripture speaks of the moon as the lesser of the "two great lights," even though it technically has no light of its own but simply reflects light from the sun, and even though Saturn is actually larger than the moon (Gen. 1:16). Calvin, therefore, noted (on v. 14) that "Moses does not speak with philosophical acuteness," rather he "relates those things which are everywhere observed, even by the uncultivated, and which are in common

---

29. From a scientific perspective, there is of course no way to provide absolute proof that the sun is motionless and the earth moves since "to determine absolute motion we need an absolute reference point," which is an impossibility. So emeritus professor of astronomy, John Byl, "A Moving Earth?," *Bylogos* (blog), July 18, 2011, http://bylogos.blogspot.com/2011/07/moving-earth.html.

30. John Calvin, *Commentaries on the First Book of Moses, Called Genesis*, trans. John King (Grand Rapids: Eerdmans, 1948), 1:79; John Calvin, *Commentary on the Book of Psalms*, trans. James Anderson (repr., Grand Rapids: Eerdmans, 1963), 5:184. See also the warning of Vern S. Poythress, *Redeeming Science: A God-Centered Approach* (Wheaton, Ill.: Crossway, 2006), 93–96.

use." He further observed (on v. 15) that Moses was not "ignorant of the fact, that the moon had not sufficient brightness to enlighten the earth, unless it borrowed from the sun; but he deemed it enough to declare what we all may plainly perceive, that the moon is a dispenser of light to us." Similarly, Calvin commented (on v. 16) that "if the astronomer inquires respecting the actual dimensions of the stars, he will find the moon to be less than Saturn; but this is something abstruse, for to the sight it appears differently. Moses, therefore, rather adapts his discourse to common usage."[31]

We must also see the description of the process of creation in Genesis 1 and 2 as revelation accommodated to common human understanding. These chapters are not scientific treatises, although it is possible that processes that scientists know about today are hidden in the simple language of Genesis 1 and 2.[32] The point is that God accommodates to our understanding, and what He tells us in the first chapters of Scripture is accurate and factual, for God does not lie (Titus 1:2). As Theodore Van Raalte put it, "Accommodation is not an accommodation of the truth as such (the end), but of the means or modes of revealing this truth."[33] In other words, "Precisely because God has accommodated His revelation to our understanding, we may have confidence that it is true. If He had not accommodated to us, He might have given His Word in a heavenly language that we could not understand or He could have supplied His infinite thoughts in some manner which we finite beings have no capacity to comprehend."[34] And so in His short powerful description of His work of creation, God has accurately revealed all we need to know about how the world began so that we can give glory to the Creator. God's accommodating the creation process to our understanding and making it accessible to us means that

---

31. Calvin, *Genesis*, 1:84–87. For Calvin on Scripture, accommodation, and science, see R. Hooykaas, *Religion and the Rise of Modern Science* (Grand Rapids: Eerdmans, 1972), 117–24. For the notion of accommodation as a long-standing hermeneutical principle in the history of the church, see Peter Harrison, *The Bible, Protestantism, and the Rise of Natural Science* (Cambridge: Cambridge University Press, 2001), 133–38.

32. W. H. Gispen, *Schepping en paradijs: Verklaring van Genesis 1–3* (Kampen: Kok, 1966), 12.

33. Theodore G. Van Raalte, "Another Wax Nose? Accommodation in Divine Revelation," in *Correctly Handling the Word of Truth: Reformed Hermeneutics Today*, ed. Mees te Velde and Gerhard H. Visscher (Eugene, Ore.: Wipf & Stock, 2014), 236. Similarly, accommodation "did *not* mean that God tolerated a process in which human writers of Scripture would include in their writings erroneous conceptions of their time, in order to serve a higher theological purpose." Vern S. Poythress, *Interpreting Eden*, 325–26, earlier published as Vern S. Poythress, "Rethinking Accommodation in Revelation," *WTJ* 76 (2014): 145. In this article Poythress helpfully highlights potential pitfalls in understanding accommodation.

34. Theodore G. Van Raalte, in a written communication with the author (June 6, 2018).

scientists need to remain very humble when attempting to rhyme Genesis 1 and 2 with current science. The account is not a scientific one.

In this general connection it is good to be reminded of the words of Herman Bavinck, who also emphasized that Scripture is not a scientific textbook and "does not take sides between the Ptolemaic and the Copernican worldview." He perceptively continued by saying that

> Holy Scripture uses the language of everyday experience, which is and remains always true. If, instead of this, Scripture had used the language of the academy and spoken with scientific precision, it would have stood in the way of its own authority. If it had decided in favor of the Ptolemaic worldview, it would not have been credible in an age that supported the Copernican system. Nor could it have been a book for life, for humanity. But now it speaks in ordinary human language, language that is intelligible to the most simple person, clear to the learned and unlearned alike. It employs the language of observation, which will always continue to exist alongside that of science and the academy.[35]

There is, nevertheless, the temptation for some scientists who accept the Genesis account as factually true to try to read scientific theories into the biblical passages that were not meant to carry that kind of freight. But God's condescension in giving us Genesis does not mean that we can scientifically and precisely reconstruct what happened when God created everything. It is another matter for believing scientists to determine whether their scientific understanding or theory is consistent with what Scripture teaches or converges with the biblical account of creation. We will see an example of this at the end of this chapter. But if on the basis of Genesis 1 and 2 we think we can establish scientifically what happened in the beginning, then we contradict the purpose of this part of Scripture. This takes us to a consideration of creationism.

Creationism

Creationist scientists want to do full justice to what Scripture teaches about the creation and the history of the world. They strive to do their scientific work on the basis of biblical presuppositions. Their desire to take seriously the historicity of the events Scripture describes is to be applauded.[36] We can be thankful

---

35. Bavinck, *Reformed Dogmatics*, 1:446.
36. For a history, see Ronald L. Numbers, *The Creationists: From Scientific Creationism to Intelligent Design*, expanded ed. (Cambridge, Mass.: Harvard University Press, 2006); George M. Marsden, *Understanding Fundamentalism and Evangelicalism* (Grand Rapids: Eerdmans, 1991), 153–81.

for the good scientific work they do, and we can benefit from it where possible. Unfortunately, their use of Scripture has not always been proper or helpful. For example, the late Henry Morris sometimes used the Bible as if it were a scientific textbook. Although it is not pleasant to criticize someone like Henry Morris, a pioneer in this field from whose work I have also benefited, this misuse of Scripture needs to be addressed. It has been a problem in the past, and although, happily, it appears less so today, it nevertheless remains an issue that we must be on our guard against, as we will see shortly. It is important that we address the way Scripture is abused in scientific discussions so that we may defend the integrity of the first-rate work of creationist scientists who do not fall into this temptation.

Henry Morris, who has been called "the founder, patriarch, architect, and chief proselyte of the modern scientific creationism movement," wrote an article emphatically titled "The Bible *Is* a Textbook of Science." It is regrettable that at the time of writing this essay was still hosted on the website of the Institute for Creation Research.[37] It is, however, not right to read into Scripture modern scientific concepts that go beyond the meaning and intent of the biblical text. Here are some examples taken from Morris's article.[38]

Regarding Hebrews 1:3, which says that God's Son is "upholding all things by the word of His power," Morris explained, "Jesus Christ, through the continual outflow of His limitless divine energy is thus sustaining all of the material stuff of the universe which He had once created. Here is clearly spelled forth the modern truth of the equivalence of matter and energy. Here is also revealed the ultimate source of the mysterious nuclear forces, the binding energy of the atom. One might also refer to Colossians 1:16–17 for the same teaching."[39] One can rightly question whether reading scientific data about Einstein's notion of the equivalence of matter and energy into the biblical text is justified. Rather, Scripture here teaches that the Son through whom God created the world continues to rule this world by upholding and sustaining all things by the word of His power (Heb. 1:2–3; cf. Isa. 55:11). The world does not run on its own. The Son keeps it going moment by moment and holds everything together (Col. 1:17). To attempt to read modern scientific insights on the equivalence of

---

37. For the characterization of Morris, see Robert Charles Williams, "Scientific Creationism: An Exegesis for a Religious Doctrine," *American Anthropologist* 85 (1983): 93. Morris's article is found in Henry M. Morris, *Studies in the Bible and Science; or, Christ and Creation* (Philadelphia: Presbyterian and Reformed, 1966), 108–20 (italics in the original) and is available at: http://www.icr.org/home/resources/resources_tracts_tbiatos/.

38. Morris, *Studies*, 108–20 (ch. 11).

39. Morris, *Studies*, 113.

matter and energy into this passage is to misuse it. The text was never written to convey that kind of information. It may be that what Hebrews 1:3 teaches does not contradict what we now understand scientifically, with our limited human comprehension, about matter and energy. But to say that such and such a scientific theory "is clearly spelled forth" in the biblical text not only goes far beyond the intent and meaning of the text but abuses it.

Another example relates to Isaiah 40:12, which asks the rhetorical question, who has "weighed the mountains in scales and the hills in a balance?" The obvious answer in the context of Isaiah 40 is God. Morris, however, commented on this passage in the context of geology: "The basic principle of isostasy (meaning 'equal weights'), which is the foundation of geophysics, is indicated by Isaiah 40:12, which speaks of God 'weighing the mountains in scales, and the hills in a balance,' from which the pre-eminent importance of gravitational forces in geophysical calculations should easily be inferred."[40] But all this geologic reasoning is hardly the point of the passage in question. The message is the greatness of God. He is so great that He can even hold the dust of the earth in a basket and weigh the mountains and hills. What man cannot even conceive of doing, the God of Israel is able to do, for He is omnipotent.

Isaiah 40:22 says of God: "It is He who sits above the circle of the earth." Morris commented, "The 'shape of the earth' is the peculiar domain of the sub-science of *geodesy*, and the fact of its basic 'roundness' is pointed out by Isaiah 40:22." But it is hardly the intent of the text to inform the science of geodesy about earth's roundness. E. J. Young rightly commented that "it does not seem warrantable to conclude that Scripture here teaches that the earth is round."[41]

In all these examples Morris has read into Scripture scientific data that was not intended by the biblical text. This approach should be rejected as an explanation of the text. In this connection it is well to remember the words of Herman Bavinck: "Holy Scripture has a purpose that is religious-ethical through and through. It is not designed to be a manual for the various sciences." A little further on he notes, "Scripture does not satisfy the demand for exact knowledge in the way we demand it in mathematics, astronomy, chemistry, etc. This is a standard that may not be applied to it.... Scripture has a criterion of its own, requires an interpretation of its own, and has a purpose

---

40. Morris, *Studies*, 118–19.
41. Morris, *Studies*, 119 (italics in the original); Edward J. Young, *The Book of Isaiah* (Grand Rapids: Eerdmans, 1965–1972), 3:57n73.

and intention of its own. That intention is no other than that it should make us 'wise unto salvation.'"[42]

Subsequently, Bavinck correctly rejects any attempt to draw the opposite conclusion, namely, that Scripture is less than accurate when it portrays historical events or that Scripture is irrelevant for science. "Precisely as the book of the knowledge of God, Scripture has much to say also to the other sciences. It is a light on our path and a lamp for our feet, also with respect to science and art. It claims authority in all areas of life." And so "a great deal of what is related in Scripture is of fundamental significance also for the other sciences. The creation and fall of humankind, the unity of the human race, the flood, the rise of peoples and languages, etc. are facts of the highest significance also for the other sciences." Yet, Bavinck reaffirms that "Scripture never intentionally concerns itself with science as such."[43]

In this connection it is also good to listen to Geerhardus Vos, a younger contemporary of Bavinck. When commenting on interpreting Genesis 1 and 2 he characterizes it as an error "to give a hyperscientific exegesis that satisfies the latest perception and newest fashion. All sorts of theories from physics, geology, and astronomy have been projected onto the narrative…it is bad exegesis." Vos says it well when he subsequently notes:

> That science has discovered this or that, or thinks to have discovered it, is not enough to cause us to discover it in Genesis. The creation narrative provides pure truth, but in such a general form that it can serve equally for the instruction of God's people in centuries past and His children at the present time. (The hyperscientific interpretation loses sight of that.) That is precisely what makes the creation narrative such a great artistic achievement of the Spirit of God.[44]

Christian scientists, however, can be encouraged when their research leads them to articulate theories that are consistent with Scripture. After all, the events that Genesis records are factually true.

Although Henry Morris was emphatic in asserting that the Bible is a textbook of science, creation scientists currently appear to be much more cautious. Indeed, important creationists specifically deny this characterization. This is a good development. For example, creationist Andrew Snelling in his major

---

42. Bavinck, *Reformed Dogmatics*, 1:444.
43. Bavinck, *Reformed Dogmatics*, 1:445.
44. Geerhardus Vos, *Reformed Dogmatics*, trans. and ed. Richard B. Gaffin Jr. et al. (Bellingham, Wash.: Lexham, 2012–2016), 1:162.

work, *Earth's Catastrophic Past*, specifically states that "the Bible never claims to be a textbook on history or science." Paul Garner had similarly written that "the first book of the Bible is not, in the words of the cliché, 'a scientific textbook.'" Carl Wieland acknowledged the same. Jason Lisle's helpful book, *Understanding Genesis*, also avoids calling Scripture a scientific textbook and gives sound hermeneutical advice.[45] Remarkably though, Lisle in an earlier work, *Taking Back Astronomy*, used Isaiah 40:22 to show that the Bible indicates that the earth is round (a notion dismissed earlier in this chapter) and that the universe has increased in size since creation. He based the latter claim on the statement that God "stretches out the heavens like a curtain" (Isa. 40:22).[46] But the point of the text is not to inform us that the universe has expanded. Rather, this is simply a poetic way of describing the ease with which God has fashioned the heavens at creation (cf. Isa. 42:5; 44:24; 45:12). Another creationist, John G. Hartnett, has rightly concluded that Scripture (including Isa. 40:22) nowhere teaches an expanding universe.[47]

It is a most noble enterprise for Christian scientists to show that there is hard scientific data that is incompatible with and contrary to the theory of evolution. But this desire to disprove evolution and vindicate God's truth should not result in an unwarranted reading of scientific theory into the biblical text, although it may be tempting to do so.[48] Scripture does not need human efforts to prove its veracity. It stands on its own authority. Indeed, science is incapable

---

45. Andrew A. Snelling, *Earth's Catastrophic Past: Geology, Creation, and the Flood* (Green Forest, Ariz.: Master; Petersburg, Ky.: Answers in Genesis, 2014), 3, also 10; Paul A. Garner, *The New Creationism: Building Scientific Theories on a Biblical Basis* (Welwyn Garden City, U.K.: EP Books, 2009), 15; Carl Wieland, "Editorial: 'But the Bible's Not a Science Textbook, Is It?,'" *Creation* 22, no. 2 (2000): 4; Jason Lisle, *Understanding Genesis: How to Analyze, Interpret, and Defend Scripture* (Green Forest, Ariz.: Master, 2015); cf. also the issue of whether there are two kinds of creationists: Robert E. Snow, "A Critique of the Creation Science Movement," in *Portraits of Creation: Biblical and Scientific Perspectives on the World's Formation*, by Howard J. Van Till et al. (Grand Rapids: Eerdmans, 1990), 184–202.

46. Jason Lisle, *Taking Back Astronomy* (Green Forest, Ariz.: Master, 2006), ch. 2, Kindle.

47. John Hartnett, "Does the Bible Really Describe Expansion of the Universe?," *Journal of Creation* 25 (2011): 125–27; also see John Byl, *God and the Cosmos: A Christian View of Time, Space, and the Universe* (Edinburgh: Banner of Truth, 2001), 179–80.

48. On the hazard of letting the creationist (or for that matter the evolutionist) agenda dominate, see Kirsten Birkett, "Science and Scripture," in *The Enduring Authority of the Christian Scriptures*, ed. D. A. Carson (Grand Rapids: Eerdmans, 2016), 962; and J. A. van Delden, *Schepping en Wetenschap* (Amsterdam: Buijten & Schipperheijn, 1977), 50. Morris describes his work on Genesis as "a study of the scientific and historical accuracy of Genesis." Henry M. Morris, *The Genesis Record: A Scientific and Devotional Commentary on the Book of Beginnings* (Grand Rapids: Baker, 1976), xii, also see xiii; and Robert Charles Williams, "Scientific Creationism."

of giving any lasting assurance of the Word's truthfulness. Scripture is divine truth and needs to be read and interpreted according to its own agenda and its testimony of itself. Scripture is its own interpreter.

At the same time, the creation science movement is to be applauded for its defense of the infallibility of the Bible and taking seriously the historicity of the creation account and all that followed. Scripture gives information that excludes some theories (such as evolution), and Scripture reminds us that creation is a great work of God and as such will never be fully comprehended. Any information that Scripture does give is therefore vitally important, also for the scientific endeavor. Scientists, especially those trying to reconstruct the past history of the earth, impoverish themselves if they do not reckon with the history the Bible narrates, including the account of creation, the fall, the Noachian flood, the confusion of tongues, and more. Old Testament scholar Edward J. Young acknowledged that "the Bible is not a textbook of science," but he rightly also went on to say that "inasmuch as the Bible is the Word of God, whenever it speaks on any subject, whatever that subject may be, it is accurate in what it says. The Bible may not have been given to teach science as such, but it does teach about the origin of all things."[49] Science needs to take into consideration all the historical facts, including those recorded in Scripture. We owe a debt of gratitude to creationist scientists for their taking seriously the truth of God's Word and its ongoing relevance for the scientific endeavor. As subsequent chapters will show, this book gratefully makes use of their work where appropriate. However, as is true of all scientific work, although God's Word is infallible, the work of scientists, whether creationist or evolutionist, is not.

What General Revelation Reveals
If Scripture does not reveal the intricacies found in a scientific textbook, what does God reveal in His creation, or in what is often described as general revelation? What does Scripture tell us about general revelation? The short answer is that God reveals Himself. He is the object of general revelation. This biblical truth was articulated in Protestant confessions in the time of the Reformation. Article 2 of the Belgic Confession states that we know God "by the creation, preservation, and government of the universe; which is before our eyes as a most beautiful book, wherein all creatures, great and small, are as so many

---

49. Edward J. Young, *Studies in Genesis One* (Philadelphia: Presbyterian and Reformed, 1964), 43.

letters leading us to perceive clearly God's 'invisible attributes, namely, his eternal power and divine nature,' as the apostle Paul says in Romans 1:20."[50]

The context of the Romans passage is the apostle noting that God's wrath
is revealed against all ungodly people "who suppress the truth in unrighteous-
ness, because what may be known of God is manifest in them, for God has
shown it to them. For since the creation of the world His invisible attributes
are clearly seen, being understood by the things that are made, even His eternal
power and Godhead, so that they are without excuse" (Rom. 1:18–20). General
revelation reveals God and His greatness so plainly that all are held responsible
for knowing His glory. Commenting on Romans 1:19, Calvin wrote that man
was created as a spectator of God's world "for the purpose of his being led to
God Himself, the Author of the world, by contemplating so magnificent an
image." A similar message is heard when David exclaims, "The heavens declare
the glory of God; and the firmament shows His handiwork" (Ps. 19:1). As is
typical of parallelism in Hebrew poetry, the message of both the first and second part of this passage is basically the same. Calvin noted on this passage that
"the heavens proclaim to us the glory of God, namely, by openly bearing testimony that they have not been put together by chance, but were wonderfully
created by the supreme Architect. When we behold the heavens, we cannot but
be elevated, by the contemplation of them, to him who is their great Creator."[51]

For our present purpose, general revelation can therefore be defined as
God's revelation of Himself to everyone through His work of creation. Note that
creation is only a means by which He reveals His glory. General revelation does
not have creation as its object. The natural world is only the instrument to show
God's attributes such as His wisdom and glory. Now, if creation reveals God
and if science studies the created world, then one of the first conclusions that
science should arrive at is the reality and glory of God who reveals Himself in
the physical world that is studied (Ps. 8:1, 9; 19:1). Secular scientists who deny
God suppress or reject this revelation. Cornelius Van Til rightly asked, "Is it not
a *wrong* reading of *nature* if it is not seen to be clearly revelatory of God?"[52]

---

50. The Westminster Confession of Faith, ch. 1, begins with: "Although the light of nature
and the works of creation and providence do so far manifest the goodness, wisdom, and power
of God, as to leave men unexcusable; yet they are not sufficient to give that knowledge of God,
and of his will, which is necessary unto salvation."

51. John Calvin, *The Epistles of Paul the Apostle to the Romans and to the Thessalonians*,
trans. Ross MacKenzie (Grand Rapids: Eerdmans, 1960), 31; Calvin, *Commentary on the Book
of Psalms*, 1:309.

52. Cornelius Van Til, "Bavinck the Theologian: A Review Article," *WTJ* 24 (1961): 57 (italics in the original).

The fact that creation reveals God and His glory means that the concern of general revelation is not information about creation or scientific data as such. General revelation is often associated with science, but "the idea is not that *data* are divinely revealed but that *God* is revealed through the created order."[53] This fundamental point is often missed. Because general revelation reveals God, a scientist cannot say that new scientific data are new revelation given by God through general revelation.[54] The results of scientific research are not part of God's general revelation. As G. C. Berkouwer noted, "It is wrong to say, as is sometimes done, that the natural sciences 'investigate' God's general revelation; and surely it is just as wrong to state that we owe our knowledge of God's revelation in nature primarily to the natural sciences." He also noted that "the revelation of God in his works is a matter of God's self-revelation, and that is not apprehended first of all by scientific investigation, but through faith, as is evident already in the Psalms of Israel. These psalms of praise are not based on scientific investigation."[55]

John C. Whitcomb Jr. has correctly said that if we affirm that God has given two revelations of truth, one in Scripture and the other in nature, then we will consequently hold that "modern science provides an independent and equally authoritative source of information with the Bible concerning such doctrines as the original creation...and that science alone is competent to tell us when and how such things occurred (or even *whether* they occurred!), while the Bible merely informs us 'in non-technical language' as to *who* brought these things

---

53. Davis A. Young, "Where Are We?," in *Portraits of Creation: Biblical and Scientific Perspectives on the World's Formation*, by Howard J. Van Till et al. (Grand Rapids: Eerdmans, 1990), 4–5 (italics in the original); coming to a similar conclusion is Mary L. VandenBerg, "What General Revelation Does (and Does Not) Tell Us," *PSCF* 62 (2010): 16–24; John Bolt, "Getting the 'Two Books' Straight: With a Little Help from Herman Bavinck and John Calvin," *CTJ* 46 (2011): 315–32.

54. Such statements have been made. An ecclesiastical report on creation and science stated approvingly that "the facts of biology are just as much words of God as the Scriptures, and to be accepted in faith." In such a context it is also stated that "the authority of general revelation, no less than that of special revelation, is a divine authority, which must be acknowledged without reservation." A. Wolters et al., "Report 28: Committee on Creation and Science," in *Agenda for Synod 1991* (Grand Rapids: Christian Reformed Church in North America, 1991), 404, 407. Bavinck goes too far when he writes that scientific "facts are just as much words of God as the content of Holy Scripture and must therefore be believingly accepted by everyone." The problem is this: who defines the "facts"? Bavinck recognized this problem, and so to make such a statement is not helpful and blurs the distinction between God's revelation of His glory in Scripture and in creation. Bavinck, *Reformed Dogmatics*, 2:501. See also Nicolaas H. Gootjes, "General Revelation and Science: Reflections on a Remark in Report 28," *CTJ* 30 (1995): 94–107.

55. G. C. Berkouwer, *General Revelation* (Grand Rapids: Eerdmans, 1955), 289.

about and *why.*" The revelation that God does give in the material universe is the revelation of Himself.[56]

To prevent possible misunderstanding, we should make clear that when we assert that God reveals Himself and not scientific data in His work of creation, we do not deny that God's work of creation gives us information that Christians can and should investigate and scientifically analyze. Christian scientists have the glorious privilege of examining and studying God's handiwork. It is part of the mandate God has given to humans. They should have dominion over the earth and subdue it (Gen. 1:26, 28).[57] Creation certainly gives much information that should be researched. But Scripture does not call all this data revelation. The data of creation is the means by which God reveals His glory and greatness (Rom. 1:20). Nicolaas Gootjes put it well using a concrete example: "Scientific results never have the status of revelation. What God reveals in the Grand Canyon is not facts about the world (how it was made and when) but his own great power and glory. For that reason, not even correct scientific results should be seen as revelations from God. A qualitative difference exists between revelation and scientific results."[58] The first is infallible; the second is fallible human investigation.

In spite of the clear testimony of Scripture that God's general revelation in creation reveals God and His glory and power, attempts have been made in evangelical or conservative circles to extend the scope of general revelation to include our knowledge of nature and scientific theories. I will mention two examples. In 1987 David Diehl published an important article, which is still being discussed, in which he set forth his case that general revelation revealed

---

56. John C. Whitcomb Jr., "Biblical Inerrancy and the Double-Revelation Theory," *Grace Journal* 4, no. 1 (1963): 17 (italics in the original). Astrophysicist Jason Lisle has expressed similar sentiments: Lisle, *Understanding Genesis*, 297–308.

57. For more biblical justification to study creation, see Kurt P. Wise, *Faith, Form, and Time: What the Bible Teaches and Science Confirms about Creation and the Age of the Universe* (Nashville, Tenn.: B&H, 2002), 31–33.

58. Nicolaas H. Gootjes, "What Does God Reveal in the Grand Canyon?," in *Teaching and Preaching the Word: Studies in Dogmatics and Homiletics*, ed. Cornelis Van Dam (Winnipeg: Premier, 2010), 21; see also VandenBerg, "General Revelation," 19–20. VandenBerg, however, creates a false dilemma when she later (20–22) seems to suggest that the content of creation and scientific research into creation have little to do with each other. In her view, there is "no basis for advocating concordance between the findings of science and the information about creation found in the various types of literature of the Bible" (22). What God, who is true, says in His Word about creation cannot contradict true knowledge of His actual handiwork, the world in which we live.

not only God, but also scientific discoveries.[59] He supported his case by outlining what he called four agenda items to which evangelicals should pay attention. The first is "the objective authority of general revelation," which entails that "general and special revelation are equally authoritative and infallible for the respective truths that they in fact reveal."[60] The second is "the 'creational' specificity of general revelation," by which he meant that "the message of general revelation, while general about the character and will of God, is quite specific when it comes to matters of creation." Consequently, general revelation also gives us knowledge "of creation's specific nature and laws."[61] His third agenda item is "the epistemological priority of general revelation," that is, "all biblical statements are dependent on general revelation for rational, empirical and personal meaning."[62] The final item Diehl brought forward is "the Christological progressiveness of general revelation." Since special revelation is progressive until the closing of the biblical canon, "we need to recognize that general revelation continues to be progressive throughout the whole human history. This of course is the basis for the increase in our scientific knowledge."[63]

Although Diehl has set forth an impressive list of action items, it all hinges on one critical point. Does general revelation authoritatively reveal scientific knowledge? In other words, is such knowledge to be considered divine, infallible revelation? How did Diehl justify the notion in his second item that general revelation also gives us knowledge "of creation's specific nature and laws"? Diehl pointed to Psalm 19:1 about which he observed that "nature not only reveals the 'glory of God' but also 'the work of his hands.' In this natural revelation there is knowledge not only of the Maker but also of the things he has made. God causes the creation to be self-revealing as well as God-revealing."[64]

The biblical passage in question reads as follows:

---

59. David W. Diehl, "Evangelicalism and General Revelation: An Unfinished Agenda," *JETS* 30 (1987): 441–55. Reactions to this article include: Andrew S. Kulikovsky, "Scripture and General Revelation," *Journal of Creation* 19, no. 2 (2005): 23–28; Jason Van Vliet, "The Two Books Debate: What if Scripture and Science Seem to Say Different Things?," in *Correctly Handling the Word of Truth: Reformed Hermeneutics Today*, ed. Mees te Velde and Gerhard H. Visscher (Eugene, Ore.: Wipf & Stock, 2014), 1–16; John Byl, "General Revelation and Evangelicalism," *Mid-America Journal of Theology* 5 (1989): 1–13.

60. Diehl, "Evangelicalism and General Revelation," 445, 448.

61. Diehl, "Evangelicalism and General Revelation," 448–49.

62. Diehl, "Evangelicalism and General Revelation," 450.

63. Diehl, "Evangelicalism and General Revelation," 453.

64. Diehl, "Evangelicalism and General Revelation," 448.

The heavens declare the glory of God;
And the firmament shows His handiwork. (Ps. 19:1)

As is typical of Hebrew poetry, the author, David, uses the technique of parallelism whereby the second line repeats the main thought of the first line. In other words, when the firmament or sky proclaims God's handiwork, it is proclaiming God's glory. This fact has already been briefly noted earlier in this section and this understanding is not controversial. It is and has been widely accepted.[65] In other words, Psalm 19 cannot be used to suggest that the object of general revelation is to reveal "creation's specific nature and laws" or, to put it differently, that such laws as deduced by scientists are infallible revelation from God.

Diehl's second justification for his position comes from the book of Romans. He noted that "Rom 1:20 teaches that the invisible attributes of God are perceived and understood by the things he has created. In other words, knowledge of God comes by and with the knowledge of creation."[66] It is true that God's attributes such as His wisdom and glory are perceived by the things He has created. In that sense one can also say that knowing creation helps us to see God's glory. But all this is no basis for saying that general revelation gives us knowledge "of creation's specific nature and laws." Romans 1:20 says that God's "invisible attributes are clearly seen, being understood by the things that are made, even His eternal power and Godhead, so that they are without excuse." This passage makes clear that we can see God's attributes through His handiwork. There is nothing here to suggest that we can include in this revelation scientific laws and theories.[67] General revelation reveals God's greatness and glory. Scientific discoveries are not divine revelation.

As part of his justification, Diehl also mentioned Acts 14:17, which states that God "did not leave Himself without witness, in that He did good, gave us rain from heaven and fruitful seasons, filling our hearts with food and gladness." It is unclear how this passage can serve Diehl's claim that general

---

65. See, e.g., Calvin, *Commentary on the Book of Psalms*, 1:309; Peter C. Craigie, *Psalms 1–50* (Waco, Tex.: Word, 1983), 180; Nic. H. Ridderbos, *De Psalmen* (Kampen: Kok, 1962), 1:208–9; Hans-Joachim Kraus, *Psalms 1–59: A Commentary*, trans. Hilton C. Oswald (repr., Minneapolis: Augsburg, 1988), 270. Early Christian commentators understand Ps. 19:1 similarly: Craig A. Blaising and Carmen S. Hardin, eds., *Psalms 1–50*, ACCS (Downers Grove, Ill.: InterVarsity, 2008), 146–48.

66. Diehl, "Evangelicalism and General Revelation," 448.

67. On Rom. 1:20, see John Murray, *The Epistle to the Romans* (repr., Grand Rapids: Eerdmans, 1968), 1:38–40; Thomas R. Schreiner, *Romans* (Grand Rapids: Baker, 1998), 86.

revelation reveals scientific laws. He himself correctly noted on this passage that as we contemplate the things of creation "we gain a knowledge of God."[68]

In conclusion, Diehl's arguments for extending general revelation to include scientific findings as authoritative revelation from God are not convincing.[69]

In conservative circles, another attempt to extend the scope of general revelation to include scientific findings can be found among the adherents of the philosophical system of Herman Dooyeweerd.[70] These authors have attempted to connect general revelation to the results of scientific research by saying that general revelation reveals God's wisdom and science discovers that wisdom.

One biblical passage in particular has been used to try to justify the claim that the results of science are general revelation and that the findings of science therefore present new revelation from God. Isaiah 28:23–29 tells of God teaching the farmer. The farmer knows how to prepare a field for sowing "for He instructs him in right judgment; His God teaches him" (v. 26). His harvesting technique "also comes from the LORD of hosts, Who is wonderful in counsel and excellent in guidance" (v. 29). The point of this passage, then, is that the farmer learned "through the revelation of creation…by listening to the voice of God in the work of his hands."[71]

Can Isaiah 28, however, be used as a prooftext for understanding general revelation in this way? It has never been used in this manner in the history of Reformed theology. Bavinck does mention the passage when discussing general revelation as God's self-revelation. However, he mentions it in the context of showing that general revelation is not normally considered the source of our knowledge of creation. He writes that "in a sense we can say that…all knowledge of nature and history as we acquire and apply it in our occupation and business, in commerce and industry, in the arts and sciences, is due to the revelation of God." Under God's guidance, human beings gradually learn to understand.

---

68. Diehl, "Evangelicalism and General Revelation," 448–49.

69. Coming to the same conclusion are: Byl, "General Revelation"; Andrew S. Kulikovsky, *Creation, Fall, Restoration: A Biblical Theology of Creation* (Geanies House, Scotland: Mentor, 2009), 17–27 (similarly, Kulikovsky, "Scripture and General Revelation"); Van Vliet, "The Two Books Debate," 4–9.

70. For a general discussion of Dooyeweerd on creational revelation, see J. Douma, *Another Look at Dooyeweerd*, trans. J. M. Batteau (Winnipeg: Premier, n.d.), 28–34.

71. Albert M. Wolters, *Creation Regained: Biblical Basics for a Reformational Worldview*, 2nd ed. (Grand Rapids: Eerdmans, 2005), 33; similarly, Michael Goheen, "Scriptural Revelation, Creational Revelation and Natural Science: The Issue," in *Facets of Faith and Science*, ed. Jitse M. van der Meer, vol. 4, *Interpreting God's Action in the World* (Lanham, Md.: University Press of America, 1996), 333–34.

Scripture itself testifies to this when it says that it is God who teaches the farmer about the way he has to work the fields (Isa. 28:24–29). But since the creation's existence is distinct from God, and nature and history can also be studied by themselves and for their own sake, knowledge of God and knowledge of his creatures do not coincide, and in the latter case we usually do not speak of revelation as the source of knowledge.... In revelation, God becomes knowable.[72]

According to Bavinck, therefore, in general revelation God, not scientific facts, becomes knowable.

We need to take a closer look at Isaiah 28:23–29. These verses describe how a farmer does his plowing, seeding, and harvesting according to God's instruction. Verse 26 can also be translated, "His God instructs him; he teaches him the principles of agriculture" (NET). The harvesting techniques vary according to the crop being taken in. "This also comes from the LORD of hosts, Who is wonderful in counsel and excellent in guidance" (v. 29). The point seems to be that God enabled the farmer to have the necessary wisdom so that by observing the seasons and deducing principles from the laws of nature ("the principles of agriculture") he was able to determine the best time to prepare the ground, sow the crops, and eventually harvest. All this takes place within the larger context of God judging His people. Just as people who do not know anything about farming might ridicule and question the wisdom of what a farmer is doing, so they scoff at God and think there is no rhyme or reason to what He is doing to His people (cf. Isa. 28:21–22). It would be better for such people to acknowledge their ignorance and acknowledge God's wisdom, which can even be seen in the ways of a farmer. In granting the necessary insight and wisdom to the farmer to learn from creation's laws of nature, God was teaching him. The point of this passage is not to inform us that general revelation reveals scientific facts as divine revelation, but it is a general statement that the farmer's agricultural insight is God's gift.[73]

Gootjes has rightly pointed out that if Isaiah 28 can be used to support the notion that science brings us new revelation from God, "then correct results of the natural sciences must be treated as revelatory truths." Further, "this general

---

72. Bavinck, *Reformed Dogmatics*, 1:341–42. Also for more on Bavinck and this issue, see Nicolaas H. Gootjes, "Farming According to General Revelation? The Meaning of Isaiah 28:22–29," in *Teaching and Preaching the Word: Studies in Dogmatics and Homiletics*, ed. Cornelis Van Dam (Winnipeg: Premier, 2010), 26–29.

73. Edward J. Young, *Isaiah*, 2:298–99; John N. Oswalt, *The Book of Isaiah, Chapters 1–39* (Grand Rapids: Eerdmans, 1986), 520–24; Klaas Schilder, *Schriftoverdenkingen*, ed. L. Doekes et al. (Goes: Oosterbaan & Le Cointre, 1956–1958), 2:151–53; Gootjes, "Farming," 31–32.

revelation then becomes not only an ongoing revelation but also a still continuously expanding revelation." As a result, discoveries of the natural sciences will "come to stand on par with scriptural data as general revelation beside special revelation."[74] But, the results of science can never be equated with general revelation. General revelation reveals God and not scientific data. The two need to be distinguished. God's creation reveals God's glory.

Furthermore, Scripture tells us that this revelation of God is plain and obvious. It is so clearly perceived in God's work of creation that it renders us without excuse (Rom. 1:19–20). However, scientific data is not always plain and obvious. It has taken centuries to get to the point where we are now. And God does not expect us to see the scientific data as obvious. Did he not challenge Job about the knowledge of creation that was beyond his reach and ability to perceive (Job 38–39)? The heavens declare the glory of God (Ps. 19:1). This is clearly revealed, but the scientific facts of the heavens are still being discovered; they are not so obvious.

Thus, to sum up, both Scripture and general revelation reveal God's glory. Scripture does so especially in recounting the history of God's love for His creation, culminating in the coming of Christ. Creation does so by showing something of the glory and power of the Creator.

It is beneficial at this point to take a closer look at a particular aspect of Psalm 19, a biblical passage often referenced in discussions of general revelation. It helps us to see the relationship between God's revelation of Himself in creation and in His Word. In the way this psalm speaks of an aspect of creation—namely, what we call the laws of nature—it also gives us a good example of how we can see something of God's glory.

An Example: Psalm 19 and the Laws of Nature

This psalm is divided into two main parts.[75] In the first six verses we are told how creation—the heavens—declares God's glory. In verses 7–14 we read of the glory of the LORD revealed in the law, His Word. In this arrangement the psalm moves to a climax. One can marvel, for example, at the starry night sky and see something of the greatness and glory of God. But when one reads the Word written, God's glory and power are seen in a much richer way. It is striking

---

74. Gootjes, "Farming," 25. This was also the concern expressed by Berkouwer, *General Revelation*, 287–90.

75. For what follows, see Cornelis Van Dam, "How Does God Reveal Himself in His Works and Word?" *Clarion* 41 (1992): 154–56, 179–81, 201–2. Although the Hebrew verse numbering begins with the heading of this Psalm, I will use the versification as found in English translations.

that in the first half of the psalm, the Creator is referred to once as "God" (v. 1), while in the second half of the psalm only the name "LORD," the covenant name of God, is used, even seven times (vv. 7, 8, 9, 14). The message is clear. Creation, general revelation, while accessible to all mankind, cannot fully reveal the God of the covenant. He is only fully known through special revelation.[76] It is also evident from this psalm that one cannot truly understand the created world and the glory of God it reveals without knowing about the LORD, the God of the covenant.

Psalm 19 begins: "The heavens declare the glory of God; and the firmament shows His handiwork" (v. 1). How do the heavens declare this? This is done without words. In quiet majesty the heavens proclaim the glory of God. "There is no speech nor language where their voice is not heard" (v. 3); that is, to put it differently, "there is no actual speech or word, nor is its voice literally heard" (v. 3 NET). But how do the heavens and the firmament, or sky, then declare the glory of God? As N. H. Ridderbos explains, they do this by carrying out the task God has given them to do according to His norms. What is that task? The firmament was created to separate the waters (Gen. 1:6–8; cf. Job 38:8–11). The heavenly bodies—the sun, moon, and stars—have as their task to separate or measure off the day from night and to be for signs, for seasons, and for days and years (Gen. 1:14). So faithfully do the heavens and the heavenly bodies do their task that they appear to be the norm or measuring line itself, so regular and predictable is their behavior. That is the context of the Hebrew text that literally reads, "Their measuring line goes out through all the earth" (Ps. 19:4).[77] One can therefore also render it: "their law is proclaimed throughout all the world." As Artur Weiser notes, "The knowledge of the world's divine ordering (literally, plumb-line or canon) penetrates into every country."[78] The psalmist gives an example by mentioning the sun. It regularly rises and sets (vv. 4–6). And so the heavens and the heavenly bodies declare and reveal God's glory by doing the task that God gave them to do at creation according to His

---

76. Nic. H. Ridderbos, *De Psalmen*, 1:204, 206–7; Nic. H. Ridderbos, *Die Psalmen. Stilistische Verfahren und Aufbau met besonderer Berücksichtigung von Ps 1–41* (Berlin: De Gruyter, 1972), 176–77; more recently, James K. Hoffmeier, "'The Heavens Declare the Glory of God': The Limits of General Revelation," *TJ*, n.s., 21 (2000): 17–24.

77. Nic. H. Ridderbos, *De Psalmen*, 1:210; the ESV emends the original Hebrew text ("their measuring line") to read: "Their voice goes out through all the earth." For the exegesis and a justification for why the original Hebrew text is followed (as in NASB, NKJV), see Cornelis Van Dam, "Duidelijke taal. De boodschap van de hemelen volgens Psalm 19:5a," in *Een sprekend begin: opstellen aangeboden aan Prof. Drs. H. M. Ohmann*, ed. R. ter Beek et al. (Kampen: Van den Berg, 1993), 86–93 (for an English abstract, see *OTA* 21 [1998], #1482).

78. Artur Weiser, *The Psalms* (Philadelphia: Westminster, 1962), 197, 199.

norms. God expects the same obedience from the head of creation, human beings, according to the norms He spelled out in His special revelation, the law (vv. 7–14).[79]

So faithfully does creation heed God's creational will that we speak of laws of nature and normal, natural phenomena. These laws of nature are, however, in fact creation's ongoing obedience to God's creational decrees. There are no autonomous laws of nature. God has a covenant with creation so that day and night come at the appointed time (Jer. 33:20). This covenant parallels "the ordinances [*ḥuqqôt*] of heaven and earth" (Jer. 33:25), that is, the obligations heaven and earth have received from God (similarly, Jer. 31:35–36; cf. Ps. 119:89–91). God gives His orders to the sun, moon, stars, seas, and all creation (e.g., Job 38:31–35; Ps. 148:6; Prov. 8:29; Jer. 5:24; cf. also Ps. 65:5–10). He makes the wind His messengers, fire and flame His ministers (Ps. 104:4). All creation's elements are His servants.

God does not give His orders haphazardly. He does so as the one who is faithful to the promise spoken to Noah: "While the earth remains, seedtime and harvest, cold and heat, winter and summer, and day and night shall not cease" (Gen. 8:22). We therefore experience a certain regularity and predictability in creation. But, it is only predictable because God is faithful and is consistent in His wishes for His creation. What scientists therefore conclude as recurring and predictable from a study of creation are strictly speaking not laws of nature, but evidence of the faithfulness of our God to His creation work as He designed it, a work He is still involved in moment by moment, seeing to it that it carries out what He has ordained and commanded.

Because God is in total control at all times, therefore, the "laws of nature" cannot be treated as autonomous and unchanging. Phenomena of creation are God's servants. God has therefore used the heavens in order to have them serve His people in special ways. Think, for example, of how God threw great stones down from heaven on the Amorites and caused the sun to stand still in the sky so that Joshua could achieve a full victory (Josh. 10). Or think of how the stars were involved in the battle against Sisera (Judg. 5:20). God also used the heavens to punish Israel. Thus, for example, God kept the rain from falling in Israel for three and a half years in the days of Ahab and Jezebel (1 Kings 17:1; James 5:17).[80]

God is active in creation. The order and regularity we see in creation do not reside in the creation but in God who commands the regularity, but who can

---

79. Nic. H. Ridderbos, *De Psalmen*, 1:210; Nic. H. Ridderbos, *Die Psalmen*, 177.
80. Other examples include 1 Sam. 7:10 and 2 Sam. 22:8–16 (Ps. 18:7–15).

also command irregularity! He even used His position as creator to destroy and cleanse the world with a great flood. While the deluge lasted, God erased the separation between land and water that He had set at creation. God made a covenant with Noah and every living creature that this type of destruction would never happen again (Gen. 9:8–11). But God has also acted in less momentous ways. For example, God can also intervene in the law of wear and tear. Things get older, not newer. Books get tattered, clothes get worn, and shoes get holes. But this is not an absolute law operating independently from God. He can also command otherwise. After Israel had wandered in the wilderness for forty years, God could say to His people, "Your clothes have not worn out on you, and your sandals have not worn out on your feet" (Deut. 29:5).

God's past and ongoing management of creation in a manner pleasing to Him must be taken into consideration by present-day science. There are no autonomous and absolutely unchanging laws of nature. Instead, creation obeys God's ongoing direction. His will for creation can change from time to time, as revealed in His Word. Scientists, especially when dealing with origins and earth history, must therefore consider the possibility that things did not always transpire as they might expect. Models such as uniformitarianism, by which changes in the earth's crust took place according to rates as we measure them today, can never be taken for absolute truth when Scripture tells of incredibly catastrophic events in the past that have impacted earth history. Rejecting the Creator will not help the scientific enterprise.

Having seen how both Scripture and creation reveal God's glory, let us now turn to other aspects of science and general revelation.

The Nature and Limitations of Science
The authority of science is enormous, and its prestige is understandable. In a matter of a few generations, science has given us a wide array of inventions and technologies. Travel has been revolutionized with cars and airplanes. Communication has taken a quantum leap forward with radio, television, internet, and cell phones. Computers and medical advances have made what was formerly impossible achievable. So who would dare contest scientific findings? It is obvious that scientists are on to something. The results of their work show that they have truth on their side. At this point one needs to pause and make some necessary distinctions.

The above examples all deal with current processes and repeatable events that can be verified through experiments under controlled conditions. However, theorizing about the origin of the universe is an entirely different matter. The processes that occurred then can be neither retrieved nor repeated. One can speculate, but one cannot be sure, scientifically speaking, exactly how Planet Earth came to its present form. As Nobel laureate Peter Medawar has acknowledged, it is simply beyond the competence of science to answer the question "How did everything begin?"[81] We need to be very humble when speaking about the origin of the world. We do not know in a scientific way how God brought the present creation into being. We have no idea what processes were set in motion when "by the word of the LORD the heavens were made, and all the host of them by the breath of His mouth.... He spoke, and it was done; He commanded, and it stood fast" (Ps. 33:6, 9).

Whatever human beings with their finite minds and limited understanding do say about origins is very much dependent on the presuppositions informing their interpretation of the scientific data they are working with. The vast majority of scientists are working with evolutionary presuppositions since evolution is the current reigning scientific paradigm. But what is current today may not be so in the future. Serious questions continue to be raised about the theory of evolution, also by scientists who do not critique the theory as Christians. Scientific paradigms change as scientific knowledge expands, and new perspectives open up.[82]

---

81. Peter Medawar, *The Limits of Science* (Oxford: Oxford University Press, 1987), 55–103, esp. 66, 88. At one time Bruce Waltke noted, "Since science is the systematic analysis of *presently* observed processes and their phenomena, science cannot and ought not attempt to answer the question of the origin of the universe. The answer is beyond the range of empirical proof." Bruce K. Waltke, "The Creation Account in Genesis 1:1–3. Part I: Introduction to Biblical Cosmology," *BSac* 132 (1975): 28; but cf. more recently, Bruce K. Waltke with Cathi J. Fredricks, *Genesis: A Commentary* (Grand Rapids: Zondervan, 2001), 73–78, where he gives considerable weight to science in concluding that Genesis 1 is not a strict historical account.

82. As explained in the landmark work of Thomas S. Kuhn, *The Structure of Scientific Revolutions*, 4th ed. (Chicago: University of Chicago Press, 2012). For a scientific assessment of the quality of the evidence for evolution, see the recent work of Rob Stadler, *The Scientific Approach to Evolution* (self-pub., CreateSpace, 2016). The results are not encouraging for supporters of the theory of evolution, and Stadler argues that educators should admit the limitations of the theory. There are many solid critiques of the theory of evolution. See, e.g., the review article by Yale University professor of computer science, David Gelernter, "Giving Up Darwin," *Claremont Review of Books* 19, no. 2 (2019): 104–9, which reviews Stephen C. Meyer, *Darwin's Doubt* (2013), David Berlinski, *The Deniable Darwin* (2010), and David Klinghoffer, ed., *Debating Darwin's Doubt* (2015). Also see Douglas Axe, *Undeniable: How Biology Confirms Our Intuition That Life Is Designed* (San Francisco: HarperOne, 2016); Michael Denton, *Evolution: Still a Theory in Crisis* (Seattle: Discovery Institute, 2016); Michael J. Behe, *Darwin Devolves: The New Science about DNA That Challenges Evolution* (New York: HarperOne, 2019); W. R. Bird, *The Origin of Species Revisited: The Theories of Evolution and of Abrupt Appearance*, 2 vols. (New York: Philosophical Library, 1989); and Phillip E. Johnson, *Darwin on Trial*, 20th anniversary ed. (Downers Grove, Ill.: InterVarsity, 2010).

We need to recognize the tentative nature of scientific claims. As geology professor Nigel Brush has made clear in his helpful book, *The Limitations of Scientific Truth*, scientific theory does not provide us with absolute truth since there is "the constant flux in scientific knowledge and scientific truth."[83] And as already noted, especially with respect to the origin of Planet Earth, the scientific enterprise is unable to make any demonstrable truth claims. Those wanting to uphold the plain sense of Genesis 1 and 2 have nothing to fear from science. Scientific truth is not superior to biblical truth. For example, contrary to mainstream scientific thinking that the world came into being by chance, believers may know for a certainty that this scientific "truth" is false for, according to Scripture, God created all things. Our world did not come into being by chance. While scientific theories and conclusions have changed and will continue to do so, we may know that "the word of our God stands forever" (Isa. 40:8).

So where does this leave us when it comes to science and interpreting Scripture? Should we keep creation and Scripture totally separate as two hermetically sealed areas of research that do not communicate with each other? Such two solitudes cannot be justified. Although we can recognize that the purpose of studying Scripture and the purpose of studying creation are different, yet we are faced with the fact that God is the ultimate author of both. Since the opening chapters of Genesis deal with creation, we cannot avoid the question of how to relate Scripture to the sciences, and vice versa.

God's Word and Science

There are at least four major points to be made when considering the relationship of God's Word to science:

1. Doing science is consistent with the creation mandate.
2. Scripture provides relevant information for science.
3. Science needs the guidance of God's Word.
4. If there is a true contradiction between what science theorizes and Scripture clearly states, then Scripture should be followed.

First, as briefly noted earlier, the scientific endeavor is completely consistent with the creation mandate of subduing the earth and having dominion over creation (Gen. 1:28). Not surprisingly, modern science is to a great extent a

---

83. Nigel Brush, *The Limitations of Scientific Truth* (Grand Rapids: Kregel Academic and Professional, 2005), 264.

product of Judeo-Christian influence on Western thought.[84] Christians have been in the forefront in the history of science. There is no conflict between believing Scripture and pursuing the natural sciences. It is of interest to note that pioneers of modern science like Isaac Newton, Robert Boyle, and John Locke fostered the approach of first canvassing Scripture when dealing with a scientific topic. These scholars saw the Bible as a sourcebook of great importance when doing science.[85] Peter Harrison has put forward the credible thesis that "the Bible—its contents, the controversies it generated, its varying fortunes as an authority, and most importantly, the new way it was read by Protestants— played a central role in the emergence of natural science in the seventeenth century."[86] That important new way of reading the Bible was to understand the text in its literal and historical sense. The Protestant Reformation highlighted the importance of this literal approach by limiting the allegorical and symbolic way of interpreting Scripture. The literal reading of the opening chapters of Genesis was especially important in providing a crucial motivation for scientific investigation.[87] Given this thesis, it is quite ironic that "today it is the literalists in the creation science movement who are considered the great opponents of truly scientific enquiry."[88] Although Scripture is not a scientific textbook, scientists should make use of any information relevant to their investigations that is found in Scripture. Such information is truly reliable.

---

84. See Hooykaas, *Religion and the Rise of Modern Science*.

85. Roy Clouser, "Is Theism Compatible with Evolution?," in *Intelligent Design, Creationism, and Its Critics: Philosophical, Theological, and Scientific Perspectives*, ed. Robert T. Pennock (Cambridge, Mass.: MIT Press, 2001), 516; Vishal Mangalwadi, *The Book That Made Your World: How the Bible Created the Soul of Western Civilization* (Nashville: Thomas Nelson, 2011), 235. For the influence of Christianity on science, see also Alvin Plantinga, *Where the Conflict Really Lies: Science, Religion, and Naturalism* (New York: Oxford University Press, 2011), 266–303.

86. Peter Harrison, *Rise of Natural Science*, 4–5. For a critique of this thesis, see Jitse M. van der Meer and Richard J. Oosterhoff, "God, Scripture, and the Rise of Modern Science," in *Nature and Scripture in the Abrahamic Religions: Up to 1700*, ed. Jitse M. van der Meer and Scott Mandelbrote (Leiden: Brill, 2008), 363–96; Jitse M. van der Meer and Richard Oosterhoff, "The Bible, Protestantism and the Rise of Natural Science: A Response to Harrison's Thesis," *S&CB* 21 (2009): 133–53. Harrison replies in "The Bible, Protestantism and the Rise of Natural Science: A Rejoinder," *S&CB* 21 (2009): 155–62.

87. Peter Harrison, *Rise of Natural Science*, 127, 205–65 (esp. 208, 263–65), 266–73; Peter Harrison, "Subduing the Earth: Genesis 1, Early Modern Science, and the Exploitation of Nature," *JR* 79 (1999): 96–107; Peter Harrison, "Hermeneutics and Natural Knowledge in the Reformers," in *Nature and Scripture in the Abrahamic Religions: Up to 1700*, ed. Jitse M. van der Meer and Scott Mandelbrote (Leiden: Brill, 2008), 341–62.

88. Rowland Ward, review of *The Bible, Protestantism, and the Rise of Natural Science*, by Peter Harrison, *RTR* 58, no. 3 (1999): 169; cf. Peter Harrison, *Rise of Natural Science*, 267–68.

This observation brings us to our second major consideration, namely, that Scripture does provide us with information vital for the proper execution and expectations of science. Now, some would say that since the Bible is not a scientific textbook, and in order to avoid conflict between the Bible and science, we should realize that Scripture answers questions about "who" and "why" while science takes care of the "how" questions. In this approach, the Bible and science complement each other and cannot be antagonistic. However, such a dichotomy is too neat and simple. It does not work in practice. The reality is far more complex because Scripture does indeed speak of the actual world in which we live.[89] When it does so, it can provide information that is relevant for scientists to consider, especially concerning origins. No one witnessed creation, but God was there and He has provided an account in His Word that needs to be studied and taken into consideration. The results of such study should have a bearing on scientific theorizing about origins. The fall into sin and the Genesis flood are other examples of biblical data that may have real consequences for scientific studies. Scientists who ignore Scripture may ignore pertinent facts that can help them in their work. The Bible is also reliable when it touches on topics of scientific interest. The fact that "all Scripture is given by inspiration of God" so that the believer may be "equipped for every good work" (2 Tim. 3:16–17) means that it can be trusted for whatever it teaches or for whatever information it communicates. In this sense, Scripture can help and enable a person also in the scientific endeavor. And so, although it is true, as Bavinck noted, that "Scripture never intentionally concerns itself with science as such" and that "it is not a scientific book in the strict sense," yet "a great deal of what is related in Scripture is of fundamental significance also for the other sciences" (besides theology). "This truth may in no way be discounted."[90]

Bavinck consequently rightly maintained the primacy of Scripture, although he was open to correction from the *facts* of science.

> When Scripture…comes in contact with other sciences and also sheds its light on them, it does not all at once cease to be the Word of God but remains that Word. Even when it speaks about the genesis of heaven and earth, it does not present saga or myth or poetic fantasy but offers, in accordance with its own clear intent, history, the history that deserves

---

89. J. P. Moreland, *Christianity and the Nature of Science* (Grand Rapids: Baker, 1989), 12; and Poythress, *Redeeming Science*, 36.

90. Bavinck, *Reformed Dogmatics*, 1:445; see also the discussion in Richard B. Gaffin Jr., *God's Word in Servant-Form: Abraham Kuyper and Herman Bavinck on the Doctrine of Scripture* (Jackson, Miss.: Reformed Academic Press, 2008), 93–100.

credence and trust. And for that reason Christian theology, with only a few exceptions, continued to hold onto the literal historical view of the creation story.[91]

It is unfortunate that Benjamin B.Warfield, stalwart Princeton defender of the infallibility of Scripture, is often cited as an example of someone who honored Scripture and yet accepted the theory of evolution. Although Warfield certainly left himself open to misinterpretation on this point, to state that Warfield endorsed evolution goes beyond the facts. As Fred Zaspel concluded on the basis of his studies,

> Although at times speaking with allowance of the possibility of evolution (carefully defined), Warfield never expressly affirmed it. Rather, he affirmed that he had rejected it sometime about age thirty and that he remained unconvinced. The Livingstone-Noll thesis does not reflect the evidence, and the prevailing understanding of Warfield as an evolutionist must be rejected.[92]

As Nancy Pearcey observed, "When Warfield explained what he *meant* by evolution, he spoke of the constant supervision of divine providence, punctuated by 'occasional supernatural inference.' Anyone expressing those views today would be branded a flaming creationist."[93]

---

91. Bavinck, *Reformed Dogmatics*, 2:495; also see Herman Bavinck, *Essays on Religion, Science, and Society*, ed. John Bolt, trans. Harry Boonstra and Gerrit Sheeres (Grand Rapids: Baker Academic, 2008), 115–16.

92. Fred G. Zaspel, "Princeton and Evolution," *The Confessional Presbyterian* 8 (2012): 91–98. It is beyond the scope of this study to go into Warfield's writings, but see further Fred G. Zaspel, "Additional Note: B. B. Warfield Did Not Endorse Theistic Evolution as It Is Understood Today," in Moreland et al., *Theistic Evolution*, 953–72; Fred G. Zaspel, "B. B. Warfield on Creation and Evolution," *Themelios* 35 (2010): 211. Warfield as an evolutionist is especially defended by David N. Livingstone and Mark A. Noll, "B. B. Warfield (1851–1921): A Biblical Inerrantist as Evolutionist," *Journal of Presbyterian History* 80 (2002): 153–71; also, David N. Livingstone, *Darwin's Forgotten Defenders: The Encounter between Evangelical Theology and Evolutionary Thought* (Grand Rapids: Eerdmans; Edinburgh: Scottish Academic Press, 1987), esp. 119; Mark A. Noll, *The Scandal of the Evangelical Mind*, 206–8; cf. Bradley J. Gundlach, *Process and Providence: The Evolution Question at Princeton, 1845–1929* (Grand Rapids: Eerdmans, 2013), 262, 287, 311–13.

93. Nancy Pearcey, *Total Truth: Liberating Christianity from Its Cultural Captivity* (Wheaton, Ill.: Crossway, 2005), 309 (italics in the original). The quotation is from Warfield's 1888 lecture "Evolution or Development," as quoted in Warfield, *B. B. Warfield—Evolution, Science, and Scripture: Selected Writings*, ed. Mark A. Noll and David N. Livingstone (Grand Rapids: Baker Books, 2000), 29.

Warfield, like Bavinck, emphasized the necessity of irrefutable facts and maintained the primacy of Scripture, as have more recent Reformed scholars, such as John Frame, who has clearly rejected the theory of evolution.[94]

A third major consideration of relating science to the Bible is that in light of the primacy of Scripture, we need, as Calvin has reminded us, the spectacles of God's Word because our minds have been darkened by sin.[95] We cannot understand creation properly without the guidance of God's Word. Creation is His handiwork. He designed it and we do well to listen to Him. Cornelius Van Til has reminded us that God's thought as the creator is behind every fact, and we need to think God's thoughts after Him. "There is not a single fact that man can interpret rightly without reference to God as the creator of that fact.... It is God who has 'caused' all facts to stand in a certain relation to one another. Man must seek to discover that relation as far as he can." Van Til subsequently maintained that "unless God has created the existence of the universe, there would be no possibility of scientific thought. Facts would then be utterly unrelated."[96]

It is therefore a great tragedy that current mainline science is captive to naturalism, which is atheistic, and thus refuses to attach any value to the fact that God created all things and that His Word is therefore also relevant for scientific endeavors. There is a good case to be made that scientists hold on to the theory of evolution, with all its weaknesses, because that is the only option open to them if they deny God as creator. The theory of evolution is the god they worship.[97] By doing so these scientists not only dishonor God (cf. Rom. 1:20–21),

---

94. For a summary of Warfield's priority of Scripture, and on the need for facts, see Zaspel, "B. B. Warfield on Creation and Evolution," 202–5; also see John Frame, *The Doctrine of the Knowledge of God* (Phillipsburg, N.J.: P&R, 1987), 316; John Frame, *Systematic Theology: An Introduction to Christian Belief* (Phillipsburg, N.J.: P&R, 2013), 202–3.

95. John Calvin, *Institutes of the Christian Religion*, ed. John T. McNeill, trans. Ford Lewis Battles (Philadelphia: Westminster, 1960), 1.6.1; 1.14.1; and Calvin, *Genesis*, 1:62.

96. Cornelius Van Til, *Christian-Theistic Evidences* (Phillipsburg, N.J.: Presbyterian and Reformed, 1978), 102–3. Concerning thinking God's thoughts after Him, see the clear summary of Van Til's thought in Greg L. Bahnsen, *Van Til's Apologetic: Readings and Analysis* (Phillipsburg, N.J.: P&R, 1998), 220–35.

97. A point made in Phillip E. Johnson, *Darwin on Trial*, 162. The entire book underlines the way that science, when it excludes God, seeks to embrace a religion of scientific naturalism espousing the theory of evolution, which Johnson characterizes as a pseudoscience (see 179–89). Christian philosopher Alvin Plantinga correctly argues that there is no conflict between science as such and Christian belief. He contends that the real conflict is between science and naturalism, a quasi-religion. Unfortunately, in his view, the theory of evolution as such is not incompatible with Christian belief, but unguided evolution is. He would therefore speak of a guided (theistic) evolution. Plantinga, *Where the Conflict Really Lies*, xii, 62–63, 309–11, 349–50. His discussion does not include any biblical exegesis. Also see Alvin Plantinga, "When Faith and Reason Clash: Evolution and the Bible," in *Intelligent Design, Creationism, and Its Critics:*

but also do not benefit from the information that Scripture does give about God's creation. That information includes not only the origin of creation at the beginning of time, the fall into sin, the Genesis flood, and the realization that all things hold together in Christ (Col. 1:17), but also the humbling reality that no human being will ever be able to fully understand creation or the laws by which God governs it. Humans are part of creation and as such will always have limited knowledge. Scientists will never be able to assume God's position as designer and sustainer of creation. God made this very clear to Job (Job 38–39), and he continues to make this clear to us today. Every scientific breakthrough seems to lead to more questions and more puzzles. In view of all of this, a question arises: how can a science that ignores the Creator speculate and hypothesize adequately about the earth's origins? At the very least, the theories of science need to be placed and evaluated in the light of God's Word.

Fourth, if there is a true contradiction between what science theorizes and what Scripture makes clear, then Scripture should be followed.

Herman Bavinck has correctly noted that no one can object to scientific facts as such. But, in using the example of geology, he noted that "these facts must be rigorously distinguished from the exegesis of these facts that geologists present. The phenomena that the earth exhibits are one thing; the combinations, hypotheses, and conclusions that the students of earth science connect with these phenomena are quite another."[98] Bavinck goes on to note geologic facts that all are agreed on, such as that the earth's crust is composed of different layers apparently deposited by water and that they occur in a certain order. However, Bavinck cautioned against accepting the mainstream science of his day, which concluded that protracted, long geologic periods were involved. Scientists have their own worldviews that influence their interpretation of the data. Geology cannot produce a history of creation. We have that in Scripture. Bavinck concluded that the limitations of the science of geology should make us wary of accepting as fact conclusions currently drawn on the basis of the raw geological data. Bavinck held out hope that eventually the science that contradicts Scripture would correct itself.[99]

Philosophical, Theological, and Scientific Perspectives, ed. Robert T. Pennock (Cambridge, Mass.: MIT Press, 2001), 131, 138.

98. Bavinck, *Reformed Dogmatics*, 2:501. A similar point is made by John Byl, "Scripture and Geologists," *WTJ* 51 (1989): 144–46.

99. Bavinck, *Reformed Dogmatics*, 2:501–7. For his recognition that reliable scientific facts necessitate changing exegesis, also see Bavinck's unpublished personal remarks in G. Harinck, C. van der Kooi, and J. Vree, eds., *"Als Bavinck nu eens kleur bekende"* (Amsterdam: VU Uitgeverij, 1994), 77. These remarks have been interpreted to mean that Bavinck thought that the results of

Bavinck's observations on geology can be applied to other sciences as well. One can readily agree on the raw data, but it is the interpretation that is given that can raise questions and doubts. How can one be sure that an interpretation is correct? When it comes to science's probing of the origin of this world, such assurance is virtually impossible to obtain on the basis of the available scientific data. The only canonical and true account that we can be sure of is given to us in God's Word. This account also needs to be taken into consideration when dealing scientifically with the origin of the world.

It is therefore of utmost importance that our faith and our understanding of Scripture are not bound to a particular scientific theory. If we do bind our faith to the latest insights, we will need to adjust our faith constantly to fit the latest scientific consensus. The result is that we would soon find ourselves "adrift on a sea of subjectivism with no solid ground on which to stand."[100] We need to remain humble and recognize that what happened when God created heaven and earth is beyond our understanding. God's interrogation of Job from the whirlwind underlines our ignorance and inability to say a wise scientific word about origins. "Where were you when I laid the foundation of the earth?" (Job 38:4). The work of creating heaven and earth is the incredible and deep work of God, which for finite minds is too profound to comprehend.

The lesson from all of this is that when science presents a theory that is speculative and cannot be proven, especially on the issue of origins, Scripture, as God's true record of earth's beginnings, has priority. When the Reformed Churches in the Netherlands were embroiled in a dispute about the meaning of the first chapters of Genesis almost a century ago, Dutch theologian Klaas

---

science in fact necessitate a new exegesis of Genesis 1 and 2: Ab Flipse, *Christelijke wetenschap. Nederlandse rooms-katholieken en gereformeerden over de natuurwetenschap, 1880–1940* (Hilversum: Verloren, 2014), 104. This interpretation, however, was strongly denied by one of Bavinck's doctoral students: H. W. van der Vaart Smit, *Bavinck's schriftbeschouwing in verband met de eerste hoofdstukken van Genesis* (Wageningen: H. Veenman, 1933). Bavinck has been faulted for working with out-of-date information and for not understanding fundamental geological principles: Davis A. Young, "The Reception of Geology in the Dutch Reformed Tradition: The Case of Herman Bavinck (1854–1921)," in *Geology and Religion: A History of Harmony and Hostility*, ed. Martina Kölbl-Ebert (London: The Geological Society, 2009), 289–300. These factors, however, do not address the issue of the limitations of scientific theory and interpretation, especially as relating to origins—issues Bavinck addressed. For a brief historical overview on the attempts to harmonize geological science with Scripture, and how these failed to respect the integrity of both Scripture and science, see Francis Watson, "Genesis Before Darwin: Why Scripture Needed Liberation from Science," in *Reading Genesis After Darwin*, ed. Stephen C. Barton and David Wilkinson (New York: Oxford University Press, 2009), 28–35.

100. Brush, *The Limitations of Scientific Truth*, 269; also Bavinck, *Reformed Dogmatics*, 2:507.

Schilder noted that *in principle* justice is done to Scripture if three things are definitely established:

1. That not a single notion finds acceptance in our thinking as a believer unless one is truly convinced that it may be derived from Scripture or can be linked with Scripture.

2. That extrabiblical scholarly research can never be a *binding norm* for our thinking as a believer. (It can, may, and must always be an *inducement* for further evaluating our insights because we may have been mistaken in our assertion: "this is what Scripture says." But it may never be the *norm*, so that when it is *certain* that Scripture teaches such and such, then no science can ever place itself as judge over Scripture.)

3. That the reality of which one speaks remains the reality of the *time* in which we live here on earth with all creation and of the *space* in which God has placed the world.[101]

A more recent example of similar sentiments comes from Kirsten Birkett of Oak Hill Theological College in London, who concluded her article on science and Scripture by writing, "When we let our interpretation of what Scripture says be led by philosophies found outside the Scripture, we are not giving Scripture its due as an integrated and coherent—although not exhaustive—guide to understanding reality." She also noted that "Scripture is our solid foundation; other knowledge should be understood and interpreted in its light, not the other way around."[102]

In light of that reality, it is most regrettable that the BioLogos Foundation is currently making a concerted effort to convince conservative Christians to accept the present-day scientific paradigm of evolution. This organization wrongly assumes that the theory of the evolutionary origin of the world has been proven true and should therefore be accepted by all. One of its core commitments on its website states, "We affirm evolutionary creation, recognizing God as Creator of all life over billions of years." As noted in the first chapter, conservative Old Testament scholars, who could have been expected to defend the historicity of Genesis 1 and 2, are embracing theistic evolution and helping BioLogos.[103]

---

101. Klaas Schilder, *Een hoornstoot tegen Assen? (Antwoord op een 'conscientiekreet')*, 2nd ed. (Kampen: Kok, 1929), 44 (my translation; italics in the original).

102. Birkett, "Science and Scripture," 984–85.

103. Helpful resources critical of the theory of evolution and written by specialists include Moreland et al., *Theistic Evolution*; and Norman C. Nevin, ed., *Should Christians Embrace Evolution? Biblical and Scientific Responses* (Nottingham, U.K.: Inter-Varsity, 2009). The answer to the question in the latter book's title is no.

In the face of such a campaign for the theory of evolution, we need to assert that God speaks more clearly in Scripture than through His handiwork. His special revelation is normative and, therefore, has priority over any scientific deductions or theories made from His work of creation.[104] Scripture must be our guiding light in understanding the biblical text, and not prevailing scientific hypotheses. Faith in the veracity of God's Word seeks understanding. Such a believing approach is especially important so that we may listen carefully to Genesis without preconceived notions. Science can speculate, but it is not able to say anything certain about origins.

At the same time, the biblical account of creation may be consistent with current scientific understanding in surprising ways and increase our sense of wonder at what God did at the very beginning of creation. For example, Scripture says that God brought heaven and earth into being by His word. God spoke and it came to be (Ps. 33:6, 9). When "God said" and gave the command, creation took place (Gen. 1:3, 6, 9, 11, 14, 20, 24, 26). The result of God's speaking—namely, the creation of all things in a systematic order—must have involved enormous physical processes that are beyond our understanding. John Lennox, professor of mathematics at the University of Oxford, has interestingly observed how the biblical revelation that "God by his Word imparts energy and information to create and structure the universe…converges with some of the deepest insights of a modern science that has come to realize the fundamental nature of information and its irreducibility to matter and energy." He clarified that

> I am not, of course, claiming that the Bible can inform every branch of science, but I am claiming that there are certain fundamental points of convergence of such immense significance for our understanding of the universe and ourselves that it is worth pointing them out. Such convergences between the Bible and contemporary science add to the Bible's credibility in a sceptical world—as Scripture itself would warrant us in thinking (Rom. 1:19–20).[105]

In such cases, a scientist who accepts Scripture as God's Word does not use the biblical text to spell out a scientific theory or to be the origin for such a theory. He only acknowledges that what Scripture says does not contradict his

---

104. For a careful and nuanced discussion on the priority of Scripture, see Poythress, *Redeeming Science*, 41–47.

105. John C. Lennox, *Seven Days That Divide the World: The Beginning According to Genesis and Science* (Grand Rapids: Zondervan, 2011), 141, 142; also see John C. Lennox, *God's Undertaker: Has Science Buried God?* (Oxford: Lion, 2009), 177–78.

scientific knowledge and is consistent with his scientific insights. Needless to say, such insights, while encouraging, do not bring us any closer to actually fully comprehending God's work, in this case His work of creating by His word.

Also in the above case, we need to recognize that in Scripture God accommodates Himself to our understanding and that the Bible is not a scientific textbook. We need to interpret Scripture according to its own intentions and within the context of the entire Word of God. At the same time, if certain current scientific insights are consistent with the historical account of creation, such limited insights into God's incomprehensible work of creation can be acknowledged with gratitude. In this book, as we listen to God's word in Genesis 1 and 2, such insights will be noted from time to time.

Although there cannot be a real conflict between the facts of creation and what Scripture tells us when both are rightly understood, conflict does arise when scientific theorizing goes beyond the evidence or the competence of science, when science does not take into consideration all of God's Word, or when science is influenced by a denial of what the Word of God teaches. Conflict between what creation and special revelation teach can also arise if Scripture is wrongly understood. In the pages that follow, we will need to listen very carefully to God's Word and conclude neither more nor less than what Scripture teaches. An ecclesiastical report on creation and science aptly observed that we may have to conclude that "our inability to find an intellectually satisfying solution" to the problem of harmonizing the Bible and science "is one of the ways in which our faith in God and his Word is being put to the test in the modern world. Yet we have no reason to lose heart, because we have the promise that our faith is the victory that overcomes the world (1 John 5:4)."[106] Our faith is not to rest "in the wisdom of men but in the power of God" (1 Cor. 2:5).

As we proceed to study the opening chapters of Genesis, we need above all to take the time to hear what Scripture says and allow the text to speak for itself. With all the noise about Genesis and science around us, we must first pay attention to what God is saying. After all, His Word should set the agenda for a correct understanding and not the dominant science and philosophies of the day. If we humbly bow before the Word as authoritative, that same Word will also work and confirm in our hearts faith that the creation account can be accepted as true and reliable in all respects.

We also need to be realistic. With our limited perception as creatures in a fallen world, we do well to realize that we cannot expect to resolve all the

---

106. Wolters et al., "Report on Creation and Science," 405.

conflicts between current scientific theories and God's revelation about creation in Genesis 1 and 2. Did the Preacher not acknowledge that the task God has given humans "to seek and search out by wisdom concerning all that is done under heaven" is a heavy burden to be busy with, and that in the end whatever we accomplish seems futile, like "grasping for the wind" (Eccl. 1:13–14)? It is good to keep such biblical realism in mind. We are, after all, dealing with God's incomprehensible work of creating, which He has been pleased to reveal to us in a form that we can comprehend, even if we cannot comprehend it exhaustively.

Summary

Genesis needs to be understood first of all within the context of Scripture. The value of using ancient myths to help elucidate the meaning of Genesis 1 and 2 is quite limited. Genesis is divine revelation and stands in a class by itself. As inspired Scripture, its origin is from heaven. It is not the result of humans borrowing from pagan myths and stripping them of polytheistic elements. Furthermore, to make proper use of any potentially relevant material in pagan writings, one needs to factor in the original provenance, purpose, and world-view of the ancient texts in question and recognize the vast differences between pagan religions and the biblical one.

Modern evolutionary science has greatly influenced the interpretation of the biblical creation account. However, we need to recognize that science has limitations, and scientists speak from outside their competence when they pontificate about the origin of the world. We also have to recognize that Scripture is not a scientific textbook, and we need to be careful not to read more into the biblical text than is warranted. At the same time we can accept as true what Genesis clearly tells us about the events of God's work of creation.

Scientists study the book of nature or, as it is also called, general revelation. This general revelation reveals God and His glory. It is a high calling, also for Christians, to study God's work of creation, but the results of scientific research are not infallible divine revelation. Science is not an independent authoritative source of revelation about earth's beginnings.

Science can and should make use of the information that Scripture gives. Indeed, a good case can be made for the notion that a literal understanding of the first chapters in the Bible played a crucial role in the development of natural science in the seventeenth century. Scripture is the primary authority, and thus if there is a genuine contradiction between a scientific hypothesis and the clear teaching of Scripture, then Scripture should be followed.

3

The Historicity of Genesis 1:1–2:3

When we consider the historicity of the opening chapters of Genesis, it is obviously essential that we focus on what the biblical text actually says. In order to listen carefully to the text, we must include consideration of the literary and canonical context in which the passage is found. This chapter therefore looks at the place Genesis 1:1–2:3 has within the book of Genesis as a whole. Next, it considers the genre of the account. Since Scripture is one revelation from God, when it comes to the question of this part of Scripture's historicity we must also note the manner in which the Bible elsewhere refers to it. Finally, this chapter looks at some general developments or trends in biblical interpretation that have contributed to a dehistoricized understanding of the Genesis account in spite of what we hope to demonstrate is the plain historical intent of the text.

The Context of This Account within the Book of Genesis
The book of Genesis opens with the majestic creation account, which runs from 1:1 to the first three verses of chapter 2. In order to understand the significance of this account and its historicity, we need to see its place within the larger context of Genesis.

The book of Genesis has been carefully put together and organized into sections beginning with the words translated as "this is the history of" (NKJV), "these are the generations of" (ESV), or "this is the account of" (NIV).[1] The Hebrew phrase is difficult to translate. The word rendered "history" or "generations" (*tôlədôt*) derives from the Hebrew verbal root *yld*, which means "to beget, to bear (children), bring forth." It can therefore be used as a heading to describe

---

1. The phrase occurs in Gen. 2:4; 6:9; 10:1; 11:10, 27; 25:12, 19; 36:1, 9; 37:2. See *DCH* 8:604–5; Sarah Schwartz, "Narrative *Toledot* Formulae in Genesis: The Case of Heaven and Earth, Noah, and Isaac," *JHebS* 16 (2016): 11–13.

the generations that followed the person named, and thus translated "gene-alogy." For example, the expression "this is the genealogy [tôlǝdôt] of Shem" (Gen. 11:10) introduces a genealogy that tells about the descendants of Shem and what happened to them. However, the phrase "these are the generations [tôlǝdôt] of" can also introduce a narrative that tells what became of the people mentioned in the text prior to this phrase. This usage is then metaphorical. We see this, for example, in Genesis 11:27, where the expression "these are the gen-erations of Terah" (ESV) introduces not a major genealogy but the narrative of Abram (11:27–25:11). The sense is that the phrase "these are the generations of" indicates what became of Terah's descendants, that is, the history of those who came later. Thus the phrase "these are the generations of" or "this is the history of" reaches back to the preceding and then moves the account forward, telling what happened to those mentioned in the preceding pericope.

This phrase is also found in Genesis 2:4: "This is the history of the heavens and the earth when they were created, in the day that the LORD God made the earth and the heavens." According to the significance of these words as just noted, Genesis 2:4 must therefore stand at the beginning of a new section and introduce it. It does not belong with chapter 1, but with Genesis 2:4–4:26, which tells what became of the perfect creation described in Genesis 1. Although not belonging to Genesis 1 it is nevertheless linked to it in the sense that it tells what became of the perfect creation described there.[2] There are a significant number of scholars, however, who divide Genesis 2:4 into two parts so that verse 4a ("this is the history of the heavens and earth") belongs with the pre-ceding section and does not introduce what follows in chapter 2. The words in verse 4b ("in the day that the LORD God made the earth and the heavens") then belong with what follows. This view is also reflected in some Bible translations. The main reason for this approach is the desire to maintain that 1:1–2:4a is of a different origin than what follows.[3]

---

2. P. J. Wiseman (followed by R. K. Harrison) has argued that the phrase "these are the generations of" constitutes part of a colophon concluding the preceding section. P. J. Wiseman, *Clues to Creation in Genesis*, ed. Donald J. Wiseman (repr., London: Marshall, Morgan & Scott, 1977), 25–45; R. K. Harrison, *Introduction to the Old Testament* (Grand Rapids: Eerdmans, 1969), 543–53. This creative and interesting approach, however, fails to convince and has few supporters today. See the critique in Garrett, *Rethinking Genesis*, 93–96; Schwartz, "Narrative *Toledot* Formulae," 29–30; and W. H. Gispen, *Genesis* (Kampen: Kok, 1974), 1:92–95.

3. See, e.g., the discussions in Victor P. Hamilton, *The Book of Genesis: Chapters 1–17* (Grand Rapids: Eerdmans, 1990), 151–52; and Gordon J. Wenham, *Genesis 1–15* (Waco, Tex.: Word, 1987), 6. Translations associating Gen. 2:4 with what precedes include the NEB, JB, and NJPS. It is interesting that the REB, the successor to the NEB, places Gen. 2:4 at the beginning of the next section.

There are, however, convincing arguments showing that Genesis 2:4 is a unit introducing a new section and should not be broken into two parts. First, the Masoretic Text, the generally accepted standard Hebrew text, indicates that a new pericope or section starts with verse 4. This ancient understanding rings true for, in the second place, the expression "this is the history of" always begins a new section elsewhere (Num. 3:1; Ruth 4:18; 1 Chron. 1:29) and can therefore be expected to do the same in Genesis. Indeed, as already noted above, the expression denotes what came after or what became of what was narrated earlier and so properly belongs at the beginning of a new paragraph. Third, verse 4 has a beautiful chiastic structure that can be pictured as follows:

This is the history

    A of the heavens

      B and the earth

        C when they were created

        C* in the day that the LORD God made

      B* the earth

    A* and the heavens.

Thus this verse is a wonderful literary unity, and it would do violence to the text to separate the first part from it.[4]

One can therefore conclude that Genesis 2:4 introduces a new section that relates what became of the perfect creation in Genesis 1. And what is true of Genesis 2:4 also holds for other instances of the phrase "this is the history of" or "these are the generations of" or "the genealogy of." Every instance introduces a new section. The structure of the book of Genesis, using the NKJV translation of *tôlədôt* for all the occurrences, can therefore be outlined as follows:

This is the history of the heavens and the earth (2:4–4:26)

This is the book of the genealogy of Adam (5:1–6:8)

This is the genealogy of Noah (6:9–9:29)

---

4. For the Masoretic Text, see David Noel Freedman, ed., *The Leningrad Codex: A Facsimile Edition* (Grand Rapids: Eerdmans; Leiden: Brill, 1998), 15 (print editions indicate a new paragraph here with the Hebrew letter *pe*). On the place and unity of Gen. 2:4 and the chiastic structure, see U. Cassuto, *A Commentary on the Book of Genesis*, part 1, *From Adam to Noah* (Jerusalem: Magnes, 1989), 96–99; Nahum M. Sarna, *Genesis: The Traditional Hebrew Text with the New JPS Translation* (Philadelphia: Jewish Publication Society, 1989), 16–17; Wenham, *Genesis 1–15*, 55; see also Terje Stordalen, "Genesis 2,4: Restudying a *Locus Classicus*," *ZAW* 104 (1992): 163–77. See further on Gen. 2:4, chapter 10 below.

This is the genealogy of the sons of Noah: Shem, Ham, and Japheth
(10:1–11:9)

This is the genealogy of Shem (11:10–26)

This is the genealogy of Terah (11:27–25:11)

This is the genealogy of Ishmael (25:12–18)

This is the genealogy of Isaac (25:19–35:29)

This is the genealogy of Esau (36:1–8; 36:9–37:1)

This is the history of Jacob (37:2–50:26)

This outline displays the inherent unity of Genesis. The entire book is structured in such a way that every time a new section begins it is introduced with the phrase "these are the *tôlədôt* of." Now, if we accept the account of Abraham (within the *tôlədôt* of Terah) or Joseph (within the *tôlədôt* of Jacob) as historically true, then why not the account of Adam and Eve's creation? The book of Genesis is one beautifully constructed, unified narrative that intends to recount history. At no point is there any indication that we move from non-historical to the historical. The idea that the first chapters are somehow of less value for passing on true information from the past than the later chapters, and thus are identified as saga or legend, does not arise from Scripture but from critical scholarship.[5]

One other matter of interpretation should be noted. Since the phrase "this is the history of the heavens and the earth" (2:4a) introduces what follows and tells what became of the heavens and the earth after their creation in chapter 1, Genesis 2:4–25 consequently cannot be understood as a second creation account as some have maintained. It focuses on what happened in and to God's perfect creation. In the process, chapter 2 gives more detail about the events that took place on day six of creation. The phrase "these are the generations of" in Genesis 2:4a therefore ties Genesis 1 and 2 together in a tight unity even though each chapter has its own distinctive style and purpose.[6] Such a

---

5. For the historicity also of the first chapters of Genesis, as evidenced by the "these are the generations" structure, see James K. Hoffmeier, "Genesis 1–11 as History and Theology," in *Genesis: History, Fiction, or Neither? Three Views on the Bible's Earliest Chapters*, by James K. Hoffmeier, Gordon J. Wenham, and Kenton L. Sparks (Grand Rapids: Zondervan, 2015), 28–32.

6. For more on the relationship between the section starting with Gen. 2:4 and what precedes it, see David A. Dorsey, *The Literary Structure of the Old Testament: A Commentary on Genesis–Malachi* (Grand Rapids: Baker, 1999), 49.

close relationship also argues for the historicity of Genesis 1. This observation brings us to the literary style of the first chapter.

The Genre of the Creation Account

Does the literary style of Genesis 1:1–2:3 support the notion that this passage is an account of historical events that actually relates what took place at creation? There has been much discussion about the genre of Genesis 1, with characterizations ranging from poetic myth and legend to a factual historical account. When speaking of genres there is a danger that modern scholars with their presuppositions will superimpose an idea of what genre fits the text best and read the text through that particular lens. It is critically important to let the text speak. When we do, it becomes evident that the literary style of the opening chapter of Scripture shows that its intent is to relate historical events. This is not fictitious mythology or legend but a sober historical account, a narrative with a plot and connected events.[7] It is also not "theological history" that should not be taken literally. Such a characterization is in no small part influenced by the perceived interplay of Genesis 1–2 with ancient Near Eastern creation accounts. As we shall see, there is every reason to accept the biblical account as a faithful historical account of God's work of creation.[8]

The Hebrew style is normal narrative prose. The text does not employ parallelism as one would find in poetry. A poetic description of creation is found in Psalm 104, but such is not the case in Genesis 1. To be sure, the text is written in an exalted style, and it is obviously a magnificent literary composition, but that does not change its basic genre of narrative prose, nor does it compromise its intent to convey true historical information. John Collins introduces a false dilemma when he uses the exalted prose narrative style of Genesis 1 as a reason "not to impose a 'literalistic' hermeneutic on the text," implying that Genesis 1 should not be read as a historical narrative as traditionally

---

7. On Gen. 1–11 not being myth, see Hamilton, *Genesis*, 56–59; Walter C. Kaiser Jr., "The Literary Form of Genesis 1–11," in *New Perspectives on the Old Testament*, ed. J. Barton Payne (Waco, Tex.: Word, 1970), 48–65. Also see chapter 2 above. For a brief general discussion on narrative, see Tremper Longman III, "Biblical Narrative," in *A Complete Literary Guide to the Bible*, ed. Leland Ryken and Tremper Longman III (Grand Rapids: Zondervan, 1993), 69–79.

8. On "theological history" and the influence of ancient Near Eastern texts, see Longman, "What Genesis 1–2 Teaches," 103–28, esp. 110; also see Todd S. Beall's response to Longman (131–35) and Beall's own essay: "Reading Genesis 1–2: A Literal Approach," in J. Daryl Charles, *Reading Genesis 1–2*, 45–59.

understood.[9] Exalted styles as often found in poetry are used to recount historical events as, for example, in the Song of Moses (Deut. 32). The biblical text of Genesis 1 describes sequential action with one event following another over the span of six days. As such it is narrating historical events.[10] As Edward J. Young put it, "The events recorded in the first chapter of the Bible actually took place. They were historical events, and Genesis one, therefore, is to be regarded as historical."[11] The six-day sequence has a beginning. The opening verse states that "in the beginning God created the heavens and the earth." There was no creation prior to this beginning. God created the heavens and the earth from nothing.[12] This opening verse therefore also indicates the beginning of time and as such should be considered part of the first day. (More will be said about that in the next two chapters.) Indeed, Genesis 1 describes for us the beginning of history. As the six days of creation indicate, creation took place in time.

Other aspects regarding the historicity of chapter 1 can be noted at this point. This chapter has a special place in Genesis. It begins the book and precedes the organizational phrase "this is the history of." Now, due to the nature of the case, it would be impossible for the book of Genesis to start with the phrase "this is the history of" since this phrase not only refers to what follows but, as we saw earlier, it also links to what preceded, telling what became of the preceding history. This arrangement presumes the historicity of Genesis 1. Yet that first chapter is unique. It has a special place with a majestic style of its own that sets it off from the chapters that follow. What makes this chapter so distinctive? Its style and placement at the very beginning of Scripture emphasize that the history of creation as recounted in Genesis 1:1–2:3 is like no other history.

How is this account at the beginning of Scripture unique and different from other records of events found in the Old Testament? The events described

---

9. C. John Collins, *Genesis 1–4: A Linguistic, Literary, and Theological Commentary* (Phillipsburg, N.J.: P&R, 2006), 44; also see 122–24, 249–67.

10. There is broad scholarly agreement on the historical narrative style of Gen. 1:1–2:3. This passage "constitutes a historical narrative text type." Thus Daniel Bediako, *Genesis 1:1–2:3: A Textlinguistic Analysis* (Saarbrücken, Ger.: VDM, 2011), 257. It is a "literal historical account." Thus, on the basis of a statistical determination of the genre, Steven W. Boyd, "The Genre of Genesis 1:1–2:3: What Means This Text?," in *Coming to Grips with Genesis: Biblical Authority and the Age of the Earth*, ed. Terry Mortenson and Thane H. Ury (Green Forest, Ariz.: Master, 2008), 174. For a concise overview of the basic scholarly agreement that Genesis 1 is prose, see Todd S. Beall, "Reading Genesis 1–2," 48–49.

11. Edward J. Young, *Studies in Genesis One*, 50.

12. Cf. Ps. 33:9; Isa. 48:13; Rom. 4:17; Heb. 11:3. The expression "create out of nothing" does not occur in the canonical Scriptures, but it is found in 2 Macc. 7:28. See the discussion in Bavinck, *Reformed Dogmatics*, 2:416–20.

here are the works of God alone.[13] No human being witnessed or was involved in the work of creation. It is only God's doing. "In the beginning God created," and that creation work of God was perfect. It was all "very good." It is against this clear historical backdrop of Genesis 1, stylistically set apart for emphasis, that the history of redemption develops under the heading "this is the history of the heavens and the earth" (2:4). It is therefore absolutely essential that we acknowledge the historicity of Genesis 1. Without it the subsequent history of the unfolding of God's plan of salvation, which covers many centuries, would be meaningless. It is ultimately the restoration of the creation described in Genesis 1—restoration from the ravages of sin—that is the focus not only of Genesis but of all Scripture.

Since the canonical text of Scripture is a unit, the question arises whether other biblical passages also support the notion that Genesis 1 should be understood as a historical narrative describing events that took place in the past.

Testimony from Other Scripture

God's creating the heavens and the earth and all that they contain is often referred to in Scripture.[14] For the purpose of this study, the following passages will be briefly examined primarily with a view to determining whether they are consistent with and support the understanding that Genesis 1 relays historical events: Exodus 20:8–11; Job 38:4–11; Psalm 33; Psalm 104; Proverbs 8:22–31; Isaiah 44–45; and a few corroborating texts from the New Testament. Some of these passages will be revisited in subsequent chapters in the course of trying to determine the precise meaning of passages in Genesis 1.

Exodus 20:8–11
The fourth commandment as recorded in Exodus 20:8–11 clearly attests to the historicity of the creation events. The reason for the rest on the seventh day is that "in six days the LORD made the heavens and the earth, the sea, and all that is in them, and rested on the seventh day. Therefore the LORD blessed the Sabbath day and hallowed it" (v. 11). The entire rationale for the fourth commandment obviously rests on the assumption that God actually did create the

---

13. Gispen, *Genesis*, 1:30. Schwartz, "Narrative *Toledot* Formulae," 35–36, concludes similarly that the first chapter "focuses on the acts of God without description of human actions, sins or shortcomings."

14. See, e.g., the following recent studies: Alexej Murán, "The Creation Theme in Selected Psalms," in Gerald A. Klingbeil, *Genesis Creation Account*, 189–223; Martin G. Klingbeil, "Creation in the Prophetic Literature of the Old Testament: An Intertextual Approach," in Gerald A. Klingbeil, *Genesis Creation Account*, 257–89.

heavens and the earth in six days. Now it is sometimes said that Genesis 1 describes creation as taking six days because it is modeled after the human pattern of work. However, the opposite is true. God's work in six days came first, and he set the pattern of work in six days for us.

The narrative style used in the fourth commandment (Ex. 20:11), which summarizes the events of Genesis 1:1–2:3, is also consistent with the historicity of what is recounted. Furthermore, the vocabulary employed corresponds in important ways with that found in Genesis. The verb translated "made" is the same as that used in Genesis 1:7 and 2:2, 3, and the noun rendered "heavens" is identical to the term used in Genesis 1:1 and 1:8.

Job 38:4–11

Of special interest when dealing with the matter of the historicity of the creation account are God's speeches to Job (Job 38:2–40:5). In response to all the inexplicable misery he experienced, Job had expressed the wish to take up his case before God (23:1–7) and had even challenged the Almighty to answer him (31:35). When God eventually appeared and answered Job out of the whirlwind, He confronted Job for his impudence and asked him: "Where were you when I laid the foundation of the earth? Tell Me if you have understanding" (38:4). God's question and demand not only set the tone for His response to Job's demands for answers from God, but they also clearly underline the modesty with which we are to approach the subject of creation. We were not there, but God was. We need to listen to Him. In responding to Job, God certainly treated the creation events as historical, identified Himself as the Creator, and in His response appears to allude in a non-chronological way to events mentioned in Genesis 1.

It may be helpful by way of example to take a brief look at the beginning of God's discourse in Job 38:4–11. After God identified Himself as the creator by asking, "Where were you when I laid the foundations of the earth?," God continued using the terminology of a builder by asking, "Who determined its measurements?" and "Who stretched the [measuring] line upon it?" God also mentioned the footings and the cornerstone of the earth (vv. 5–6). These events refer to the creation of the earth on the first day of creation. God continued by asking Job about events that transpired on the third day of creation: "Who shut in the sea with doors, when it burst forth and issued from the womb...when I fixed My limit for it, and set bars and doors; when I said 'This far you may come, but no farther, and here your proud waves must stop?'" (38:8, 10–11). These questions remind us of day three, which Genesis 1:9–10 describes in part: "God said, 'Let the waters under the heavens be gathered together into one place, and let dry land appear'; and it was so. And God called the dry land Earth, and the gathering together of the waters He called Seas. And God saw that it was good." Although Genesis 1 does not use the language and imagery found in the book of Job, God's response to Job does not contradict the Genesis account of days one and three. Both parts of Scripture refer to the same historical events.

God's response to Job also includes information not found in Genesis 1. After God had asked Job who laid the cornerstone of the earth, He continued "when the morning stars sang together, and all the sons of God shouted for joy" (Job 38:7). What does this mean? There appears to be no reference to anything like this in Genesis 1. The sons of God were already mentioned at the beginning of the book of Job (1:6; 2:1) and are rightly usually identified as angels.[15] In this poetic passage, we have a typical parallel construction. "The morning stars sang together" corresponds with "all the sons of God shouted for joy." Such a personification of natural phenomena as the stars is not unusual. In Psalm 104:4 the winds are God's messengers or angels and the flaming fire or lightning His ministers. And so "the morning stars" and "the sons of God" (or angels) can be considered synonymous here. In other words, the "morning stars" do not refer to the creation of the stars on the fourth day and so there is no contradiction with the account in Genesis 1.[16]

We can also note that when God spoke to Job about the containment of the waters, He related to Job that He said, "This far you may come, but no farther, and here your proud waves must stop!" (Job 38:11). When God so commands and determines the limits of the sea, this manner of describing His work of creation is compatible with the Genesis account of God creating by His word. "Then God said, 'Let the waters under the heavens be gathered together into one place, and let the dry land appear'; and it was so" (Gen. 1:9).

Psalm 33

There are many references and allusions to creation in the Psalms. God's having created the world is accepted as a historical fact (Ps. 8:3; 89:11–13; 121:2; 124:8; 134:3; 136:4–9) and details such as that God created by speaking are mentioned (Ps. 33:6, 9; 148:5). For our purpose, two psalms illustrate the historicity of the Genesis creation account: Psalms 33 and 104. Psalm 33 is a psalm of praise.

---

15. "The sons of God" was understood as angels in the Targum of Job and translated as such in the LXX; the NIV is a modern version with this rendering. See note 33 on Job 1:6 in the NET. For the creation of the angels, see the Appendix below.

16. John E. Hartley, *The Book of Job* (Grand Rapids: Eerdmans, 1988), 495n21; Gert Kwakkel, "Er is meer dan Genesis 1. Andere oudtestamentische teksten over de schepping," in *In den beginne en verder: een bijbels-theologische reflectie op de schepping*, ed. G. Kwakkel and P. H. R. van Houwelingen (Barneveld: Vuurbaak, 2011), 31.

Among the reasons for giving praise to the LORD is His ability to create by His word.

> By the word of the LORD the heavens were made,
> and all the host of them by the breath of His mouth.
> He gathers the waters of the sea together as a heap;
> He lays up the deep in storehouses.
> Let all the earth fear the LORD;
> let all the inhabitants of the world stand in awe of Him.
> For He spoke, and it was done;
> He commanded, and it stood fast. (Ps. 33:6–9)

This psalm is obviously referring to historical events throughout. Otherwise the whole reason for praising and fearing the LORD would be lost. Thus also His work of creation by speaking His word of command is treated as historically true.

Psalm 104

Psalm 104 is entirely devoted to the theme of creation. This psalm can in a sense be called "a poetic retelling of the Genesis story." However, to characterize it as "dischronologizing" the Genesis account is, as we shall see, not warranted.[17] There is good reason for Richard M. Davidson's observation that "there is a wide recognition among Old Testament scholars that Psalm 104...follows the same basic order as the days of creation in Genesis 1."[18] At the same time, we need to realize that this psalm has its own purpose and thus is far from a simple reflection of Genesis 1. We therefore need to be careful not to read more into this psalm than is warranted.

This psalm is in the first place an exuberant song glorifying God, who not only made but also maintains all of creation. For that reason, as the psalm praises God for His original works of creation, mentioned in the order of Genesis 1, it also speaks of what followed. Indeed, this psalm also relates to the present state of affairs. An example of the psalm referring both to creation and to a subsequent situation is found in the poet's description of God dividing the

---

17. For the characterizations "poetic retelling" and "dischronologizing," see Adele Berlin, "The Wisdom of Creation in Psalm 104," in *Seeking Out the Ancients: Essays Offered to Honor Michael V. Fox on the Occasion of His Sixty-Fifth Birthday*, ed. Ronald L. Troxel, Kelvin G. Friebel, and Dennis R. Magary (Winona Lake, Ind.: Eisenbrauns, 2005), 75–76.

18. Richard M. Davidson, "The Creation Theme in Psalm 104," in Gerald A. Klingbeil, *Genesis Creation Account*, 153–54. In the pages that follow, Davidson surveys key scholars to make his point.

water and the land (Ps. 104:6–9). When read carefully, these verses not only speak of God's work on the third day of creation, but also appear to refer to the Noachian flood. The expression "the waters stood above the mountains" (v. 6) is not found in Genesis 1, but there is a similar reference in Genesis 7. "The waters prevailed exceedingly on the earth, and all the high hills under the whole heaven were covered. The waters prevailed fifteen cubits upward, and the mountains were covered" (Gen. 7:19–20). Also, the assurance that the water will never again cover the earth (Ps. 104:9) alludes to God's promise after the great flood (Gen. 9:11, 15).[19] Another example of the psalm referring to creation, but also pointing ahead, is the reference to grass and plants. This can certainly be seen as a reference to the creation of vegetation. At the same time, the poet notes that it is food for the animals, and so the reference to such creatures anticipates their subsequent creation (Ps. 104:14). Similarly, the reference to ships points ahead to what human beings will make to navigate the waters (v. 26). When one understands the basic organization and flow of Psalm 104, with its dual references to creation and to later situations, the basic chronological order of creation as given in Genesis 1 is clearly evident and is justifiably recognized as such.

Jacques B. Doukham has outlined the following thematic structure of Psalm 104 that reflects the order of Genesis 1. This outline is further supported by the fact that Psalm 104 shares significant common wording with Genesis 1.[20]

Day One: Motif of light (Ps. 104:2a)

Day Two: Creation of firmament, reference to waters above (Ps. 104:2b–4)

Day Three: Appearance of the ground: formation of the earth plants (Ps. 104:5–18)

---

19. See the discussion in Kwakkel, "Er is meer dan Genesis 1," 38. It has been said that Ps. 104 says nothing about the flood. So, e.g., Paul H. Seely, "Creation Science Takes Psalm 104:6–9 Out of Context," *Perspectives on Science and Christian Faith* 51 (1999): 170–74. However, this position goes too far and does not adequately consider that the psalm was written post-flood and for the purpose of praising God's goodness. Noel K. Weeks, "Cosmology in Historical Context," *WTJ* 68 (2006): 290–91; also see, with further literature, Richard M. Davidson, "Creation Theme," 162–63.

20. Jacques B. Doukhan, *The Genesis Creation Story: Its Literary Structure* (Berrien Springs, Mich.: Andrews University Press, 1978), 83–86. The outline (including footnotes) used in the text here is a quotation from Richard M. Davidson, "Creation Theme," 156. A similar analysis of Ps. 104 can be found in Derek Kidner, *Psalms 73–150* (Downers Grove, Ill.: InterVarsity, 1975), 368; and James B. Jordan, *Creation in Six Days: A Defense of the Traditional Reading of Genesis One* (Moscow, Idaho: Canon, 1999), 247–51.

Day Four: Luminaries to indicate seasons and time (Ps. 104:19–23)

Day Five: First mention of animals in terms of creatures;[21] allusion to birds;[22] sea and living beings in it (Ps. 104:24–26)

Day Six: Food for animals and man; gift of life by God for animals and man[23] (Ps. 104:27–30)

Day Seven: Glory of God;[24] allusion to the revelation on Sinai[25] (Ps. 104:31–32)

This outline highlights some noteworthy elements that are relevant for and underline the historicity of Genesis 1. As already noted, the order of creation is the same as in Genesis 1. Thus light, which was created on day one, is mentioned separately from and before the creation of the luminaries on day four (Ps. 104:2, 19). It is, however, remarkable that unlike Genesis 1, in Psalm 104 the moon is mentioned prior to the sun. "He appointed [*lit.* made] the moon for seasons; the sun knows its going down" (Ps. 104:19). The next two verses then mention night and then day. Davidson notes that, "this seems to be a poet's way of highlighting the evening-morning sequence of the days in creation without explicitly stating as much."[26] Parallel with Genesis 1:14 is the statement in Psalm 104:19 that God made the moon to mark the seasons.

Also, in points of detail there are important similarities. Both accounts show that God is the creator, and both reflect the goodness of creation for which He is to be praised. The Spirit is also mentioned in both passages as participating in creation (Gen. 1:2; Ps. 104:30). Both accounts use similar vocabulary for creation, though Psalm 104 uses additional terms. Furthermore, in addition

---

21. Up to now the animals are mentioned merely in connection with the creation of the earth (as inhabitants) and the creation of the luminaries (as their indications of daily life); only from day five on, are the animals concerned as created.

22. The word *qnyn* which means "properties or riches," echoes the word *yĕqannēnû* of v. 17 ("to make the nest") and may therefore, by means of the alliteration, refer to the idea the former word conveys. This is a common practice in Hebrew poetry.

23. Man is implied here in the reference back to the ships of v. 26.

24. The concept of *kābôd* [glory] belongs especially in the Psalms to the imagery of God as king of the earth, i.e., its Creator (see Ps. 145:11; 19:2; 29:2, 3 etc.). On the other hand, this concept is clearly associated with the theophany on Sinai (see Ex. 24:16, 17).

25. See Ex. 19:18. The Israelites did not know volcanoes.... This reference to Sinai in direct association with the very concern of creation points to the Sabbath.

26. Richard M. Davidson, "Creation Theme," 165. Leupold and Delitzsch are cited as authorities. This order supports the notion that the days of creation began with the evening. See further chapter 5 below.

to the similarities, Psalm 104 sometimes gives more detail, which fills out the Genesis account somewhat.[27]

The objection has been made that Psalm 104 is poetry and therefore cannot be interpreted as recounting literal history.[28] As pointed out above in regards to the same negative approach to Genesis 1, such an objection creates a false dilemma between the poetic genre and historical reliability and overlooks the historical information communicated in poetic passages like Exodus 15 and Judges 5. Some psalms, such as 78, 105, 106, and 135, are specifically designed to recall past events.[29] The point has even been made that "biblical writers often wrote in poetry to *underscore* what is literally and historically true."[30]

In conclusion, the basic outline of this psalm reflects the chronology of Genesis 1. This fact shows that the author accepted the historical trustworthiness of the opening chapter of Scripture and used its sequence of events to compose a joyful praise to the LORD for His magnificent work of creation and His ongoing care for it.

Proverbs 8:22–31

Proverbs 8:22–31 reads as follows:

The LORD possessed [*qnh*] me at the beginning of His way,
before His works of old.
I have been established from everlasting,
from the beginning, before there was ever an earth.
When there were no depths I was brought forth,
when there were no fountains abounding with water.
Before the mountains were settled,
before the hills, I was brought forth;
while as yet He had not made the earth or the fields,

---

27. Richard M. Davidson, "Creation Theme," 184–88.

28. Patrick D. Miller, *The Way of the Lord: Essays in Old Testament Theology* (Grand Rapids: Eerdmans, 2007), 186.

29. See further, e.g., David Noel Freedman, "Early Israelite Poetry and Historical Reconstructions," in *Symposia Celebrating the Seventy-Fifth Anniversary of the Founding of the American Schools of Oriental Research (1900–1975)*, ed. Frank Moore Cross (Cambridge, Mass.: American Schools of Oriental Research, 1979), 85–96; and Peter C. Craigie, "The Conquest and Early Hebrew Poetry," *TynBul* 20 (1969): 76–94.

30. Richard M. Davidson, "Creation Theme," 176 (italics in the original). In a footnote he writes, "Often in Scripture when something of special importance is being stated, the writer or speaker breaks forth into poetry! Note already in Genesis 1 through 3 the poetic summary of God's creation of humanity (Gen 1:27), the record of the clearly poetic, ecstatic utterance of the first man after the creation of woman (Gen 2:23) and God's legal sentence upon the guilty after the fall (Gen 3:14–19)" (176–77n94).

or the primal dust of the world.
When He prepared the heavens, I was there,
when He drew a circle on the face of the deep,
when He established the clouds above,
when He strengthened the fountains of the deep,
when He assigned to the sea its limit,
so that the waters would not transgress His command,
when He marked out the foundations of the earth,
then I was beside Him as a master craftsman;
and I was daily His delight,
rejoicing always before Him,
rejoicing in His inhabited world,
and my delight was with the sons of men.

The intent of this poetic pericope is not to give another account of creation; however, it does say some helpful things for our present discussion concerning the historicity of Genesis 1. This part of Proverbs speaks of wisdom and creation. Wisdom is personified as a woman in Proverbs 8, as elsewhere in Proverbs (Prov. 1:20–33; 7:4; 9:1). Proverbs 8:22–31 has two parts. The first section (vv. 22–26) speaks of Wisdom before the creation of the earth, and the second part (vv. 27–31) concentrates on Wisdom being present during the creation process.

In verse 12 Wisdom begins narrating from her own perspective. She continues speaking in Proverbs 8:22. The Hebrew verb (*qnh*) in this verse has been rendered in different ways: "possessed," "brought forth," and "created." Thus, there are three main translations of this passage: "The LORD possessed me at the beginning of His way, before His works of old" (NKJV; similarly, ESV),[31] or "The LORD brought me forth as the first of his works, before his deeds of old" (NIV), or "The LORD created me as the beginning of his works, before his deeds of long ago" (NET).[32]

This passage has sparked enormous theological discussion in the history of the church because the New Testament alludes to this passage in terms of the Son of God, who is wisdom and the beginning of God's creation (1 Cor. 1:24; Col. 1:15–17; 2:3; Rev. 3:14). So what exactly is Proverbs 8:22 saying and how does it relate to the second person of the Trinity? Clarity on this point is desirable before we discuss this pericope further.

---

31. Similarly, KJV, NKJV, NASB, and DSV.

32. Similarly, CSB. A good overview of the pros and cons of these translations can be found in Bruce K. Waltke, *The Book of Proverbs: Chapters 1–15* (Grand Rapids: Eerdmans, 2004), 408–9.

We need to keep in mind that the purpose of this part of Scripture is to underline the desirability and blessings of wisdom (Prov. 8:1–11). It is not to guide us into the mysteries of the Trinity. Wisdom, personified as a woman, is a figure of speech. A major implication is that not too much should be made of the differences in the translation of the verb (*qnh*), whether it is rendered "possessed" or "brought forth" or "create." We are dealing with a metaphor. This figure of speech represents wisdom and does not speak of the eternal Son of God. This pericope does, however, in a sense prepare us for the New Testament revelation of the Son as the wisdom of God (1 Cor. 1:24), but Proverbs 8 does not directly speak of Him. The Son cannot be identified with the figure of speech, that is, Woman Wisdom.

A related matter is the next part of verse 22, which has been translated as "as the beginning of his works" (NET) or "as the first of his works" (NIV). Here too one cannot say that this refers to the eternal Son of God. But the passage and its manner of speaking can be said to prepare us for New Testament statements that allude to Proverbs 8, such as that the Son is "the firstborn over all creation" (Col. 1:15) and "the Beginning of the creation of God" (Rev. 3:14). But Proverbs 8:22 does not directly speak of the eternal Son of God.[33] Once it is clear what the passage is not saying, we can consider more closely the meaning of verse 22 as it introduces this pericope.

When all the evidence is considered, the translation of the first part of the verse as "The LORD brought me forth" has the most to commend it. The birth metaphor is also used subsequently in this pericope ("I was brought forth," vv. 24, 25). The translation, "The LORD possessed me," can be considered compatible. The point of the figure of speech seems to be, as Waltke puts it, that "wisdom comes from God's essential being; it is a revelation that has an organic connection with God's very nature and being." Furthermore, "since this wisdom existed before creation and its origins are distinct from it, wisdom is

---

33. Waltke correctly states that "Augustine and Calvin, et al. erred in that they wrongly interpreted Wisdom as a hypostasis of God that they equated with Jesus Christ and not as a personification of the sage's wisdom." Waltke, *Proverbs 1–15*, 409n104. Similar views are expressed by Derek Kidner, *Proverbs* (Downers Grove, Ill.: InterVarsity, 1964), 78–79; and W. H. Gispen, *De Spreuken van Salomo* (Kampen: Kok, 1952), 1:133–34. For a discussion on how Prov. 8 functioned in christological disputes and for Wisdom as a type of Christ, see Waltke, *Proverbs 1–15*, 127–33. The Son as "the firstborn of all creation" (Col. 1:15) refers to the rights and privileges of the firstborn son who inherits sovereign rule (cf. Ps. 89:27). The Son as "the beginning of God's creation" (Rev. 3:14) does not mean that God made Him first, but that "all things were made through him" (John 1:3). See Douglas J. Moo, *The Letters to the Colossians and to Philemon* (Grand Rapids: Eerdmans, 2008), 119–20; and Grant R. Osborne, *Revelation* (Grand Rapids: Baker Academic, 2002), 204–5.

neither accessible to humanity nor can it be subdued by human beings, but it must be revealed to people and accepted by them."[34]

The LORD brought forth or possessed this wisdom "at the beginning of His way, before His works of old" (v. 22). As the following verses indicate, this refers to the time before the creation of the earth, when there were no springs or mountains (vv. 23–26). Genesis 1 does not speak of the time prior to creation, but Proverbs 8 does. However, it does so in negative terms. It was a time "when there were no [watery] depths" and "no fountains abounding with water." It was before the mountains and hills had been shaped and before the LORD had "made the earth or the fields, or the primal dust of the world" (vv. 24–26). The term used to refer to the watery depths (təhôm) is the same word used in Genesis 1:2 for "the deep." In Genesis 1 there is no explicit statement that God created the waters, but the fact that prior to creation they did not exist confirms that these waters were indeed part of God's creation work.[35]

Psalm 90 also speaks of the time prior to creation. "Before the mountains were brought forth, or ever You had formed the earth and the world, even from everlasting to everlasting, You are God" (Ps. 90:2). By speaking of a time when there was no earth or waters, Psalm 90 and Proverbs 8 support the notion that God created the world from nothing.

After describing Wisdom's existence before creation, the focus moves to her presence at creation. In the context of Wisdom being with the LORD, mention is made of 'āmôn, traditionally translated as "master craftsman" (Prov. 8:30). This rendering has been much contested but it has the support of a long, ancient tradition with strong justification both lexically and contextually.[36] How does this master workman or craftsman relate to Wisdom? The passage is often translated "I was beside Him as a master craftsman," or some variation

---

34. Waltke, *Proverbs 1–15*, 409. For a concise discussion on the pros and cons of the various translations, see Waltke, *Proverbs 1–15*, 408–9. For the compatibility between "possess" and "bring forth" in this context, see Kidner, *Proverbs*, 80. For the argument that the meaning "create" may be implied only for Gen. 14:19, 22, but probably is not (and rendered "possess" in ESV and NASB), see E. Lipiński, "*qānâ; miqneh, miqnâ; qinyān*," in *TDOT* 13:58–63.

35. So also George M. Landes, "Creation Tradition in Proverbs 8:22–31 and Genesis 1," in *A Light Unto My Path: Old Testament Studies in Honor of Jacob M. Myers*, ed. Howard N. Bream, Ralph D. Heim, and Carey A. Moore (Philadelphia: Temple University Press, 1974), 286; *pace* Kwakkel, "Er is meer dan Genesis 1," 46.

36. It has the support of Jewish tradition, the LXX, and Vulgate. See further *HALOT*, 62. For a full and detailed analysis and justification for this translation, see Cleon L. Rogers III, "The Meaning and Significance of the Hebrew Word אָמוֹן in Proverbs 8:30," *ZAW* 109 (1997): 209–14.

thereof.[37] The difficulties with this translation include the fact that nowhere in Proverbs is Wisdom pictured as actually doing the work of creating.[38] For that reason some exegetes and translations have emended the Hebrew vocalic text and translated the term as "nursling" so that as a little child Wisdom delighted and rejoiced in the LORD's work (v. 30).[39] However, such an emendation is not necessary, and the context does not favor it. As Derek Kidner notes, the translation "nursling" "makes wisdom's role completely irresponsible; and if this is done to avoid unduly exalting her, it is overdone."[40] Retaining the traditional meaning of 'āmôn, the text can be rendered: "I was beside Him, who is a master workman." "Master workman" is then understood to be in apposition to the preceding object, "Him." The message of the text then correctly stays focused on the LORD as the creator and on Wisdom as being present at His creation work. There is no reference in this context to Wisdom actually doing the work of creation. The LORD does that.[41]

Although the sequence of creation is the same as in Genesis 1, in Proverbs 8:27–29 a different vocabulary is used to describe the events. The LORD's creative acts are described poetically and the term for "create" (br') is not used. Instead, various other words are used. The LORD is pictured as a builder or architect[42] who "prepared the heavens" and "drew a circle on the face of the deep [təhôm], when He established the clouds above" (vv. 27–28a). With respect to the waters, the LORD "strengthened the fountains of the deep" and "assigned to the sea its limit" (vv. 28b–29a). He also "marked out the foundations of the earth" (v. 29b). All of this is compatible with the description of the very beginning of creation, the events of the second day, and the beginning of the third day in Genesis 1:1, 6–10. In agreement with the fact that God created

---

37. So, e.g., NASB, NIV (1984), NRSV, ESV, and NET.

38. It has been suggested that Prov. 8:30 suggests that Wisdom as a master workman was instrumental in the work of creation. Kidner, *Proverbs*, 80–81. But "it is one thing to be an instrument in a creator's hands; it is quite another to be the artisan who advises and/or does the work." Waltke, *Proverbs 1–15*, 417.

39. This translation is found in the JPS 1917 and DSV. See also the arguments for "child" or "nursling" in Waltke, *Proverbs 1–15*, 418–19; Gispen, *Spreuken*, 1:149. For further contextual and grammatical arguments against the translation "I was beside him like a master workman," see Rogers, "The Meaning and Significance," 218–19.

40. Kidner, *Proverbs*, 81. For arguments for translating as "nursling" or "child" and evaluation, see Rogers, "The Meaning and Significance," 214–18.

41. For a more detailed contextual and grammatical defense of the translation "I was beside him who is a master workman," see Rogers, "The Meaning and Significance," 218–21.

42. Ángel M. Rodríguez, "Genesis and Creation in the Wisdom Literature," in Gerald A. Klingbeil, *Genesis Creation Account*, 246–47.

by issuing commands, Proverbs 8:29 informs us that the LORD "assigned to the sea its limit, so that the waters would not transgress His command" (similarly, Job 38:11).

In terms of what was created, Proverbs 8 repeats what is recounted in Genesis 1: the creation of the heavens (Prov. 8:27; Gen. 1:1, 6–8), the earth (Prov. 8:29b; Gen. 1:1, 9–10), the deep (təhôm) (Prov. 8:27, 28; Gen. 1:1, 2), the waters (Prov. 8:29; Gen. 1:2, 6), and the sea (Prov. 8:29; Gen. 1:26, 28).[43]

Proverbs 8:30–31 speaks of the delight and joy of Wisdom in the creation work of the LORD, especially in the creation of humanity (cf. Job 38:7). This happiness reflects the fact that as God created, He saw that His handiwork was good (Gen. 1:4, 10, 12, 18, 21, 25). This observation climaxed on the sixth day, after creating humankind, when "God saw everything that He had made, and indeed it was very good" (Gen. 1:31).

In sum, Proverbs 8 presupposes and supports the historical character of the events recounted in Genesis 1 and in some ways elaborates on God's creation work. This chapter also confirms that God called the earth into being from nothing. Furthermore, the personification of wisdom prepares us for the New Testament revelation of the Son as the wisdom of God and as a participant in the work of creation (1 Cor. 1:24; 8:6; Col. 1:16). This participation presupposes the historicity of the creation account in Genesis 1.

Isaiah 44–45

God's work of creation is well attested in Isaiah.[44] The LORD as creator is found especially frequently in chapters 40 through 48, and for our purposes we will focus on some passages from Isaiah 44 and 45. A major theme is that the LORD is the only true God. All the idols are as nothing; it is absurd to worship them (Isa. 44:6–20; 45:5–6, 21–25). In this manner the LORD asserts Himself as Israel's redeemer and so comforts His people. In this context, God also highlights His identity as the one who created all things and who as sovereign LORD will even draft Cyrus as His instrument for the benefit of His people Israel (Isa. 44:24–45:4). While thus encouraging His people, the LORD emphasizes that He is the creator and thus the Lord of history. In the course of this prophetic discourse, our understanding of Genesis 1 as a historical account is also deepened. The

---

43. For a detailed listing of differences in the terminology of what was created in Genesis 1 and Proverbs 8, see Landes, "Creation Tradition," 282 and passim.

44. Isa. 17:7; 29:16; 37:16; 40:21–28; 41:20; 64:8. See Ben C. Ollenburger, "Isaiah's Creation Theology," *ExAud* 3 (1987): 54–71.

following passages and themes from Isaiah poignantly highlight God as creator and redeemer.

The fact of creation is asserted in different ways. "Thus says the LORD, your Redeemer, and He who formed you from the womb; 'I am the LORD, who makes all things, who stretches out the heavens all alone, who spreads abroad the earth by Myself'" (Isa. 44:24). All the verbs in this verse are participles in the original and clearly refer to God's identity as redeemer and creator.[45] The context of speaking of God the creator can justify the use of the past tense in English instead of the present tense so that the reference is clearly to God's creative work in the past. On the other hand, it should be noted that the use of the participles in the original text expresses God's abiding relationship with His work of creation.[46] The reference to "all things" (in "who makes all things") reminds us of "the heavens and the earth" of Genesis 1:1. God alone is the creator (cf. Isa. 44:6). No one else was with God when He made all things—a reality emphasized by His spreading out the earth by Himself (v. 24). The last two words of the Hebrew text of verse 24 can be understood as a rhetorical question: "Who was with Me?" No one was there besides God![47]

When Isaiah says that God stretched out the heavens and spread out the earth (v. 24), he perhaps provides additional insight into God's work during the first three days of creation.[48] The descriptive notion of stretching out the heavens is also found elsewhere in Isaiah, where the same Hebrew term for "stretch" is used (Isa. 45:12; 51:13). The LORD "created the heavens and stretched them out" (Isa. 42:5) and, most colorfully, He today "stretches out the heavens like a curtain, and spreads them out like a tent to dwell in" (Isa. 40:22; cf. Ps. 104:2). This type of figurative language seems to intimate that the creation and the calling into existence of the heavens (Gen. 1:1) involved a process about which we are not further informed. It is interesting that the Targum on Isaiah 44:24 adds that the LORD stretched out the heavens by His Word.[49] The idea of a process

---

45. For the use of participial titles for God, see *IBHS*, 618n28; for the omission of the article in such cases in poetic style, see Joüon, §138e.

46. J. Alec Motyer, *The Prophecy of Isaiah* (Downers Grove, Ill.: InterVarsity, 1993), 354. For the use of the past tense in translating the participles, see, e.g., CSB, ESV, NIV (1984), NET, NJPS; the use of the present tense for the last three participles is also found, e.g., in KJV, NASB, and JPS 1917.

47. See the text note on Isa. 44:24 in the NASB. For a concise summary of the textual evidence, see John Goldingay and David Payne, *A Critical and Exegetical Commentary on Isaiah 40–55* (London: T&T Clark, 2006), 2:9–10.

48. Also see Edward J. Young, *Isaiah*, 3:188.

49. For an English translation, see Bruce D. Chilton, ed., *The Isaiah Targum: Introduction, Translation, Apparatus and Notes* (Collegeville, Minn.: Liturgical Press, 1987), 88.

in God's creation activity is also suggested by the fact that the Hebrew term for "spread" (as in the LORD "spreads abroad the earth," Isa. 44:24) is also used elsewhere in the context of creation for spreading out the earth (Ps. 136:6; Isa. 42:5). The idea is that of spreading out by stamping and beating. The picture is one of God "flattening out the surface of the earth with a hammer as he would a piece of metal."[50]

The figure of the heavens as a tent (Isa. 40:22) suggests that the heavens are there to shelter those living on earth. This is made explicit in Isaiah 45:18, a passage which gives further background information on the creation event. "For thus says the LORD, who created the heavens, who is God, who formed the earth and made it, who has established it, who did not create it in vain, who formed it to be inhabited." The Hebrew original stresses that it was God Himself who created the heavens and the earth. Indeed, this verse ends with the words: "I am the LORD, and there is no other."

The LORD "did not create it in vain" (v. 18). The word for "in vain" (tōhû), which can also be translated "empty," is the same one that is translated "without form" in Genesis 1:2: "The earth was without form [tōhû], and void." The fact that the LORD "did not create it in vain [tōhû]" or "empty" does not deny the reality that at one time the earth was "without form [tōhû]" during the process of creation. The point is that God's purpose was not to have an empty world, but one that could be inhabited.[51]

Isaiah 45:18 also suggests that the creation of the earth involved a process. God "created," but he also "formed," "made," and "established" his handiwork. The term "create" is used exclusively for divine creation. It expresses "clearly the incomparability of the creative works of God in contrast to all secondary products and likenesses made from already existing material by man."[52] Because God is always the subject of the verb "create," what actually happens is beyond our conceptualization.[53] The other terms used do, however, indicate that some sort of process took place in God's creating work. He "formed," "made," and "established" the earth. It has been suggested that these "three images of shaping, making, and establishing…point to initial design and purposefulness, effective execution, and consequent firmness and security."[54] Whatever the case

50. John N. Oswalt, The Book of Isaiah, Chapters 40–66 (Grand Rapids: Eerdmans, 1998), 117; also HALOT, 1292; Goldingay and Payne, Isaiah 40–55, 1:225.

51. Edward J. Young, Isaiah, 3:211.

52. Helmer Ringgren, "bārā," TDOT 2:246.

53. W. H. Schmidt, "br' to create," TLOT 1:255.

54. John Goldingay, The Message of Isaiah 40–55: A Literary-Theological Commentary (London: T&T Clark, 2005), 290; see also Goldingay and Payne, Isaiah 40–55, 2:52.

may be, the use of these verbs indicates that when God created by His word of command, much more took place than we can possibly comprehend. We need to accept God's work of creating the heavens and the earth in faith—a point underlined by the closing words of the next verse: "I the LORD speak the truth; I declare what is right" (Isa. 45:19 ESV).

One final feature of Isaiah 44–45 needs to be mentioned. A detail not specifically recorded in Genesis 1 is that God is the one who creates darkness. "I form the light and create darkness" (Isa. 45:7). This passage occurs in the context of the LORD addressing Cyrus, His anointed, through whom He will show His sovereignty. The LORD's absolute control includes literally everything. "I form the light and create darkness, I make peace and create calamity; I, the LORD, do all these things" (v. 7). The immediate context speaks of God's ongoing providential control of all things, including light and darkness, well-being and calamity (cf. Prov. 16:4; Amos 3:6)—ultimately all for the rescue and refining of His chosen people. However, at the same time, the passage clearly indicates that God is the one who created darkness. Indeed, the text alludes to the creation of light and its separation from darkness in Genesis 1:4 and thus here provides an extra detail not expressly noted in the opening chapter of Scripture. By His word of power, the LORD brought darkness into existence. Everything, including darkness, was brought into being by God. When God named darkness by calling it night (Gen. 1:5), He showed His complete control over it as part of His creation. Nothing existed prior to creation, not even darkness.[55]

Although darkness is often associated in Scripture with evil and sin (see, e.g., Isa. 5:20), darkness is also a blessing and part of His good creation. Darkness is a gift that allows humans to sleep and refresh. It enables the wild animals to seek their food (Ps. 104:20–21). One cannot therefore equate the creation of darkness with the introduction of sin into the world.[56]

Some New Testament Testimony

The historicity of the events that took place in Genesis 1 is also affirmed in the New Testament. For example, Christ used the phrase "since the beginning of the creation which God created" (Mark 13:19) and said that "He who made

---

55. Edward J. Young, *Isaiah*, 3:200; Geoffrey W. Grogan, "Isaiah," in *The Expositor's Bible Commentary*, vol. 6, *Isaiah, Jeremiah, Lamentations, Ezekiel*, ed. Frank E. Gaebelein (Grand Rapids: Zondervan, 1986), 271; Helmer Ringgren and L. A. Mitchel, "*ḥāšak, ḥōšek*," *TDOT* 5:249.

56. As Westermann appears to do when he denies that God created darkness. Claus Westermann, *Isaiah 40–66*, trans. David M. G. Stalker (repr., Philadelphia: Westminster, 1969), 162; also see Claus Westermann, *Genesis 1–11*, trans. John J. Scullion (Minneapolis: Augsburg, 1984), 113–15; cf. Edward J. Young, *Isaiah*, 3:200–201.

them at the beginning 'made them male and female'" (Matt. 19:4; cf. Gen. 1:27). The apostle John clearly alluded to Genesis 1 when he wrote: "In the beginning was the Word, and the Word was with God, and the Word was God. He was in the beginning with God. All things were made through Him, and without Him nothing was made that was made" (John 1:1–2; cf. Col. 1:16–17; Heb. 1:2). It was "God who commanded light to shine out of darkness" (2 Cor. 4:6). Barnabas and Paul exclaimed to the pagans at Lystra that they should turn "to the living God, who made the heaven, the earth, the sea, and all things that are in them" (Acts 14:15). In Athens, the apostle Paul proclaimed "God, who made the world and everything in it, since He is Lord of heaven and earth" (Acts 17:24). We can only accept this by faith. "By faith we understand that the worlds were framed by the word of God, so that the things which are seen were not made of things which are visible" (Heb. 11:3). God should be praised and worshiped as the one who created all things (Rev. 4:11; 14:7).

Before considering Genesis 1 and 2 in detail, we need to ask why, in spite of such abundant evidence for the historicity of these chapters, there are such powerful trends in biblical interpretation that continue to assert that these chapters do not aim to convey a historical account.

General Dehistoricizing Developments

The readiness of scholars to accept the historical reliability of Genesis has been undermined by both philosophical developments and the dominance of the theory of evolution in science. Let us briefly examine these factors.

Two Types of History

Accepting the historicity of the opening chapter of Scripture was the mainstream thinking of the Christian church from earliest times. However, that situation changed. Eventually, under the growing pressure of the Enlightenment and scientific discoveries, commentators began to waffle on the historicity of Genesis 1.[57] Philosophers and theologians began to reject whatever they could not observe or reproduce by experiment, such as miracles, the virgin birth, the

---

57. For an overview of the history of interpretation on the first chapters of Genesis from patristic times to the present, see VanDoodewaard, *Quest*, 21–280. For a survey of sixteenth- and seventeenth-century Reformed commentators on Genesis 1, see David W. Hall, Lux Supra Tenebrae: *Essays on Calvin and Calvinism*, vol. 3 (Powder Springs, Ga.: The Covenant Foundation, 2015), 4–35. For commentators from the early nineteenth century, see Terry Mortenson, *The Great Turning Point: The Church's Catastrophic Mistake on Geology—Before Darwin* (Green Forest, Ariz.: Master, 2004), 43–47; and from the nineteenth and early twentieth century, see Nigel M. de S. Cameron, *Evolution and the Authority of the Bible* (Greenwood S.C.: Attic, 1983), 72–77.

divine nature of Christ, and even God's active role within history generally. This reliance on human reason became more and more determinative as to what constituted truth and history in the biblical record. This reliance on human reason severely undermined the authority of Scripture as divine revelation and resulted in the historical-critical method of interpreting the Bible. Rationalism became the new hermeneutic, which in its most consistent form denied any supernatural event as actually having happened in real-time history. Instead of divine revelation being the source of the Old Testament writings, Scripture became the product of Israel's religious development.[58]

With the abandonment of divine revelation and the historical value of the Old Testament, it was said that what was important was the message of Scripture, not whether something actually happened. One had to focus on the religious truth and moral value of what was written. Such bifurcated thinking led many scholars to distinguish between two types of history, often referred to by their German terms, *Historie* and *Geschichte*. *Historie* is what actually happened, as determined and reconstructed by modern scholars. Such history is true since it could be reasonably demonstrated as likely to have occurred. *Geschichte* is what Israel believed to have happened based on their inferences from events they experienced. For example, it was said that when Israel escaped from Egypt, they deduced from this miraculous event that this was an act of God. He was behind it. They concluded that this was God's hand at work, and so they recorded their conviction in Scripture. This history is therefore also called confessional history (*Heilsgeschichte*). Such a history is true for what it means for the believer—true in terms of its significance. They believed that God led them out. But this confession is not objectively verifiable as something that really happened, namely, that God actually came down and set His people free. This way of thinking of history in a twofold manner—the real verifiable history and what Israel deduced had happened—still dominates the critical study of the Old Testament.

Modern scholarship now wrestles with these distinctions since they pose a dilemma for scholars with respect to the historical reliability of what Scripture records. However, this dilemma is one of their own making. There is no need to speak of two types of history, a verifiable history and what Israel believed

---

58. For brief overviews, see Alan F. Johnson, "The Historical-Critical Method: Egyptian Gold or Pagan Precipice?," in *Quo Vadis, Evangelicalism? Perspectives on the Past, Direction for the Future*, ed. Andreas J. Köstenberger (Wheaton, Ill.: Crossway, 2007), 91–108; J. Robert Vannoy, "Divine Revelation and History in the Old Testament," in *Interpretation and History: Essays in Honour of Allan A. MacRae*, ed. R. Laird Harris, Swee-Hwa Quek, and J. Robert Vannoy (Singapore: Christian Life, 1986), 67–74; Edward J. Young, *Introduction*, 19–26.

happened, because there was only one history for Israel. God worked as creator and as savior of His people in real time and space. The biblical account of the past, including the account of creation, is not the product of the thinking or inferences of a believing community, but it is a record of God's actions as written down under the inspiration of the Holy Spirit for the instruction and direction of God's people. Each of God's mighty acts in saving His people was accompanied by His Word. We know that God was the one who delivered Israel out of Egypt because He told Moses so and had it written in Scripture for our benefit. We do not rely on human inferences and deductions but on God's own explanation of the events, which He accompanied with His Word. To accept the distinction between *Historie* and *Geschichte* is to deny that the events as recorded in Scripture actually happened and to remove a firm historical basis from the faith that Israel confessed.[59]

Story and Historicity

Not satisfied with a historically unreliable Old Testament, critical scholars turned to literary and genre studies to salvage some meaning from the biblical account. The importance of the historicity of narratives was downplayed and the accounts were called stories. The emphasis was not on whether they were really history but on what message was conveyed by them.

What exactly is a story? A prominent biblical scholar, James Barr, mentioned the following characteristics. A story is considered to have "large elements which no one seriously considers as history and which belong rather to the area of myth and legend." A story "moves back and forth, quite without embarrassment, between human causation and divine causation." Stories explain how something came to be and provide analogies "in which experience, past or future, can be understood and expressed." Stories also have no "critical evaluation of sources and reports."[60]

According to this definition, Genesis 1 and 2 qualify as stories without any real historical value in the eyes of critical scholars. Thus this part of Scripture has been called a myth or legend. Its main purpose was not to answer the question of what happened and to give a historical account of what actually

---

59. For a critique of the distinction, see Edward J. Young, *The Study of Old Testament Theology Today* (London: James Clarke, 1958), 7–33. For an overview of modern scholarship wrestling with the distinction, see Gerhard Hasel, *Old Testament Theology: Basic Issues in the Current Debate*, 4th ed. (Grand Rapids: Eerdmans, 1991), 115–38.

60. The quotes are from James Barr, "Story and History in Biblical Theology," *JR* 1 (1976): 7–8.

occurred in real time and space. Rather, it is a story that answers the "who" and "why" questions and explains the origin of the Sabbath.[61] With this assessment of the opening chapters as less than a historical account, there is no reliable history of what actually took place.

The Influence of Mainstream Science on the Issue of Historicity
Another general development that has contributed to the dehistoricizing of the Genesis creation account is the growing influence of scientific theories on biblical interpretation. Rather than simply letting the plain meaning of the biblical text and context guide them, various Old Testament scholars, even some conservative ones, are succumbing to evolutionary hypotheses on the origin of creation. The historicity of the account presented in Genesis 1 and 2 as historically understood invariably suffers.

Bruce Waltke, for example, struggles both to affirm the historicity of Genesis and to deny that it is a normal historical account. He writes that Genesis "certainly has historical elements. It is factual in the sense that God created the cosmos and all that is in it." But, "it is not straightforward or positivistic history." Later he comments that, "it is not concerned with presenting a strict historical account.... The narrator has an agenda very different from the modern historian. He has a theological agenda: to tell us that God created the earth and that it is all very orderly."[62] According to Waltke, "The best harmonious synthesis of the special revelation of the Bible, of the general revelation...and of science is the theory of theistic evolution."[63]

We find another example in C. John Collins's work. He states that Genesis 1 and 2 is not a scientific account. Such a statement is correct when understood to mean that God does not explain in any scientific detail all the processes that occurred for creation to physically take place when He issued His creative words of command. However, Collins elucidates his understanding of the nonscientific character of Genesis 1 by writing that the biblical text "has used language geared to its communicative purpose, which was to tell the story in order to inculcate a particular view of God and the world—a view shot through with wonder, delight, and awe at the boundless energy and creativity of God." Such a characterization seems to suggest that what the text recounts is not what actually took place. Indeed, "it is unlikely that the author makes a strong claim

---

61. Bill T. Arnold, *Genesis* (Cambridge: Cambridge University Press, 2009), 51–52; Hermann Gunkel, *The Legends of Genesis* (Chicago, Ill.: Open Court, 1901), 16–17.
62. Waltke, *Genesis*, 75–77; similarly, Waltke, *Old Testament Theology*, 189–93.
63. Waltke, *Old Testament Theology*, 202.

for the sequence of events," although the text has a "historical impulse" and occurs in a book that "purports to tell history."[64]

Approaches that minimize the historical character of Genesis 1 help scientists, such as Denis Alexander, Emeritus Director of the Faraday Institute for Science and Religion in Cambridge, to conclude that the language of Genesis 1 "should be taken figuratively" and Genesis 1 can be characterized as a "theological essay" and a "theological manifesto."[65]

The writings of Bruce Waltke, John Collins, and many other like-minded evangelical Old Testament scholars give credibility to the work of the BioLogos Foundation, whose scholars affirm "evolutionary creation, recognizing God as Creator of all life over billions of years." Scholars associated with this foundation also "believe that the diversity and interrelation of all life on earth are best explained by the God-ordained process of evolution with common descent." They "believe that God created humans in biological continuity with all life on earth."[66] Armed with such evolutionary presuppositions, BioLogos reads Scripture through the eyeglasses of current evolutionary hypotheses on the earth's origins. The result is a rejection of the biblical account of creation. For example, evangelical scholars associated with BioLogos say that Adam is not the historical first man. Rather, he is the first spiritual hominid, probably a neolithic farmer, who was endowed with a soul.[67] BioLogos's efforts have not been ineffective: the organization published a book in which twenty-five evangelical leaders share their stories about how they embraced the theory of evolution.[68]

Our age is the age of evolutionism. Evolution is the reigning paradigm in which science and other disciplines operate today. As a result, there continue to be many ongoing attempts to harmonize the interpretation of Genesis 1 and 2 with evolutionary theory. We must, however, remember that our generation is not the first to experience difficulties with Genesis and the prevailing philosophical and scientific worldviews. There has always been the tendency to accommodate the biblical creation account to whatever was the dominant

---

64. Collins, *Genesis 1–4*, 252–53, 266–67.

65. Denis R. Alexander, *Creation or Evolution: Do We Have to Choose?* 2nd ed. (Oxford: Monarch, 2014), ch. 7, "What kind of literature is Genesis 1:1–2:3?"

66. The quotations are from the BioLogos website: http://biologos.org/about-us/our -mission/.

67. Former Senior Fellow of Biblical Studies for Biologos, Peter Enns, *Evolution of Adam*, 122–23; BioLogos Advisory Council's Denis R. Alexander, *Creation or Evolution*, ch. 10, "Model C" and "Comparing the Models." Also see James K. Hoffmeier, "Response to Kenton L. Sparks," in *Genesis: History, Fiction, or Neither? Three Views on the Bible's Earliest Chapters*, by James K. Hoffmeier, Gordon J. Wenham, and Kenton L. Sparks (Grand Rapids: Zondervan, 2015), 144–45.

68. Applegate and Stump, *How I Changed My Mind*.

philosophy of the day. Beginning with the first-century Jewish thinker and exegete Philo, "throughout Christian, Moslem and Jewish philosophy, there was a general tendency to disregard the literalness of the story of creation and to harmonize it with what each particular philosopher happened to believe with regard to the origin of the world."[69] As Noel Weeks notes, "It was such an accommodation that allowed Aristotelian cosmology to be accepted by the late Medieval church and set the stage for the church's defence of Aristotle against Galileo."[70] We today must not be caught in the situation where we are defending an evolutionary cosmology, only to find out in the next scientific revolution that we have been duped. We must insist on the priority of Scripture. Science must not dictate an understanding of Genesis 1 and 2 that contradicts what is obviously intended to be a historical account.

A final methodological point to note is that if we allow science to determine whether the biblical text of Genesis recounts history or not, then what about other miraculous biblical accounts such as the resurrection of Christ from the dead? If science has determined that a corpse cannot be raised to life, does that mean we should reject the bodily resurrection of the Lord Jesus? As with creation, so also with other divine miracles recorded in Scripture, no biological or scientific explanation is possible. Scripture's determination of what is historical must be accepted and not science's. We will be returning to the issue of the influence of science on biblical interpretation from time to time as we go through Genesis 1 and 2.[71]

The Philosophy of the Cosmonomic Idea

Another dehistoricizing factor that has played an important part in Dutch Reformed circles both in the Netherlands and in North America is the influence of Herman Dooyeweerd's philosophy. His main work is the three-volume *Philosophy of the Law Idea* (*De wijsbegeerte der wetsidee*, 1935–1936), also known as *The Philosophy of the Cosmonomic Idea*. Dooyeweerd's work was revised and enlarged when translated into English as *A New Critique of Theoretical*

---

69. H. A. Wolfson, "The Veracity of Scripture in Philo, Halevi, Maimonides and Spinoza," in *Alexander Marx Jubilee Volume*, ed. Saul Lieberman (New York: Jewish Theological Seminary of America, 1950), 608, as quoted in Noel K. Weeks, *The Sufficiency of Scripture* (Edinburgh: Banner of Truth, 1988), 97n1.

70. Weeks, *Sufficiency of Scripture*, 97; also see Cornelis Van Dam, "A Lesson from Galileo's Trial," *Clarion* 65 (2016): 90–92; and Birkett, "Science and Scripture," 949–56.

71. Another example of an interpretation made, in part at least, because of the influence of science is the framework hypothesis. It will be discussed in chapter 5.

Thought.[72] The philosophy is also known as the Amsterdam or Reformational philosophy. This intricate philosophical system has many positive features but has also faced considerable criticism.

Briefly, with respect to the topic at hand, Dooyeweerd affirmed that God, the Creator, has so structured reality that it can be analyzed as having fifteen modal law spheres, each with its own laws and limits that can be discovered through scientific or philosophic inquiry. These spheres or modalities are all aspects of reality. One of these fifteen law spheres is the "historical." However, Dooyeweerd does not use the terms "history" and "laws of history" as they are normally understood.[73] Cosmic time, not historical time, constitutes the basis of the philosophical theory of reality in Dooyeweerd's thinking. "The entire empirical reality in its overrich diversity of structures is enclosed and determined by universal cosmic time."[74] However, time takes on a special meaning in the uppermost sphere or modality, called faith; it could be called "faith time." The entire redemptive history, although it also takes place in the historical aspect of time's horizon, can only be understood as *redemptive* history in the chronology and duration of the faith aspect. It has an eschatological perspective that points to the fulfillment of the expectation of faith, the full revelation of the kingdom of God in the return of Christ.[75]

According to Dooyeweerd, faith time is outside cosmic time and the days of creation related in Genesis 1 belong not to historical time but to this "faith time." They belong to the "in the beginning" with which the book of Genesis begins and do not fall within any chronological sequence since that is part of

---

72. Herman Dooyeweerd, *A New Critique of Theoretical Thought*, trans. David H. Freeman and William S. Young, 4 vols. (Amsterdam: H. J. Paris; Philadelphia: Presbyterian and Reformed, 1953–1958). For introductions, see J. M. Spier, *An Introduction to Christian Philosophy*, trans. D. H. Freeman, 2nd ed. (Nutley, N.J.: Craig, 1966); Andree Troost, *What Is Reformational Philosophy? An Introduction to the Cosmonomic Philosophy of Herman Dooyeweerd*, ed. Harry Van Dyke, trans. Antony Runia (n.p.: Paideia, 2012); and Willem J. Ouweneel, *Wisdom for Thinkers: An Introduction to Christian Philosophy* (Jordan Station, Ontario: Paideia, 2014). For Dooyeweerd's influence in North America, see C. T. McIntire, "Herman Dooyeweerd in North America," in *Dutch Reformed Theology*, ed. David F. Wells (Grand Rapid: Baker, 1989), 55–70.

73. A helpful summary of some of Dooyeweerd's thinking on the historical law sphere is Nick Van Til, "Dooyeweerd's 'History' and the Historian," *Pro Rege* 2, no. 2 (December 1973): 7–15; also see L. Kalsbeek, *Contours of a Christian Philosophy: An Introduction to Herman Dooyeweerd's Thought*, ed. Bernard Zylstra and Josina Zylstra (Toronto: Wedge, 1975), 151–59; and Troost, *What Is Reformational Philosophy?*, 121–63.

74. Dooyeweerd, *A New Critique*, 1:29; see also Gordon H. Clark, "Cosmic Time: A Critique of the Concept in Herman Dooyeweerd," *The Gordon Review* 2, no. 3 (September 1956): 94–99.

75. Herman Dooyeweerd, "De verhouding tussen wijsbegeerte en theologie en de strijd der faculteiten - II," *PhRef* 23 (1958): 67.

created reality. God has revealed His words of creation in the faith aspect of time. In this way Dooyeweerd wishes to avoid any conflict between the natural sciences and the creation account in Genesis.[76] In his *In the Twilight of Western Thought*, he explained in part: "God's creative deeds surpass the temporal order because they are not subjected to it. But as a truth of faith God has revealed these creative deeds in the faith-aspect of this temporal order which points beyond itself to what is supra-temporal."[77] In his magnum opus he asserted that, "in this eschatological aspect of time faith groups the 'eschaton' and, in general, that which is or happens beyond the limits of cosmic time. In this special sense are to be understood the 'days of creation', the initial words of the book of Genesis.... I cannot agree with the tendency of some modern Christian theologians, who identify the eschatological aspect of time with the historical."[78] Elsewhere he wrote, "The creative act of God is not subject to time.... The days of creation must be understood in terms of *faith* time, not in human terms of the [physical] time measure of the earth's rotation."[79]

Thus this philosophy imposes a meaning on the Genesis creation account that runs counter to the clear intent of the biblical text, which presents the events of creation as historical and occurring in real time. Just as Dooyeweerd limited the sphere of Scripture's message about Genesis 1 to "faith time," so he also denied that Scripture can give us philosophical notions and knowledge that are relevant to science, economics, or legal theory. According to Dooyeweerd, the Bible does not speak in a propositional way; it speaks in the faith modality; or to put it differently, Scripture is limited to the realm of "faith." Not surprisingly, Dooyeweerd has been criticized for not basing his philosophy on Scripture and instead imposing it on Scripture.[80]

---

76. Dooyeweerd, "De verhouding - II," 67–68.

77. Herman Dooyeweerd, *In the Twilight of Western Thought: Studies in the Pretended Autonomy of Philosophical Thought* (Nutley, N.J.: Craig, 1968), 150.

78. Dooyeweerd, *A New Critique*, 1:33.

79. Proposition 29 in Herman Dooyeweerd, "De leer van de mensch in de Wijsbegeerte der Wetsidee," *Correspondentie-Bladen* 7 (December 1942): 134–44. English text available at http://www.members.shaw.ca/aevum/32Propositions.html. For a summary of Dooyeweerd's position on the days of creation, see J. Glenn Friesen, "95 Theses of Herman Dooyeweerd," *PhRef* 74 (2009): 91–92 (thesis 60). Spykman notes, "Let us call that primeval time *creating* time, and our present time *creational* time." Gordon J. Spykman, *Reformational Theology: A New Paradigm for Doing Dogmatics* (Grand Rapids: Eerdmans, 1992), 154 (italics in the original). This speaking of the six days of creation as "creating time" appears to be analogous to Dooyeweerd's faith time; see Spykman, *Reformational Theology*, 154–56.

80. For the place of Scripture in formulating philosophical and other concepts, see the discussion between Dooyeweerd and Cornelius Van Til in Herman Dooyeweerd (with response by C. Van Til), "Cornelius Van Til and the Transcendental Critique of Theoretical Thought," in

Nevertheless, Dooyeweerd's influence has led Reformed scholars to deny the historicity of Genesis 1 and 2. N. H. Ridderbos, professor in Old Testament disciplines at the Free University in Amsterdam (1950–1975), helped give legitimacy to Dooyeweerd's views on creation by saying that they were not in conflict with Genesis 1, although he added that they could not appeal to Genesis 1 for support. Ridderbos himself was in favor of the framework hypothesis, which also denied the reality of the days of creation as recorded in Genesis 1.[81] Disciples of Dooyeweerd can be expected to continue to promote the view that Genesis 1 and 2 are not relating historical events.[82]

Summary and Conclusion

The context and genre of the creation account within the book of Genesis support the historicity of Genesis 1 as do references to creation elsewhere in Scripture. If we accept the biblical account of creation as trustworthy, then we acknowledge that God, the ultimate author of Scripture, presents us with a record of historical events that really took place at the beginning of time. We therefore agree with Edward J. Young when he writes, "The events recorded in the first chapter of the Bible actually took place. They were historical events and Genesis one, therefore, is to be regarded as historical."[83]

In the chapters that follow, we will turn to the text of Genesis 1 itself and listen carefully in order to understand what Scripture tells us about how and when this world came into being.

Jerusalem and Athens: Critical Discussions on the Theology and Apologetics of Cornelius Van Til, ed. E. R. Geehan (n.p.: Presbyterian and Reformed, 1971), 74–127. For a summary of Dooyeweerd's views, see Friesen, "95 Theses," 87–88 (thesis 42). Happily there has recently been a call for a fresh or continued engagement with Scripture among Dooyeweerd's philosophical heirs: Al Wolters, "What is to Be Done...Toward a Neocalvinist Agenda?," *Comment*, December 2005, 39.

81. Nic. H. Ridderbos, *Beschouwingen Over Genesis I*, 2nd ed. (Kampen: Kok, 1963), 66–67, 122–26. This view will be discussed in chapter 5.

82. E.g., Clouser, "Is Theism Compatible with Evolution?," 514–23, esp. 516–18.

83. Edward J. Young, *Studies in Genesis One*, 50. It is interesting that even a liberal observer outside evangelicalism noted that Scripture demands to be read literally in Genesis but pressures from science have led conservative biblical scholars to deny the obvious literal sense of the biblical text. James Barr, *Fundamentalism* (London: SCM, 1977), 40–45.

4

"In the Beginning"

In order to understand as well as possible the historical events Genesis 1 is communicating, we need to determine the meaning and significance of the words "in the beginning." For example, is this part of a heading or summary of what follows, or is this the actual beginning of the narrative? Different answers have been given to such questions. It is therefore essential that we comprehend the import of these very first words of Scripture and investigate the different interpretations that have been given. What do these words communicate?

The Translation

The traditional translation of Genesis 1:1 is, "In the beginning God created the heavens and the earth." This rendering of verse 1 as an independent clause or stand-alone sentence is consistent with the punctuation of the passage by the Masoretes, who were instrumental in passing the Hebrew text down to us. The translation "in the beginning" is grammatically justifiable and is also supported by the earliest Aramaic interpretations of Scripture, the Targums;[1] by the ancient translation of the Hebrew into Greek, the Septuagint; and by the ancient Latin translation, the Vulgate.[2] Consequently, it is not surprising that

---

1. For a detailed discussion and defense of the traditional translation on grammatical and other grounds, see Edward J. Young, *Studies in Genesis One*, 3–7; Gispen, *Genesis*, 1:34–36; Westermann, *Genesis 1–11*, 78, 93–98; and Hamilton, *Genesis*, 103–8. For the Targums, see Gary Anderson, "The Interpretation of Genesis 1:1 in the Targums," *CBQ* 52 (1990): 22–23. Although the Targums on the Pentateuch traditionally go back to the time of the biblical Ezra, the texts in our possession are from a much later date. For the dating, background, and text of Gen. 1, see Bernard Grossfeld, ed., *The Targum Onqelos to Genesis* (Collegeville, Minn.: Liturgical Press, 1988), 30–35, 42–43; Martin McNamara, ed., *Targum Neofiti 1: Genesis* (Collegeville, Minn.: Liturgical Press, 1992), 43–46, 52; Michael Mahler, ed., *Targum Pseudo-Jonathan: Genesis* (Collegeville, Minn.: Liturgical Press, 1992), 11–16.

2. The Septuagint translation of Genesis dates from about the middle of the third century BC. For a recent English translation, see Albert Pietersma and Benjamin G. Wright, eds., *A New*

this rendering is found in the majority of modern translations.[3] According to this translation, this verse indicates that time itself began when God created the heavens and the earth. This was the beginning of all things. Prior to this beginning there was no time, but only eternity. God always was and His existence is here presupposed. "Before the mountains were brought forth, or ever You had formed the earth and the world, even from everlasting to everlasting, You are God" (Ps. 90:2). The first verse therefore mentions the absolute beginning of all history and time. In the nature of the situation, this verse therefore also refers to the beginning of the material world.

This traditional understanding has been challenged by an interpretation of this verse that does not treat it as a stand-alone sentence. Instead, some scholars render the first verse of Genesis as a dependent clause that needs the following verse to complete its meaning. We then get a translation such as, "When God began to create heaven and earth—the earth being unformed and void" (NJPS). However, the technical grammatical and stylistic arguments for such a rendering are not convincing, as has been ably demonstrated by scholars and therefore need not be rehearsed here.[4] Also, the wording of John 1:1, "in the beginning," alludes to and supports the traditional rendering of Genesis 1:1. This observation brings us to the importance of taking into account the larger context of Scripture.

It is necessary when determining the meaning of an important biblical passage, such as the opening verse of Scripture, to keep in mind the teaching of the entire Word of God. Does the nontraditional translation do justice to what the Bible teaches elsewhere? If Genesis 1:1 is interpreted as a dependent clause as in the translation noted above, then the earth was already there when God began his creation work. There was preexisting matter before God created. In other words, there was no absolute beginning of creation. But this understanding contradicts Scripture, which informs us that "the universe was created by the word of God, so that what is seen was not made out of things that are visible"

English Translation of the Septuagint and the Other Greek Translations Traditionally Included under That Title (New York: Oxford University Press, 2007). Jerome (342–420) translated the Hebrew text into Latin. The English translation of the Vulgate can be found in *The Holy Bible. Douay Rheims Version* (Rockford, Ill.: Tan, 1971); the Old Testament part of this English translation of the Vulgate dates from 1609.

3. E.g., ASV, CSB, JB, NASB, NET, NIV (1984 and 2011), NJB, NKJV, REB (this revision of the NEB reverted to the traditional translation), and RSV.

4. A key technical Hebrew language argument in favor of the traditional rendering is that the very first Hebrew term can best be understood as being in the absolute state and not the construct. See Edward J. Young, *Studies in Genesis One*, 1–7; Westermann, *Genesis 1–11*, 93–98; Wenham, *Genesis 1–15*, 11–13.

(Heb. 11:3 ESV). Indeed, this truth is already apparent in the Old Testament. The LORD "spoke, and it [the earth] was done [i.e., came to be]" (Ps. 33:9). There was no preexisting matter before God began His work of creation. It was creation from nothing. These considerations bring us to the question of how the first verse of Genesis is related to the two verses that follow.

These first two verses of Scripture read in part: "In the beginning God created the heavens and the earth. The earth was without form, and void; and darkness was on the face of the deep." How do these two statements relate to each other? Let us begin with the traditional explanation. If the first verse marks the beginning of God's creative work, then verse two describes the earth as it was called into existence (Ps. 33:6; Heb. 11:3). Since Exodus 20:11 informs us that "in six days the LORD made the heavens and the earth, the sea, and all that is in them," it would appear that Genesis 1:2 is part of the first day. It also seems clear from the same Exodus passage that the very beginning of the creation work of God (referred to in Gen. 1:1) was on that first day as well. We will be coming back to this matter of whether verses 1 and 2 are indeed part of the first day of the six days of creation in the next chapter.

The understanding of the first two verses of Scripture as just outlined is not accepted by everyone. It appears that the majority of scholars today hold that the opening verse is either a superscription or summary of what follows. Other notable interpretations include the classic gap theory, the precreation chaos theory, and positing an initial creation and an indeterminate length of time followed by six days of creation. All these understandings would make it easier to reconcile current mainstream scientific theories with the Genesis account of creation primarily because Scripture would then leave room for a very old earth as required for the theory of evolution. Let us take a closer look at these understandings of the first verse.

A Title or Summary

For our purposes, the title or summary view holds, as Claus Westermann articulated it, that Genesis 1:1 "is not the beginning of an account of creation, but a heading that takes in everything in the narrative in one single sentence." Similarly, Bruce Waltke calls verse 1 a summary "which encapsulates the entire narrative" and "refers to the entire created event, the six days of creation, not something before the six days, nor part of the first day."[5] Waltke argues that the phrase "the heavens and the earth" is a figure of speech (merism) that

---

5. Westermann, *Genesis 1–11*, 94, also 97; Waltke, *Genesis*, 58; cf. Arnold, *Genesis*, 35.

designates the organized universe. Since Hebrew does not have a word for the "universe," the terms "heaven" and "earth" are used together to designate the ordered universe in Genesis 2:1 and 4. In view of that usage, the phrase must mean the same in the opening verse of Genesis. As a result, according to Waltke, "the earth" referred to in verse 1 cannot be the same as "the earth" in verse 2 since in that verse the "earth" is in a formless state (and not part of an ordered universe).[6]

Using the writings of Waltke, Vern Poythress has critically and helpfully examined the notion that the opening verse is a summary and has found that the main arguments for this view have "superficial plausibility, but none has weight." Poythress maintains that Genesis 1:1 records the first event and is not a summary.[7] He advances three compelling arguments against Waltke's understanding, given here in a brief summary form.

First, Poythress shows that

> if, in Gen 1:1, we replace the expression "the heavens and the earth" with some other expression, like "all things" (John 1:3) or "visible and invisible" (Col 1:16), we lose the key connection between "the earth" in Gen 1:1 and "the earth" in Gen 1:2, which is important for determining the state of the earth in v. 1. Similarly, if we assume that the compound expression in v. 1 must be isolated from the expression "the earth" in v. 2 (because the compound is somehow a seamless whole), we arrive at a similar result, wherein v. 2 is disconnected from v. 1. We fail to do justice to the significance of the occurrence of "the earth" in both verses.[8]

In other words, viewing verse 1 as a summary results in an unwarranted disconnect between Genesis 1:1 and Genesis 1:2.

Secondly, although the expression "the heavens and the earth" usually refers to the organized universe, its sense or meaning in a particular context need not necessarily include the idea of organization. This is the case with the opening verse of Genesis. Although there is already some minimal organization in verse 2 (the deep, its surface, and space above where the Spirit of God was hovering), it is not justifiable to read back into the expression "the heavens and the earth"

---

6. Bruce K. Waltke, "The Creation Account in Genesis 1:1–3. Part III: The Initial Chaos Theory and the Precreation Chaos Theory," *BSac* 132 (1975): 218–21.

7. Vern S. Poythress, *Interpreting Eden*, 321, previously published as Vern S. Poythress, "Genesis 1:1 is the First Event, not a Summary," *WTJ* 79 (2017): 97–121 (the quote is from p. 121). Poythress is especially responding to Waltke, "The Creation Account: Part III," 216–28. For similar arguments for Gen. 1:1 as the first event, see C. John Collins, *Reading Genesis Well: Navigating History, Poetry, Science, and Truth in Genesis 1–11* (Grand Rapids: Zondervan, 2018), 161–62.

8. Poythress, *Interpreting Eden*, 298–99.

as used in verse 1, the meaning or sense that expression has attained after God's creating work was done. Its usage in verse 1, at the very beginning of creation, is unique and its meaning needs to be derived in the first place from the immediate context and not from its use in the rest of the Old Testament.[9]

In the third place, Waltke argues that Isaiah 45:18 tells us that "the LORD did not create it [the earth] a formless mass." Consequently, according to him, it is theologically inappropriate to say that God would create a formless entity as He apparently did if Genesis 1:1 is taken as the first act of creation. Poythress, however, shows that Isaiah 45:18 speaks broadly about creation. The context of this passage indicates that the formless entity was not the endpoint of God's work of creation because the rest of the passage goes on to say that God created the world to be inhabited.[10]

Another objection to seeing the opening verse as a heading is that it forms part of the narrative and is connected to it with the Hebrew word *wə* ("and"). This conjunctive in verse 2 connects it to verse 1 and so continues the narrative, making it impossible for verse 1 simply to be a formal heading. Furthermore, no historical narrative begins with *and*. The *and* at the beginning of books such as Exodus and Leviticus connects these books to the ones preceding them. Verse 2 is a circumstantial clause, as we will see shortly, qualifying an element in the independent clause (v. 1) that precedes it. Verse 2 describes the earth as it came from the hands of the Creator and thus belongs with the first verse.[11]

Furthermore, Nathan Chambers has argued for understanding Genesis 1:1 as God's first work of creation by noting that if this passage is a summary, then it is a very odd summary because Genesis 1 "describes how God creates the heavens, the earth, *and seas;* names all three; creates creatures peculiar to each zone; and then gives humans dominion over the creatures of each [of] these three zones." Since a tripartite formula—heavens, earth, and seas—is used in the Decalogue in a summarizing way (Ex. 20:4, 11), you could expect a similar summary in Genesis 1:1 if that verse was intended to be a summary.[12]

Finally, mention can be made of Jeremy D. Lyon's point that the way Genesis 1:1 appears in Hebrew manuscripts seems to support interpreting that verse as part of the first day. Scribal practices evident both in ancient Qumran

---

9. Poythress, *Interpreting Eden*, 301–13.

10. Waltke, "The Creation Account: Part III," 220; Poythress, *Interpreting Eden*, 313–14.

11. Mark F. Rooker, "Genesis 1:1–3: Creation or Recreation? Part 2," *BSac* 149 (1992): 415–16; G. Ch. Aalders, *Genesis*, trans. William Heynen (Grand Rapids: Zondervan, 1981), 1:52–53.

12. Nathan Chambers, "Genesis 1.1 as the First Act of Creation," *JSOT* 43 (2019): 391 (italics in the original). Chambers understands "heaven" in Gen. 1:1 as "the realm of God within creation" (391). See further on this issue the Appendix: The Creation of Heaven and the Angels.

texts of Genesis and in medieval texts like the Leningrad Codex consistently show that the first five verses of Scripture are in their own paragraph or scribal unit. Since each subsequent day also has its own clearly marked textual unit, one can assume that the creative acts described in Genesis 1:1–5 belong to the first day. Lyon further noted that ancient Jewish literature also supports understanding verse 1 as being part of the first day.[13]

In light of the above, one can conclude that the first verse of Genesis is not a heading or summary but describes the very first act of creation on the first day.

The Classic Gap Theory

In its barest essentials this theory postulated a large time gap between verses 1 and 2. During this time gap, the perfect creation of verse 1 was ruined, presumably by the fall of Satan. This ruined earth is pictured in verse 2. The conditions there described were caused by God's judgment in the form of a flood, followed by a global ice age when the light and the heat from the sun were somehow removed. All the fossils, whether of plants, animals, or humans, which are found on the earth today date from that destructive time period. These fossils do not bear any genetic relationship with life now found on the earth. Proponents of this theory "have almost uniformly appealed to it for the harmonization of huge quantities of time required by evolutionary scientists and the rather recent creation Genesis seems to present."[14] With the first world ruined, a subsequent restoration was needed. This we find recorded beginning with Genesis 1:3.

What are the arguments for such a time gap? This was a rather popular theory widely disseminated through the influential *Scofield Reference Bible* (1917), and it deserves our attention. The *Scofield Bible*'s note on the word "created" in Genesis 1:1 states, in part, "The first creative act refers to the dateless past, and gives scope for all the geologic ages." A note on the phrase "without form and void" begins, "Jeremiah 4:23–26; Isaiah 24:1 and 45:18, clearly indicate that the earth had undergone a cataclysmic change as the result of the divine judgment. The earth bears everywhere the marks of such a catastrophe."[15] The sense

---

13. Jeremy D. Lyon, "Gen 1:1–3 and the Literary Boundary of Day One," *JETS* 62 (2019): 281–85.

14. Weston W. Fields, *Unformed and Unfilled* (Nutley, N.J.: Presbyterian and Reformed, 1976), 7.

15. See notes on Gen. 1:1 in C. I. Scofield, ed., *The Scofield Reference Bible. The Holy Bible, Containing the Old and New Testaments. Authorized King James Version, with a New System of Connected Topical References to All the Greater Themes of Scripture* (New York: Oxford University Press, 1917). The headings are also telling. Before v. 2 the heading reads, "Earth made waste and

conveyed by this approach is that "in the beginning God created the heavens and the earth, and the earth became without form and void." On the face of it, this interpretation has appeal and seems to point to a solution in reconciling current mainstream science and the text of Scripture. There are, however, grammatical and exegetical reasons to question and to reject this approach.

With respect to the grammar, in order to have a time gap between the first two verses of Scripture, one needs to interpret the Hebrew word translated "and" as signifying sequential action. So, first what is described in verse 1 occurred and then later what we read in verse 2. First, God created the heavens and the earth, and then at a later time the earth became without form and void. By then translating *hāyǝtâ* as "became" instead of the traditional "was," one leaves room for an indeterminate span of time between the two opening verses.[16]

In response, it should be noted that translating *wǝ* ("and") as indicating sequence is misreading the original Hebrew. According to Hebrew grammar, something that happened subsequently would be expressed by the following order: "and" + verb + subject. That is the normal narrative order in a verbal clause. In verse 2, however, the order is "and" + subject + verb. This is the order normally used for circumstantial clauses. Such a clause describes the condition or circumstance. In this case, verse 2 then describes the earth as God originally created it. These were the circumstances and the condition of the earth when God had called it into being and when He created light. Verse 2, therefore, does not describe what happened to the earth at some point in time after the creation of everything. It is for this reason that some translations (like the NKJV and ESV) do not even include "and" in order to avoid the wrong impression that verse 2 expresses sequential action. The NIV rendering, "now the earth was formless and empty," accurately conveys the disjunctive, explanatory sense of the Hebrew. Since verse 2 does not indicate chronological sequence, one cannot translate it as "and the earth became (or had become) without form and void." As a circumstantial clause, Genesis 1:2 describes the condition of the earth when God called it into being on the first day.[17]

---

empty by judgment (Jer 4:23–26)," and prior to v. 3, "The new beginning—the first day: light diffused." The revised edition (1967) is not as dogmatic and gives an additional interpretation for "without form and void" in a note on Gen. 1:1. The gap theory is mentioned in a note on Isa. 45:18.

16. Defending the notion that the verb in Gen. 1:2 should be translated "had become" is the focus of the study of Arthur C. Custance, *Without Form and Void: A Study of the Meaning of Genesis 1.2* (Brockville, Ontario: Custance, 1970).

17. For the grammatical points made, see Ronald J. Williams, *Hebrew Syntax: An Outline*, 3rd ed., revised and expanded by John C. Beckman (Toronto: University of Toronto Press, 2007), §495a; Joüon, §154m; *IBHS*, §30.3a; GKC, §§141i, 156a. For a detailed discussion for and against

There are also exegetical and theological arguments that need to be mentioned. The *Scofield Reference Bible* reasons that the phrase "without form and void" has negative connotations and reminds one of God's judgment. So when verse 2 tells us that "the earth was without form and void," the *Scofield Bible* draws the conclusion that Genesis 1:2 refers to God having judged the earth because of a preceding fall into sin. As proof that the phrase speaks of God's judgment, the *Scofield Bible* refers to Jeremiah 4:23–26 where God's wrath is pictured in terms of the earth being "without form and void," a cosmic catastrophe, a veritable undoing of creation. However, this argument does not hold. Although God's judgment in Jeremiah 4 yields a world "without form and void," that does not mean that this judgment also refers to the situation in Genesis 1:2. A similar observation applies to Isaiah 24:1, which does not use the same vocabulary as Genesis 1:2, but does speak of judgment and devastation.[18]

The phrase "without form and void" does not in and of itself speak of judgment or God's wrath. The usage of these terms elsewhere makes that clear. The first word, "without form" (*tōhû*), means "wilderness, emptiness." It speaks of a trackless waste, inhospitable territory (Job 12:24; Ps. 107:40). It pictures the loneliness and desolateness of a barren desert. This is clear from the parallelism in Job 26:7, where the first part reads, "He stretches out the north over empty space [*tōhû*]." The second part of that verse corresponds to this: "He hangs the earth on nothing."

The second expression in the pair "without form [*tōhû*] and void [*bōhû*]" only occurs with *tōhû* in the Old Testament (Gen. 1:2; Isa. 34:11; Jer. 4:23). It is therefore difficult to evaluate it separately. The term *bōhû* appears to be used to strengthen the meaning of *tōhû*. The sense is that the earth was as empty as it could be. Thus the meaning of "without form and void" is that the earth in its initial state was without vegetation and animals, as well as human beings.[19] There is no mention of a fall of creation and God's judgment or any implication that creation had to be remade. The earth as God first created it could simply not be inhabited yet. The rest of Genesis 1 will show how God transformed this empty desolation to become an earth fully prepared to receive human beings. This objective reminds one of Isaiah 45:18: "For thus says the LORD, who created the heavens, who is God, who formed the earth and made it, who has

---

chronological sequence, see, respectively, Custance, *Without Form and Void*, 41–116; and Fields, *Unformed and Unfilled*, 87–112.

18. See also Bruce K. Waltke, "The Creation Account in Genesis 1:1–3. Part II: The Restitution Theory," *BSac* 132 (1975): 139–42.

19. This is also the understanding of the Targum Pseudo-Jonathan and Targum Neofiti; Mahler, *Targum Pseudo-Jonathan: Genesis*, 16; McNamara, *Targum Neofiti 1: Genesis*, 52.

established it, who did not create it in vain [*tōhû*], who formed it to be inhabited." The emptiness (*tōhû*) was but a first, initial phase in His creation work.
The earth was not yet as God had intended it to be.[20] This Isaiah passage therefore also should not be used by the *Scofield Bible* to speak of God's judgment.

Two other arguments have been used to defend the gap theory. Proponents
of this theory have suggested that the Hebrew verb meaning "to create" must
be rigidly separated from the Hebrew verb "to make." "To create" means to
make from nothing, and "to make" never means that, but refers, among other
things, to "working on something that already exists in order to effect a change
in it until it becomes something further."[21] With this line of thinking, Genesis
1:1 refers to the original creation ("In the beginning God created the heavens
and the earth"), but the reference to creation in the fourth commandment in
Exodus 20:11 does not refer to the original creation. It relates to a completely
different event because the verb "make" is used and not the verb "create." So
when Exodus 20 tells us that God made the heavens and the earth in six days,
this divine activity refers to a reworking of the original creation. This work of
the six days was not a time of creation from nothing but "a time in which a
ruined cosmos was re-ordered as a fit habitation for man. And when the reor-
dering was completed, God rested."[22]

There is, however, no evidence warranting such a rigid distinction between
"to create" and "to make." Although it is true that the verb "to create" expresses
better than any other word the idea of an absolute creation, a making from
nothing, yet, we should not drive a wedge or artificial division between "to create" and "to make." After all, both are used of God's work with respect to the
origin of the world. Scripture must be compared with Scripture. When this is
done, the only conclusion that can be drawn is that the statement "God created
the heavens and the earth" (Gen. 1:1) and the statement "the LORD made the
heavens and the earth" (Ex. 20:11) both refer to the same event and not to two
different ones. The reason for this conclusion is that the verbs "to create" and
"to make" are used interchangeably in speaking of God's creation work.

This interchangeability can be demonstrated from Genesis 1 and 2. About
the creation of man we read, "Let Us make man" (1:26), "God created man"
(1:27), and compare also "the LORD God formed man" (2:7). Although there are

---

20. David Toshio Tsumura, *Creation and Destruction: A Reappraisal of the* Chaoskampf
Theory in the Old Testament (Winona Lake, Ind.: Eisenbrauns, 2005), 33, also 25–26; Edward J.
Young, *Studies in Genesis One*, 38.

21. Custance, *Without Form and Void*, 181.

22. Custance, *Without Form and Void*, 181.

different connotations of the verbs employed with the creation of man (cf. 2:7), they are mutually compatible and highlight different aspects of God's work. There is also variety in the work of creation on the fourth and fifth days. We read that "God created great sea creatures" (1:21) and that "God made the beast of the earth" (1:25). The terms are used interchangeably. When God called the sea creatures into being (1:20), He created them (1:21). When He called the creatures of the earth into being (1:24), He made them (1:25). This synonymous usage is also found in Genesis 2:4. "This is the history of the heavens and the earth when they were created, in the day that the LORD God made the earth and the heavens." So, just from Genesis 1 and 2 it is already evident that "to create" and "to make" are used interchangeably. This can also be demonstrated from elsewhere in the Old Testament,[23] but these examples may suffice.

Another argument for a time gap between verses 1 and 2 of Genesis 1 concerns the reference to darkness in verse 2. It is said that this implies the presence of evil and judgment since darkness symbolizes sin and judgment in Scripture (e.g., John 3:19; Jude 13). It is therefore supposed that God originally created the world in light and that the darkness resulted from the fall into sin and God's subsequent judgment. However, just because darkness can symbolize evil does not make darkness itself a manifestation of evil or inherently bad. God's Word teaches otherwise. Darkness is part of the cycle of day and night as God created it (Gen. 1:5; cf. Ps. 104:20–24). Human beings need the darkness so they can have rest. It is beneficial to them.[24] As a matter of fact, darkness is part of God's creation work. "I form the light and create darkness" (Isa. 45:7).

In conclusion, there is no scriptural basis for the theory that Genesis 1:2 describes the earth after it fell under God's judgment because of sin. What verse 2 does describe is the first stage in the preparation of the earth for man. "It is the first picture of the created world that the Bible gives.... The earth was desolation and waste, but all was in God's hand and under his control; nothing was contrary to his design."[25] And so verse 1 states that God created the heavens and the earth. This was His first act of creation. Verse 2 describes the earth as the Creator called it into being (cf. Ps. 33:9).

The Precreation Chaos Theory

Another understanding, similar in some ways to the gap theory, is that the creation account in Genesis 1 describes God using existing material when he

---

23. Fields, *Unformed and Unfilled*, 56–74.

24. Edward J. Young, *Studies in Genesis One*, 34–35n33; Fields, *Unformed and Unfilled*, 131–33.

25. Edward J. Young, *Studies in Genesis One*, 38.

made the heavens and the earth. This understanding can be called the precreation chaos theory. A prominent advocate for this position is Bruce Waltke, who holds that in Genesis 1 God was dealing with preexisting matter that was without form and void. As he put it, Genesis 1:1–2 "cannot mean that God created the 'heaven and the earth' and what he brought into existence was an 'unformed and unfilled' earth. The cosmos of verse 1 and the chaos of verse 2 cannot have co-existed.... *In sum, Genesis one represents the Heavenly King transforming the pre-existing chaos into the present cosmos.*"[26] Chronologically, verse 2 "must describe the state of the earth prior to verse 1."[27] He justifies this position by understanding verse 1 as an introductory summary statement, a broad general declaration that God created the cosmos. Verse 2 does not merely denote an inferior stage of creation but rather the contrary of creation. The phrase "unformed and unfilled" (or "without form and void") means utter chaos and is the opposite of "the heavens and the earth," which is the total cosmos.[28] Waltke therefore holds that verse 1 does not describe the absolute beginning of creation; rather, "this is a relative beginning. As verse 2 seems to indicate, there is a pre-Genesis time and space."[29] An implication of this is that Genesis 1 does not describe creation from nothing.[30]

Part of Waltke's concern in this understanding of the text appears to be his desire to remove the Genesis account as a factor in determining the age of the earth. He writes that the Genesis account "teaches only that God brought the pre-Genesis darkness and chaotic waters within his protective restraints, not when or how they happened.... If one wishes to form a concord between natural theology and Genesis 1, which I for one do not, then let it be noted that the age of the earth cannot be decided by this text and that one must commence one's thinking about cosmic origins with chaotic waters already in existence."[31]

However, does Waltke's explanation do justice to the available evidence and especially the text of Genesis? The idea that Scripture alludes to God having conquered and transformed a preexisting chaos into the present cosmos is

---

26. Bruce K. Waltke, "The Literary Genre of Genesis, Chapter One," *Crux* 27, no. 4 (1991): 4 (italics in the original); similarly, Waltke, "The Creation Account: Part III," 221.

27. Waltke, *Genesis*, 60.

28. Waltke, "The Literary Genre," 4; Waltke, "The Creation Account: Part III," 227; also see Waltke, *Genesis*, 59–60.

29. Waltke, *Genesis*, 58n12, also 59.

30. "Though Waltke would deny the eternality of matter, he opens the door to the idea of preexisting matter in Genesis 1 by saying the creation account in Genesis 1 assumes that physical existence is present at 'the beginning.'" Rooker, "Creation or Recreation? Part 2," 424.

31. Waltke, "The Literary Genre," 4–5.

controversial and dubious. Indeed, the whole idea can be discredited. There is no solid biblical basis for it.[32]

More specifically, Waltke's view that the opening verse of Genesis is a summary statement reflecting the finished work of God rather than the beginning of a process of creation means that Waltke associates verse 2 and its circumstantial clauses with what follows and not with what precedes. In other words, according to this understanding, God did not and could not create something that could be characterized as being "without form and void." He did not, as Waltke puts it, create disorder and darkness.[33] There are some major problems with this approach.[34] If God had not created what is mentioned in Genesis 1:2, where then did the earth come from? The fourth commandment clearly teaches that God created all (Ex. 20:11). Furthermore, as we saw earlier, the phrase "without form and void" does not mean disorder and darkness and is not negative in and of itself. There is thus no reason that God could not have called the earth into existence in that empty and dark state and worked from there. Indeed, there is a clear progression in the work of creation. It did not happen all at once. God worked to complete it over a span of time. The expression "the heavens and the earth" in Genesis 1:1 encompasses all created reality. As the late Jewish biblical scholar Nahum Sarna put it, "The combination of opposites expresses the totality of cosmic phenomena."[35] In other words, the opening verse declares that at the very beginning God called the entire universe into existence (cf. Ps. 33:6). The verses that follow mention the initial condition of the earth and God's subsequent acts of creation.

Another problem with the precreation chaos understanding is that the Hebrew verb "to create" is interpreted to satisfy the theory and is not explained according to the immediate and broader biblical context. Since, as noted earlier, Genesis 1:1 speaks of the absolute beginning of time and matter, the verb "to create" here means to call into existence what previously was not there. This verb is admirably suited to convey that meaning since God, not a foreign deity, is always the subject of this verb. This fact underlines God's sovereignty in calling

---

32. See especially the thorough study by Rebecca S. Watson, *Chaos Uncreated*; cf. Bernard F. Batto, "The Combat Myth in Israelite Tradition Revisited," in *Creation and Chaos: A Reconsideration of Hermann Gunkel's Chaoskampf Hypothesis*, ed. John Scurlock and Richard H. Beal (Winona Lake, Ind.: Eisenbrauns, 2013), 217–36. Against the view that there was a chaos that had to be conquered to produce order, including the supposed origin of the notion in the pagan Enuma Elish and its supposed reflection in Gen. 1, see Millard, "From Weal to Woe," 195–99.

33. Waltke, "The Creation Account: Part III," 221.

34. See also in this connection Rooker, "Creation or Recreation? Part 2," 414–25.

35. Sarna, *Genesis*, 5.

the world into being and ordering it according to His will.[36] The broader biblical context also supports creation from nothing. God is the one who "calls into existence the things that do not exist" (Rom. 4:17 ESV). "By faith we understand that the worlds were framed by the word of God, so that the things which are seen were not made of things which are visible" (Heb. 11:3).

Initial Creation Plus Six Days

One other interpretation of the first verses needs to be mentioned, namely, the notion that there was an initial creation followed at some undetermined length of time by the seven days of the creation account. According to Old Testament scholar C. John Collins, "the first verse…narrates the initial creation event; then verse 2 describes the condition of the earth just before the creation week gets under way. These two verses stand outside the six days of God's workweek, and—just speaking grammatically—say nothing about the length of time between the initial event of 1:1 and the first day of 1:3." In a footnote he adds, "that is, Gen. 1:1–2 is background to the six days, with verse 1 describing an event that took place before the main storyline got going. The grammar itself tells us nothing about *how long before* the storyline."[37] What are the arguments for this understanding?

Collins has approached the text on the basis of discourse analysis, by which the modern scholar seeks to read the text as a competent original reader would have done. This includes determining the genre, which is narrative. Now since "the verb *created* in Genesis 1:1 is in the perfect, and the normal use of the perfect at the very beginning of a pericope is to denote an event that took place before the storyline gets under way," Collins considers the first two verses to describe what had happened prior to the six days of creation that are subsequently described. He would therefore translate the verb in the English pluperfect tense: "God had in the beginning created the heavens and the earth."[38] Some examples

---

36. This interpretation is the traditional one and remains widely accepted. See, e.g., W. H. Schmidt, *"br'* to create," in *TLOT* 1:255; Raymond C. Van Leeuwen, *"br'* I," in *New International Dictionary of Old Testament Theology and Exegesis*, ed. Willem VanGemeren (Grand Rapids: Zondervan, 1997), 1:732; Arnold, *Genesis*, 35–36. See further, Rooker, "Creation or Recreation? Part 2," 417–19.

37. Collins, *Genesis 1–4*, 78 (italics in the original). Agreeing with Collins in a recent essay is Richard M. Davidson, "The Genesis Account of Origins," in Gerald A. Klingbeil, *Genesis Creation Account*, 87–99.

38. Collins, *Genesis 1–4*, 51 (italics in the original), also see 42–43; C. John Collins, "Reading Genesis 1:1–2:3 as an Act of Communication: Discourse Analysis and Literal Interpretation,"

he gives lend support to this application of his discourse analysis (Gen. 24:1; 3:1), but by his own admission not all passages do (Ex. 19:1).[39]

In response, it is doubtful whether it is appropriate to apply to a unique passage like Genesis 1:1 such a general rule derived from discourse analysis (i.e., that the use of a perfect at the beginning of an account refers to preceding events). In the first place, one would expect an account of the distant past to begin with the Hebrew perfect.[40] The book of Job, for example, also begins with a Hebrew perfect, but one would not think of translating with the pluperfect, "There had been a man in the land of Uz whose name was Job" (Job 1:1). The narrative is only starting, and Job is just being introduced. There is no need for a pluperfect, and a simple past tense is appropriate ("there was a man in the land of Uz, whose name was Job"). Likewise, there is little to justify a pluperfect understanding of the Hebrew perfect in Genesis 1:1. After all, we have here an account of the very beginning and what God did from that point on as relayed in the rest of the chapter. To project a time prior to the six days is not honoring the unity of the text as we have it. The phrase "in the beginning" is placed in a most emphatic position at the front of the sentence and so before the entire pericope (Gen. 1:1–2:3). That factor should override considerations of discourse analysis that would chronologically separate what the text suggests belongs together. As the very first verse in Scripture, this passage occupies a very special place announcing the absolute beginning of creation, including the commencement of time and thus the days of creation.[41]

A variant of the position of an initial creation followed by seven days is articulated by Old Testament scholar John H. Sailhamer. He claims that the term "beginning" in Genesis 1:1 "could refer to billions of years, to a few thousand years, or to a period as brief as a few months or days." The duration of time is unspecified. So, "two distinct time periods are mentioned in Genesis 1. In the first period (the 'beginning,' Genesis 1:1), God created the universe; no time limitations are placed on that period. In the second period (Genesis 1:2–2:4a), God prepared the garden of Eden for man's dwelling; that activity occurred in one week." The billions of years, geological ages, and dinosaurs as postulated by

in *Did God Create in Six Days?*, ed. Joseph A. Pipa and David W. Hall (Taylors, S.C.: Southern Presbyterian Press, 1999), 131–35.

39. Collins, *Genesis 1–4*, 51–52.

40. A rule to be noted and relevant for Gen. 1 is that "in representing a series of events, only the first verb stands in the perfect, and the narration is continued in the imperfect." GKC, §49.1.

41. On not translating as a pluperfect, see Gispen, *Genesis*, 1:37–38. The perfect, rather than the pluperfect, is suggested for Gen. 1:1 in Joüon, §112c.

mainstream science would all fit into the period called "the beginning."[42] When understood this way, Genesis 1:1 "does not say that God created the universe in the first moment of time; rather it says that God created the universe during an indeterminate period of time before the actual reckoning of a sequence of time began."[43] How does Sailhamer justify his position that "in the beginning" does not refer to a point in time but to "a *period* or *duration* of time which falls before a series of events"?[44]

There are some Old Testament examples of the word "beginning" used in the sense that Sailhamer highlights. In Job 8:7 the term refers to the first part of Job's life, and in Genesis 10:10 it has reference to the beginning of the reign of Nimrod. In both cases a period of time is involved. More examples could be given.[45] The question is, of course, whether such an understanding fits the context of Genesis 1, for there are also examples of the term "beginning" having reference to a point of time, the beginning of time per se, rather than a duration of time, although Sailhamer denies this.[46] In Isaiah 46:10 God declares "the end from the beginning," referring to his ability to predict the end of an event from its very beginning. Deuteronomy 11:12 says that the eyes of the LORD were always on the land "from the beginning of the year to the very end of the year," clearly indicating a beginning point of time.[47] The meaning of "beginning" as a point of time can justly be assigned to Genesis 1.[48] That sense of the term fits the context of this passage as the start of the six days of creation, the point at the beginning of time when creation was instantly called into existence by the Word of God (Ps. 33:6, 9; Heb. 11:3). It also fits the wider context of Scripture since Exodus 20:11 speaks of the entire creation process as lasting six days.

The view that the first two verses of Genesis are outside the creation week has also been set forth in the Netherlands. Dogmatician Herman Bavinck wrote that "the first verse needs to be read as the account of an independent fact. In verse 2 the earth already exists, though in a disordered and vacuous state. And verse 1 reports the origin of that earth." In other words, "the creation of heaven

---

42. John H. Sailhamer, *Genesis Unbound: A Provocative New Look*, 2nd ed. (Colorado Springs: Dawson Media, 2011), ch. 2, Kindle.

43. Sailhamer, *Genesis Unbound*, ch. 3, Kindle.

44. Sailhamer, *Genesis Unbound*, ch. 3, Kindle (italics in the original).

45. H.-P. Müller, "*rō'š* head," in *TLOT*, 1190.

46. Sailhamer writes that the term in question "always refers to an extended, yet indeterminate duration of time—not a specific moment." Sailhamer, *Genesis Unbound*, ch. 3, Kindle.

47. H.-P. Müller, "*rō'š*," 1190; and *DCH* 7:381, where other examples are found as well.

48. H.-P. Müller, "*rō'š*," 1190. Also see the critique of Sailhamer's position in Jordan, *Creation in Six Days*, 133–38.

and earth in verse 1 and the unformed state of the earth in verse 2 are ante-
rior to the first day." In Bavinck's view the time elapsed between the first and
second creation would have been short.[49] Old Testament scholar G. Ch. Aalders,
Bavinck's younger colleague at the Free University, likewise wrote of a first
and second creation as being distinct from each other, but suggested that the
second creation followed immediately after the first. He made no such distinction in the commentary on Genesis that he wrote for a popular readership.
Klaas Schilder also wrote of a first and second creation but made it very clear
that this distinction does not mean that we now have room for many millions
of years within the account of creation. More recently the Dutch dogmaticians
J. van Genderen and W. H. Velema distinguished between a first and second
creation as well and suggested that "the earth could have been there already for
a long time before man was created."[50]

What are we to make of the notion of a first creation in Genesis 1:1–2
that took place prior to the six-day creation that followed in verses 3–31? This
understanding cannot be found in the work of John Calvin or in the work of
Calvinist theologian Francis Turretin (1623–1687), who specifically rejected
the idea that verses 1 and 2 refer to a time before the six days. The Westminster
Standards likewise affirm that all things were created in the space of six days.[51]
Of course, the biggest problem with positing a separate creation event preceding the first day is the fourth commandment's stating that "in six days the LORD
made the heavens and the earth, the sea, and all that is in them" (Ex. 20:11).
Bavinck anticipated that objection and responded that "this can only be understood, however, of the second creation" (Gen. 1:3–31).[52] But such reasoning is
arbitrary and has no basis in Scripture. No distinction is made between a first
creation (Gen. 1:1–2) and a separate second creation comprised of the six-day
period. Scripture rather underlines that in six days everything was created. The

---

49. What was called into being in Gen. 1:1 "lasted for some time, however short." Bavinck,
Reformed Dogmatics, 2:478; cf. Herman Bavinck, *Our Reasonable Faith*, trans. Henry Zylstra
(Grand Rapids: Baker, 1977), 172–73.

50. G. Ch. Aalders, *De Goddelijke openbaring in de eerste drie hoofdstukken van Genesis*
(Kampen: Kok, 1932), 217–18, 229; Aalders, *Genesis*, 1:50–58; Klaas Schilder, *Heidelbergsche
Catechismus toegelicht* (Goes: Oosterbaan & Le Cointre, 1947–1951), 3:304; J. van Genderen and
W. H. Velema, *Concise Reformed Dogmatics*, trans. Gerrit Bilkes and Ed M. van der Maas (Phil-
lipsburg, N.J.: P&R, 2008), 274.

51. Calvin, *Institutes*, 1.14.2; Calvin, *Genesis*, 1:78; Benjamin B. Warfield, "Calvin's Doctrine
of the Creation," *PTR* 13 (1915): 204; Francis Turretin, *Institutes of Elenctic Theology*, ed. James T.
Dennison Jr., trans. George Musgrave Giger (Phillipsburg, N.J.: P&R, 1992), 1:447; James Benjamin
Green, ed., *A Harmony of the Westminster Presbyterian Standards* (n.p.: Collins, World, 1976), 34.

52. Bavinck, *Reformed Dogmatics*, 2:479.

object of God's creation work is "the heavens and the earth" both in Genesis 1:1 and in the fourth commandment, which speaks of this creation as occurring within six days.

The view of a first creation taking place prior to the six days of creation appeals to those who accept the current conclusions of mainstream science since this leaves the age of the earth undetermined. One can therefore both believe in an earth billions of years old and accept the Genesis creation account. Oxford professor John Lennox has been quick to note this point.[53] However, the benefit of holding to a prior first creation for harmonizing Scripture with science is dubious. Theologian John Frame rightfully notes that this theory (of a time gap between Genesis 1:1 and 1:3) "creates more problems with science than it solves" since "during such a period the heavens and earth would have existed (1:1), but there would have been no light (1:3) or heavenly bodies (1:14–19). But most scientists would deny that such a situation ever existed."[54]

Summary and Conclusions

The first two verses of Scripture describe the very beginning of God's creation work. There is no convincing evidence of an indeterminate time gap within the first verses of Genesis 1. There was no precreation chaos and no initial creation that preceded the six days of God's work of creating. No created thing yet existed. Verse 1 relates God's bringing the heavens and the earth into being. By His word, God made it all. He spoke and it came to be (Ps. 33:6, 9). Verse 2 describes the world that God had made as it existed at the very beginning. It was not yet ready to receive the crown of creation, man. The subsequent narrative focuses on God preparing the world for human habitation.

---

53. Lennox, *Seven Days*, 52–53.
54. Frame, *Systematic Theology*, 200.

5

The Days of Creation

The meaning of the creation days is an important element in the consideration of the historicity of the Genesis account. This is a hotly debated issue, and in response to the question of what constitutes a day in Genesis 1, scholars have offered a variety of answers, from a normal, twenty-four-hour day to extremely long periods of time. All participants in this debate can acknowledge that the meaning of the term *yôm* ("day") is not constant in Hebrew, nor for that matter is the term *day* in English. After all, this expression can indicate daytime, the opposite of night (Gen. 1:5), as well as a longer period of time as in Genesis 2:4, when the Hebrew word for "day" refers to all six days of creation ("in the day that the Lord God made the earth and the heavens"). Our concern here is with what is meant with each of the six days of creation. We will consider the case for understanding the days of Genesis 1 as literal days. Subsequently, we will look at some other proposals, both ancient and current. But first we need to ask, when did the first day begin?

When Did the First Day Begin?

In the previous chapter we concluded that Genesis 1:1 describes the absolute beginning of all history and time. "In the beginning God created the heavens and the earth." If that is the absolute beginning, does that mean that it also describes the start of the first day? We need to take a closer look.

The answer to this question has been and continues to be a matter of some dispute. The majority of scholars today seem to favor the view that the first day began with the creation of light. The arguments for this position include the following. After God called the heavens and the earth into being, the first act of creation specifically noted in the text was the creation of light. The text reads, "Then God said, 'Let there be light'; and there was light. And God saw the light, that it was good; and God divided the light from the darkness. God called the light Day, and the darkness He called Night. So the evening and the morning were the first day" (Gen. 1:3–5). This text is understood as narrating what God did during that day. There was a progression from the creation of light to the time that evening came and then eventually morning. Once morning came, it was light again and the first day was completed. Thus a day is reckoned as beginning with the light and ending when dawn brings a new day.

In this view, the first day must therefore have started with the creation of light.[1] However, if you insist on six days for all creation, without any preliminary unknown time, then the first day of history does not fit the pattern of a day beginning with light, since at the very beginning there was no light. The very first day must therefore be considered special and exceptional.[2] But such an approach is not very satisfying exegetically since it takes the first day as beginning not with light but with darkness (Gen. 1:2), making this day different from those that followed, which all are understood to begin with light.

Another approach, which gets around this inconsistency, separates the work of creation in verses 1 and 2 from what follows in verse 3. The first day then starts with the creation of light. Genesis 1:1–2 is then said to describe "the first creation," which took place prior to the first day, and verse 3 begins the narrative of "the second creation," which occurred "in time." The basis for distinguishing two creation works is, in the words of Herman Bavinck, that there is "a distinction between what God did 'in the beginning' (Gen. 1:1; cf. John 1:1) and what he did 'by the words of his mouth' in six days (Gen. 1:3ff.)"[3] However, as we have seen in the previous chapter, this reasoning does not convince. God's work of creation is always pictured in Scripture as one work done in six days. It is never divided into a first and second enterprise. As a matter of fact, precisely the same words that occur in Genesis 1:1 as the object of God's creation work ("the heavens and the earth") recur in the fourth commandment as the result of God's creation work in six days (Ex. 20:11).

We need to take a step back and ask, what according to Scripture constituted a day? We then note that the view that has the day begin with the creation of light, and thus the morning, does not jive with ritual law, which

---

1. So, e.g., Cassuto, *Genesis*, 28–30; Benno Jacob, *The First Book of the Bible: Genesis*, ed. Ernest I. Jacob and Walter Jacob (New York: Ktav, 1974), 4; Carl J. Lawrenz and John C. Jeske, *A Commentary on Genesis 1–11* (Milwaukee: Northwestern, 2004), 50–51.

2. So H. C. Leupold, *Exposition of Genesis* (Grand Rapids: Baker, 1950), 1:42, 56–57; Edward J. Young, *Studies in Genesis One*, 87, 89.

3. Bavinck, *Reformed Dogmatics*, 2:478–79, also see 496–97. His contemporary Abraham Kuyper made a similar distinction. Abraham Kuyper, *Locus de sacra scriptura, creatione, creaturis: college-dictaat van een der studenten* (Kampen: Kok, 1910), 3:82.

places the beginning of the day in the evening. Unleavened bread was to be eaten from the evening of the fourteenth day of the first month to the evening of the twenty-first day of the month (Ex. 12:18), and the Day of Atonement was to be observed from evening to evening (Lev. 23:32; also cf. Lev. 15:5–27). Those who consider the day to begin with light have suggested that these ritual laws were exceptions to the rule, and thus the evening had to be noted as the beginning of the day for the purpose of these special days.[4] However, Daniel 8:14 and 26 also speak of "evenings and mornings" as an indication of days.[5]

The traditional interpretation has held that the day began with the evening. This understanding is reflected in the New King James translation of the second half of Genesis 1:5. "So the evening and the morning were the first day." The objection has been raised that the evening is only a fraction of the day, and so is the morning. How can those two add up to a day? In response, it can be noted that the phrase "so the evening and the morning" is a merism, a figure of speech in which contrasting elements are paired to signify a whole. In this case it signifies an entire day, "one day" (Gen. 1:5 NASB). Thus "evening" includes all the darkness (Gen. 1:2), which was also created by God (Isa. 45:7), and "morning" covers the entire period of light.[6] Over against the objection that "morning" usually means only the first hours of light, it can be noted that the author could not have used the word for "day" instead of the word for "morning" because "day" designated "light" earlier in the verse. It was therefore necessary to save the word *yôm* ("day") for the conclusion of the verse when the entire period is called "one day" (Gen. 1:5, so literally, NASB).[7] Thus, with this way of reckoning, the first day started from the beginning of creation when all was still dark and continued through the time of light. All this is then reflected in the words "there was evening and there was morning,

---

4. David Miano, *Shadow on the Steps: Time Measurement in Ancient Israel* (Atlanta: Society of Biblical Literature, 2010), 12.

5. Edward J. Young, *The Prophecy of Daniel* (Grand Rapids: Eerdmans, 1949), 174–75; NKJV simply translates "days" in Dan. 8:14, but the text literally says "evenings and mornings" (cf. ESV).

6. Andrew E. Steinmann, "Night and Day, Evening and Morning," *BT* 62 (2011): 145–47, in response to C. John Collins, "The Refrain of Genesis 1: A Critical Review of Its Rendering in the English Bible," *BT* 60 (2009): 127. Similarly, Andrew E. Steinmann, "A Note on the Refrain in Genesis 1: Evening, Morning, and Day as a Chronological Summary," *JESOT* 5 (2016–2017): 125–40; Andrew E. Steinmann, "אֶחָד as an Ordinal Number and the Meaning of Genesis 1:5," *JETS* 45 (2002): 583; and John Calvin, *Sermons on Genesis, Chapters 1:1–11:4*, trans. Rob Roy McGregor (Edinburgh: Banner of Truth, 2009), 29.

7. A. van Selms, *Genesis* (Nijkerk: Callenbach, 1989), 1:27–28. Also see H. Niehr, "'*ereḇ*," *TDOT* 11:338. On the complexity of the issue with respect to Gen. 1, see also H. R. Stroes, "Does the Day Begin in the Evening or in the Morning?" *VT* 16 (1966): 473–75.

one day" (Gen. 1:5 NASB).[8] It is also of interest to note that Psalm 104, which poetically retells the creation account of Genesis 1, also places the evening and night before the light of day (Ps. 104:19–23), apparently reflecting the evening-morning sequence of the days of creation.[9] When David complained to the LORD all day long, he expressed that fact by saying, "evening and morning and at noon I will pray, and cry aloud" (Ps. 55:17). Again, in describing a day, darkness came first.

When all factors are considered, the view that the day begins with darkness seems to do the most justice to the text of Genesis 1:1–5, is in agreement with the ritual laws, is also reflected in the current Jewish understanding that the Sabbath begins around sunset on Friday, and fits most naturally with the fourth commandment, which tells us that the earth was created in six days (Ex. 20:11; also Ex. 31:17).

The Case for Literal Days
What Constituted a Day?

There has been an enormous amount of discussion about this point throughout the history of the Christian church up to the present. This is not the place to trace that development, though it is very interesting, especially when we understand the various philosophical and cultural influences involved.[10] When it comes to interpreting what is meant with the days of Genesis 1, it should be stated at the outset that as far as the Hebrew text and language, as well as the larger context of Scripture, are concerned, there is nothing to suggest that these

---

8. For a detailed defense of the day starting with the evening, see J. Amanda McGuire, "Evening or Morning: When Does the Biblical Day Begin?" *AUSS* 46 (2008): 201–14 (esp. 201–5). Others who have supported this position include E. A. Speiser, *Genesis* (New York: Doubleday, 1964), 5; Van Selms, *Genesis*, 1:27; those supporting with some reservation include Stroes, "Does the Day Begin," 473–75; Wenham, *Genesis 1–15*, 19. E. J. Young notes that the commencement of the first day was at the very beginning. Edward J. Young, *Studies in Genesis One*, 89.

9. Richard M. Davidson, "Creation Theme," 165, and see n55 where he quotes H. C. Leupold, *Exposition of the Psalms*, 728: "The beginning is made with the moon, perhaps because the Hebrew day began with the evening."

10. The best current treatment up to 1860 is Andrew J. Brown, *The Days of Creation: A History of Christian Interpretation of Genesis 1:1–2:3* (Blandford Forum, U.K.: Deo, 2014). For more selective and briefer overviews up to the twentieth century, see Stanley L. Jaki, *Genesis 1 through the Ages*, 2nd ed. (Royal Oak, Mich.: Real View; Edinburgh: Scottish Academic Press, 1998); Jack P. Lewis, "The Days of Creation: An Historical Survey of Interpretation," *JETS* 32 (1989): 433–55; also see Robert Letham, "'In the Space of Six Days': The Days of Creation from Origen to the Westminster Assembly," *WTJ* 61 (1999): 149–74. Since Augustine's influence was huge, it is beneficial for an understanding of his views to consult Louis Lavallee, "Augustine on the Creation Days," *JETS* 32 (1989): 457–64, and of course. Andrew J. Brown, *Days of Creation*, 44–53.

days were anything other than literal days. This does not yet indicate that we can fully understand what that means in terms of God's creation work. But grammatically, textually, and contextually speaking, it is difficult to evade the force of the text as simply referring to a day as the term is customarily used. Indeed, on this point there is near unanimity among current scholars.

The reasons for this wide agreement are clear. First, each day is literally defined as "there was evening and there was morning," indicating as clearly as possible the passage of a single day six times. Second, whenever the word for "day" is modified by an ordinal number (and this happens about 150 times in Scripture), it always refers to a literal day.[11] Not surprisingly, in light of these two considerations, standard Hebrew lexicons give the meaning "day" and not "a long indeterminate period of time" for these particular occurrences of the Hebrew term *yôm* in Genesis 1. Commentators, both liberal and conservative, agree.[12] Third, the fourth commandment clearly states that "in six days the LORD made the heavens and the earth, the sea, and all that is in them" as the reason for us to work six days (Ex. 20:9–11; similarly, Ex. 31:15–17).[13] It is difficult to imagine that each of these days means an indeterminate length of time. This commandment very precisely sets God as the example that we

---

11. E. Jenni, "*yôm* Day," in *TLOT*, 528–29; John C. Whitcomb Jr., "The Science of Historical Geology in the Light of the Biblical Doctrine of Mature Creation," *WTJ* 36 (1973): 66–67; Robert V. McCabe, "A Defense of Literal Days in the Creation Week," *Detroit Baptist Seminary Journal* 5 (2000): 104–5. The fact that numeral "one" is cardinal and the rest of the numerals in Gen. 1 are ordinal is not a problem since the Hebrew numeral "one" can function both as a cardinal and an ordinal in many texts. Sarna, *Genesis*, 8, 353; but also see GKC, §98a; and 186–87 below.

12. Standard lexicons on Gen. 1 define the term as "day of twenty-four hours" (*HALOT*, 399) and "day, of 24 hours" (*DCH* 4:166; Jenni, "*yôm* Day," 528). Commentators include John Skinner, *A Critical and Exegetical Commentary on Genesis*, 2nd ed. (repr., Edinburgh: T&T Clark, 1930), 21; Van Selms, *Genesis*, 1:45; Gispen, *Genesis*, 1:50; Wenham, *Genesis 1–15*, 19. Critical scholar James Barr affirmed that "a literal interpretation would hold that the world was created in six days, these days being the first of the series which we still experience as days and nights." Barr, *Fundamentalism*, 40. Barr even stated in a letter to a certain David Watson (April 23, 1984): "so far as I know, there is no professor of Hebrew or Old Testament at any world-class university who does not believe that the writer(s) of Genesis 1–11 intended to convey to their readers the ideas that: (a) creation took place in a series of six days which were the same as the days of 24 hours we now experience" (available at https://web.archive.org/web/20170612180930/http://members .iinet.com.au:80/~sejones/barrlett.html). There is some exaggeration here for there are reputable scholars who think otherwise, but the point is nevertheless well taken in terms of the obvious meaning of the text. For an additional reference to this letter, as well as more examples of critical scholars taking Genesis 1 literally, see Alvin Plantinga, "Evolution, Neutrality, and Antecedent Probability," in *Intelligent Design, Creationism, and Its Critics: Philosophical, Theological, and Scientific Perspectives*, ed. Robert T. Pennock (Cambridge, Mass.: MIT Press, 2001), 216–17.

13. The fact that a duration of time, six days, is in view is indicated by the Hebrew usage of the accusative of temporal determination. Joüon, §126i.

should follow. There is no analogical sense of long periods of time here, but rather the requirement to imitate God by working for six days, which are therefore days as we know them.[14]

On the basis of these three major considerations, we can conclude that these were days defined by evening and morning, days as we are accustomed to reckon days. They were not long periods of geologic time or allegorical days or a figure of speech. At the same time, we must acknowledge that these were days that we have enormous difficulty comprehending. After all, these were very special days, witnessed by no human being and full of God's creative activity. This first week of creation included three days without the sun and yet with light provided in some other manner. How can we picture such extraordinary days? Also, as finite humans it is impossible for us to comprehend the unique processes that made the creation of this present world possible. Furthermore, these were days before the cataclysmic changes wrought by the fall into sin and before the judgment of the Noachian flood, which had possible cosmic consequences.[15] It is therefore appropriate to speak humbly about these days. Although it is not so intended, yet for us to call these "twenty-four-hour days" sounds somewhat haughty, as though we were there and timed everything exactly. Such clock precision also smacks of scientism, as if we can more accurately describe the days than God who revealed them to us.[16] Scripture gives no precise length but does say that each day was marked by an evening and a morning, as we would reckon days. They are indeed, as Bavinck put it, "to be considered days and not to be identified with the periods of geology," but they "have an extraordinary character." They were very special and unique days. They were truly "workdays of God."[17] As such they are beyond our comprehension.

Max Rogland has given a helpful overview of important Dutch Reformed theologians and their views of the creation days. His survey shows that not only

---

14. So also Terence E. Freitheim, "Were the Days of Creation Twenty-Four Hours Long? Yes," in *The Genesis Debate: Persistent Questions about Creation and the Flood*, ed. Ronald F. Youngblood (Grand Rapids: Baker, 1990), 20.

15. See Snelling, *Earth's Catastrophic Past*, 613–21.

16. In a similar context, Poythress noted, "One may wonder whether this approach has unconsciously given in to the *philosophical* primacy of a modern scientific orientation toward precise, quantitative measurement of time. In other words, it may have swallowed an ideological, philosophical assumption that it fervently wants to avoid!" Poythress, *Redeeming Science*, 222 (italics in the orginal), cf. 140–43, esp. n16.

17. Bavinck, *Reformed Dogmatics*, 2:499–500. For a cautionary note not to use Bavinck's characterization of the day as extraordinary at the expense of its historicity, see James Visscher, "Bavinck on Creation," in *Living Waters from Ancient Springs: Essays in Honor of Cornelis Van Dam*, ed. Jason Van Vliet (Eugene, Ore.: Pickwick, 2011), 150.

Bavinck, but also other conservative Reformed theologians of the late nineteenth and early twentieth centuries, such as Abraham Kuyper, A. G. Honig (Bavinck's successor as professor of dogmatics in Kampen), and G. Ch. Aalders (Old Testament professor at the Free University), considered the days to be real days (and not ages), but were very careful not to equate the creation days with an exact twenty-four-hour time span.[18] Klaas Schilder was also very careful not to define precisely what constituted the six days of creation. For him it was critical that one understood the word for "day" in its true and literal sense and that these days occurred in time and space.[19] As noted earlier in chapter 1, Schilder insisted that justice is done to Scripture if one maintains "that the reality of which one speaks remains the reality of the *time* in which we live on earth with all creation and of the *space* in which God has placed the earth."[20] As Rogland rightly summarized Schilder's thinking, "If one accepts that Gen 1 narrates *historical realities*, he [Schilder] thinks that legitimate differences of exegetical opinion can exist as to the precise length of the creation days."[21] It is thus clear that the Dutch Reformed theologians just noted did not think in terms of deep time of millions or billions of years in understanding the days of Genesis 1.

An acknowledgment of the limitations of what the biblical text actually tells us about the nature of these days is most commendable. E. J. Young has also underscored the need for caution. In his *Studies in Genesis One*, he noted that "the length of the days is not stated. What is important is that each of the days is a period of time which may legitimately be denominated יוֹם ('day')."[22] Elsewhere he wrote, "There arises the question as to the length of these days. That is a question which is difficult to answer. Indications are not lacking that they may have been longer than the days we now know, but the Scripture itself does not speak as clearly as one might like."[23] More recently, Vern Poythress has underlined, in a detailed study on time in Genesis 1 and the unusual character of the days of creation, the need for caution in trying to measure or explain those days with scientific theories. He concluded, "A simple affirmation of creation in six days by people unfamiliar with technical timekeepers is simpler

---

18. Max Rogland, "*Ad Litteram*: Some Dutch Reformed Theologians on the Creation Days," *WTJ* 63 (2001): 212–17.

19. Schilder, *Een hoornstoot*, 45–46.

20. Schilder, *Een hoornstoot*, 44 (my translation; italics in the original). Also see Rogland, "*Ad Litteram*," 221–22.

21. Rogland, "*Ad Litteram*," 221 (italics in the original).

22. Edward J. Young, *Studies in Genesis One*, 104.

23. Edward J. Young, "Creation," in *The Encyclopedia of Christianity*, ed. Philip E. Hughes (Marshallton, Del.: National Foundation for Christian Education, 1964–1972), 3:243.

than any of the detailed theories, and is compatible in principle with several of them, because it is less specific."[24]

Such carefulness and reticence in determining the exact length of the days of creation is nothing new. J. V. Fesko has shown that while the Westminster Confession was being drafted, the divines differed on the length of the days. "John Lightfoot (1602–75), for example, believed that the first day of creation was thirty-six hours long."[25] It is significant that the Westminster Confession did not define the length of the days as twenty-four hours. This is proper, for it would have gone beyond what Scripture clearly conveyed.

The bottom line is that the days of creation were actual days defined by evening and morning. Scripture does not tell us the exact number of hours in these days. They were special days without doubt, and one can call them God's workdays. But this description does not make the days of Genesis 1 any less real.

Chronological Sequence

Although the typical reader of Genesis 1 will assume that the days follow each other in chronological sequence, some, like David Sterchi, have questioned this assumption. He does not deny the possibility of a chronological sequence, but asserts that the syntax of the text does not require it. "To claim that the text requires us to read it chronologically is to err by exceeding the meaning in the text."[26] So the question is whether the Hebrew text is ambiguous with respect to chronological sequence.

Sterchi's main syntactical argument is that the absence of the Hebrew definite article ("the") from day one through day five and the use of the definite article for days six and seven suggest that the order may not be chronological. He tries to support this claim by giving examples of other numeric sequences in the Old Testament. The grammatical evidence is, however, not compelling, and in spite of his investigations Sterchi himself acknowledges that Genesis 1 may be

---

24. Poythress, *Interpreting Eden*, 213–58, esp. 258; an earlier form of this study appeared as Vern S. Poythress, "Time in Genesis 1," *WTJ* 79 (2017): 213–41.

25. J. V. Fesko, "The Days of Creation and Confession Subscription in the OPC," *WTJ* 63 (2001): 245; also see William S. Barker, "The Westminster Assembly on the Days of Creation: A Reply to David W. Hall," *WTJ* 62 (2000): 113–20; and the caution of G. I. Williamson, "Some Thoughts on Creation," *Ordained Servant* 9 (2000): 24–25.

26. David A. Sterchi, "Does Genesis 1 Provide a Chronological Sequence?," *JETS* 39 (1996): 536; another example is Mark A. Throntveit, "Are the Events in the Genesis Creation Account Set Forth in Chronological Order? No," in *The Genesis Debate: Persistent Questions about Creation and the Flood*, ed. Ronald F. Youngblood (Grand Rapids: Baker, 1990), 36–55.

giving a chronological account.[27] However, in coming to a decision on whether there is chronological sequence or not, we also need to consider the overall context of the chapter. When that is done, one must accept that Genesis 1:1–2:3 relates a series of events, one following the other over a period of seven days.

The entire narrative in the Hebrew text is linked together with sentences beginning with the Hebrew word for "and." With the exception of the first and seventh days, the account of each day begins and ends with "and" ("And God said…and there was evening and there was morning"). Furthermore, the account follows a clear progression from the basics that make life possible to the climax of the creation of humanity in the image of God Himself. The very fact that chronological markers like days are used leaves no doubt that the creation acts of God followed one after the other. E. J. Young rightly states that "it is this remarkable fact of progression, both in method of statement and in actual content, which proves that the days of Genesis are to be understood as following one another chronologically. When to this is added the plain chronological indications, day one, day two, etc., climaxing in *the* sixth day…all support for a non-chronological view is removed."[28]

The view that the days are sequential agrees with the conclusion reached in chapter 3, namely, that the genre of Genesis 1 is historical narrative. As a historical record of what transpired while God created all things, the creation account demands to be read as it presents itself—a series of God's creation acts spread over six consecutive days.

Did Calvin Affirm a Six-Day Creation?

Some have understood John Calvin to have denied that God created all things in six days. When Calvin commented on the phrase "the first day" in Genesis 1:5, he noted that these words show the error of those "who maintain that the world was made in a moment. For it is too violent a cavil to contend that Moses distributes the work which God perfected at once into six days, for the mere purpose of conveying instruction. Let us rather conclude that God himself

---

27. Sterchi, "Does Genesis 1 Provide a Chronological Sequence?," 533, 535, 536. Grammatically, "one day" in Gen. 1:5 can mean "the first day." *IBHS*, 274; GKC, §98a. The use of ordinal numbers for the days that follow indicates a chronological order in spite of the lack of an article with the first five days. Robert C. Newman, "Are the Events in the Genesis Creation Account Set Forth in Chronological Order? Yes," in *The Genesis Debate: Persistent Questions about Creation and the Flood*, ed. Ronald F. Youngblood (Grand Rapids: Baker, 1990), 36–38; also cf. Steinmann, "Genesis 1:5," 583.

28. Edward J. Young, *Studies in Genesis One*, 99 (italics in the original); also see Derek Kidner, *Genesis* (Downers Grove, Ill.: InterVarsity, 1967), 55.

took the space of six days, for the purpose of accommodating his works to the capacity of men." A little further on he wrote that God "distributed the creation of the world into successive portions, that he might fix our attention, and compel us, as if he had laid his hand upon us, to pause and to reflect."[29]

Does Calvin's use of accommodation in this context mean that according to him God did not actually create in six days? Some scholars have so concluded. For example, Alister McGrath opines that for Calvin "the biblical stories of creation (Genesis 1–2) are accommodated to the abilities and horizons of a relatively simple and unsophisticated people; they are not intended to be taken as literal representations of reality."[30] Elsewhere he states that for Calvin "the phrase 'six days of creation'…is simply an accommodation to human ways of thinking to designate an extended period of time."[31] Similarly, Kenton Sparks states that

> Calvin…argued that accommodation was at work in the chronological system used to enumerate the various creation days of Genesis 1. Because the text reflects an accommodation to the ancient view of time, says Calvin, "It is useless to dispute whether this is the best and legitimate order or not." In other words, for Calvin, accommodation was a useful interpretive tool because it made irrelevant in such cases any questions about the Bible's correctness.[32]

Other examples of scholars maintaining that Calvin's notion of accommodation allowed for scientific mistakes in Scripture could be mentioned.[33] The question is, however, whether Calvin's use of accommodation in Genesis 1 does indeed undermine the literal reading of the text. The issue is important, for such a perception of Calvin's use of accommodation is seen as a justification for

---

29. Calvin, *Genesis*, 1:78.

30. Alister E. McGrath, *The Foundations of Dialogue in Science and Religion* (Malden, Mass.: Blackwell, 1998), 125; similarly, Alister E. McGrath, *A Life of John Calvin: A Study in the Shaping of Western Culture* (Oxford: Blackwell, 1990), 256–57.

31. As quoted by Peter M. Van Bemmelen, "Divine Accommodation and Biblical Creation: Calvin vs. McGrath," *AUSS* 39 (2001): 113, from Alister E. McGrath, *Science and Religion: An Introduction* (Malden, Mass.: Blackwell, 1999), 11.

32. Kenton L. Sparks, *God's Word in Human Words: An Evangelical Appropriation of Critical Biblical Scholarship* (Grand Rapids: Baker Academic, 2008), 235, quoting Calvin, *Genesis*, 1:77, where Calvin discusses whether the day began with evening or morning.

33. E.g., Jack B. Rogers, *The Authority and Interpretation of the Bible: An Historical Approach* (San Francisco: Harper & Row, 1979), 111–14; and Davis A. Young, as discussed below in this section.

emancipating the natural sciences from the literal text of Scripture and from theological restrictions.[34]

So does Calvin's use of accommodation undermine a literal understanding of the creation account? The answer is no. Indeed, a careful reading of Calvin's Genesis commentary, as quoted earlier, shows that he did not deny that creation took six days, rather he affirmed this fact. Although God could have made the world "in a moment," he took six days "for the purpose of accommodating his works to the capacity of men." In other words, his manner of creating was tailored to our being able to follow God's work, as much as that is possible for finite creatures.[35] Calvin made the same point in his preaching. In his sermon on Genesis 1:1–2, Calvin noted that God created "the way he did for our sakes and for our instruction.... Afterwards, since he took six days to create the things we now see and laid them out and directed them in an orderly fashion, he did not do so, I say, out of any necessity laid upon him, but to hold us back and cause us to consider more attentively his power, his goodness, his righteousness, and his infinite wisdom in the whole of his creation."[36] Elsewhere he noted, "Six days were employed in the formation of the world; not that God, to whom one moment is as a thousand years, had need of this succession of time, but that he might engage us in the consideration of his works."[37]

In view of the above, Peter Van Bemmelen rightly critiques McGrath's assertions as "a serious misreading of Calvin's words. Nowhere does Calvin say that the six days of Creation in Gen 1 are an accommodation to designate an extended period of time. On the contrary, Calvin holds that God created the world in six days...thus accommodating himself to the capacity of his creatures."[38]

In his detailed discussion of Sparks's reading of Calvin, Vern Poythress points out that Sparks erroneously speaks of "the ancient view of time," as if there was only one ancient view. Moreover, Calvin made no mention of this and, contrary to Sparks's understanding, Calvin did not view the sequence of six days as an accommodation. Rather, as Poythress notes, "the 'accommodation' lies in the fact that God spreads out his works in time, *not* in the language in Gen 1

---

34. See McGrath, *Foundations*, 124; and McGrath, *Life of John Calvin*, 256–57.

35. Similarly, Calvin, *Institutes*, 1.14.2.

36. Calvin, *Sermons on Genesis*, 14, also see 19.

37. Calvin, *Genesis*, 1:105; see also Arnold Huijgen, *Divine Accommodation in John Calvin's Theology: Analysis and Assessment* (Göttingen: Vandenhoeck & Ruprecht, 2011), 220–21.

38. Van Bemmelen, "Divine Accommodation," 113.

describing those works."[39] Indeed, Poythress rightly says that "Calvin thinks that the language in Genesis 1 actually describes six days of God's works, but accommodation takes place in the way God accomplishes *the works* themselves."[40] Another critic of Sparks's views, Hoon J. Lee correctly concludes that "Calvin's doctrine of accommodation did not challenge the authority of Scripture, nor did he maintain that the Bible contains errors in science or doctrine."[41]

In his comprehensive study of Calvin's view of accommodation, Arnold Huijgen notes that "Calvin did not address the Copernican world view, nor did he employ the idea of accommodation to demarcate the place of natural sciences."[42] Also, this fact warns against employing Calvin's use of accommodation as a tool for dehistoricizing Genesis 1. Huijgen further observes that the idea of accommodation has in the past opened up the way for a thoroughly rationalistic understanding of Scripture that left little room for miracles.[43]

In light of all of the above, we can say that Davis A. Young, a prominent proponent of the view that the earth is billions of years old, misuses Calvin's notion of accommodation in Genesis 1 when he attempts to employ it for his position. Whereas Calvin accepted as true all statements Scripture makes, Young leaves open the possibility that biblical references touching on the natural world can be untrue, since the primary concern of Scripture is to present salvation in Jesus Christ. In his view we need to invoke the principle of accommodation whenever "Scripture includes a statement about the natural world that is clearly contrary to firmly established and empirically verified knowledge." But when it comes to origins and the creation of the world, what exactly has been empirically verified by science? As discussed above in chapter 2, verification of scientific theory on the world's origin is impossible. Young unjustly dismisses the idea that Genesis 1 uses phenomenal language, that is, that Scripture describes the natural world as humans see it.[44] We will be returning to some of these exegetical issues below.

---

39. Poythress, *Interpreting Eden*, 351 (italics in the original). An earlier version of this study appeared as Vern S. Poythress, "A Misunderstanding of Calvin's Interpretation of Genesis 1:6–8 and 1:5 and Its Implications for Ideas of Accommodation," *WTJ* 76 (2014): 157–66.

40. Poythress, *Interpreting Eden*, 352 (italics in the original).

41. Hoon J. Lee, "Accommodation—Orthodox, Socinian, and Contemporary," *WTJ* 75 (2013): 347.

42. Huijgen, *Divine Accommodation*, 374; also see 222–24.

43. Huijgen, *Divine Accommodation*, 375.

44. Davis A. Young, *John Calvin and the Natural World* (Lanham, Md.: University Press of America, 2007), 168–71, 221–30 (quote on 230); cf. Calvin, *Genesis*, 1:78–81.

To sum up, Ford Lewis Battles concluded decades ago in his own study of Calvin's use of accommodation that, in Calvin's view, "accommodation as practiced by the Holy Spirit so empowers the physical, verbal vehicle that it leads us to, not away from, the very truth. Thus accommodating language and the truth to which it points are really a unity."[45] Indeed, as Poythress points out, "until the Enlightenment, the classical idea of accommodation took care not to deny the full truthfulness of Scripture."[46]

Summary

The text of Genesis 1 presents each of the six days of creation as we normally understand a day, with an evening and a morning—a day measured in hours, not millennia. Either we accept the plain historical sense of Genesis 1 as narrating real history covering six days of creation, or we consider it all as some sort of literary construction with a historical message that is far from being clear. Accepting the days as historical and real does not mean that we can fully understand what those days entailed. They were certainly not ordinary or normal days, but truly workdays of God, and we must be modest in speaking of their length and character. As created beings, we cannot fathom the work of the Creator, and we must therefore refrain from dogmatic assertions.

God's creation work as described in Genesis 1 no doubt raises questions in our minds, and we will attempt to address specific difficulties when we discuss each day in subsequent chapters.

We now need to turn to nonliteral views, especially those held by scholars who seek to do justice to the Scriptures as God's Word. Their desire to listen to the text also needs to be honored by carefully considering their understanding of the text and weighing their arguments in the light of God's revelation.

Nonliteral Day Views

There have been many challenges to the historicity of the account of creation. This chapter deals with four important challenges. First, since Augustine has

---

45. Ford Lewis Battles, "God Was Accommodating Himself to Human Capacity," *Int* 31 (1977): 37.

46. Poythress, *Interpreting Eden*, 325, previously published in Poythress, "Rethinking Accommodation," 145. For an overview of how the idea of accommodation has changed to include an errant Scripture, see D. A. Carson, "Recent Developments in the Doctrine of Scripture," in *Hermeneutics, Authority, and Canon*, eds. D. A. Carson and John D. Woodbridge (Grand Rapids: Zondervan, 1986), 26–28; and Wayne A. Grudem, "Scripture's Self-Attestation and the Problem of Formulating a Doctrine of Scripture," in *Scripture and Truth*, ed. D. A. Carson and John D. Woodbridge (repr., Grand Rapids: Baker, 1992), 53–57.

been used to justify dehistoricizing Genesis 1, his view of the days will be considered. Next, the framework hypothesis and the analogical days view will come under scrutiny, followed by a look at the notion that the seven-day structure is an ancient literary device.

Augustine and the Days of Creation
In the patristic period there was a widespread understanding that Genesis 1 narrated six, literal, and consecutive days of creation.[47] Augustine of Hippo (354–430), highly regarded also by Reformed churches, however, reached a different conclusion. He believed that everything was created in one moment and not in six days. Many scholars appeal to him in support of a nonliteral reading of the text of Genesis 1. We, therefore, need to consider how and why he came to his conclusion. There are several basic interrelated reasons.

First, Augustine read Genesis 1 through the lens of Sirach 18:1 in the Old Latin translation. This passage reads, in part, "creavit omnia simul," which can be translated as "he created everything together" or "he created everything at the same time."[48] Augustine understood these words as proof that God created everything in one moment. He explained that

> Holy Scripture has said of the Creator that He completed His works in six days; and elsewhere, without contradicting this, it has been written of the same Creator that he created all things together [Sir. 18:1]. It follows, therefore, that He, who created all things together, simultaneously created these six days, or seven, or rather one day six or seven times repeated. Why, then, was there any need for six distinct days to be set forth in the narrative one after the other? The reason is that those who cannot understand the meaning of the text, *He created all things together*, cannot arrive at the meaning for Scripture unless the narrative proceeds slowly step by step.[49]

In other words, according to Augustine, God accommodated the narrative to our understanding. It should be noted, however, that the Latin translation of

---

47. Andrew J. Brown, *Days of Creation*, 16–29 (passim); Jaki, *Genesis 1*, 76–81. A handy resource of the relevant texts is William A. Dembski, Wayne J. Downs, and Justin B. A. Frederick, eds., *The Patristic Understanding of Creation: An Anthology of Writings from the Church Fathers on Creation and Design* (Riesel, Tex.: Erasmus, 2008); also see J. Ligon Duncan III and David W. Hall, "The 24-Hour View," in *The Genesis Debate: Three Views on the Days of Creation*, ed. David G. Hagopian (Mission Viejo, Calif.: Crux, 2001), 46–47, 99–102.

48. See further Roger A. Bullard and Howard A. Hatton, *A Handbook on Sirach* (New York: United Bible Societies, 2008), 358.

49. Augustine, *The Literal Meaning of Genesis*, ed. John Hammond Taylor (New York: Paulist Press, 1982), 1:142 (bk. 4, ch. 33, §52) (italics in the original).

the Greek that Augustine used is a mistranslation. A more accurate rendering would be that God "created everything in common" (Sir. 18:1 NETS).[50]

Second, Augustine did not know Hebrew and knew but little Greek. So for his exegesis he relied on the Old Latin translation of the Old Testament, which was not based on the original Hebrew text, but on the Greek of the Septuagint.[51] His reliance on a translation of a translation did not help him make sound exegetical decisions of the original text. This handicap becomes evident when Augustine thought that he had found additional evidence for his notion of God creating everything simultaneously in the Old Latin translation of Genesis 2:4. "This is the book of the creation of heaven and earth. When day was made, God made heaven and earth and every green thing of the field." Augustine subsequently wrote, "Now perhaps we have here a confirmation of what we tried to show in the previous book, that God created everything at one time. The earlier narrative [Gen. 1] stated that all things were created and finished on six successive days, but now to one day everything is assigned, under the terms 'heaven' and 'earth,' with the addition also of 'plants.'"[52] This, however, is not the meaning of Genesis 2:4 that is conveyed by the Hebrew text or an English translation like the New King James Version ("This is the history of the heavens and the earth when they were created, in the day that the LORD God made the earth and the heavens"). But Augustine could not check the Hebrew, and so relying on the faulty Latin text he came to his flawed conclusion.[53]

In sum, Augustine's understanding of everything being created in one day was largely due to his interpreting Genesis 1 in light of Sirach 18:1, his inability to read Hebrew, and his limited knowledge of Greek. These factors greatly diminish the value of using Augustine as an example and model of someone who argued for a nonliteral reading of the days of Genesis 1. Furthermore, two additional extrabiblical factors can be mentioned as well. The philosophies of his day, such as the notion of spontaneous generation, played their part. Augustine also desired to harmonize Scripture with the science current in his day.

---

50. The Latin *simul* ("together," "at one time") seems to be an incorrect translation for the Greek *koinē*. See also Augustine, *Literal Meaning of Genesis*, 1:254n69. On the text of Sirach, see Bullard and Hatton, *Handbook*, 2–3.

51. K. E. Greene-McCreight, *Ad Litteram: How Augustine, Calvin, and Barth Read the "Plain Sense" of Genesis 1–3* (New York: Peter Lang, 1999), 38; Augustine, *Literal Meaning of Genesis*, 1:5, 271n103.

52. Augustine, *Literal Meaning of Genesis*, 1:149–50 (bk. 5, ch. 3, §§5–6); also see Greene-McCreight, *Ad Litteram*, 58–59.

53. For the Old Latin text and the improved translation by Jerome, see Lavallee, "Augustine on the Creation Days," 459–60.

In addition, a nonliteral interpretation would silence the scorn and criticism of those enemies of Christianity who heaped abuse upon the idea that God would need six literal days to create all things. Augustine had been an auditor among the Manichees for about nine years, and they rejected the creation of the world in six days. A desire to deflect criticism from the members of this sect could also have influenced Augustine in his interpretation of the days. But it is important to note that Augustine acknowledged the priority of Scripture over scientific theory in his exegetical work when seeking to understand the text of Genesis 1.[54]

In spite of the high esteem that Augustine enjoyed during the Reformation, neither Luther nor Calvin accepted his interpretation of an instantaneous creation. Contrary to Augustine's view that the world was made in an instant, both Reformers asserted that the days in Genesis 1 are to be understood literally as six days of God's work of creating.[55] In agreement with the Reformers, the confessional formulations of the Irish Articles (1615) and the Westminster Standards affirm that God created everything "in the space of six days," the very phrase Calvin used.[56]

The Framework View

Another nonliteral approach to the sequence of creation days argues that Genesis 1 only provides a "figurative framework" and not a chronological account. The current exposition of the framework hypothesis has its roots in the work of a Dutch scholar, Arie Noordtzij (1871–1944), of the Reformed Churches in the Netherlands. Though his views were criticized, these views or variations thereof still find favor among some Dutch conservatives.[57] His

---

54. Andrew J. Brown, *Days of Creation*, 45–47; Lavallee, "Augustine on the Creation Days," 461–64; Van Bemmelen, "Divine Accommodation," 110–11.

55. Martin Luther, *Luther's Works*, vol. 1, *Lectures on Genesis: Chapters 1–5*, ed. Jaroslav Pelikan, trans. George V. Schick (St. Louis, Mo.: Concordia, 1999), 4–5; Calvin, *Genesis*, 1:78, 105.

56. The phrase is found in Calvin, *Genesis*, 1:78 ("*sex dierum spatium*"; CO 23:18); Irish Articles, art. 18; Westminster Confession of Faith 4.1; Westminster Shorter Catechism 9; Westminster Larger Catechism 15; see James Benjamin Green, *Harmony*, 34; also see David W. Hall, "What Was the View of the Westminster Assembly Divines on Creation Days?," in *Did God Create in Six Days?*, ed. Joseph A. Pipa and David W. Hall (Taylors, S.C.: Southern Presbyterian Press, 1999), 41–52; David W. Hall, "The Evolution of Mythology: Classic Creation Survives as the Fittest Among Its Critics and Revisers," in *Did God Create in Six Days?*, ed. Joseph A. Pipa and David W. Hall (Taylors, S.C.: Southern Presbyterian Press, 1999), 279–305.

57. A. Noordtzij, *Gods Woord en der eeuwen getuigenis: het Oude Testament in het licht der oostersche opgravingen*, 2nd ed. (Kampen: Kok, 1931), 116–20; for critiques see J. Ridderbos, *GTT* 25 (1924–25): 275–78, and Aalders, *De Goddelijke openbaring*, 232–40. Noordtzij was regarded with some suspicion by his contemporaries as indicated by the title of a recent biography: C. M.

ideas came to North America through the translation of a work by another Old Testament scholar, N. H. Ridderbos.[58] Today this interpretation has found some acceptance in North America due mostly to the work of Meredith Kline.[59] Lee Irons and Meredith Kline gave an articulate exposition and defense of the framework hypothesis. The main points of their approach are as follows.[60]

Irons and Kline describe Genesis 1 thus: "the seven-day scheme is a figurative framework." Although the six days of creation are presented as normal days, yet, in their view, "the total picture of God's completing His creative work in a week of days is not to be taken literally." It is a "literary structure in which the creative works of God have been narrated in a topical order." The events that took place are real historical events but "they are narrated in a nonsequential order within the literary structure or framework of a seven-day week."[61] The main exegetical arguments that support this understanding are the triadic or topical structure of Genesis 1, the claim that Genesis 2:5–6 indicates that God employed ordinary providence during the creation period, and the notion that the days of Genesis 1 are heavenly days (from the upper register) and not earthly ones. Let us consider each of these arguments and pay particular attention to the matter of historicity.

Only a triad? Irons and Kline consider the structure of Genesis 1 to consist of two parallel triads. Days 1–3 form the first triad and deal with the creation kingdoms; days 4–6 form the second triad and deal with the creature kings who rule those kingdoms. "The fact that the first six days form a two-triadic unit highlights the uniqueness of the seventh day, which depicts the Creator King enthroned in His heavenly Sabbath rest over all creation."[62] They therefore outline Genesis 1 as follows.

---

van Driel, *Gewantrouwd gereformeerd: het omstreden leiderschap van neocalvinist Arie Noordtzij (1871–1944)* (Barneveld: Vuurbaak, 2010). For the continuing influence of his views, see, e.g., Jochem Douma, *Genesis* (Kampen: Kok, 2005), 42–43; J. J. T. Doedens, "Taal en teken van trouw: over vorm en functie van Genesis 1," in *Woord op Schrift: theologische reflecties over het gezag van de Bijbel*, ed. C. Trimp (Kampen: Kok, 2002), 95–102.

58. Nic. H. Ridderbos, *Is There a Conflict between Genesis 1 and Natural Science?*, trans. John Vriend (Grand Rapids: Eerdmans, 1957), 11–12, 29–46.

59. Meredith Kline has been influential in promoting the framework understanding. See Meredith G. Kline, "Because It Had Not Rained," *WTJ* 20 (1958): 146–57; and Meredith G. Kline, "Space and Time in the Genesis Cosmogony," *PSCF* 48 (1996): 2–15.

60. Lee Irons and Meredith G. Kline, "The Framework View," in *The Genesis Debate: Three Views on the Days of Creation*, ed. David G. Hagopian (Mission Viejo, Calif.: Crux, 2001), 217–56.

61. Irons and Kline, "Framework View," 219.

62. Irons and Kline, "Framework View," 224.

Creation Kingdoms		Creature Kings	
Day 1	Light	*Day 4*	Luminaries
Day 2	Sky	*Day 5*	Sea Creatures
	Seas		Winged Creatures
Day 3	Dry land	*Day 6*	Land animals
	Vegetation		Man

The Creator King
Day 7 Sabbath

Since this is a literary structure, Irons and Kline maintain that Genesis 1 has no literal sequential chronology. Rather, there is chronological recapitulation along with the thematic parallelisms. The exegetical consequences are obviously far reaching with respect to how one understands the history of God's creation work. It is crucial that Irons and Kline understand days one and four as reporting the creation of the same thing, light, which accomplishes the same purpose in both days. So, they ask, over against those who see chronology in Genesis 1, why would God discard the arrangement concerning light made in day one with a new arrangement in day four, especially when the work in day one was considered good? So they treat days one and four, and the differences between them, simply as a literary device with no chronological meaning. Indeed, Irons and Kline assert that "the temporal recapitulation of Day 1 on Day 4 justifies taking the whole week of seven days as a figurative framework that provides a literary and theological structure for the narrative of the divine work of creation."[63] Since the relationship of these days provides indispensable justification for the framework view of Irons and Kline, this relationship needs a closer look.

In response to their work, it can be noted that God's work on day one and day four are not the same and therefore cannot refer to the same event. On day one, God created light and separated the light from the darkness. On day four, God made and set light-bearers in the expanse or firmament of the sky or heavens. This firmament was made on day two and thus was not present on day one. Also, the light of day one is called "day," but on day four the lights set in the expanse of the heavens are designated "the greater light to rule the day, and the lesser light to rule the night" (Gen. 1:16). While there is some parallelism of light and light-bearers between day one and day four, the differences are telling, and there is no basis for saying that the events of day one and day four

---

63. Irons and Kline, "Framework View," 228–30 (quote on 229).

are the same. Indeed, Scripture clearly teaches that light was created before the light-bearers. God's creation of light was not dependent on light-bearers. When we compare Scripture with Scripture the creation of light before light-bearers poses no problem. Elsewhere the Bible speaks of light existing independent of the sun. Isaiah prophesied about the time when "the sun shall no longer be your light by day, nor for brightness shall the moon give light to you; but the LORD will be to you an everlasting light, and your God your glory. Your sun shall no longer go down, nor shall your moon withdraw itself; for the LORD will be your everlasting light" (Isa. 60:19–20). Other places can be mentioned as well.[64] If light can exist independently of the sun and moon in the future, why could light not have existed independently at the beginning of creation?

Since the evidence is wanting for what Irons and Kline consider the critical justification for the notion of chronological recapitulation—namely, the parallel between days one and four—the framework view of Irons and Kline cannot be justified and collapses. One must therefore simply follow the text of Genesis 1 and acknowledge that the sea creatures and winged creatures were created on day five and not simultaneously with the sky and seas on day two. Likewise, the dry land and vegetation were created days before the land animals and man came into being. When we consider the different works of God on the days that are supposedly parallel, we discover they are in fact not parallel, even if they have some common elements.[65]

Genesis 2:5. Another reason why proponents of the framework hypothesis insist on denying chronological sequence in Genesis 1 is their understanding of Genesis 2:5. They consider the plant life in this verse to be the same as that mentioned on the third day. Since the plants in Genesis 2 were not there before the creation of man, then, according to this understanding, the plants mentioned on the third day could not have been created prior to man's creation on the sixth day. However, as we will see in chapter 10, the plants referred to in Genesis 2 are not the same as those mentioned in Genesis 1. There is thus no contradiction, and we do not need to deny temporal sequence in Genesis 1 or suggest that God used only ordinary providence as we experience it today for his work of creation. This point of course raises the question, how exactly do proponents of the framework hypothesis understand the term *yôm* ("day")? This brings us to their final argument.

---

64. Zech. 14:6–7; Rev. 21:23; 22:5; also cf. Isa. 24:23; 30:26.
65. For more detail, see the critiques in Edward J. Young, *Studies in Genesis One*, 68–73; Paulin Bédard, *In Six Days God Created* (n.p.: Xulon, 2013), 74–83.

Upper-register time. Irons and Kline speak of the upper and lower registers. These refer to the two realms that compose the created order. The upper register is the invisible dwelling place of God, and the lower register is the earth, but includes the whole cosmos that is visible from the earth.[66] This distinction is used to counter the criticism that the framework hypothesis turns the day merely into a manner of representation with no significance for the essential knowledge of the divine creative activity. Irons and Kline asserted that although they are not ordinary days, they do have genuine significance. But they are days of the upper register.[67] The days of Genesis are not literal but "an instance of lower-register terms being used metaphorically to describe the upper register.... Scripture uses the language of earthly time to speak of the progress of heavenly time."[68]

But there are problems with this distinction. The existence of heaven and the upper register does not mean that heaven, as part of creation, has a different time with little or no connection to time on earth. There is no basis in Scripture for two distinct created time dimensions, each linked to a different created spatial realm. To the contrary, the heavenly and earthly spatial realms seem to mesh seamlessly within one time continuum. When Satan was in God's presence and received permission to take everything away from Job, he immediately went down to earth to do just that (Job 1:6–12). When a spirit appeared before the LORD in heaven and volunteered to entice Ahab to his destruction and received permission to do so, he subsequently did it (1 Kings 22:19–22). Heavenly and earthly time correlate with each other. There is of course the mystery of the eternal God coming into our time, which is created, but that is not the issue here. Heavenly time, which is also part of creation, is synchronous with earthly time.[69] There is no basis for divorcing created time on earth from created time in heaven.

Now that we have evaluated three major arguments for the framework hypothesis, we need to address the consequences of this theory for the historicity of Genesis 1 and 2.

Framework and history. Proponents of the framework hypothesis argue that the six days are not literal days. "The complete seven-day framework is a

---

66. Irons and Kline, "Framework View," 237.
67. Irons and Kline, "Framework View," 239, 247.
68. Irons and Kline, "Framework View," 240; also see 247.
69. See Poythress, *Redeeming Science*, 345. Also see Bédard, *In Six Days*, 164–71. On the matter of the eternal God and time, see Bavinck, *Reformed Dogmatics*, 2:426–30, esp. 429.

metaphorical appropriation of lower-register [earthly] language denoting an upper-register [heavenly] temporal reality. With their evenings and mornings, the six days do not mark the passage of earthly time in the lower register, but of heavenly time in the upper register."[70]

This position is very problematic for the framework hypothesis itself and at the very least quite confusing. For although on this theory the days do not mark the passage of earthly time, and the arrangement is topical and not chronological, yet the seventh day is the final day of the creation week and human beings were created last.[71] Also, in the framework theory the animals created on days 5 and 6 needed the conditions created on days 2 and 3. This raises the question whether the framework hypothesis contains a false dilemma when it sets topical order against chronological order. In other words, could an arrangement of events that is topical not also be chronologically accurate? Even if one were to grant that the arrangement is topical, does that necessarily mean that there is no temporal sequence? It appears that the topical does not exclude the temporal order, especially since Genesis 1 so strongly emphasizes a chronological sequence. One cannot escape the stress on one day following the next in the account. The sequence is even numbered (one, two, three, etc.). It is difficult to imagine how a text could more strongly express chronological sequence than Scripture does in its opening chapter.[72]

Proponents of the framework hypothesis hold that the days of Genesis 1 are upper-register days. Consequently, they separate the account of creation from earthly time and relegate the events to heavenly days and times. As a result those favoring this hypothesis assert that Genesis 1 does not tell us anything about how long God's work of creation actually took because it is all described for us in heavenly language, and the use of the Hebrew term for "day" is just a figure of speech that is not meant to be taken literally. In other words, Genesis 1 does not tell us whether the earth is old or young, although it would appear that this hypothesis clearly prefers an old earth. Indeed, if the normal working of providence was used by God in His work of creation, then a very long period of time must be allowed.[73] As Kline mentions elsewhere, the conclusion of the matter is that "as far as the time frame [of creation] is concerned, with respect

---

70. Irons and Kline, "Framework View," 248.
71. Irons and Kline, "Framework View," 221.
72. These and similar points are also made by Poythress, *Redeeming Science*, 144–45, 341–42.
73. Irons and Kline, "Framework View," 218, 230–36.

to both the duration and sequence of events, the scientist is left free of biblical restraints in hypothesizing about cosmic origins."[74]

Conclusion. Although proponents insist that the framework hypothesis "does *not* teach that creation was a nonhistorical event,"[75] this hypothesis nevertheless does undermine the historicity of Genesis 1. Consider the examples we looked at. If day one and day four recount the same event, then on which day did the event take place, or did it take place on only day one and therefore not on day four? We are left to ask, does Genesis 1 really record what actually happened or not?[76] By making Genesis 1 a literary construction with no earthly time, what is left of its historical value as a narrative in which God has presented his account of creation? Irons and Kline emphasize the message, the theological proclamation of God being the creator.[77] It is true that Genesis 1 gives this message, but this message only has impact if the events as recorded actually happened as God revealed them. The framework hypothesis denies the historicity of the events as they are described to have transpired on day one and day four, and for that matter what happened on all the other days as well. It is all a figurative framework; only the ideas have value for the reader. But that is not what the text says. God in His Word takes us from one day to the next and tells us in language we can understand what happened on each day. The framework hypothesis must therefore be rejected, for all the reasons already mentioned, but also because it undermines the historicity of Genesis 1, in spite of its claims to the contrary.[78]

The Analogical Day View

Another important nonliteral way of reading Genesis 1 is the analogical day view. C. John Collins is professor of Old Testament at Covenant Theological Seminary, and he has a background in both science and theology. He is currently at the forefront of promoting what he calls "anthropomorphic" or "analogical" days.[79] But what exactly constitute such days? How do his views relate to the historicity of Genesis?

---

74. Kline, "Space and Time," 2.
75. Irons and Kline, "Framework View," 219 (italics in the original).
76. See further Bédard, *In Six Days God*, 132–35.
77. Irons and Kline, "Framework View," 218.
78. See further on historicity of Gen. 1 and the framework view, Jordan, *Creation in Six Days*, 82–95.
79. For an early study, see C. John Collins, "How Old is the Earth? Anthropomorphic Days in Genesis 1:1–2:3," *Presb* 20 (1994): 109–30.

Anthropomorphic days? Collins is not the first to speak of anthropomorphic expressions when discussing the creation account. A Dutch scholar from an earlier generation, N. H. Ridderbos, asked, "Does the author [of Genesis] mean to say that God completed creation in six days, or does he make use of an anthropomorphic mode of presentation?...God is the Eternal One. Are we really to take literally the representation that for every great work (or two works) of creation He used a day?"[80] These questions suggest that when Genesis 1 speaks of days we should not take that terminology literally but realize it is simply an anthropomorphic or nonliteral mode of speech.

Collins also follows this line of thinking. He supports his claim that the six days are anthropomorphisms by noting that Genesis 1–2 "pictures God as a craftsman, industriously making and shaping his creation. Indeed, 2:7 portrays God as potter when it says he 'formed' man; and of course when God 'breathed' into the man that is a recognizable anthropomorphism."[81] Although it is true that such expressions have been described as anthropomorphic, this does not mean that the language used is merely figurative and does not designate a specific divine activity.[82] E. J. Young correctly noted in the context of Genesis 1 and 2 that

> if the term "anthropomorphic" may legitimately be used at all, we would say that whereas it might apply to some elements of Genesis 2:7, it does not include all of them. In other words, if anthropomorphism is present, it is not present in each element of the verse. The words "and God breathed" may be termed anthropomorphic, but that is the extent to which the term may be employed. The man was real, the dust was real, the ground was real as was also the breath of life. To these elements of the verse the term "anthropomorphism" cannot legitimately be applied.[83]

It is good to remind ourselves that anthropomorphisms in theological discourse can, properly speaking, only be used of God. It can be defined as "the

---

80. Nic. H. Ridderbos, *Conflict*, 30–31.

81. Collins, "How Old is the Earth?," 117; "the seven 'days' of the creation week are an anthropomorphism to describe God's activity" (120).

82. The question can even be raised whether one should speak of anthropomorphisms in the context of God's self-revelation. All God's revelation is given in human language in order to accurately communicate what the LORD wanted to convey to His people. See on this Edward J. Young, *Studies in Genesis One*, 55–56n36. Visee's study, to which Young refers, can also be found in G. Visee, *Onderwezen in het koninkrijk der hemelen* (Kampen: Van den Berg, 1979), 1–51.

83. Edward J. Young, *Studies in Genesis One*, 57.

portrayal of God in human form," as in references to God's hands (1 Sam. 5:11), mouth (Ps. 33:6), eyes, ears, or face (2 Chron. 16:9; Ps. 34:15–16).[84]

So can one speak of days as being anthropomorphic? The answer must be no. As E. J. Young summed up his discussion, "We do not believe that it is accurate to speak of the six days as an anthropomorphic mode of expression."[85] In other words, the days mentioned in Genesis 1 are not some sort of figure of speech signifying something other than a day, but the word "day" is meant to convey exactly what it means: a day—not a metaphorical day, but a real, and therefore historical day.

Analogical days? When describing the days of creation as God's workdays, Collins notes that they are not identical to our days, but rather analogous. By identical he means "24 hours long, following in direct contiguous sequence." By analogous he means that these days "have a point of similarity, with a basis in our experience, by which we can understand something about God and his historical activity."[86] He also commented that the length of these days "is neither specified nor important, and not everything in the account needs to be taken as historically sequential." According to Collins, "This position found advocates in the American Presbyterian William Shedd and the Dutch Reformed Herman Bavinck."[87] However, it should be noted that Bavinck's interpretation does not agree with that of Collins. Although Bavinck considered the days to be extraordinary, God's "workdays," they were in his view nevertheless days that followed each other in a real historical sequence.[88]

---

84. Murray A. Rae, "Anthropomorphism," in *Dictionary for the Theological Interpretation of the Bible*, ed. Kevin J. Vanhoozer (Grand Rapids: Baker Academic; London: SPCK, 2005), 48. Anne Knafl in her study broadly defines divine anthropomorphism as "*any description that applies human characteristics, actions, abilities, or feelings to a deity, specifically the Israelite God.* I will use 'anthropomorphism' as a broad category that encompasses divine form, along with divine emotion (anthropopathism), activity (anthropopraxis), and location." Anne K. Knafl, *Forming God: Divine Anthropomorphism in the Pentateuch* (Winona Lake, Ind.: Eisenbrauns, 2014), 35 (italics in the original). For God accommodating "the knowledge of him to our slight capacity" through anthropomorphic expressions, see Calvin, *Institutes*, 1.13.1.

85. Edward J. Young, *Studies in Genesis One*, 58. Similarly, "time indicators are not anthropomorphic." Joseph A. Pipa Jr., "From Chaos to Cosmos: A Critique of the Non-Literal Interpretations of Genesis 1:1–2:3," in *Did God Create in Six Days?*, ed. Joseph A. Pipa and David W. Hall (Taylors, S.C.: Southern Presbyterian Press, 1999), 171.

86. Collins, "Reading Genesis 1:1–2:3," 139n19.

87. Collins, *Genesis 1–4*, 124.

88. See Bavinck, *Reformed Dogmatics*, 2:499–500; Bavinck, *Our Reasonable Faith*, 172–73.

According to Collins, "The six workdays are a literary device to display the creation week as a careful and artful effort."[89] As a consequence "the reader is invited to sit lightly on sequence and time lengths," although Collins is reluctant to abandon the sequence of the six days altogether.[90] Collins even leaves open the possibility of a different sequence and overlap of the days of Genesis 1. He writes, "Whatever the degree of overlap and topical arrangement, still they are 'broadly sequential,' and extend over some span of elapsed time."[91]

Collins continues the analogy beyond the days as such. God is presented as a workman going through His workweek and enjoying His Sabbath rest. "To speak this way is to speak analogically about God's activity; that is, we understand what he did by analogy with what we do; and in turn, that analogy provides guidance for man in the proper way to carry out his own work and rest."[92] If we are to understand by analogy what God did by what we do, then Collins is consistent in terms of his own thinking, because he views God not as creating during the six days but as working on that which He had already called into being in Genesis 1:1.[93]

In light of this analogy, Collins thus translates parts of the fourth commandment as "*In the space of six days* you are to cultivate and *work* all your labor…for *in the space of six days* the LORD *worked on* the *sky* and the *land*, the sea and all that is in them" (Ex. 20:9, 11).[94] This translation clearly shows Collins's analogical ideas and also demonstrates that Collins, for example, denies that light and the light-bearers were called into being on the first and fourth days, respectively. God's activity on these days did not involve "ontological origination," but a working on that which had already been created in the very beginning (Gen. 1:1). "The six 'days' represent periods of God's special ('supernatural') activity in preparing and populating the earth as a place for humans."[95] A problem with Collins's understanding is his translation of the key verb (*āśâ*) in Exodus 20:9 and 11 as "to work upon" rather than "to make." The description in Exodus 20 is based upon Genesis 1:3, where the same verb is used and is translated as "made" ("God saw everything that He *had made*").

---

89. Collins, *Genesis 1–4*, 73.

90. Collins, *Genesis 1–4*, 74.

91. Collins, "Reading Genesis 1:1–2:3," 142.

92. Collins, *Genesis 1–4*, 125.

93. For Collins's view of an initial creation plus seven days, with my critique, see chapter 2 above.

94. Collins, "Reading Genesis 1:1–2:3," 141–42 (italics in the original); also see 135–39; Collins, *Genesis 1–4*, 56–58, 67–68.

95. Collins, "Reading Genesis 1:1–2:3," 143–44; also see 67–68.

This verb is also used to explain the verb "to create" in Genesis 2:3 (literally, "God rested from all His work that He had created *by making*"). A well-known Hebrew authority, Umberto Cassuto, notes that the arrangement of these verbs ("make" and "create") in Genesis 2:3 specifies "the kind of creation of which the verse speaks, namely, an act of creation that is also a 'making,' that is, a wondrous work implying the making of things that never existed before."[96] It has therefore been rightly concluded that "since Exodus 20:11 is based on Genesis 2:3, we know that by the term 'made' God means 'created.'"[97]

Andrew Steinmann has rightly critiqued the analogical day theory by noting the obvious point that "the Scriptures do not state that God's work of creation is 'like six days' followed by a Sabbath. Instead, they state that God did his work of creating the world in six days and then rested on the seventh day, and that Israel must do the same every week (Exod 20:11; 31:17)."[98] In other words, God's work is not patterned after man's work week but the reverse is the case. It is not a matter of our understanding God's work by what we do, but the point is that God's work of six days is the pattern we are to follow. Steinmann therefore correctly notes that "the Israelite seven-day working week is compared to God's work of creation, not vice versa" in Exodus 20:8–11 and 31:12–17.[99]

A justification that Collins gives for his analogical day view is that Genesis 2:5–7 involves a climate cycle that "had been in effect for at least a year, if not longer."[100] We will deal with the entire pericope (Gen. 2:5–7) in chapter 10. A close examination of this passage will show that Collins cannot claim support for his views in this part of Scripture. Another exegetical rationale for his analogical approach is his understanding of the seventh day as unending. This interpretation will be addressed in chapter 9 and found wanting. The analogical day view allows Collins to read Genesis in a manner compatible with current scientific theories on origins.[101] However, the desire to have one's exegesis in harmony with mainstream science can lead to some questionable results and a confusing interpretation of the opening chapters of Genesis.

---

96. Cassuto, *Genesis*, 70. Cassuto translates the passage in question as "God abstained from all His work which He had creatively made" (60). The idea is that God created by making. See GKC, §114o; Gispen, *Genesis*, 1:87.

97. Pipa, "From Chaos to Cosmos," 170.

98. Andrew E. Steinmann, *Genesis: An Introduction and Commentary* (Downers Grove, Ill.: IVP Academic, 2019), 60.

99. Steinmann, *Genesis*, 60.

100. C. John Collins, "Reading Genesis 1–2 with the Grain: Analogical Days," in J. Daryl Charles, *Reading Genesis 1–2*, 88.

101. Collins, *Genesis 1–4*, 56–57, 123–24, 249–67.

Science and historicity. Current mainstream science maintains that the earth is billions of years old. Collins's exegesis makes such a dating possible. He does this mainly in several ways. First, as already noted in chapter 3, he translates Genesis 1:1 as "God had, in the beginning, created the heavens and the earth" and then separates the first two verses from what follows. The length of time between the initial event of creation and the beginning of the first day in verse 3 is unknown. Second, with his analogical day view, he gives himself room to accommodate current scientific theory.

While it is understandable that Collins would want to leave room open for incorporating current scientific theories on origins, this desire has led to confusing and inconsistent exegesis. For example, the Hebrew text clearly states that God called light into being on the first day and the light-bearers on the fourth day (Gen. 1:3, 14–18). Indeed, the text specifically says that on the fourth day God "made two great lights…God set them in the firmament of the heavens" (Gen. 1:16–17). As just noted above, in the context of Genesis 1 "to make" is synonymous with "create," the making of things that never existed before.[102] But Collins denies the clear statement of the text because it does not conform with mainstream science.[103] He says, without any proof and in spite of God saying "let there be lights" on day four (Gen. 1:14), that when it says that God made the lights (Gen. 1:16) "this does not necessarily assert the origin of their being; instead it says that God carried out some operation on them, without saying just what it was."[104] However, when Collins comes to the use of the verb "to make" for God's work of creating Adam in verse 26, he takes a different approach, arguing that the verb refers to God making man in the sense of originating him. This is because the verb "to create" is used in verse 27 as a parallel description of God's making of man.[105] Such a contradictory handling of the same Hebrew verb ("to make") within the same chapter does not enhance the credibility of his exegesis.

Another source of confusion is that Collins does not want to impose a "literalistic hermeneutic" on the "exalted prose narrative" of Genesis 1. This way of interpreting means, with respect to the six days, that, as he states in his book *Genesis 1–4*, the length of "God's workdays…is neither specified nor important, and not everything in the accounts needs to be taken as historically

102. Cassuto, *Genesis*, 70.
103. Collins, *Genesis 1–4*, 56–57.
104. Collins, *Genesis 1–4*, 67–68.
105. Collins, *Genesis 1–4*, 68.

sequential."[106] In an earlier essay he had written that "if we wish to specify their relationship to time as we know it, perhaps we may view them as successive periods of undefined length (with perhaps some overlap)."[107] In any case, he affirms in his *Genesis 1–4* that "the order of events and even the lengths of time are not part of the author's focus.... The six workdays are a literary device to display the creation week as a careful and artful effort."[108] These sentiments clash with Collins's other statements in the same book that the Hebrew text clearly indicates sequential events; indeed, he makes the confusing statement that "I find it easiest to imagine that sequence—of *some* kind, anyhow— matters in the author's presentation of events."[109] Elsewhere in the same book he writes, "The days are broadly sequential...; but since this sequence is part of the analogy, it is possible that parts of the days overlap and that events on a particular day may be grouped for logical rather than chronological reasons."[110] With respect to days overlapping, he adds to the confusion by having earlier admitted that the refrain, "there was evening and there was morning," is "marking the end points of each of the workdays."[111]

Consistent with this somewhat confused thinking is Collins's taking Genesis 1–11 as giving "attention to history without undue literalism."[112] Although he says that the length of the creation days is not important, it is clear that he prefers to view the creation week as a long period of time. According to his understanding of Genesis 2:5–6, the creation week must be some years long in order for the climate cycle to function.[113] We will see in chapter 10 that the reference in this passage is to domesticated plants that needed man to work the soil, and it points ahead to man tending the garden. Whether a climate cycle needs to take place is thus irrelevant, and such a lengthy cycle contradicts the very concept of a day.

---

106. Collins, *Genesis 1–4*, 44, 124; Collins, "Reading Genesis 1–2," 87–89. Collins claims that this was Bavinck's position, but Bavinck never indicated any doubt about the historical sequence of the six days. Furthermore, while Collins leaves the length of the creation week completely open, Bavinck emphasizes that each day is characterized by one evening and morning and that these days are not to be identified with geologic ages. See Bavinck, *Reformed Dogmatics*, 2:497–500.
107. Collins, "How Old is the Earth?," 120.
108. Collins, *Genesis 1–4*, 73.
109. Collins, *Genesis 1–4*, 74 (italics in the original).
110. Collins, *Genesis 1–4*, 129.
111. Collins, *Genesis 1–4*, 56.
112. Collins, "Reading Genesis 1–2," 77.
113. Collins, *Genesis 1–4*, 126–29.

When a scholar seeks to incorporate the current scientific understanding of the earth's origins into his or her interpretation of the text, and when this obscures what is normally regarded as the clear intent and meaning of the text, it raises the issue of the historical value of Genesis 1. In this regard we may simply ask, are the days historical or just some literary device?

Collins is unclear on the point of historicity. He asserts that the creation account "is intended to be a record of something that actually happened."[114] But he also notes, "If by 'historical' we mean what the word means in ordinary language, namely 'a record of something that the author wants us to suppose actually happened in the space-time world that we experience,' then we need have no hesitation in calling this narrative 'historical'.... At the same time we should acknowledge that in saying the account is 'historical' we have not settled every question we might ask about whether, for example, things are narrated in the order in which they occurred."[115] He also comments, "We must not impose a 'literalistic' hermeneutic on the text." Because it is "exalted prose narrative," the text "points us away from ordinary narration and leads us to suppose that its proper function extends well beyond its information to the attitudes it fosters."[116]

In a chapter on history and science Collins concludes that the truth claim of Genesis, with respect to the days of creation, is that the six days "took some length of time, longer than an ordinary week (in order to allow the climate cycle of Gen. 2:5–6 to be established)."[117] In that context he says nothing about a creation day being characterized by evening and morning, presumably because these are not real days but only analogical days. When it comes to the historical truth value of Genesis 1, Collins rejects a young earth and asserts that his interpretation of the creation account is compatible with the Big Bang theory (or family of theories) of mainstream science.[118] Clearly, the days for Collins are not real historical days as defined in Genesis 1, that is, with an evening and a morning. Furthermore, the entire narrative is not straightforward history, for Collins questions the clear statements that light and the light-bearers were created on the first and fourth days, respectively, and that God's work of creating followed in the order of the days as narrated.[119] Indeed, if the days are analogical and integral to a literary device, the entire narrative is surely less than an account of historical events.

---

114. Collins, "How Old is the Earth?," 116; also see Collins, *Genesis 1–4*, 13.
115. Collins, "Reading Genesis 1:1–2:3," 140.
116. Collins, *Genesis 1–4*, 44; also Collins, "Reading Genesis 1:1–2:3," 140–41.
117. Collins, *Genesis 1–4*, 254.
118. Collins, *Genesis 1–4*, 256–59, 267.
119. Collins, "Reading Genesis 1:1–2:3," 132, 135.

Conclusion. The analogical day view as set forth by Collins dehistoricizes Genesis 1 and for that reason should be rejected. If the six days are simply a literary device to display God's work of creation in a careful and artful manner, as he suggests,[120] then Genesis 1 is no longer a historical narrative. Indeed, Collins acknowledges that in his view "the literary reading of Genesis 1:1–2:3... shows why it is unlikely that the author makes a strong claim for the sequence of events."[121]

The notion of analogy as developed by Collins places an unhelpful hermeneutical barrier to understanding the days of Genesis 1. Scripture presents the six days of creation work followed by the seventh day of rest as the first historic week of Planet Earth. Subsequent weeks follow. Scripture indicates no break in the narrative to indicate a transition from analogical days in Genesis 1 to literal, historical days in subsequent chapters. Furthermore, the fourth commandment does not speak of the creation days as analogous but as days as we know them.[122] By speaking of the creation days as analogous one separates the first week from the days that follow. The biblical text does not justify such a separation. In Collins's case, this approach has also led to undermining the passage's historicity. It appears that current scientific theory is hindering Collins's acceptance of the obvious meaning of the text when it describes creation in six days.

Seven-Day Structure as an Ancient Literary Device
Scholars have also appealed to ancient Near Eastern literary conventions to suggest that the days of Genesis 1 should not be understood as days recounting an actual succession of events. Instead, the convention of a seven-day structure means that the narrative has a metaphorical character.

For example, Old Testament scholar John Stek has suggested that Genesis 1 is structured with the number seven as an ancient Near Eastern literary device. According to Stek, although Genesis 1 "is narrated in the form of a series of distinct divine acts distributed over a period of seven 'days'...it ought not to be read as though it were a record of events." He continues, "What occurs in the arena of God's action can be storied after the manner of human events, but accounts of 'events' in that arena are fundamentally different in kind from all

---

120. Collins, *Genesis 1–4*, 73.
121. Collins, *Genesis 1–4*, 253.
122. Gerhard F. Hasel, "The 'Days' of Creation in Genesis 1: Literal 'Days' or Figurative 'Periods/Epochs' of Time?," *Origins* 21 (1994): 29.

forms of historiography." They are "metaphorical narrations."[123] The metaphorical nature of the account raises the question of, "why the narrator distributed the creation acts of God over a period of time and why he then employed a seven-day (sabbatical) structure." Although, according to Stek, we are not given the answer to that question, he turns to ancient Near Eastern "theogonic and cosmogonic myths" and suggests that "as regards the seven-day structure, any other temporal order would appear to have been unfitting in that ancient world. Throughout the ancient Near East the number seven had long served as the primary numerical symbol of fullness/completeness/perfection, and the seven-day cycle was an old and well-established convention."[124] Geologists Davis Young and Ralph Stearley have used this approach in their defense of a nonliteral Genesis 1 that would allow for an earth billions of years old.[125]

This way of reasoning disregards the obvious historical intent of the passage. Furthermore, rather than interpreting Genesis 1 within the immediate and broader context of Scripture, appeal is made to a Near Eastern literary convention that in turn is employed to dehistoricize the biblical narrative despite the fact that the text presents itself as historical. Such a use of ancient Near Eastern literature is not a sound hermeneutical approach. It results, in this case, in the historical value of the biblical text being determined by nonbiblical sources.

More specifically, the ancient Near Eastern pattern that Stek adduces does not really fit the Genesis narrative. Stek does not mention the fact that the ancient Near Eastern literary device in question is always in the pattern of an action continuing for six days and climaxing on the seventh day. Three examples can be mentioned from second-millennium-BC Ugaritic literature discovered on the Mediterranean coast in northern Syria. The Baʿlu Myth describes the building of the god's house. In that context each of the first six days is characterized by fire and flames consuming fuel in the palace, probably as part of a giant casting process. On the seventh day, the fire is removed and the silver has turned into plaques and the gold into bricks, and Baʿlu rejoices. Another example is found in the description of the military campaign in the Kirta Epic, where the first six days are all the same, characterized by the word "go." The climax is the seventh day when Kirta's army is to reach ʾUdmu, the great city. A final example is from the Aqhatu Legend, where for each of the first six days Daniʾilu gave the

123. John H. Stek, "What Says the Scripture?," in *Portraits of Creation: Biblical and Scientific Perspectives on the World's Formation*, by Howard J. Van Till et al. (Grand Rapids: Eerdmans, 1990), 236.

124. Stek, "What Says the Scripture?," 238–39.

125. Davis A. Young and Ralph F. Stearley, *The Bible, Rocks and Time: Geological Evidence for the Age of the Earth* (Downers Grove, Ill.: IVP Academic, 2008), 192–202.

gods food and drink. On the seventh day, the account climaxes with the appearance of Baʻlu and his intercession on Daniʾiluʾs behalf.[126] In contrast to these patterns, the biblical account of creation does not repeat the same action and wording for each of the six days but rather details specific and different events. Jewish scholar S. E. Loewenstamm notes that although Genesis 1 is often cited as a classic example of the ancient Near Eastern seven-day scheme, the biblical account "differs fundamentally...in that a new event takes place on each of the six days of creation, and each day contains a narrative of its own." After the six days, the Genesis account "proceeds to mention the principal subject in the seventh and last part."[127] Once we have noted this fundamental difference— namely, a different activity on each of the six days followed by a seventh day with rest and no action at all—we should acknowledge that the opening chapter of Scripture must be interpreted on its own terms and not through the lens of certain literary features of texts from the ancient Near East.

In conclusion, if we interpret the Genesis narrative of seven days metaphorically because it appears to reflect an ancient Near Eastern literary convention, we do injustice to the historical character of this part of Scripture. This interpretation also does not give due recognition to the unique character of the Genesis narrative within the context of ancient Near Eastern literature.

Summary and Conclusions

The first day began at the very beginning of God's creation work. There is nothing to suggest that the days that followed in Genesis 1 are anything other than literal days. Indeed, grammatically, textually, and contextually the text clearly refers to a day as customarily understood. This conclusion does not mean that we can fully comprehend what those days entailed. We must be modest as we try to understand the text and careful not to go beyond what it clearly states. Contrary to the views of some, Calvin also affirmed a six-day creation, a view echoed in the confessional formulations of the Irish Articles and the Westminster Standards.

Augustine is often cited as an example to follow or to consider when scholars propose a nonliteral understanding of the days of creation. However,

---

126. See, respectively, *COS* 1:261 (*CTA* 4.vi.16–40 and note 174); 1:335 (*CTA* 14.ii.103– iii.123); 343–44 (*CTA* 17.i.1–34).

127. S. E. Loewenstamm, "The Seven Day-Unit in Ugaritic Epic Literature," *Israel Exploration Journal* 15 (1965): 132n33. For a similar conclusion on the uniqueness of the Genesis account, see Sarna, *Genesis*, 4; Daniel C. Timmer, *Creation, Tabernacle, and Sabbath* (Göttingen: Vandenhoeck & Ruprecht, 2009), 65–66.

Augustine's view that creation took place in an instant is not very persuasive when the factors that influenced his view are considered.

The framework view, the analogical days view, and the view that interprets Genesis 1 through the lens of an ancient Near Eastern literary device should be rejected for exegetical reasons and because the role of Scripture's self-testimony must be prioritized over any witness from extrabiblical literary sources. Furthermore, all these approaches undermine the historicity of Genesis 1. While these views are considered compatible with today's scientific consensus and thus find support among many biblical interpreters, current scientific theories on the origin of the world should not be decisive for our understanding of Genesis 1.

6

"God Created"

God's work of calling our world—and indeed the universe—into existence is beyond our understanding. Yet, Scripture invites us to take a closer look. What do those words in the opening verse of Scripture—"God created"—mean? Not all scholars agree. As we will see in this chapter, one popular academic defends the notion that "to create" is merely to give a function to existing things and not to bring them into being. Another scholar suggests that "to create" means "to separate." Does Scripture support such meanings? Some of the proposed meanings relate to God's providence. How are God's works of creation and providence related to each other? This chapter addresses these and related issues.

The Creator

"In the beginning God created." What powerful opening words! The first thing to notice is the simple and unquestionable affirmation of God's existence. This foundational passage refutes atheism. No argumentation about God's existence or His role as creator is needed; it is plain and obvious for all to see. God's attributes, His eternal power and divine nature, are evident to all human beings from what He has made "so that they are without excuse" (Rom. 1:20).

Genesis 1:1 is also remarkable within the context of the ancient Near East. The nations around Israel all had their theogonies, that is, their accounts of the origins and descent of their gods. Here there is no such account tracing the genealogies of the gods. Instead, there is a simple declaration of God, the Creator. There is no question about where God came from, as pagans would ask. The opening words of Genesis make clear that to raise questions about God's origin is off limits. God is eternal. He alone is eternal without beginning and end. Matter is not eternal. God created it. There is no place for materialism or the belief that physical matter is eternal or that it alone is the fundamental reality.

A major implication of accepting the truth of God the Creator, and the reality not only of His being but also of His work, is that we must then also accept His account of His work of creation and not question its historicity or accuracy. He alone was there to witness it, and He alone is able to reveal it. He does so in Genesis.

What Is the Meaning of "Create"?

Usage in Scripture

There is for us, as human beings with our limitations, a profound mystery in the opening words of Scripture. "In the beginning God created the heavens and the earth." We cannot comprehend this creating act of God. We can only go by what Scripture says and try to discern its meaning. What does Genesis convey with the words "God created"? The subject of the Hebrew verb (*bārā'*) is always God, the true God of Israel. The agent of creation is never a false god or a human being. It is always God who creates.

When God creates, something new and special always results. Two different scenarios are possible. First, when God creates something new it can refer to His creative activity on an already existing entity. For example, God's opening up the ground to swallow the rebels Korah, Dathan, and Abiram is described as "the LORD creates a new thing" (Num. 16:30). Another example of God's creative work on an existing entity is found in David's prayer, "Create in me a clean heart, O God" (Ps. 51:10). In Genesis 1, God said, "Let Us make man," and a little later we read, "God created man" (vv. 26, 27), whom He made by forming man of dust from the ground (Gen. 2:7; cf. v. 4). So, the creation of man is another example of God's creating something new from existing material, in this case dust from the ground.[1]

The second scenario in which God creates something new is His making something from nothing. It is a remarkable fact that no substance or material from which God created is ever mentioned with the verb "to create" (*bārā'*). In the context of God creating heaven and earth, we read in Psalm 33:9 that God "spoke, and it was done." Elsewhere Scripture tells us, "He commanded and they [sun, moon, stars, etc.] were created" (Ps. 148:5). From such usage of this verb elsewhere in Scripture, and from its context in Genesis 1 where no material source for creation is mentioned, we can deduce that in the beginning God

---

1. There are many examples of "to create" (*bārā'*) being used with other verbs expressing God's creative acts. See Karl-Heinz Bernhardt, "*bārā'*," *TDOT* 2:246; Stek, "What Says the Scripture?," 208–13.

created the heavens and the earth from nothing. Later in this chapter we will return to the discussion of God's creating by speaking. The point now is that God's work of creation meant the appearance of our planet and universe from no prior existing material. "He spoke, and it was done." Also consistent with creation from nothing (*creatio ex nihilo*) is Hebrews 11:3: "By faith we understand that the universe was created by the word of God, so that what is seen was not made out of things that are visible" (ESV; also cf. John 1:3; 2 Macc. 7:28).[2]

If God created from nothing—and He did—what process did He follow? Was there a process? Such questions cannot be answered on the basis of the verb "to create." It does not tell us how God did the actual creating. The term "to create" in and of itself does not imply or suggest a process that led to that which was created. This does not mean that some sort of process in the act of creating is excluded. Process may have been part of the creative activity of God, but the verb "to create" simply does not tell us one way or the other. Outside Genesis 1, we know from the context that some process could be involved when the term "to create" is used. For example, when God calls Himself "the Creator of Israel" (Isa. 43:15), we know from the rest of Scripture that a long historical process was involved before there was a nation called Israel.[3] In Genesis 1 we are told that "God created man in His own image" (Gen. 1:27), a creation subsequently described in some detail in 2:7. But we would not have been able to deduce that process from the usage of the term "to create" as such. That understanding came from the larger context. The use of verbs like "to make" or "bring forth" during the days of creation also suggests some sort of process was involved as God did His work of creating (Gen. 1:7, 9, 11, 16, 20, 24). In conclusion, Scripture does not describe a process when the verb "to create" is used, but neither does it deny that some processes might have been involved.

God's work of creation is incomprehensible to us. His work is done with His divine power, wisdom, and understanding (Ps. 136:5; Prov. 3:19; Jer. 10:12; 51:15). His understanding has no limit (Ps. 147:5) and is unsearchable (Isa. 40:28).

---

2. For a concise study showing that God created from nothing, see John Oswalt, *"Creatio Ex Nihilo*: Is It Biblical and Does It Matter?" *TJ* 39 (2018): 165–80; for a more detailed study, see Paul Copan and William Lane Craig, *Creation Out of Nothing: A Biblical, Philosophical, and Scientific Exploration* (Grand Rapids: Baker Academic, 2004). Remarkably, no reference to Heb. 11:3 is made in Young and Stearley, *The Bible, Rocks and Time*, 189–92, in spite of the fact that the authors discuss verbal fiat creation and other related biblical passages. Heb. 11:3 is also not mentioned in the biblical index at the back of that book. See also Gary A. Anderson's and Richard J. Clifford's essays in *Creation ex nihilo: Origins, Development, Contemporary Challenges*, ed. Gary A. Anderson and Markus Bockmuehl (Notre Dame: University of Notre Dame Press, 2018), 15–35, 55–76.

3. Isa. 44:24 and related passages also imply process, as discussed in chapter 3.

There is no way that our finite minds can grasp and comprehend the infinite power and wisdom of God in His work of creating the world in which we live.[4]

John Walton

The understanding of "create" outlined above has been challenged by Old Testament scholar John H. Walton. According to him, Genesis 1 must be seen within the context that "in the ancient world, something was created when it was given a function." In Genesis, therefore, "'to create something' means to give it a function." According to Walton, "The text is making no comment on material origins. It is more interested in indicating how God set up the cosmos to function for human beings in his image. These functions define the idea of existence; the ancients had little interest in the material."[5]

Several questions arise. Even if we were to grant that Walton was completely accurate in his assessment of a more or less universal ancient mindset of functional thinking (a position that has been convincingly challenged),[6] the issue is whether Genesis is simply a product of an ancient Near Eastern environment or whether it is revelation from the living God of heaven and earth. In other words, does Scripture need to be read through ancient Near Eastern glasses or should it be read on its own terms as divine revelation and as Scripture explains itself? To posit the former means that we can only be sure that we know what Genesis 1 is communicating to us after we have studied the ancient Near Eastern writings. In other words, our understanding of Genesis 1 is then held hostage to whatever new discoveries from antiquity are made and to whatever interpretation influential scholars give to these discoveries. With that premise interpreters of Genesis during the previous two millennia who were not informed of the ancient Near Eastern mind as we understand it today were not able to truly comprehend the biblical text. Giving such a normative importance to extrabiblical findings is unacceptable and militates against God's ability to clearly convey the meaning He intended to readers of His revelation in all times and places. Walton is overrating the importance of ancient Near

---

4. For a discussion on wisdom and creation in Prov. 8, see chapter 3.

5. Walton, *Genesis 1 as Ancient Cosmology*, 120, 139. A popular presentation of his ideas can be found in Walton, *Lost World of Genesis One*.

6. E.g., in a response to Walton (in J. Daryl Charles, *Reading Genesis 1–2*, 172), Richard Averbeck states that "it is simply not true that material creation was not a major concern in the ANE world surrounding ancient Israel" and follows this up with examples; similarly, Ronald Hendel, review of *Genesis 1 as Ancient Cosmology*, by John H. Walton, *Journal of Semitic Studies* 58 (2013): 221; also see Weeks, "The Bible and the 'Universal' Ancient World," esp. 10–12.

Eastern materials for a proper understanding of Genesis and not fully factoring in the differences between the pagan and biblical worldviews.

When we come to the specific issue of Walton's understanding of the verb "to create" (*bārā'*), we find his reasoning is somewhat confusing. He writes that "it is still best to consider the verb *bārā'* as meaning 'to bring something into existence.'" But then he goes on to suggest that "it is highly unlikely that *material* existence is in view." His conclusion is that "the nuanced meaning of *bārā'* that best suits the data is that it means 'to bring something into (functional) existence.'"[7] Even with his nuanced definition, "to create" still means to bring something into existence. This "something" is, according to normal English parlance, a material object. Is Walton creating a false dilemma here? Why try to exclude the material or ontological aspect of creation and instead insist on the sense of "to create" as functional only? How can the functional exist without the material objects or entities in view? The problems he encounters can be illustrated by his discussion of part of the fourth commandment where the verb "to make" (*'āśâ*) is used rather than "to create" ("For in six days the LORD made the heavens and the earth, the sea, and all that is in them," Ex. 20:11). He suggests that it "would be entirely justifiable to understand Exodus 20:11 as discussing God *doing* his work.... The creative activities of the six days are better classified as 'doing work' rather than as 'making things.'"[8] Remarkably, Walton gives no complete translation of verse 11. It would indeed be difficult to translate the verse in the sense he suggests given his understanding that God is not making things, for the text of verse 11 gives an object to God's activities. He "made heaven and earth, the sea, and all that is in them."[9] Another example of the difficulties Walton encounters is God's creation of the "great sea creatures and every living thing that moves" (Gen. 1:21). How can God create the functions without creating their actual physical existence?

A further consequence of Walton's view of *bārā'* is that he denies that Genesis 1 teaches creation from nothing. In his view verse 1 means that "in the initial period, God brought cosmic functions into existence." The condition of "without form" described in the next verse "could refer to the precosmic condition, the functionless cosmic waters."[10] If that is so, then matter preceded God's

---

7. Walton, *Genesis 1 as Ancient Cosmology*, 132–33.

8. Walton, *Genesis 1 as Ancient Cosmology*, 134.

9. Critical responses by Richard E. Averbeck, Todd S. Beall, and C. John Collins to Walton's view on the verb "to create" can be found in Charles, *Reading Genesis 1–2*, 170–81.

10. Walton, *Lost World of Genesis One*, 133, 143. In the course of his discussion, Walton refers to the work of David Tsumura, who deplores Walton's misuse of an argument of his. David T. Tsumura, review of *Genesis 1 as Ancient Cosmology*, by John H. Walton, *JAOS* 135 (2015):

work of six-day creation. But such speculation flies in the face of the obvious intent of the passage to describe the creation of the material world around us *and* the functions God gave to its various parts. This is particularly obvious with the creation of humankind. Human beings first had to be created before being given their task or function (Gen. 1:26–30). Since Genesis 1:1 speaks of the very beginning of creation (as we discussed in chapter 3), Walton has no biblical basis for conjecturing that matter existed before the six day creation.

In summary, when Walton tries to redefine the Hebrew term for "to create" by rendering "to give a function," he gives far too much weight to a supposed ancient Near Eastern notion that creating means giving a function. Furthermore, this redefinition creates a false dichotomy between the objects of God's creation and their function. The two belong together. Walton's redefinition also means that Scripture says nothing about the origin of the material world, and Genesis is thus of no relevance to scientific investigations of origins.

Ellen van Wolde

Another recent attempt to redefine *bārā'* that has caused a lot of discussion is Ellen van Wolde's suggestion that the verb does not mean "to create," but can best be translated "'to separate', designating an action of a very concrete, spatial and physical character."[11] Consequently, she translates Genesis 1:1 as follows: "In the beginning in which/when God separated the heaven and the earth." This rendition shows that there is no absolute beginning but the beginning of the action of separating heaven and earth. God started a process. She seeks support from ancient Mesopotamian creation texts that also speak of the divine opening act in terms of separation of heaven and earth. This line of evidence has been challenged.[12] In any case, it is the biblical evidence that must be decisive.

---

354. Elsewhere Walton affirms "God's creation of the material cosmos," but his reasoning is confusing given that he emphatically stated that Gen. 1 is not the account of material origins. Apparently Scripture has no such account, although occasional references to God's work of creating the material cosmos can be found. Walton, *Lost World of Genesis One*, 96–97.

11. Ellen van Wolde, "Why the Verb ברא Does Not Mean 'to Create' in Genesis 1.1–2.4a," *JSOT* 34 (2009): 20; also see Ellen van Wolde, "Semantics and the Semantics of ברא: A Rejoinder to the Arguments Advanced by B. Becking and M. Korpel," *jHebS* 11, no. 9 (2011): 1–39; Ellen van Wolde, "Separation and Creation in Genesis 1 and Psalm 104, a Continuation of the Discussion of the Verb ברא," *VT* 67 (2017): 611–47. Van Wolde's thesis deals with the root br' in qal. In piel, br' means "to shape by cutting" or "to cut" and br' is then usually considered to be a different root; *HALOT*, 153–54; *DCH* 2:258–59; also see note 21 below.

12. Van Wolde, "Why the Verb ברא Does Not Mean Create," 7–13, 21; also see Van Wolde, "Separation and Creation," 631–32. Her appeal to Sumerian literature has been challenged by

Another example of how she applies her unique understanding can be ascertained from the way she deals with Genesis 1:21. Traditionally, it is translated as "God created great sea creatures and every living thing that moves, with which the waters abounded, according to their kind, and every winged bird according to its kind." Van Wolde, however, argues that this means that God separated the sea creatures from the birds that fly in the air. That is, God "placed the animate inhabitants of the aerial and liquid parts of the earth in spatially distant positions and thus assigned each to its own spatial environment."[13]

One final example: in 1:27 the term *bārā'* occurs three times. The traditional translation reads, "God created man in His own image; in the image of God He created him; male and female He created them." This is interpreted to indicate three processes of separation: "the twice mentioned spatial separation of the human being from God and the separation of human beings into males and females."[14] As further support for her thesis, Van Wolde writes that "in the Hebrew Bible the noun 'creator' is never expressed with the participle of *br'*." Other verbs are used instead to convey this notion.[15]

What are we to think of this? In short, Van Wolde's arguments are not convincing. To begin with the last point mentioned above, she errs because, as Bob Becking and Marjo Korpel note in their critique, the participle of *bārā'* is actually used at least thirteen times in the Old Testament to describe God as creator.[16] With respect to Van Wolde's main thesis that *bārā'* means "to separate," Becking and Korpel respond that "a Hebrew verb with the meaning 'to separate' requires at least one preposition" to complete the verb. Otherwise, "'separate' has to be taken as 'split, cleave.' In that case, however, the text of Gen 1:1

JoAnn Scurlock, "Searching for Meaning in Genesis 1:2," in *Creation and Chaos: A Reconsideration of Hermann Gunkel's* Chaoskampf *Hypothesis*, ed. John Scurlock and Richard H. Beal (Winona Lake, Ind.: Eisenbrauns, 2013), 50–51n9; and Terrance Randall Wardlaw Jr., "The Meaning of ברא in Genesis 1:1–2:3," *VT* 64 (2014): 504–5. For a response, see van Wolde, "Semantics," 18–19.

13. Van Wolde, "Why the Verb ברא Does Not Mean Create," 13–14, 21; also see Van Wolde, "Separation and Creation," 634–35.

14. Van Wolde, "Why the Verb ברא Does Not Mean Create," 17, 21–22; also see Van Wolde, "Separation and Creation," 636.

15. Van Wolde, "Why the Verb ברא Does Not Mean Create," 20.

16. Eccl. 12:1; Isa. 40:28; 42:5; 43:1, 15; 45:7 (twice), 18; 57:19; 65:17, 18 (twice); Amos 4:13; see further Bob Becking and Marjo C. A. Korpel, "To Create, to Separate or to Construct," *jHebS* 10, no. 3 (2010): 9–10; cf. Van Wolde, "Semantics," 19–20.

would mean that heaven and earth are each split into two halves."[17] Such a sequence of events is clearly not Van Wolde's intent.

Another problem for Van Wolde's thesis is that there is no place in Scripture where it can be proven that *bārā'* has the meaning "to separate." On the contrary, the relatively frequent usage of this verb in Isaiah makes it abundantly clear that the verb means "to create" since the context demands it or it is used in parallel with verbs denoting making something new. For example, the LORD is "the Creator of the ends of the earth" (Isa. 40:28). It would make no sense to say that He is "the Separator of the ends of the earth." Indeed, the context points back to the LORD who "stretches out the heavens like a curtain, and spreads them out like a tent to dwell in" (Isa. 40:22). Similar comments can be made on other passages (such as Isa. 40:26; 42:5; 43:1, 15). In other texts the parallel constructions make it impossible to give the meaning "to separate" to *bārā'*. For example, in Psalm 102:18 "the generation to come" is parallel to "a people yet to be created." It would make no sense to translate "a people yet to be separated."[18]

With respect to Genesis 1, let us take verse 27 as an example. "So God created man in His own image; in the image of God He created him; male and female He created them." Van Wolde's understanding of this passage as describing three processes of separation makes little sense. She argues that the verb *bārā'* refers to the separation of humanity from God and then to the separation of human beings into male and female. But this understanding runs counter to the fact that there is no indication of a separation through a preposition of separation, namely, "from." Instead, God created male and female, summed up as "man" (*'ādām*), mentioned as a singular twice in verse 27. This indicates that the later reference to "male and female" in this verse should be taken as coreferential, referring to "man." The notion that *bārā'* indicates separation is highly unlikely.[19]

A further factor to take into consideration is that there is no evidence in the ancient Greek translation of the Old Testament (the Septuagint) or in the earliest Jewish interpretations of Genesis 1 (the Targums) that *bārā'* was ever understood to mean "to separate." Not surprisingly, the history of research on

---

17. Becking and Korpel, "To Create," 7–8. Cf. Van Wolde, "Semantics," 16–17. Van Wolde's rejoinder is unconvincing. The verbs implying separation that do not take a preposition (which she mentions in her defense) have the meaning "to split" or "divide" (an entity) and do not refer to separating unlike entities.

18. For these and other examples, see Becking and Korpel, "To Create," 12–14.

19. Wardlaw, "The Meaning," 509–10.

this verb and the current consensus also do not support the rendering "to separate" but rather "to create."[20]

Last but not least, *bārāʾ* meaning "to create" is also attested in the New Testament. With an obvious reference to Genesis 1, the apostle John wrote, "In the beginning was the Word.... All things were made through Him" (John 1:1, 3). Elsewhere we read, "By faith we understand that the universe was created by the word of God" (Heb. 11:3 ESV). There is no mention of separation.

Although it is clear that the verb *bārāʾ* has the meaning "to create," God in His wisdom did use separation in His work of creation. In fact, the account of creation uses a different Hebrew verb (*bdl* in the *hiphil* stem) to indicate the work of separation. "God separated the light from the darkness" (Gen. 1:4 ESV). The expanse separated the waters below (seas, rivers, springs) from those above (the clouds) (vv. 6–7). The lights in the expanse of the heavens separated day from night (v. 14) and light from darkness (v. 18). There was also a separation between the dry land and the waters (v. 9), although the verb "to separate" is not used in this instance. So, while we need to recognize that God's work involved making separations, we also need to maintain the meaning "to create," with all its rich biblical connotations, for the verb *bārāʾ*.[21]

Creation Is the Work of the Triune God

Since God is the only subject of the verb "to create" (*bārāʾ*), his work is "beyond conceptualization: divine activity can be perceived only insofar as it remains comparable to human activity. Therefore the verb expresses nothing further concerning the method of creation."[22] It is good to remember our human limitations when speaking of God's work of creating. The verb "to create" in itself does not give any indication how God created.

We are, however, not completely uninformed on the mode of God's creative activity. Scripture tells us that He has created by the word of His command. "God said, 'Let there be light,' and there was light" (Gen. 1:3). This pattern is found ten times in the creation account (vv. 3, 6, 9, 11, 14, 20, 24, 26, 28, 29).

---

20. Becking and Korpel, "To Create," 3–7; Grossfeld, *The Targum Onqelos to Genesis*, 42–43; Mahler, *Targum Pseudo-Jonathan: Genesis*, 1, 19, 20; McNamara, *Targum Neofiti 1: Genesis*, 52, 54, 55.

21. For God creating by successive acts of separation (Gen. 1:4, 6–7, 14, 18) and possible relations to the root *brʾ*, see Arnold, *Genesis*, 37; cf. Karl Möller, "Images of God and Creation in Genesis 1–2," in *A God of Faithfulness: Essays in Honour of J. Gordon McConville on His 60th Birthday*, ed. Jamie A. Grant, Alison Lo, and Gordon J. Wenham (New York: T&T Clark International, 2011), 10–11.

22. Schmidt, "*brʾ* to create," 255.

God's speaking is a command. "He commanded and they [sun, moon, stars, etc.] were created" (Ps. 148:5). In Psalm 33, there is the parallelism of speaking and commanding in the context of God's work of creation. "He spoke, and it was done; he commanded, and it stood fast" (Ps. 33:9). This psalm also parallels God's word with the breath of His mouth. "By the word of the LORD the heavens were made, and all the host of them by the breath of His mouth" (v. 6). By faith we understand that the world was created "by the word of God" (Heb. 11:3). What an awesome display of God's power! He merely said the word, and it came to be.

Within the context of the entire Scripture, we can say more. The apostle John began his gospel with a clear allusion to Genesis 1 when he wrote of the Son of God: "In the beginning was the Word, and the Word was with God, and the Word was God. He was in the beginning with God. All things were made through Him, and without Him nothing was made that was made.... And the Word became flesh and dwelt among us, and we beheld His glory, the glory as of the only begotten of the Father, full of grace and truth" (John 1:1–3, 14). There is clearly a relationship between the Word who was with God as recounted in John 1 and the word spoken by God at creation. The fact that the second person of the Trinity is called the Word indicates that at creation, in Calvin's words, "God did not speak as humans do, but he demonstrated the power of his eternal Word, that word which has been manifested in the flesh: it is God, our Lord Jesus Christ, by whose power the world was created in all its fullness."[23]

It is a mystery how exactly the Son related to the Father in the creation of the heavens and the earth. From the fullness of Scripture we know that the Father created through the Son. "By Him all things were created that are in heaven and that are on earth, visible and invisible, whether thrones or dominions or principalities or powers. All things were created through Him and for Him. And He is before all things, and in Him all things consist" (Col. 1:16–17). We can scarcely begin to comprehend what this means. One thing is sure. It is through the eternal Son that God unleashed unimaginable energy and power as He spoke into being a material universe, governed by intricate laws that He had designed. By His Word, God imparted the information needed to create and structure the universe.[24] As we read in Hebrews 1:2, it is through the Son that God created the world, and He is "upholding all things by the word of His power" (1:3; cf. 1 Cor. 8:6; 2 Peter 3:5).

---

23. Calvin, *Sermons on Genesis*, 20; also see Calvin, *Institutes*, 1.13.7.
24. Lennox, *Seven Days*, 97, 141.

The Holy Spirit was also involved. When God called the earth into being it "was without form, and void; and darkness was on the face of the deep. And the Spirit of God was hovering over the face of the waters" (Gen. 1:2). The use of the participle ("hovering") denotes the continuing, active presence of the Spirit. He was involved with God's creation work. The only other place where the verb "hovering" is used is in a description of God's protective care over Israel, as an eagle fluttering over its young (Deut. 32:11). This image suggests that the newly created earth, as yet not suitable for habitation, was not left on its own. The Spirit moved over it in a caring manner.

Vern Poythress ventures to go further in describing the Spirit's activity in Genesis 1, plausibly suggesting that the Spirit was "making effective the speech of God," and that this work of the Spirit is also alluded to in Psalm 33:6: "By the word of the LORD the heavens were made, and all the host of them by the breath of his mouth" ("the breath of his mouth" being the Spirit). Poythress is in line with Nic. H. Ridderbos who suggested that the expression "breath of his mouth" denotes the power going out from God and that reference here is to the Spirit. Although with this understanding of Psalm 33:6 there is not a lot of difference between the Word and Spirit, since they are in parallel here, nevertheless, "the breath of his mouth" probably does allude to the Spirit's involvement in the work of creating. In Poythress's words, "The Spirit empowers and makes effective the speech of God. The Spirit produces the effectiveness of the word."[25] This truth is seen elsewhere as well. When God renews the earth in spring and makes, as it were, a new creation, He sends forth His Spirit (Ps. 104:30).[26] Of course, with respect to the new creation, the Spirit makes effective God's Word by writing it on our hearts (2 Cor. 3:3; also Heb. 10:16).

In sum, the triune God—Father, Son, and Holy Spirit—is active in the work of creation described in Genesis 1.

---

25. Vern S. Poythress, "Reforming Ontology and Logic in the Light of the Trinity: An Application of Van Til's Idea of Analogy," *WTJ* 57 (1995): 201; Nic. H. Ridderbos, *De Psalmen*, 1:343–44; similarly, J. Ridderbos, *De Psalmen* (Kampen: Kok, 1955), 1:283. Calvin hesitates to see a reference to the Spirit in "the breath of his mouth." Calvin, *Commentary on the Book of Psalms*, 1:543. Tsumura translates "breath of God" (Gen. 1:2) because v. 2 "seems to describe a situation in which God's words were *not yet* uttered" since that first happened in v. 3. In v. 2 "God's breath was not articulated as a voice to pronounce his creative word but was ready to get involved in such creative actions." Tsumura, *Creation and Destruction*, 75. However, Ps. 33:6, 9 suggest that everything, including what is mentioned in Gen. 1:1, was called into being by God's command.

26. On the relationship of Ps. 104 to God's work of creation, see Jordan, *Creation in Six Days*, 247–51; and Miller, *The Way of the Lord*, 178–92.

Creation and Providence

In considering how God created, the question arises whether God used the means of ordinary providence. This issue is particularly important for those who wish to harmonize Genesis 1 with current evolutionary views on origins. After all, if there is no difference between God's works of creation and providence, one could argue that God's work of creation took place by providential processes, that is, by natural processes that we experience today. Then one could imagine that God's creation commands or decrees had been at work for billions of years before the physical universe came to be what we know it as today. This is a widely held view, and one for which Old Testament scholar John Stek (1925–2009) has clearly argued.[27]

Although Stek acknowledged that Reformed theology had traditionally distinguished between creation and providence,[28] he was convinced that this distinction was imposed on the biblical text and therefore needed to be reassessed. He therefore thought that "God's 'Let there be…' in Genesis 1 is too narrowly conceived if it be supposed that it stands only as a power word to effect origination, the means by which God brought into being creatures that had then to be maintained by a *new* divine act, another decree from the mouth of God, such as, 'Let the created be preserved.'" In other words, "God's 'Let there be…' was a sovereign establishing and sustaining word. His creation decree was and is the fundamental preserving and governing word."[29] "Let there be" describes both God's work of creation and providence.

Stek used the example of the creation of light. "Let there be light" is a creation decree that "originates, preserves, and governs light…. *God issued a decree enduring in its effect.*"[30] Stek understands the other "let there be" decrees in a similar manner. Stek's reasoning is in a sense an argument from silence and thus not strong. For him the fact that there is no explicit decree to preserve creation beyond the point of its origination means that the notion of preservation must be included in the decree. But is this not begging the question? Is it not obvious that what God created would also endure? A decree explicitly commanding the continuation of God's creation is unnecessary. That such

---

27. Stek, "What Says the Scripture?," 207–16, 242–50; see 249 for his making room for evolution over billions of years. See also, e.g., Denis R. Alexander, *Creation or Evolution*, 35–47. A critique of John Stek's position is found in Nicolaas H. Gootjes, "Is Creation the Same as Providence?," in *Teaching and Preaching the Word: Studies in Dogmatics and Homiletics*, ed. Cornelis Van Dam (Winnipeg: Premier, 2010), 242–46.

28. As also detailed in Hall, Lex Supra Tenebrae, 4–35.

29. Stek, "What Says the Scripture?," 246 (italics in the original); also see 213–16.

30. Stek, "What Says the Scripture?," 247 (italics in the original).

continuance is assumed is obvious.[31] Why else would God create if His creation was not to endure?

Furthermore, Nicolaas Gootjes has shown[32] that Genesis 1 clearly differentiates between creation and providence. On the second day, God commanded, "Let there be a firmament," and the text later notes, "God made the firmament" (Gen. 1:6–7). The reference is clearly to creation, not providence. Similarly, God issued the command for the creation of lights in the expanse of the heavens (v. 14) and subsequently we read of the actual act of creation: "God made two great lights" (v. 16). However, when God assigns their places (v. 17), this assignment belongs to God's governing His creation and so is part of God's providence. With the creation of the animals, similar observations can be made. God's command "let the waters abound with an abundance of living creatures" (v. 20) is followed by God's act of creating them. "So God created great sea creatures and every living thing that moves, with which the waters abounded" (v. 21). After this act of creation is noted, we read that "God blessed them, saying, 'Be fruitful and multiply, and fill the waters in the seas'" (v. 22). This passage speaks of God's providence by which He ensures the continuation of what He created. Likewise with the creation of man, God first declared His intent to create man and then He actually did so. He subsequently ensured the continuation of the human race by providential means (vv. 26–28). Thus Genesis 1 distinguishes between God's works of creation and providence. At the same time, it is clear that one cannot separate creation from providence. From the moment something was created, God upheld His creation. Without God's work of providence, nothing could exist. He upholds and governs all things (Neh 9:6; Acts 17:25, 28). But the specific work of creation had come to an end by the sixth day. It is not ongoing. "By the seventh day God had finished the work he had been doing; so on the seventh day he rested from all his work" (Gen. 2:2 NIV).[33]

But if God's work of creation is finished and separate from providence, why does Scripture speak of God's work of creating beyond the creation week of Genesis 1? Stek, in defense of his combining creation and providence in the verb "to create" (*bārā'*), has raised this precise point. He correctly pointed to the fact that the verb "to create," which occurs in Genesis 1, elsewhere in Scripture can include the meaning of providence. He thus defends his point that

---

31. A point also made by Gootjes, "Is Creation the Same as Providence?," 243.
32. For what follows, see Gootjes, "Is Creation the Same as Providence?," 243–46.
33. For this translation, see chapter 9 below.

God created by providential means.[34] We need to consider some of the biblical passages used to support this notion.

Texts that Stek mentions include the following: "This will be written for the generation to come, that a people yet to be created may praise the LORD" (Ps. 102:18). "You [the LORD] send forth Your Spirit, they [the creatures] are created; and You renew the face of the earth" (Ps. 104:30). In the context of Isaiah's speaking of the LORD as Israel's creator (Isa. 43:1, 15), Isaiah writes, "Thus says the LORD who made you and formed you from the womb" (Isa. 44:2). Stek then notes that the creating work of God mentioned in these passages takes place by providential means. Creatures and humans are propagated by sexual means. Thus God creates new generations. Could this usage of "create" not indicate that God also used the "normal" means provided in His providential care to create the current world over long periods of time? God is even said to "create" the wind (Amos 4:13). We know that air movement has natural causes through the laws of nature that God has given in His providential care. Yet the term "create" is used. Does this not suggest that "create" in Genesis 1 should be understood as God using providential means to make the world?[35]

In reflecting on these issues, several things need to be distinguished. In order to determine the meaning of a word, we need to take into consideration the context in which it is used. In Genesis 1 the context clearly indicates that when the verb "create" is employed, something that did not exist before was called into being, such as the heavens and the earth, the sea creatures, and human beings (Gen. 1:1, 21, 27). However, in the passages dealing with providence mentioned above, Scripture does not use the verb "to create" the way it is used in Genesis 1. Rather, these passages speak of reproducing what had already existed, such as future generations of humans who are conceived and born of human parents by normal, divinely ordained means. Now, it is not right to take the meaning of "create" as used in Psalms 102, 104, and Isaiah 44 and to read that particular meaning back into Genesis 1 so that the word "create" becomes loaded with two separate meanings—creation of the very first animal or man and the reproduction of new life by providential means from existing entities. James Barr warned about loading different meanings on a single term in a given context and called it "illegitimate totality transfer."[36] You cannot have

---

34. Stek, "What Says the Scripture?," 213–16, 246–50.
35. For the above, see Stek, "What Says the Scripture?," 213–16.
36. James Barr, *The Semantics of Biblical Language* (London: Oxford University Press, 1961), 218, 222.

all the uses or aspects of a meaning of a word actualized in a concrete occurrence of that word.

So why does Scripture use the term "to create" outside the creation narrative? In other words, why use the term "create" for what is properly understood as part of God's providence? We need to realize, of course, that although God's works of creation and providence should be clearly distinguished and not confused, these works are closely related to each other. The moment after each work of God's creation was finished, His work of providence, of causing His work of creation to persist in its existence, took over. The Reformed *Synopsis of a Purer Theology* (1620–1624) noted with regard to providence that "this power prevents created things from falling back into nothing, which would happen if God were to withdraw his strength."[37]

Another voice from the past that can be mentioned is the Heidelberg Catechism, which has appropriately defined "providence" as God's "almighty and ever present power, whereby, as with His hand, He still upholds heaven and earth and all creatures, and so governs…all things."[38] After surveying the pervasive and thorough activity of the work of God's providence, Herman Bavinck even noted that "providence as an activity of God is as great, all-powerful, and omnipresent as creation; it is a continuous or continued creation. The two are one single act and differ only in structure." He then hastened to emphasize that "creation and providence are not identical. If providence meant a creating anew every moment, creatures would also have to be produced out of nothing every moment. In that case, the continuity, connectedness, and 'order of causes' would be totally lost, and there would be no development or history."[39] So, when providence is described as "continuous creation" in Reformed theology, this means that "the same power of God is at work in both creation and providence."[40]

And that is probably the central point. When Scripture uses the term "to create" to describe what we would classify under providence, it is really emphasizing that God's ongoing power in maintaining creation is no less powerful or wonderful than His work of creation at the beginning of time. The Hebrew language can express an ongoing process by using participles. So the truth of God's ongoing power in continuing to uphold creation can be expressed with the use of Hebrew participles of verbs describing God's creative activity. For example,

---

37. Dolf te Velde, ed., Riemer A. Faber, trans., *Synopsis Purioris Theologiae. Synopsis of a Purer Theology. Latin Text and English Translation*, vol. 1 (Leiden: Brill, 2015), 269, 271.

38. Heidelberg Catechism 27, in Canadian Reformed Churches, *Book of Praise*, 525–26.

39. Bavinck, *Reformed Dogmatics*, 2:606–7.

40. Gootjes, "Is Creation the Same as Providence?," 236–37.

the first part of Isaiah 42:5, which contains three Hebrew participles, can literally be translated, "Thus says God, the LORD, creating the heavens and the stretcher of them, and the spreader of the earth." This can be correctly rendered in the past tense since God's work of creation has been completed: "Thus says God, the LORD, who created the heavens and stretched them out, who spread forth the earth." Yet the use of the Hebrew participles has a purpose, here and in other similar places (like Zech. 12:1). In the words of E. J. Young, "The participles express not only the original act of creation but also the creative power of God as exercised in the continued existence of His works."[41] God exercises this ongoing creative power, which we understand as providence, through His word.

God's powerful works of creation and providence, exercised by His word, are beautifully and profoundly both distinguished and brought together in Hebrews 1:2–3, which says that God created the world through the Son, who is "upholding all things by the word of His power." We find the same relationship between creation and providence in Colossians 1:16–17: "By Him [God's Son] all things were created that are in heaven and that are on earth, visible and invisible, whether thrones or dominions or principalities or powers. All things were created through Him and for Him. And He is before all things, and in Him all things consist." And so the Father and the Son not only worked together to create all things, but they also work together to sustain and uphold everything that was made.

In conclusion, there is no biblical justification to say that God created by providential means. God's work of providence needs to be distinguished from His work of creation. Nevertheless, the two are closely related, and as we will see in more detail when discussing the days of the creation week, God's providence is not absent from His work of creation either. But God did not call into being new life or entities by providence, but by His word of command.

Does Genesis 1 Describe Creation through Analogies with Providence?

If we are to distinguish creation and providence and to maintain that God did not create by way of ongoing providence, can we nevertheless hold that God described His work of creation in Genesis 1 by using analogies with providence? Vern Poythress proposes that "correlations between creation and providence help us to understand the meaning of details in Genesis 1."[42] One guiding prin-

---

41. Edward J. Young, *Isaiah*, 3:117.
42. Poythress, *Interpreting Eden*, 140; found in an earlier form in Vern S. Poythress, "Correlations with Providence in Genesis 1," *WTJ* 77 (2015): 71.

ciple is that "Genesis 1 shows interest not only in the events of creation but in their later effects."[43] This is a sound guideline since, as we saw above, Genesis 1 does indeed also speak of God's providence. A second guiding principle is that "God's description of his creative works in Genesis 1 instructs the Israelites through analogies with providence."[44] In other words, God revealed His work of creation by using analogies with what Israel was already familiar with through God's providence in creation. This guideline deserves a closer look.

Poythress correctly affirms that Genesis 1 uses "nontechnical language, such as is suitable to address everyone."[45] "The language of Genesis describing the world of nature is characteristically 'phenomenal language,' language describing how things appear to ordinary people." Accordingly, "it does not postulate any particular scientific cosmology." For example, "it does not 'theorize' about what the sun is made of or how far away it is."[46]

Having established that Genesis 1 uses the language of everyday life, Poythress suggests that God instructed Israel about creation using analogies. In other words, Israel was told about creation in terms they could understand and according to phenomena they were familiar with in God's providence. For example, when commenting on "the deep" in Genesis 1:2, Poythress notes that it is "a large mass analogous to the seas that we experience providentially." With respect to "the waters" in the same verse, he writes that we are not informed as to the chemical composition. "It is *analogous* to a sea, but the account does not go into details as to what are all the points of analogy."[47] So far so good.

But what if this use of analogy could distort or limit the message of Genesis 1? For example, on the creation of light, Poythress comments: "The appearance of light in creation is analogous to the providential experience of seeing light beginning to dawn after the night. Thus, we might translate 'light' as 'daylight.' Genesis 1:3 is not discussing light in a technical scientific way—for example, as electromagnetic radiation. It is saying that the coming of light on the first day is like the coming of daylight that we experience within God's providential order at the beginning of a new day."[48]

When we reflect on these statements, the question arises whether we are not in danger of limiting the meaning of the text and seeing it too much through

---

43. Poythress, *Interpreting Eden*, 140.
44. Poythress, *Interpreting Eden*, 143.
45. Poythress, "Correlations with Providence in Genesis 1," 71.
46. Poythress, *Interpreting Eden*, 133; also see Poythress, "Correlations with Providence in Genesis 1," 73.
47. Poythress, *Interpreting Eden*, 146.
48. Poythress, *Interpreting Eden*, 148.

human eyes by suggesting the analogy of daylight as we experience it at the dawn of a new day. Does calling the "light" of Genesis 1 "daylight" as we experience it at dawn not do injustice to the text? The light of verse 3 was clearly light without the sun, which had not yet been created. There was no gradual lightening of the sky on the horizon as at daybreak. This was a sudden glorious manifestation of light that came into being on God's command: "'Let there be light'; and there was light." This has no analogy in providence and it is not helpful to press the creation of light into an analogical mold lest we distort the text's meaning by considering it only from the standpoint of our present experiences.

All of this raises a larger question. While Poythress correctly underlines that the language used in the creation account is the language of everyday life, are we not taking the matter a step too far by suggesting that we can actually understand what is going on by analogous thinking? By using analogy as a tool for understanding, are we not in danger of imposing a meaning on the text that cannot be biblically justified? God's work of creating and calling into being that which did not exist is unique and totally unlike anything we experience providentially.

The danger of trying to understand Genesis 1 through the rigorous use of analogy is also seen when Poythress discusses the order of creation. He notes that

> an ordinary ancient reader of Gen 1 can observe a natural order in quite a few of the events. (1) The narrative introduces the earth at an early point. If Gen 1:1 describes early events, as I think it does, and is not merely a title, the earth in v. 2 is not necessarily the very first thing to be created in chronological order. The narrative starts there at an early point because it intends to provide an explanation for ordinary people, and this explanation will use analogies from providence. In providence human beings must have a place from which to observe. The story of creation, as analogous to providence, provides for the earth at an early point. As a sparse account, it leaves out details concerning events that may have occurred prior to the creation of the earth.[49]

Poythress continues with light, which comes next, "because in providence light is necessary if a human observer is to appreciate any of the rest of the events. Likewise, in creation, as analogous to providence, light is introduced early."[50] The other acts of creation are dealt with in a similar manner from the

---

49. Poythress, "Correlations with Providence in Genesis 1," 94; similarly, Poythress, *Interpreting Eden*, 268.

50. Poythress, "Correlations with Providence in Genesis 1," 94; similarly, Poythress, *Interpreting Eden*, 268.

perspective of the ordinary person who would see a correlation between the order of creation and his experience of providence.

Questions arise about this approach. Is what is recorded in Genesis 1 historically what actually happened in that order, or is this narrative arranged to reflect and to be analogous to providential priorities and conditions as perceived by any human today? Tensions exist here, and it seems that Poythress is leaning toward the latter. As the quote above indicates, the earth may not necessarily have been created first but is mentioned first because that would be the logical point for human beings to start, for they need a place from which to observe. Also, when discussing the division of waters, Poythress suggests that the vertical division between the waters above and below on the second day could logically be expected to come before the horizontal division of the waters on the third day, based on the more fundamental providential role the waters above play compared to those on the earth.[51] But the text gives no indication that the order of creation is based on human expectation of what ought to receive priority. Rather, the clear message of the text is that one event follows the other. In the end, Poythress concludes that "Genesis 1 does include a sense of progression and a chronological order. The use of successive numbers for each day confirms this order. But that does not mean that it cannot also, as a sparse account, stick to the main points and group together created objects of one kind for topical simplicity…. The events come basically in chronological order."[52] This is hardly a clear or robust recognition that the events of God's work of creation did indeed follow each other in the historical order as given in Genesis 1. This lack of clarity results from reading Genesis 1 with an over-emphasis on the analogies between creation and providence. This approach is not convincing.

Summary and Conclusions

God alone is eternal and He brought into being all things. He alone is able to inform us of the origin of the heavens and the earth. We therefore need to accept His account as historically accurate. The verb "to create" means "to bring something into being." The notion that "create" means "to give an existing

---

51. Poythress, *Interpreting Eden*, 268; similarly, Poythress, "Correlations with Providence in Genesis 1," 94.

52. Poythress, *Interpreting Eden*, 270–71. Initially, the first part of his conclusion read that the text "does include a sense of progression and some chronological order." Poythress, "Correlations with Providence in Genesis 1," 95.

entity a function" is to be rejected. It is based on dubious grounds, creates false dilemmas, and tends to deny that God created from nothing.

The verb "to create" as such does not tell us how God created or what processes were involved. However, in the larger context of Genesis 1 and the entire Scripture, He informs us that He created by His word of command, indeed by the Word, His eternal Son, and also with the Holy Spirit. Creation is the work of the triune God—Father, Son, and Holy Spirit.

God's work of creation in the beginning, by which He brought all things into being, needs to be distinguished from His work of providence whereby He sustains all of creation. When the verb "to create" is used of God's work of providence, the point is made that the same power of God is at work both in His work of creation at the beginning and in His subsequent sustaining of creation. His work of providence is no less wonderful than His work of creation at the beginning.

Lastly, the idea that correlations between creation and providence help us to understand the meaning of details in Genesis 1 has very limited applicability, is not very helpful, and can call into question the historical order of the creation events.

7

"The Heavens and the Earth" and Cosmology

"In the beginning God created the heavens and the earth. The earth was without form, and void" (Gen. 1:1–2a). We have concluded in previous chapters that God's work of creation began on the first day at the very beginning of time with the creation of the heavens and the earth and that the earth at that point was "without form, and void," that is, not yet suitable for human habitation.

We now need to consider a bit more closely what exactly the phrase "the heavens and the earth" entails within the context of Genesis 1 and 2, as well as in the Scriptures as a whole. Next, we will consider whether Genesis 1, in speaking of the expanse and waters above and below, teaches a normative biblical cosmology; whether it simply reflects the cosmological notions of the time; or whether it describes God's work of creating in terms understandable for those living on earth. What view of the universe does biblical revelation give us, and how does it impact our understanding of the Genesis creation account?

The Phrase "the Heavens and the Earth" and Its Biblical Context

It is important at the outset to remind ourselves of what was noted in chapters 1 and 2, namely, that in revealing His work of creation, the LORD used the language of our everyday experience. To put it differently, God's work of creation is described using geocentric expressions. The vocabulary and phrases used are understandable to us who live on Planet Earth. This fact is also evident in the phrase used to describe what God did at the beginning of the first day. He created "the heavens (šāmayim) and the earth ('ereṣ)" (Gen. 1:1; 2:1, 4). English translations of this phrase elsewhere in Scripture can also simply render the Hebrew as "heaven and earth."

From the vantage point of someone living on earth, the expression "the heavens and the earth" can readily be understood as encompassing everything. God created all that we see. Indeed, the phrase is widely understood as a merism, a literary device using opposites or extremes to indicate totality. In the context of Scripture as a whole, this expression therefore refers to the entire universe as we now know and experience it. God is the one who made "heaven and earth," that is, everything (Ex. 20:11; 31:17; 2 Kings 19:15; Jer. 32:17).

The context of Genesis 1:1 ("In the beginning God created the heavens and the earth") is of course unique since this passage refers to the very beginning of creation when God called the universe into being. He had not yet transformed the heavens and the earth into their present form. The phrase "the heavens and the earth" cannot therefore refer to the organized cosmos that we can see today. It designates "the universe as first created out of nothing in the initial, essential state and form in which God was pleased to have it appear as the first step in his work of creation."[1] We can therefore expect continuity between the phrase "the heavens and the earth" and what follows in Genesis 1. The earth that is mentioned in verse 1 is described in verse 2 as it was on the first day of God's creation week—a formless and empty entity that included "the deep" (təhôm) and "waters." On the third day of creation, God made a separation of what was without form and void by gathering the waters under the heavens into one place so that the dry land appeared, which God now called the earth (Gen. 1:10). It is this more restricted meaning of the term "earth" that is subsequently used in the creation account.

There is also continuity with the word for "heaven(s)." Given the geocentric orientation of God's revelation of His creation work as it is visible to us, it is unsurprising that we are not *specifically* informed about the creation of heaven as God's dwelling place, although as part of creation it is de facto included in the creation account of verse 1.[2] The focus in Genesis 1 is on preparing the earth for human beings to dwell in. The term "heaven" in verse 1 is used again, but this time in a more narrow sense when used as a name for the expanse that God created on the second day.[3] "God called the expanse Heaven" (v. 8 ESV). Since the vocabulary used in Genesis 1 is the language of our everyday experience, many translations render the Hebrew word for "heaven" as "sky" in verse 8 and elsewhere (vv. 9, 14, 15, 17, 20) or as "air" (vv. 26, 28, 30). One should, however, be aware that the Hebrew original (šāmayim) is the same in each instance. There is thus continuity in all these passages with verse 1. What we perceive as heaven is further in view when God sets the luminaries in the heavens (v. 17).

---

1. Lawrenz and Jeske, *Genesis 1–11*, 37–38.
2. We will return to the idea of heaven as God's home in the Appendix.
3. Gispen, *Genesis*, 1:54.

In spite of the fact that Genesis 1 uses the language of our everyday experience, some of the expressions in this chapter, including the phrase "the heavens and the earth" have raised the question whether the text is setting forth a specific biblical cosmology and if so, whether this cosmology is still valid for our age with its knowledge of space travel and the modest place of the earth in the universe.

Does Genesis Provide a Biblical Cosmology?

A cosmology, for the purpose of this discussion, is a description of the structure of the universe. Mainstream Old Testament scholarship on the whole assumes and presupposes that the biblical text, in its description of the universe, largely reflects the views of the surrounding ancient Near Eastern cultures. Genesis thus presents a view of the cosmos that is antiquated and inaccurate for readers today who have access to scientific advances in astronomy and related fields. As a result, Scripture is not a reliable source of accurate information about the cosmos, and thus it cannot be used in any way when dealing with scientific issues. One result of such thinking is that Scripture only conveys theological truth. As Galileo, quoting Cardinal Baronius, famously put it, "Scripture tells us how to go to heaven, not how the heavens go."[4]

Others utilize Scripture's descriptions that relate in some way to the cosmos to construct what is then presented as a biblical cosmology. For example, there are those who hold that Scripture teaches a cosmology that puts the earth in a fixed position near or at the center of the universe. Since the infallible Word of God teaches this geocentric view, it must be accepted as a reality and scientific fact. It is divine truth.[5]

Common to both these scenarios is the assumption that the Bible teaches us a cosmology. The first example suggests that Genesis gives us a flawed ancient Near Eastern cosmology. The second example insists that the Bible presents a normative cosmology that we must embrace. But does Genesis set forth a

---

4. For an overview of cosmological views and Galileo, see Byl, *God and the Cosmos*, 15–35, esp. 33; for the view that theological truth and not historicity is central in Genesis 1, see, e.g., Walton, *Lost World of Genesis One*, 16–22, 142–51; Robin Routledge, *Old Testament Theology: A Thematic Approach* (Downers Grove, Ill.: IVP Academic, 2008), 130–31. Denis Lamoureux goes as far as stating, "*Holy Scripture makes statements about how God created the heavens that in fact never happened.*" Denis O. Lamoureux, "No Historical Adam: Evolutionary Creation View," in *Four Views on the Historical Adam*, ed. Matthew Barrett and Ardel B. Caneday (Grand Rapids: Zondervan, 2013), 54 (italics in the original).

5. E.g., Gerardus D. Bouw, *Geocentricity* (Cleveland: Association for Biblical Astronomy, 1992); for a critique, see Danny R. Faulkner, "Geocentrism and Creation," *Journal of Creation* 15, no. 2 (2001): 110–21; cf. Byl, *God and the Cosmos*, 202–4.

cosmology, a definitive view of the structure of the universe? That is the central issue. We need to take a closer look at the biblical evidence, beginning with the biblical phrase "heaven and earth" (Gen. 1:1) and how it relates to ancient Near Eastern culture. This will be followed by looking at other elements in Genesis 1 and in Scripture elsewhere.

The Heavens and the Earth

Scholars suggest that the phrase "the heavens and the earth" indicates a universe composed of two parts. Such a bipartite understanding of the universe is also found in ancient Near Eastern myths. Similarly, the tripartite expression "heavens...earth...sea" (Ex. 20:11) or "heaven...earth...water" (Ex. 20:4; Deut. 5:8) is said to reflect a three-level understanding of the cosmos that is also found in the ancient world contemporary with Israel.[6] In the course of the next few sections we will try to determine what the Old Testament actually teaches with respect to cosmology.

On the assumption that the Old Testament is indebted for its worldview to that of Israel's neighbors, scholars have reconstructed an Old Testament cosmology, which is often diagrammed and printed.[7] G. Bartelmus has provided a typical description of heaven that many scholars today would agree is a fair representation of the biblical view: "Heaven is a solid vault (Ps 19:2[1]), which keeps the waters of chaos above and beside it from invading the cosmos (Gen 1:6–8; Ps 148:4). To it are attached as lights the sun, moon, and stars (Gen 1:14–17). It has openings through which the waters of chaos can once more invade the world during the deluge (Gen 7:11; 8:2...). According to 2 Sam 22:8 and Job 26:11, this enormous bell-shaped firmament rests on a foundation (pillars...), as do the earth (Ps 75:4[3]...) and the mountains (Ps 18:8[7])."[8]

The earth as dry land stands in the middle of this three-story cosmos. Beneath the earth lies the primal ocean, which also surrounds everything "so

---

6. Othmar Keel, *The Symbolism of the Biblical World: Ancient Near Eastern Iconography and the Book of Psalms*, trans. Timothy J. Hallett (Winona Lake, Ind.: Eisenbrauns, 1997), 26–47; Tsumura, *Creation and Destruction*, 58–72.

7. E.g., Owen C. Whitehouse, "Cosmogony," in *A Dictionary of the Bible*, ed. James Hastings (New York: Charles Scribner's Sons, 1908), 1:503; Kyle Greenwood, *Scripture and Cosmology: Reading the Bible between the Ancient World and Modern Science* (Downers Grove, Ill.: IVP Academic, 2015), 26; Routledge, *Old Testament Theology*, 131. More examples can be found in M. J. Paul, *Oorspronkelijk: overwegingen bij schepping en evolutie* (Apeldoorn: Labarum Academic, 2017), 81–90.

8. G. Bartelmus, "*šāmayim*," *TDOT* 15:211.

that the cosmos is represented as neither more nor less than a 'water-tight chamber' amid the waters of chaos, delimited by heaven and earth."[9]

But how credible is this reconstruction of an Old Testament cosmology? First, we should note that no complete image or drawing of an ancient Israelite conception of the world has ever been found.[10] The modern diagrams purporting to be a representation of such a view are simply reconstructions as envisaged by modern scholars.

Second, the accuracy and adequacy of the typical ancient Near Eastern cosmological diagram set forth today has been seriously criticized. Othmar Keel and Silvia Schroer have, for example, argued that

> people in the ancient Near East did not conceive of the earth as a disk floating on water with the firmament inverted over it like a bell jar, with the stars hanging from it. They knew from observation and experience with handicrafts that the lifting capacity of water is limited and that gigantic vaults generate gigantic problems in terms of their ability to carry dead weight. The textbook images that keep being reprinted of the "ancient Near Eastern world picture" are based on typical modern misunderstandings that fail to take into account the religious components of ancient Near Eastern conceptions and representations.[11]

Keel and Schoer have therefore come up with their own diagram in which the presence of Yahweh is acknowledged as the one who sustains the universe by His power and wisdom.[12] Assyrian specialist Wilfred G. Lambert "could find no evidence that the Mesopotamians believed in a hard-domed heaven."[13] Focusing only on the heavens, Wayne Horowitz has noted that "although the clear sky seems to us to be shaped like a dome, rather than a flat circle, there is no direct evidence that ancient Mesopotamians thought the visible heavens to be a dome."[14]

Third, in weighing the credibility of the typical ancient Near Eastern cosmological reconstruction, it should be noted that there is no single ancient Near Eastern cosmology. Different peoples envisaged the cosmos in different

---

9. Bartelmus, "*šāmayim*," 212.

10. Othmar Keel and Silvia Schroer, *Creation: Biblical Theologies in the Context of the Ancient Near East*, trans. Peter T. Daniels (Winona Lake, Ind.: Eisenbrauns, 2015), 83.

11. Keel and Schroer, *Creation*, 78.

12. Keel and Schroer, *Creation*, 83–84.

13. As noted and documented in Randall W. Younker and Richard M. Davidson, "The Myth of the Solid Heavenly Dome," in Gerald A. Klingbeil, *Genesis Creation Account*, 33.

14. Wayne Horowitz, *Mesopotamian Cosmic Geography* (Winona Lake, Ind.: Eisenbrauns, 1998), 264.

ways. Keel and Schroer note that "ancient Near Eastern images are concep-
tual, not photographic. They combine aspects of (empirical) experience of
the world and worldly outlook."[15] Thus Mesopotamians conceived the world
differently from Egyptians. There is, for example, little commonality between
what is called the "The Babylonian Map of the World" (9th c. BC) and the
Egyptian representation of the world with the sky goddess, Nut, bending pro-
tectively over the world disk (4th c. BC, but related to a much older tradition).[16]
Furthermore, even within the main ancient Near Eastern cultures there were
significant differences in how the universe was conceived.[17]

Fourth, the assumption that Israel's worldview is indebted to that of their
pagan neighbors is too simplistic. There may appear to be some superficial
commonalities in how the world is pictured, but as Gerhard Hasel has pointed
out, the account of Genesis 1 "represents not only a 'complete break' with the
ancient Near Eastern mythological cosmologies but represents a parting of the
spiritual ways brought about by a conscious and deliberate antimythical polemic
which means an undermining of the prevailing mythological cosmologies."[18]

Fifth, the images of ancient Near Eastern cosmology visualized for the biblical text fail to adequately account for the fact that Scripture's descriptions of
the cosmos are using the language of empirical observation. One can argue that
the notion of three levels—the heavens, the earth, and the waters below—is the
result of common human perception of the world. Could such a perception not
lead to the use of metaphors that are not meant to be photographically pictured?

In conclusion, there is insufficient evidence for using the phrase "heaven
and earth" as the basis of a biblical cosmology. There are, however, not a few
who push the notion that Scripture teaches that heaven is a solid vault. We need
to consider the evidence.

Is Heaven a Solid Vault?

Those who, like Paul Seely, think that Israel's cosmology owes much to the neighboring culture of the ancient Near East point especially to what is considered
the biblical picture of the heaven or sky being a solid vault or dome. Since we

---

15. Keel and Schroer, *Creation*, 79–80.

16. Horowitz, *Mesopotamian Cosmic Geography*, 20–42, esp. 21; Keel and Schroer, *Creation*,
79–80.

17. Gerhard F. Hasel and Michael G. Hasel, "The Unique Cosmology of Genesis 1 against
Ancient Near Eastern and Egyptian Parallels," in Gerald A. Klingbeil, *Genesis Creation Account*,
15–16.

18. Gerhard F. Hasel, "The Polemic Nature of the Genesis Cosmology," *EvQ* 46 (1974): 91;
also Currid, *Against the Gods*, 44–46.

today know that this is not so, Seely draws the conclusion that the Bible teaches a faulty cosmology. According to him, the purpose of Genesis 1:7 is to reveal God as the Creator and not to endorse the ordinary opinion of men that is reflected in the erroneous cosmology of Genesis 1.[19] In response, a number of things need to be said.

As noted in the previous section, there was no single cosmology in the ancient Near East and no proof that the ancients considered the visible heavens to be a solid dome. Thus this line of argument does not convince. What is more important is the biblical evidence adduced as proof that the Bible teaches heaven to be a solid vault.

The word at the center of the discussion is the Hebrew noun *rāqîaʿ*. Two older, classic dictionaries have translated this term as "extended surface, (solid) expanse" and "the beaten metal plate, or bow; firmament, the firm vault of heaven."[20] The most recent authoritative lexicon has given the more objective translation of "firmament, expanse of the sky, vault of heaven." There is no dispute about the verbal root (*rqʿ*). It means "to trample, hammer out, spread out."[21] The verb can mean "to stamp" (in protest or joy, Ezek. 6:11; 25:6) or "to trample" (the enemy, 2 Sam. 22:43). It can also denote "to spread out," and is then used of hammering out gold leaf for the high priestly ephod (Ex. 39:3). By hammering the gold, it would become thinner and thinner and could so be readily used for making threads. The verb is also used metaphorically of the LORD spreading out the earth, which is paralleled with stretching out the heavens (Isa. 42:5; 44:24), and of spreading out the skies in times of drought so that they are "strong as a cast metal mirror" (Job 37:18).

Although the verb *rqʿ* in Job 37:18 functions in a comparison with metal, it is noteworthy that the noun *rāqîaʿ* as such is never identified with a solid. It is consistently used of that which God created on the second day. To determine what that was, we need to let Scripture speak. When we check all the passages using this term, it is striking that there is no instance of this noun being used to designate a giant solid dome sitting on the earth. This fact alone should caution us against speaking of a biblical cosmology that viewed heaven as a solid vault. God called the *rāqîaʿ* ("firmament") "heaven" or "sky" (*šāmayim*) (Gen. 1:8). We can therefore understand the *rāqîaʿ* as the expanse of the sky (Gen. 1:6–8; Dan. 12:3). It is what God has spread out (*rqʿ*) (cf. Isa. 42:5). For someone looking up from earth to heaven, the expanse of the sky is also like the vault

---

19. Paul H. Seely, "The Firmament and the Water Above: Part 1," *WTJ* 53 (1991): 227–40.
20. See, respectively, BDB (1907), 956a and *HALOT* (original German 1967–1990), 1290.
21. *DCH* 7:552b–53a, 554b–55a (published in 2010).

or dome of heaven, understood metaphorically. Thus in a vision Ezekiel saw something that looked like a *rāqîaʿ*, an expanse. It was not the expanse; it only looked like it.[22] The context seems to indicate that what looked like the expanse was some sort of sparkling platform being held up by the four living creatures, above which was the likeness of God's throne (Ezek. 1:22, 23, 25, 26; 10:1).

Not surprisingly, considering the close relationship to heaven of the "firmament" or "expanse," which God also called "the sky" or "heaven" (Gen. 1:8), the phrase "the expanse (*rāqîaʿ*) of the heavens (*šāmayim*)" occurs in Genesis 1 as well (vv. 14, 15, 17, 20). That close bond between the expanse and heaven is also reflected in the parallelism of heaven (*šāmayim*) and the expanse of the sky (*rāqîaʿ*) in Psalm 19:1 (MT v. 2). We can conclude from God calling the "firmament" or "expanse" the "sky," and from the close relationship seen above, that when Scripture speaks of "heaven" with the sense of "sky," that is, heaven as visible to us, then the two terms are synonymous. In other words, when birds fly in the heaven (*šāmayim*), then we can consider them to fly in the expanse or "sky" (*rāqîaʿ*) (Deut. 4:17 NASB; "air," NKJV, ESV). From our perspective, birds fly against or across the expanse of the sky (Gen. 1:20).[23] Furthermore, since Genesis uses the language of our everyday experience and not scientific jargon, God can tell us that He put the lights in the sky (*rāqîaʿ*; Gen. 1:14–17), for that is how the sun, moon, and stars appear to us. From earth's vantage point the birds, sun, moon, and stars share the same "space," so to speak. The birds flying in the expanse and the lights being set in it are other indications that the (*rāqîaʿ*) was not a solid dome.[24]

One could sum up and say, as many commentaries conclude, that the *rāqîaʿ*, the firmament or expanse, is "the sky, the blue vault of heaven above us." It "includes not merely the lower heavens, or atmospheric sky, but the whole visible expanse up to and including the region of the fixed stars." There is no evidence that the expanse was ever conceived of as a solid dome in Scripture.[25] At the same time, as we look up into the heavens, the sky can appear as a

---

22. Contra Seely, "The Firmament: Part 1," 239; "Now over the heads of the living beings there was something like an expanse [*rāqîaʿ*], like the awesome gleam of crystal, spread out over their heads" (Ezek. 1:22 NASB).

23. Cassuto, *Genesis*, 49.

24. The above points argue against the notion of a solid dome as put forth in Seely, "The Firmament: Part 1," 237.

25. Lawrenz and Jeske, *Genesis 1–11*, 52. For further discussion, see Younker and Davidson, "Myth of the Solid Heavenly Dome," 47–52; and Aalders, *De Goddelijke openbaring*, 151–54.

dome. It is striking that Webster's dictionary's first definition of "heaven" is "the expanse of space that seems to be over the earth like a dome."[26]

If Scripture thus presents the expanse of the sky (*rāqîaʿ*) using the language of our perception and not as part of a biblical cosmology, what are we to make of the function of this expanse? Genesis 1:7 speaks of water above the firmament or the expanse of the sky. What does this mean? Is this also an indication of borrowing from a pagan cosmology, as has been suggested?

A Heavenly Sea?

"Then God said, 'Let there be a firmament in the midst of the waters, and let it divide the waters from the waters.' Thus God made the firmament, and divided the waters which were under the firmament from the waters which were above the firmament; and it was so" (Gen. 1:6–7).

Paul Seely, as so many others, has used this passage to argue that the idea of water above the firmament or expanse reflects an ancient Near Eastern concept of "a veritable sea located above a solid firmament which is in turn located above the sun, moon, and stars."[27] What are we to think of this? We have already seen that the expanse was not a solid firmament. Therefore, to suggest a physical heavenly ocean situated above a solid dome is out of the question. Since the biblical text is determinative, we need to focus on it.

First, to state the obvious, the purpose of the firmament was to separate the waters below from those above. That is the main point being communicated. Furthermore, as we have seen, God is not presenting a cosmology but a description of His work of creation in terms that we can understand and in a manner that aligns with our perception of reality. In other words, we need to consider carefully what the biblical text states without going beyond what is stated and "overloading" the meaning of the text with preconceived cosmological notions. This is especially important in this instance since we do not find the exact same wording respecting the relationship of the waters to the firmament or expanse anywhere else in Scripture.

Second, translating is interpreting, and it is not always easy for a translation to reflect precisely the intended meaning of the original. The question arises as to what exactly is meant by the Hebrew text translated "above," as in God separating the waters under the firmament "from the waters which were above the

---

26. Webster's Third New International Dictionary, Unabridged, s.v. "heaven," https://unabridged.merriam-webster.com.

27. Paul H. Seely, "The Firmament and the Water Above: Part 2," *WTJ* 54 (1992): 31. For the commonly accepted notion of waters above the heavens, see notes 6 and 7 above.

firmament" (Gen. 1:7). Normal Hebrew usage would suffice with ʿal to indicate "above," as in "above the expanse."[28] But here the word "above" renders a double Hebrew preposition (*mēʿal*) composed of "from" (*min*) and "above" (ʿal), thus literally "from above." This composite preposition is followed by *lǝ* "with respect to" (often not translated) and "firmament."[29] Thus literally we can translate, "the waters that were from above with respect to the firmament." In other words, what we have here is not simply a Hebrew word meaning "above." It is more complicated than that. The meaning is "from above" and thus not simply "above."[30] It is also noteworthy that the same construction (*mēʿal* plus *lǝ*) elsewhere conveys the meaning "beside" or "by" ("beside the incense altar," 2 Chron. 26:19). These considerations alert us to the possibility that the text does not mean that the waters were physically above the expanse of the sky. Indeed, one can understand the text to say that the waters were under and by the expanse (and not above it). Dutch Old Testament scholar G. Ch. Aalders was therefore justified in his translation, which stated that God made a separation "between the waters which were beneath the firmament and the waters which were above, at the firmament."[31] Since the passage uses the vocabulary of observation, the waters above, at the expanse, are clouds.

Third, this interpretation is confirmed by the fact that the position of clouds is described in a similar fashion elsewhere. The same composite preposition (*mēʿal*) used in Genesis 1:7 is also found in Psalm 148:4: "Praise Him, you heavens of heavens, and you waters above [*mēʿal*] the heavens." As just noted, the preposition used literally means "from above." Here it indicates direction of flow and not the position of the water above the heavens, and so a possible translation is "waters that descend from the heavens above,"[32] or one can think of a rain curtain coming down from heaven.[33] Another translation (of Ps. 148:4) is "let the highest heavens give Him praise; and the rain clouds which are in the skies."[34] In this connection it is notable that the Hebrew term

---

28. Rashi, *The Metsudah Chumash*, ed. Avrohom Davis (New York: Ktav, 1997–1998), 1:6n36.

29. Cf. BDB, 759a; *DCH* 6:397b–98a.

30. Each preposition within a composite preposition, as in Gen. 1:7, can retain its full force of meaning. GKC, §119d.

31. My translation of "tusschen de wateren die beneden het uitspansel zijn, en de wateren die boven bij de uitspansel zijn." Aalders, *De Goddelijke openbaring*, 198; also see Aalders, *Genesis*, 1:60; cf. Edward J. Young, *Studies in Genesis One*, 90n94.

32. Younker and Davidson, "Myth of the Solid Heavenly Dome," 53.

33. C. Houtman, *De hemel in het Oude Testament: een onderzoek naar de voorstellingen van het oude Israël omtrent de kosmos* (Franeker: Wever, 1974), 184.

34. The translation is by R. K. Harrison as given in Curtis Vaughan, ed., *The Old Testament Books of Poetry from 26 Translations* (Grand Rapids: Zondervan, 1973), 455.

for clouds is sometimes used in parallel with heaven; for example, "yet He commanded the clouds above, and opened the doors of heaven" (Ps. 78:23). This passage is a reminder that Old Testament Israel was well aware that the rain that came down from heaven did so by clouds shedding the moisture (Judg. 5:4; 2 Sam. 22:12; Job 36:27–29; Eccl. 11:3; Isa. 55:10).[35]

Fourth, in response to the objection that the expanse cannot possibly be the atmosphere around the earth with the clouds near the upper limit because God has set the sun, moon, and stars in this expanse (Gen. 1:14–17),[36] one must remember, as noted earlier, that Genesis 1 uses the language of human observation and experience. When we look up into the sky, we see not only the birds flying in it, but we also see the sun. The Hebrew term *rāqîaʿ* can be translated with a variety of terms, such as "firmament," "expanse," "sky," or "heaven." It is sufficiently flexible or nonspecific to include both the earth's atmosphere and what we call outer space. Also, when we read that the birds fly "across [ʿal] the face of the firmament of the heavens" (Gen. 1:20) this is how we perceive birds flying through the air.[37]

When we understand the firmament as the sky and the "waters from above the firmament" as rain-bearing clouds, that is, as waters that descend from the heavens above, then we deny that Genesis 1 is setting a biblical cosmology before us, and we affirm that God is communicating His incomprehensible work of creation in terms we can understand. Such an understanding of verse 7 is not new. Apart from those already mentioned, such diverse scholars as John Calvin, Rabbi J. H. Hertz, C. F. Keil, F. Delitzsch, H. C. Leupold, W. H. Gispen, Vern S. Poythress, and many others have held this view.[38]

Those who maintain that the text says that the waters are indeed above the expanse have made several choices in interpreting the text. First, those like Paul Seely will use it to affirm that the Genesis narrative shows indebtedness to ancient Near Eastern cosmology. We have seen that there is little basis in fact

---

35. A point made in great detail by Poythress, *Interpreting Eden*, 175–82; earlier published in Vern S. Poythress, "Rain Water Versus a Heavenly Sea in Genesis 1:6–8," *WTJ* 77 (2015): 184–89.

36. E.g., Kulikovsky, *Creation, Fall, Restoration*, 130.

37. See, e.g., Cassuto, *Genesis*, 49; Aalders, *Genesis*, 1:67. For the preposition, *DCH* 6:720b.

38. Calvin, *Genesis*, 1:80; J. H. Hertz, ed., *The Soncino Edition of the Pentateuch and Haftorahs*, 2nd ed. (repr., London: Soncino, 1961), 3; C. F. Keil, in Keil and Delitzsch, *Commentary on the Old Testament*, 1:33; Franz Delitzsch, *A New Commentary on Genesis*, trans. Sophia Taylor (repr., Minneapolis: Klock & Klock, 1978), 1:86–87; Leupold, *Exposition of Genesis*, 1:59–60; Gispen, *Genesis*, 1:53; Poythress, *Interpreting Eden*, 171–85; others include Wenham, *Genesis 1–15*, 19; and Kenneth A. Mathews, *Genesis 1–11:26* (Nashville: Broadman & Holman, 1996), 150.

to support the notion of a solid dome in the biblical account. Others have also come to this conclusion.[39]

Second, some have chosen to understand God's Word to teach that there are waters above the firmament, even today, although we cannot see them. So what does this mean? James Jordan has suggested that "those waters were taken up into the angelic heaven, where they form the sea of glass/ice/crystal" associated with the throne of God (Ezek. 1:22; Rev. 4:6).[40] However, although it is an intriguing suggestion, he gives no exegetical proof, and so this suggestion must be considered quite speculative. More in keeping with the lack of evidence are those who simply acknowledge that in their understanding of the text the waters are above the firmament and do not try to explain it, for such a circumstance is incomprehensible to us. Martin Luther, after saying that Moses wrote that there were waters above the firmament, stated, "Here I, therefore, take my reason captive and subscribe to the Word even though I do not understand it."[41] E. J. Young, in a similarly modest tone, simply noted the fact of waters above the expanse and did not try to explain it.[42] When you do try to figure it out, you run into all sorts of problems that the biblical text is unable to answer. This brings us to the third choice of those who affirm that there are waters above the expanse.

Those wishing to affirm a heavenly sea above the expanse can also try to explain this scientifically in the conviction that Scripture is here teaching something important to modern Christians. This approach has led to a number of scientific theories. At one time a popular hypothesis was that the waters above were an enormous canopy of water vapor extending high up into the atmosphere that would have been sufficient to supply rain for forty days and nights (Gen. 7:11–12). However, this theory has since been discredited.[43] Those seeking scientific data from Genesis 1:7 struggle to define what the expanse is. After all, the sun and moon are also in this expanse (Gen. 1:14–18). It would therefore, Andrew Snelling surmises, "seem logical to assume that the waters which God placed above the firmament must have been put beyond outer space at the limits of the universe. This is no easy matter to resolve scientifically." Similarly,

---

39. Most recently, Hasel and Hasel, "Unique Cosmology"; Younker and Davidson, "Myth of the Solid Heavenly Dome"; and Poythress, "Rain Water."

40. Jordan, *Creation in Six Days*, 230, also see 39, 100.

41. Luther, *Works*, 1:26.

42. Edward J. Young, *Studies in Genesis One*, 90.

43. For the theory, see Joseph C. Dillow, *The Waters Above: Earth's Pre-Flood Vapor Canopy*, 2nd ed. (Chicago: Moody, 1982); Lawrenz and Jeske, *Genesis 1–11*, 54–55. For an overview of the critique, see Douglas F. Kelly, *Creation and Change: Genesis 1.1–2.4 in the Light of Changing Scientific Paradigms*, rev. ed. (Fearn, U.K.: Mentor, 2017), 237–38.

as John Byl notes, putting the waters "beyond the observational horizon at least places the problem out of sight."[44] But all such speculation goes far beyond what Genesis 1 conveys.

Although everything the creation account relates is true, this information was not designed to carry the type of scientific details scientists are now trying to extract from it. As Geerhardus Vos noted many years ago, "Some want to give a hyperscientific exegesis that satisfies the latest perception and newest fashion. All sorts of theories from physics, geology, and astronomy have been projected onto the narrative…but it is bad exegesis."[45] When Calvin commented on what he thought were the waters above the heaven, he acknowledged that this appeared to be opposed to common sense. But he wrote, "To my mind, this is a certain principle, that nothing is here treated of but the visible form of the world. He who would learn astronomy, and other recondite arts, let him go elsewhere. Here the Spirit of God would teach all men without exception."[46] In other words, Genesis conveys God's truth according to how a typical human sees reality using the language of our observation. It was not written in the first place for astronomers. It does not give a biblical cosmology. It is therefore best to interpret the waters above simply as clouds for the reasons given earlier.

The expanse separated the waters above from those below (v. 7). We now need to turn to the latter.

The Waters Below

What were these waters "under the firmament"? Did they form part of a biblical cosmology, similar to that of the ancient Near Eastern cultures, which depicted the earth floating on a primal ocean?

The earliest description of the earth is that it was "without form, and void; and darkness was on the face of the deep [*təhôm*]. And the Spirit of God was hovering over the face of the waters [*hammāyim*]" (v. 2). "The deep" and "the waters" refer to the same liquid that initially covered the earth. On the second day, God separated "the waters from the waters" with the firmament (vv. 6–7). On the following day, "God said, 'Let the waters under the heavens be gathered together into one place, and let the dry land appear'; and it was so. And God called the dry land Earth, and the gathering together of the waters He called

---

44. Snelling, *Earth's Catastrophic Past*, 1:212; D. R. Humphreys, "A Biblical Basis for Creationist Cosmology," in *Proceedings of the Third International Conference on Creationism*, ed. R. E. Walsh (Pittsburgh: Creation Science Fellowship, 1994), 257; Byl, *God and the Cosmos*, 161.

45. Vos, *Reformed Dogmatics*, 1:162.

46. Calvin, *Genesis*, 1:79–80.

Seas [*yammîm*]" (vv. 9–10). What were these seas and how did they relate to the earth?

There are those who argue that verse 10 teaches that "the earth is a single continent in the shape of a flat, circular disk floating in the middle of a circular sea, which sea was thought to be the source of water for the earthly springs, wells and rivers." The basis for this conclusion is that Genesis 1 reflects these ancient, uniform views about the earth and sea. They were "the ordinary opinions of the writer's day" that were contemporary with Old Testament Israel. Since Paul Seely has argued the above-mentioned points in considerable detail, we will use his article in refuting these notions.[47] There are several problems with this approach.

First, Seely's conclusion is based on the unproven assumption that Genesis 1 reflects ancient cosmology. He simply assumes that words and concepts like "earth" and "seas" in Genesis 1 had the same meaning and connotations for Israel as they did in the neighboring civilizations whose cosmological beliefs he surveys. But Genesis 1 is not presenting a cosmology using terminology loaded with pagan mythological connotations. Genesis 1 is authoritative divine revelation in a historical narrative style that uses the language of normal human experience to tell how God created the world. It is therefore unique in the entire ancient Near East.[48] Indeed, scholars have suggested that the language of Genesis 1 specifically opposes mythological "creation" conceptions current in the ancient world. The word for "seas" (*yammîm*) has no connection with any purported Canaanite creation myth.[49] Gerhard Hasel has also shown that a term like the "deep" (*təhôm*) (v. 2) "lacks any mythological connotations which are part of the concept of 'primeval ocean' in ancient Near Eastern (Sumerian, Babylonian, Egyptian, Ugaritic) creation mythology." The term *təhôm* "is used in a non-mythical context, namely a 'historical' context with its different meaning and emphasis."[50] With respect to its general usage, Cornelis Houtman has noted that nowhere does the Old Testament expressly say that the deep (*təhôm*) is found under the earth or that the earth rests on it. Israelite usage of the term indicates that they did not localize the *təhôm* in a particular place but rather considered it to be a description of the power of water in its general manifestation as springs, rivers, lakes, and seas. The word *təhôm* gave expression to

47. The quotations are from Paul H. Seely, "The Geographical Meaning of 'Earth' and 'Seas' in Genesis 1:10," *WTJ* 59 (1997): 255.

48. On the genre of Gen. 1, see chapter 3 above.

49. Hasel and Hasel, "Unique Cosmology," 18; Tsumura, *Creation and Destruction*, 56.

50. Hasel, "Polemic Nature," 85; also see Tsumura, *Creation and Destruction*, 53–54; Tsumura, "Genesis and Ancient Near Eastern Stories," 31–32.

Israel's experience that water in its different manifestations is at bottom a unity. It is also a power that can be benevolent or hostile.[51] Now one could argue that in some places we could derive from the context that the *təhôm* can be seen as being below the surface of the earth; for example, prior to the Noachian flood, "the fountains of the great deep [*təhôm*] were broken up" (Gen. 7:11). Yet Houtman is correct with respect to the cosmological point he is making, and contrary to Seely's conclusion the Old Testament does not speak of *təhôm* as a deep sea below a floating earth.[52]

Second, Seely assumes that all ancient Near Eastern cultures had similar cosmological views. When he suggests that the terms for "earth" and "seas" in Genesis 1:10 were understood by the first readers as a flat earth-disk floating ("earth") on a circular body of water ("seas"), he backs up this contention by appealing to what he considers uniform Egyptian and Mesopotamian concepts that make this probable.[53] However, as mentioned earlier in this chapter, there was no uniform cosmological outlook. With respect to how the earth and sea were pictured, the notion of a single earth surrounded by water is, for instance, contradicted by a Mesopotamian drawing, dated to the ninth century BC or later, that appears to show islands or a distant land mass from the main continent. Other examples could be mentioned as well.[54]

Third, the biblical evidence adduced by Seely is not convincing. He claims that the usage of "earth" in Genesis 1:10 must be understood as the entire earth since this is the meaning of the term in verses 1 and 2. While one can agree that "earth" refers to all of terrestrial creation, an apparent mixture of water and land, as described in the first two verses of Genesis 1, Seely overlooks the fact that in verse 10 God specifically defined "earth" as the name given to dry land as opposed to the water, which He called "seas." The text gives no indication whether the earth is contiguous dry land, a single continent, as Seely assumes, or whether the dry land is distributed in continents and islands. Seely, however, argues that understanding the dry land as so distributed in continents and islands is contrary to the historical context of Genesis 1 and is thus reading into the text what is not there. After all, in his view, the first readers would probably have imagined a single earth-disk floating on a sea. This was their view of the

---

51. Houtman, *De Hemel*, 186. David Tsumura also noted that the term *təhôm* is "never treated as the third division of the tripartite cosmology in the Old Testament." Tsumura, *Creation and Destruction*, 69.

52. As concluded in Seely, "Geographical Meaning," 254.

53. Seely, "Geographical Meaning," 236, 246.

54. Horowitz, *Mesopotamian Cosmic Geography*, 20–42. On this example and others, including a critique of Seely's methodology, see Weeks, "Cosmology in Historical Context," 286–90.

dry land.[55] Such speculation is, however, an inadequate basis for Seely's position and also overlooks the fact that Genesis 1 is not presenting a cosmology. Furthermore, ancient Israel knew that besides the dry land they inhabited, there were also islands elsewhere (Isa. 11:11; 42:15; Ezek. 26:18).

Seely further holds that a phrase in the account of Nebuchadnezzar's dream supports his view of a flat earth since the tree in the vision was visible "to the ends of all the earth" (Dan. 4:11 [MT v. 8]). "The statement only makes sense if the earth is defined as a flat continent."[56] But, as E. J. Young comments, "the language [of Dan. 4:11] is hyperbolic, in keeping with the language of universality with which the Assyrian and Babylonian kings described their reigns."[57] Furthermore, if you do want to take the words of Nebuchadnezzar literally, then, as James Patrick Holding reminds us, this "passage is actually a statement by a pagan king, which doesn't mean that the Bible endorses that view. And it is a vision, and is therefore not intended to be a picture of reality."[58] Another passage Seely adduces is the LORD's questioning Job, in the course of which God says that the dawn takes hold of "the ends of the earth" (Job 38:13), which is literally "the skirts of the earth," and shakes off the wicked. Seely comments that this verse "is comparing the earth to a blanket or garment picked up at one end and shaken." Since you cannot do that with a spherical earth, the earth must have been flat. But this literalistic reading completely overlooks the beautiful imagery in this metaphor. The earth is compared to a tablecloth that is shaken to clear it of all impurities. "So the evil-doers who are active at night…are dispersed in the light of day."[59]

In an attempt to prove that Scripture teaches a cosmology of the earth floating on water as a flat circular disc, Seely also turns to a psalm of David wherein he praises the LORD's ownership of the earth, "for He has founded it upon the seas, and established it upon the waters" (Ps. 24:2), and to the psalmist who said that God "laid out the earth above the waters" (Ps. 136:6).[60] But, do these passages show that Israel thought that the earth floated on water? No. To read ancient Near Eastern cosmology into these passages is unwarranted. While there may be allusions in the vocabulary to pagan thinking, the psalmists have

---

55. Seely, "Geographical Meaning," 237.

56. Seely, "Geographical Meaning," 239; similarly, Greenwood, *Scripture and Cosmology*, 75.

57. Edward J. Young, *Daniel*, 102.

58. James Patrick Holding, "Is the 'Erets (Earth) Flat?," *Journal of Creation* 14, no. 3 (2000): 52.

59. Robert Gordis, *The Book of Job: Commentary, New Translation, and Special Studies* (New York: Jewish Theological Seminary of America, 1978), 445. For implications of a literalistic reading, see Holding, "Is the Earth Flat?," 52.

60. Seely, "Geographical Meaning," 250–52.

demythologized and depersonalized such language in extolling the Creator's greatness.[61] One should also note the difference between the earth floating on the sea (which is not indicated in the text) and being set upon the waters.[62] There is no evidence in Scripture that gives any credence to an ancient Near Eastern cosmological notion of the earth floating on water. What we do have is poetic language that portrays the earth as resting on the waters of creation.[63] A similar image of God spreading out the earth occurs in Isaiah 42:5 and 44:24. As E. J. Young sensibly observes on those passages, the Hebrew word for "spread" "is poetic and merely pictures the earth as it appears to the human eye."[64]

What about the use of terms together like "heavens...earth...sea" (Ex. 20:11) or "heaven...earth...water" (Ex. 20:4; Deut. 5:8)? Could these expressions not indicate a cosmological understanding of a tripartite, or three-layered, universe as is often said? We need to take a closer look.

Some passages simply list heaven, earth, and sea (e.g., Ex. 20:11; Ps. 146:6), but the second commandment goes into more detail and specifies not to make images of anything that is in "the water under the earth" (Ex. 20:4; Deut. 4:18; 5:8). What exactly does the phrase "under the earth" mean? At first glance such wording would appear to support the idea that under and around the earth is a world ocean. However, given the context, it would be more appropriate to see such wording, as Benno Jacob has noted, "as a reflection of the threefold *environment of all creatures.* They were respectively: the birds of the heavens, the animals of the earth, and the fish of the sea."[65] In other words, the waters referred to as being under the earth were visible to the Israelites and could therefore simply refer to seas, rivers, and springs, which are all physically lower than the land or earth adjacent to it. The usage of the Hebrew prepositional phrase translated "under" (*mittahat l*) elsewhere in geographical contexts supports this understanding. Rebekah's nurse was buried "below [lit. under] Bethel" (Gen. 35:8); the camp of Midian "was below [lit. under] him in the valley" (Judg. 7:8); the Philistines were pursued "as far as below [lit. under] Beth Car" (1 Sam. 7:11); the place Zarethan is "below [lit. under] Jezreel" (1 Kings 4:12). In all these cases

---

61. Craigie, *Psalms 1–50,* 212; Willem A. VanGemeren, "Psalms," in *The Expositor's Bible Commentary: Psalms, Proverbs, Ecclesiastes, Song of Songs,* ed. Frank E. Gaebelein (Grand Rapids: Zondervan, 1991), 221.

62. A point made by Holding, "Is the Earth Flat?," 54.

63. VanGemeren, "Psalms," 824.

64. Edward J. Young, *Isaiah,* 3:117. See also Aalders, *De Goddelijke openbaring,* 183–84; and Calvin on Ps. 24: Calvin, *Commentary on the Book of Psalms,* 1:403.

65. Benno Jacob, *The Second Book of the Bible: Exodus* (Hoboken, N.J.: Ktav, 1992), 548 (italics in the original).

the intent of the Hebrew "under" is not the rendering "underneath." Again, we are dealing with language of human perception.[66]

Those who see Scripture presenting a cosmology also contend that references such as those to "the pillars of the earth" (1 Sam. 2:8; also Ps. 75:3 [MT v. 4]) and "the foundations of the earth" (Isa. 24:18) indicate a subterranean body of water in which these pillars and foundations are established.[67] But such terminology in poetic passages hardly suffices as proof for a biblical cosmology since they can be understood most naturally metaphorically rather than literally. Even today we still speak of "pillars of the church," by which we refer not to physical attributes of the building but to strong supporters of the congregation.[68]

In light of the above we can conclude that Scripture does not present us with a cosmology that some in the ancient world held, namely, that the earth floated like a flat disk on a primal ocean.[69]

Conclusion and Consequences

We have examined the notion that Genesis 1 teaches a particular cosmology or an authoritative description of the structure of the universe that we should accept as normative today. We can conclude that this passage, and for that matter other passages often adduced, do not teach an authoritative cosmology.[70] Rather, what we have is God's work of creation being narrated using the language of observation in terms comprehensible to those who live on earth and who did not witness those enormous events at the beginning of time. This conclusion has several consequences.

---

66. Those agreeing that *mittaḥat l* has or can have the sense of "lower" rather than "under" in Ex. 20:4; Deut. 4:18; and 5:8 include Keil and Delitzsch, *Commentary on the Old Testament*, 1:396; Aalders, *De Goddelijke openbaring*, 184–85; John J. McGovern, "The Waters of Death," *CBQ* 21 (1959): 350–58; Houtman, *De hemel*, 187; Hasel and Hasel, "Unique Cosmology," 19.

67. E.g., Greenwood, *Scripture and Cosmology*, 78–80.

68. Hasel and Hasel, "Unique Cosmology," 19; For the Scripture references, see, e.g., Ralph W. Klein, *1 Samuel* (Waco, Tex.: Word, 1983), 18; David Toshio Tsumura, *The First Book of Samuel* (Grand Rapids: Eerdmans, 2007), 148; Marvin E. Tate, *Psalms 51–100* (Waco, Tex.: Word, 1990), 256; Edward J. Young, *Isaiah*, 2:175n68; Aalders, *De Goddelijke openbaring*, 187–88.

69. Similarly, Houtman, *De Hemel*, 188.

70. Those coming to this conclusion also include F. W. Grosheide, "Kan van een bijbelsch wereldbeeld worden gesproken?," *GTT* 28 (1927–1928): 17–34; Aalders, *De Goddelijke openbaring*, 199–200; Houtman, *De hemel*, 195; Paul, *Oorspronkelijk*, 111–12; R. Laird Harris, "The Bible and Questions of Cosmology," *Presb* 7 (1981): 200; C. John Collins, *Science and Faith: Friends or Foes?* (Wheaton, Ill.: Crossway, 2003), 100–102; Kulikovsky, *Creation, Fall, Restoration*, 95; also see Hasel and Hasel, "Unique Cosmology," 29.

Since Genesis 1 does not give a cosmology but simply narrates God's work of creation one day at a time, it is difficult to accept the characterization that G. K. Beale gives, namely, that "Genesis 1 is a cosmic temple building episode shot through with temple theology at every point. It is not an attempt to give an actual depiction of only visible reality but also of the invisible dimension, especially of God's heavenly temple." And, he continues, "the worldview of the Old Testament, especially Genesis 1 and 2, viewed the cosmos as a temple."[71] Now, one may claim to see allusions to temple building in Genesis 1 in the light of subsequent Scripture, but there is no evidence to affirm that Genesis 1 as it stands gives any reason for such a connection. Beale attempts to justify his position on the basis of the creation of the firmament or expanse (Gen. 1:6–8) but gives no proof from Genesis 1 for his statement that "*this expanse in Genesis 1 is associated in some integral manner with the notion of the cosmic temple, including perhaps the heavenly dimension of the temple.*"[72] The fact that later Scripture connects the likeness of an expanse with God's throne (Ezek. 1:22) does not justify concluding that when Genesis 1 speaks of the expanse it does so as part of temple imagery. The biblical text of Genesis 1 gives no evidence that the cosmos is pictured as a temple. As John Day puts it, such a conception of the cosmos on the basis of Genesis 1 "seems to be pure eisegesis," that is, reading one's own ideas into the text.[73] We should read and understand Genesis 1 within its own context and not import concepts found in later texts into what is considered the meaning of the narrative. It is an entirely different matter if we notice allusions to Genesis 1 and 2 in subsequent descriptions of the tabernacle or temple.[74]

With respect to the relationship of Genesis 1 to science, the fact that Genesis 1 does not give us a cosmology means that it neither affirms nor denies that the earth or the sun is at the center of the universe. In this connection it is also good to heed John Byl's note of caution with respect to current cosmological

---

71. See, respectively, Beale, *Erosion of Inerrancy*, 203 (also see 197); and G. K. Beale and Mitchell Kim, *God Dwells Among Us: Expanding Eden to the Ends of the Earth* (Downers Grove, Ill.: InterVarsity, 2014), 148; cf. S. Dean McBride Jr., "Divine Protocol: Genesis 1:1–2:3 as Prologue to the Pentateuch," in *God Who Creates: Essays in Honor of W. Sibley Towner*, ed. William P. Brown and S. Dean McBride Jr. (Grand Rapids: Eerdmans, 2000), 11–15.

72. Beale, *Erosion of Inerrancy*, 204 (italics in the original). For more on the notion of a cosmic temple, see chapter 10 below.

73. John Day, review of *Revisiting the Days of Genesis*, by B. C. Hodge, *JTS* 66 (2015): 693.

74. A similar point is made in Daniel I. Block, "Eden: A Temple? A Reassessment of the Biblical Evidence," in *From Creation to the New Creation: Biblical Theology and Exegesis. Essays in Honor of G. K. Beale*, ed. Daniel M. Gurtner and Benjamin L. Gladd (Peabody, Mass.: Hendrickson, 2013), 4–5, 18–21.

theories. "They are speculative, ad hoc, and not easily testable. Therefore, a large role is played by philosophical and religious beliefs, and Christians must not permit modern cosmology to unduly modify their religious beliefs."[75]

In response to those who would assume that Genesis 1 was written in terms of the science of that time, James Jordan correctly observes that "it would be better to assume that God inspired Genesis 1 in such a way that it is not written in terms of the science of any time, though it does not conflict with the true arrangement of the cosmos, rightly understood."[76] Indeed, as Geerhardus Vos taught his students in the late nineteenth century, "The creation narrative provides pure truth, but in such a general form that it can serve equally for the instruction of God's people in centuries past and His children at the present time. (The hyperscientific interpretation loses sight of that.) That is precisely what makes the creation narrative such a great artistic achievement of the Spirit of God."[77]

Because Genesis 1 does not provide a cosmology, Christian scientists who accept the historicity of Genesis 1 need to exercise care not to read more into the text than it states. On the one hand, the account can be trusted to give a sound chronological sequence of the events that took place at the beginning of time, and that basic information is important for science. On the other hand, one needs to recognize that Genesis 1 was not given for the purpose of enabling scientists to theorize and reconstruct exactly how God's creation work unfolded. This reality should cause us to be humble and very careful in making use of the historical information of Genesis 1 for the purpose of constructing scientific hypotheses. We need to remember the LORD's poignant words to Job: "Where were you when I laid the foundations of the earth? Tell Me, if you have understanding" (Job 38:4).

---

75. John Byl, "The Role of Belief in Modern Cosmology," in *Facets of Faith and Science*, ed. Jitse M. van der Meer vol. 3, *The Role of Beliefs in the Natural Sciences* (Lanham, Md.: University Press of America, 1996), 59. Byl discusses cosmologies that are compatible with Scripture in Byl, *God and the Cosmos*, 189–214.

76. Jordan, *Creation in Six Days*, 229.

77. Vos, *Reformed Dogmatics*, 1:162.

8

Days One through Six

Having covered some general issues relating to Genesis 1, we now need to build on the preceding chapters and consider each of the days of creation in turn. Of particular interest is understanding the events recorded in terms of their historicity and abiding significance for us today, including possible relevance for science. What Genesis 1 relates is true, and it is possible that what scientific theory affirms is not inconsistent with the simple straightforward account of creation. However, the task of the interpreter of Scripture is to listen to and try to understand the biblical text. Convergences with or implications for science can be noted, but the biblical text must always be the authoritative starting point. It is the abiding divine norm against which all hypotheses need to be evaluated.

It hardly needs to be said that in listening to the text of Genesis 1, we need to remember our creaturely limitations. As a sage of long ago put it: "As you do not know what is the way of the wind, or how the bones grow in the womb of her who is with child, so you do not know the works of God who makes everything" (Eccl. 11:5). Although the biblical text is clear, God's work is incomprehensible. We can only accept His revelation of His work of creation in faith. "By faith we understand that the worlds were framed by the word of God, so that the things which are seen were not made of things which are visible" (Heb. 11:3).

Although we could make many interesting comments about apparent similarities in concepts and vocabulary between the Genesis account and ancient Near Eastern texts of earth's beginnings, the temptation to mention these will be resisted. Important similarities have already been noted in chapter 2. For the purpose of this chapter, these will only be mentioned when ancient Near Eastern data helps us in a meaningful way to hear what the biblical text is communicating.

Furthermore, one could easily become bogged down with carefully considering and refuting all sorts of exegetical suggestions related to the text, regardless of whether they are relevant for this project. As mentioned, the purpose of this chapter is to listen to the text, especially respecting the historicity of God's work of creation, and to briefly explore the implications of what Scripture says for the scientific endeavor.

Day One

"In the beginning God created the heavens and the earth. The earth was without form, and void; and darkness was on the face of the deep. And the Spirit of God was hovering over the face of the waters.

Then God said, 'Let there be light'; and there was light. And God saw the light, that it was good; and God divided the light from the darkness. God called the light Day, and the darkness He called Night. So the evening and the morning were the first day" (Gen. 1:1–5).

The Creation of the Heavens, the Earth, and Darkness

As we saw in chapter 5, the first day began "in the beginning" when God "created the heavens and the earth" (v. 1), that is, He called into being what had not previously existed. "He spoke and it was done" (Ps. 33:6, 9).

As noted in chapter 3, passages such as Isaiah 42:5, which says that God stretched the heavens and spread out the earth, could be an indication that processes took place as God created the heavens and the earth and subsequently formed the firmament and dry land on the second and third days. In any case, it is important to underline that heaven and earth had a beginning. Time began at their creation. They did not exist from eternity. There was no material existence before God started His work of creation.

The earth that God called into being was initially "without form, and void; and darkness was on the face of the deep" (Gen. 1:2; cf. Ps. 104:6). There was as yet no place for human habitation (cf. Isa. 45:18).[1] Genesis 1 informs us that "the Spirit of God was hovering over the face of the waters" (v. 2).[2]

Genesis 1 does not go into any detail about the creation of heaven as the dwelling place of God. This topic will be dealt with in the appendix of this book. As we saw in chapter 7, the heavens are subsequently mentioned during the creation account from the perspective of someone living on earth. Indeed, for the purposes of this account God identified the heavens with the firmament, or sky, on day two (v. 8).

---

1. For the meaning of "without form and void," see chapter 4 above.
2. See further on the Spirit's involvement, chapter 6 above.

Up to this point, God's work of creation is in darkness. Darkness is part of God's good creation. The sovereign LORD Himself said, "I form the light and create darkness" (Isa. 45:7). Both have a real and separate existence; both are an ontological reality, as God made clear when He addressed Job. "Where is the way to the dwelling of light? And darkness, where is its place?" (Job 38:19).[3] God has full control of both light and darkness as part of His creation. This is clear from God's ability to separate light from darkness and to give both a name (Gen. 1:4–5).

In the context of Genesis 1, the creation of darkness, the opposite of light, is a good thing. After all, at the end of His work of creation, "God saw everything that He had made, and indeed it was very good" (v. 31). Darkness can be associated with calamity from which people need to be delivered. That is the case in Isaiah 45, as the parallel structure indicates. "I form the light and create darkness, I make peace and create calamity; I, the LORD, do all these things" (Isa. 45:7). But such an association is not always necessary. Humans are blessed with darkness so that they can sleep and be refreshed. God also used darkness to protect His people from the full glory of His majesty. "He made darkness canopies around Him" (2 Sam. 22:12; also Deut. 4:11; 5:23). Similarly, for the sake of His people, "He would dwell in the dark cloud," that is, thick darkness (1 Kings 8:12; also Ps. 97:2). Another benefit of darkness is that animals use the darkness of the night to feed themselves (Ps. 104:20–21).

The Creation of Light

After the description of God's first act of creating heaven and earth, the biblical text records, "then God said" (Gen. 1:3). In chapter 6, we considered the import of these words in the context of creation as the work of the triune God. The phrase "then God said" indicates that God created by His Word, that is, in and through the eternal Son, who is the Word (John 1:1–3, 14; Col. 1:16). Although God's speaking is first mentioned in Genesis 1:3, this does not mean, as Calvin noted, "that the creation work of verse 1 took place without the Word.[4] "By faith we understand that the worlds were framed by the word of God" (Heb. 11:3). Without the Word "nothing was made that was made" (John 1:3).

God's speech is authoritative command. His utterance cannot be challenged. When God speaks, He accomplishes His purpose. "Then God said, 'Let

---

3. See further on this point, Pipa, "From Chaos to Cosmos," 177–78; also for darkness as a separate created entity, David J. A. Clines, *Job 38–42* (Nashville: Thomas Nelson, 2011), 1107; on Isa. 45:7, Oswalt, *Isaiah 40–66*, 204.

4. Calvin, *Genesis*, 1:74.

there be light'; and there was light" (Gen. 1:3). Bavinck notes that "the word God speaks is not a mere sound but a force so great that by it he creates and upholds the world. He speaks and it is there."[5] The text gives the impression of an immediate fulfillment of the command. As Cassuto asserts, the terse construction of the fiat ("let there be light)" and the execution ("and there was light") shows "the precision and celerity with which the injunction was carried out: as He commanded, and as soon as He commanded."[6] The power of God's command is also clear from the reference to creation found in the parallelism within Psalm 33:9. "For He spoke, and it was done; He commanded, and it stood fast."

When the inspired psalmist penned these words, he also attested to the historicity of this event, as did the apostle Paul when he affirmed that God "commanded light to shine out of darkness" (2 Cor. 4:6). As we saw in chapter 3, the genre of Genesis 1 is historical narrative. Since God's creating through speaking was a historical event, it is impossible to understand God's speaking as part of a royal political metaphor.[7] When God's actions in Genesis 1 are understood as metaphorical expressions of divine kingship, then one cannot consequently affirm that the events of Genesis 1 actually transpired as recorded.[8]

God created light before the light-bearers, which came into being on the fourth day. By doing this, God made it clear that light did not depend on the sun and moon. These entities are but God's instruments. God saw that the light he created was good; that is, it was exactly what He had in mind and perfectly fulfilled the purpose for which He called it into being. Without light, creation could not be seen or known for what it is. Light is also a basic necessity for all life that God would create, and it is necessary in the alternating of day and night, and so also for the measuring of time.

The creation of light did not put an end to the darkness. God gave them each their own domain, a fact alluded to when God asked Job: "Where is the way to the dwelling of light? And darkness, where is its place?" (Job 38:19). Each has its own distinct realm. "God divided the light from the darkness. God called the light Day, and the darkness He called Night" (Gen. 1:4–5). In our manner of speaking, we would call this light daytime. By naming light and

---

5. Bavinck, *Reformed Dogmatics*, 2:261.

6. Cassuto, *Genesis*, 26.

7. As argued in Stek, "What Says the Scripture?," 232–35.

8. This consequence, namely, that there is no record of actual events in Gen. 1, is drawn by Stek, "What Says the Scripture?," 236, 242, 263; and by Young and Stearley, *The Bible, Rocks and Time*, 210.

darkness, God showed that He was sovereign over them and assigned them their function.

What was this light that God called into being? What was its source? The biblical text only mentions that light was created and does not mention the source. A very old Jewish interpretation is that God Himself was the source. "The splendor of his majesty shown forth from one end of the world to the other" (Genesis Rabbah 3:4). A reference is made to Psalm 104:2 where God is described as "covering yourself with light as with a garment."[9] This notion still has some adherents.[10]

We, however, need to distinguish between the fact that "God is light" (1 John 1:5) and the light as created by God on the first day. The unapproachable light in which God dwells (1 Tim. 6:16) and with which He covers Himself as with a garment (Ps. 104:2) is eternal. Since "God is light" (1 John 1:5), this divine light has not been created as was the case with the light God called into being on the first day. In chapter 3 we saw that Psalm 104 deals with God's work of creation and parallels Genesis 1 in some respects. Since this Psalm begins with God's greatness and His covering Himself "with light as with a garment" (Ps. 104:2), this feature has been used to argue that this eternal light was the source of the light of Genesis 1:3. However, this is reading into Psalm 104 far more than it states. There is no justification for concluding that the created light in Genesis 1 was a radiance of God's eternal light.[11]

In this connection it should also be noted that we need to be careful not to read back into Genesis 1 what is revealed about the new creation, where God Himself is said to be the light. "The sun shall no longer be your light by day, nor for brightness shall the moon give light to you; but the LORD will be to you an everlasting light" (Isa. 60:19); that is, God's glory will dispel the darkness (Isa. 60:1–2). As a result, the apostle John could record that the new Jerusalem "had no need of the sun or of the moon to shine in it, for the glory of God

---

9. The Genesis Rabbah dates from the late fourth to the early fifth century AD. Jacob Neusner, *Genesis Rabbah. The Judaic Commentary to the Book of Genesis: A New American Translation* (Atlanta: Scholars Press, 1985).

10. E.g., Mark S. Smith, "Light in Genesis 1:3—Created or Uncreated: A Question of Priestly Mysticism?," in *Birkat Shalom: Studies in the Bible, Ancient Near Eastern Literature, and Postbiblical Judaism Presented to Shalom M. Paul on the Occasion of His Seventieth Birthday*, ed. Chaim Cohen et al. (Winona Lake, Ind.: Eisenbrauns, 2008), 131; Richard M. Davidson, "Creation Theme," 157–58; Jonathan D. Sarfati, *The Genesis Account: A Theological, Historical, and Scientific Commentary on Genesis 1–11* (Powder Springs, Ga.: Creation Book Publishers, 2015), 116.

11. For this use of Psalm 104, see Smith, "Light," 128–29; Richard M. Davidson, "Creation Theme," 157–58. For the lack of justification for the view that the created light was a radiance of God's eternal light, see Kelly, *Creation and Change*, 108, cf. 264–65; Van Selms, *Genesis*, 1:25.

illuminated it. The Lamb is its light" (Rev. 21:23). We have no way of knowing how this prophecy will be fulfilled since prophecy, unlike Genesis 1, by its very nature can use figurative language. The point of Revelation 21:23 "is not about the astronomical situation in the renewed universe but 'to affirm the unsurpassed splendor which radiates from the presence of God and the Lamb.'"[12]

"The Evening and the Morning"

The first events of creation are concluded with the statement: "So the evening and the morning were the first day" (Gen. 1:5). Here we have another meaning of the word for "day," as this represents the entire period of time encompassing all the nighttime and daytime. It is this meaning of day that is subsequently used for days two through seven. This day also marks the beginning of normal temporal sequences of one day following another. This is the result of the separation of light from darkness and thus part of God's work of creation. As creator, God has established His "covenant...with day and night," and He "appointed the ordinances of heaven and earth" (Jer. 33:25). The Creator has instituted what science calls the laws of the natural world.

The text literally says, "and there was evening and there was morning: one day." This way of stating the matter is significant. It defines a day as consisting of an evening and a morning, and the biblical text thus tells the reader that all the subsequent days of creation need to be understood in this manner.[13] Although most Bible translations render it as "the first day," a meaning solely derived from the context,[14] it is important to realize that grammatically speaking the meaning of the text is "one day" (so, correctly, NASB). Contextually, the rendering "one day" also makes sense, for as Cassuto notes, "first" implies precedence over other entities in existence, "but in our case there was only *one day*, for the second had not yet been created."[15] The subsequent numbers are ordinal numbers.

It is noteworthy that also with days two through five the Hebrew text does not use the definite article, but the ordinal numbers are used. So after the refrain, "there was evening and there was morning," the text literally continues

---

12. Richard D. Phillips, *Revelation* (Phillipsburg, N.J.: P&R, 2017), 656, quoting George Eldon Ladd, *A Commentary on the Revelation of John* (Grand Rapids: Eerdmans, 1972), 284; also see G. K. Beale, *The Book of Revelation: A Commentary on the Greek Text* (Grand Rapids: Eerdmans, 1999), 1093.

13. Steinmann, "Genesis 1:5," esp. 583–84.

14. So, e.g., GKC, §98a. Nowhere else is this construction of the indefinite noun "day" plus the cardinal numeral "one" found to express "the first day." *IBHS*, 274.

15. Cassuto, *Genesis*, 30 (italics in the original).

with "a second day," "a third day" and so on, stressing that each day is defined by an evening and a morning.[16] The special sixth day, with the completion of the work with the making of the crown of creation, has the article but only with the ordinal numeral (literally "a day, the sixth"; Gen. 1:31), while the climactic seventh day is appropriately defined with the full use of an article: "the seventh day" (2:2).[17]

The First Day and Science

A preliminary remark is in order with respect to whether the manner of God's creating by speaking is consistent with theistic evolution. The creation account repeatedly informs us that "God said." We have seen earlier in this chapter, and also in chapter 6, that this information cannot be reduced to a metaphor. Consequently, God's speaking and commanding creation into being goes diametrically against any theory of evolution. In spite of the fact that we cannot comprehend what was all involved, it was a real speaking with real content, and within a few days it resulted in a mature creation. Although God's subsequent speaking to Adam and Eve, and to many others like Abraham and Moses, was different in that it was not speech resulting in creation, yet that was nevertheless real speaking as well. Mart-Jan Paul, professor of Old Testament at the Evangelische Theologische Faculteit, Leuven, has rightly pointed out the inconsistency evident in the fact that those who promote theistic evolution generally have no difficulty accepting that God spoke to Abraham or Moses, but doubt or reject the reality of His content-filled speaking at creation and at the creation of the woman (Gen. 2:18).[18] But you cannot have it both ways. If God's speaking to Abraham was real, so was His speaking at creation. There is no indication in Genesis 1 and 2 or elsewhere in Scripture that this was not the case.

Scientists characterized by Paul Seely as moderate concordists, who wish to correlate the first verses of Genesis 1 with mainstream science, typically consider verse 1 "as a reference to the Big Bang of 15 to 20 billion years ago."[19] But

---

16. As Steinmann noted, although the English versions generally include the definite article, "no article is present for days two through five…. Therefore the refrain deliberately and purposefully identifies each evening and morning as a particular single day." Steinmann, "A Note on the Refrain," 136n16.

17. On the use of the article because of the special character of days six and seven, see Sarna, *Genesis*, 14; Cassuto, *Genesis*, 60. For the use of the article for the sixth day, also see GKC, §126w; cf. Joüon, §138b.

18. In correspondence with the author, May 4, 2020.

19. Paul H. Seely, "The First Four Days of Genesis in Concordist Theory and in Biblical Context," *PSCF* 49 (1997): 86.

as Seely notes, one simply cannot find agreement between the first two verses of Genesis and the scenarios of earth's origins proposed by current science. While Scripture tells us that water covered the earth, "science tells us the dry land of the earth formed first, condensing out of a nebula in a molten form that was far too hot for any water to rest upon it…. The statements of Gen. 1:2 and science are exactly opposite to each other."[20] Furthermore, on the first day of creation, there was only the earth. There were as yet no stars and moon, a situation contradicting the Big Bang theory, according to which a star, the sun, would have been the source of the earth.[21] In addition, as we saw in chapters 4 and 5, that first day speaks of the absolute beginning of God's work of creating and thus a young earth. The billions of years and deep time of the Big Bang do not agree with the Genesis creation account, which speaks of six days of creation each defined by "and there was evening and there was morning."

How then do we relate God's work of creation on the first day to current scientific understanding? Vern Poythress gives helpful directives. "Genesis 1 needs to be interpreted first of all in a manner independent of modern scientific knowledge, lest we fall victim to the myth of scientistic metaphysics in our interpretation." On the other hand, since the Creator is also the ultimate author of Genesis 1, "it is legitimate for us to explore how the two might fit together within his comprehensive plan."[22]

The Spirit's hovering over the waters, indicating His involvement in the work of creation, has been connected with preparing the earth for further development to make life possible there. Already Wolfgang Capito, a sixteenth-century Reformer, pictured this action as "divine virtue from the Spirit of the Lord warmly brooding over the inchoate, confused particles, until his active presence reduces them to the most beautiful and perfect order at the conclusion of the six days' work."[23] Such thoughts are consistent with the Spirit's work of giving new life as recorded elsewhere in Scripture (e.g., Ps. 104:29–30).

To put such thoughts in scientific terms, one could speculate that the Spirit's hovering over the waters suggests motion that in modern scientific terms could be translated as "vibrated" or "energized." As Henry Morris notes, "If the universe is to be energized, there must be an Energizer. If it is set in motion, there

---

20. Seely, "First Four Days," 86–87.

21. Byl, *God and the Cosmos*, 48.

22. Poythress, *Interpreting Eden*, 272, 273; also see Poythress, "Correlations with Providence in Genesis 1," 96–97, and chapter 2 above where the relationship between the Bible and science is discussed.

23. As quoted from Capito's *Hexameron* in Kelly, *Creation and Change*, 107.

must be a Prime Mover."[24] Morris offers his scientific insights and speculations into how the vibrating activity of the Holy Spirit may have imparted successive outflows of energy to bring the world into its present form.[25] When such thoughts are consistent with Genesis 1, they could provide a possible theoretical, albeit speculative, context for current science seeking to understand something of the beginnings of the world using biblical data.

Coming now to the water over which the Spirit moved, this was apparently ordinary water. As geologist Andrew Snelling put it, "There is no hint that the initial state of what God created was not that of ordinary matter."[26] After all, the apostle Peter tells us that "the earth was formed out of water and through water" (2 Peter 3:5 ESV). On the basis of these observations from Genesis 1:2 and 2 Peter 3:5, Snelling notes that "there is no suggestion in these passages that the original state of the matter comprising the earth was a high energy ionized plasma or a state so energetic that even neutrons or protons could not form. This is in stark contrast to the secular ideas of a 'big bang' in which all the matter in the present cosmos was in a volume smaller than that of an atom at an incredibly high state of excitation. Thus we find a sharp dichotomy between the speculations of modern cosmologists as to how the cosmos began and God's account of what actually occurred."[27]

In an attempt to understand the beginning of creation, D. Russell Humphreys, a physicist, speculated that God created "a large 3-D space and within it a ball of liquid water, the 'deep.' The ball is greater than two light-years in diameter, large enough to contain all the mass of the universe." He further speculated how this could have resulted in what is recorded for God's work on the first day of creation.[28]

It obviously remains a challenge to interpret the events of the first day of Genesis in such a way that we do justice to the text and at the same time discern whether the simple language of this historical narrative contains information consistent with current scientific theories or whether it gives the necessary insights into constructing new scientific theory on the origin of Planet Earth.

Besides a literal understanding of the text, an analogous reading of the creation account has also been proposed in relating Genesis 1 to science, a method that has been applied to the creation of light. Poythress suggests that "God's

---

24. Morris, *Genesis Record*, 52.

25. Morris, *Genesis Record*, 52; also see Snelling, *Earth's Catastrophic Past*, 1:203–4; Kelly, *Creation and Change*, 107–8.

26. Snelling, *Earth's Catastrophic Past*, 1:204.

27. Snelling, *Earth's Catastrophic Past*, 1:204.

28. D. Russell Humphreys, *Starlight and Time* (Green Forest, Ariz.: Master, 1994), ch. 2, Kindle.

description of his creative works in Gen 1 instructs Israelites through analogies with providence."[29] We have considered and critiqued this approach as applied in general to the days of creation in chapter 6 above. With respect to the specifics of the first day, Poythress states, among other things, that "Genesis 1:3 is not discussing light in a technical scientific way—for example, as electromagnetic radiation. It is saying that the coming of light on the first day is like the coming of daylight that we experience within God's providential order at the beginning of a new day."[30] When trying to relate this light to current scientific understanding, Poythress writes that "light in day 1 could correspond to the time when the condensing sun begins to give off light because of heating through gravitational contraction. Or, more likely, it could correspond to the initial penetration of light to the surface of the new earth, after a period in which the planet was covered with an opaque atmosphere and was encircled by interplanetary debris."[31]

The problem with this correlation with science is that it is based on the supposition that Genesis 1 does not record a strictly chronological account of creation, since the sun was not created until the fourth day. The sun is not the light of day one.[32] Edward Young rightly asked, "In an area so filled with mystery and about which we know so little, who can dare to assert that Moses is in error in declaring that light was created before the sun? Can one prove that the presence of light demands a light-bearer?"[33] The fact that the first day is defined as encompassing evening and morning seems to indicate that the earth was now rotating on an axis with light coming from one side. The other days that follow would all be described similarly as "evening and morning."[34]

Finally, a note on the fact that on day one, God called light into being by speaking. John Lennox remarked that the recurring phrase "then God said" is

---

29. Poythress, Interpreting Eden, 143.

30. Poythress, Interpreting Eden, 148.

31. Poythress, Interpreting Eden, 273.

32. "Genesis 1 does include a sense of progression and a chronological order.... But that does not mean that it cannot also, as a sparse account, stick to the main points and group together created objects of one kind for topical simplicity." Poythress, Interpreting Eden, 270. Cf. Richard E. Averbeck, "A Literary Day, Inter-Textual, and Contextual Reading of Genesis 1–2," in J. Daryl Charles, Reading Genesis 1–2, 19.

33. Edward J. Young, Studies in Genesis One, 88.

34. It is interesting to note that in Calvin's day the earth was still considered to be stationary and at the center of the universe. Calvin therefore asked whether "light and darkness succeeded each other in turn through the whole circuit of the world; or whether the darkness occupied one half of the circle, while light shone in the other." In any case, he noted that "whether it was everywhere day at the same time, and everywhere night also, I would rather leave undecided." Calvin, Genesis, 1:61, 76–77.

loaded with meaning. Since God creates through His Word, identified in the New Testament as the eternal Son who holds all things together (John 1:1–3; Col. 1:15–17), it was He "who conceived and, with unimaginable energy and power, spoke into being a material universe, governed by intricate laws that he himself designed."[35] Lennox also observed that God's creating by His Word, and so imparting energy and information to create and structure the universe, "converges with some of the deepest insights of a modern science that has come to realize the fundamental nature of information and its irreducibility to matter and energy."[36]

Although the creation work of God on the first day is beyond our understanding, Christian scientists can attempt to think God's thoughts after Him and theorize scientific reconstructions that are consistent with God's revelation of His work on the first day of creation. Faith seeks understanding, although such an endeavor can, as we have seen, lead to much speculation.[37]

Day Two

On the second day, God called into being an expanse. "Then God said, 'Let there be a firmament in the midst of the waters, and let it divide the waters from the waters.' Thus God made the firmament, and divided the waters which were under the firmament from the waters which were above the firmament; and it was so. And God called the firmament Heaven. So the evening and the morning were the second day" (Gen. 1:6–8).

We saw in chapter 7 that this firmament or expanse is the sky or heaven as we see it. It is the blue vault above us. The context will determine whether we should think of it as referring to what is beyond the earth's atmosphere, as is the case when God places lights in the expanse of the heavens (vv. 14–18), or whether the immediate atmosphere that surrounds the earth is in view. That is the case here, for as we saw in the preceding chapter, the waters above are the clouds.

The Creation of the Firmament

God said, "Let there be a firmament." Unlike the creation of light, the narrative does not immediately continue with the words "and there was a firmament." Rather, the actual execution of the creative act is described as "thus God made

---

35. Lennox, *Seven Days*, 97.

36. Lennox, *Seven Days*, 141; for more on information as a fundamental entity on equal footing with matter and energy, see Werner Gitt, *In the Beginning Was Information* (Bielefeld, Germany: CLV, 2000), 12–137.

37. See, e.g., the reconstruction found in Morris, *Genesis Record*, 56–57.

the firmament, and divided the waters which were under the firmament from the waters which were above the firmament" (v. 7). Is the use of the Hebrew verb rendered "to make" significant? It need not be. The expression "God made" could simply mean, as Nahum Sarna has noted, "that the divine intention became a reality." In his view it does not indicate creation by deed rather than word. For example, Psalm 33:6 describes God's creation of the heavens by His word as making the heavens. "By the word of the LORD the heavens were made, and all the host of them by the breath of His mouth."[38] A process taking time is not necessary for God to make something. Furthermore, time is part of creation, and God is completely sovereign over it. He can therefore do in one day the work of a thousand years (cf. Ps. 90:4; 2 Peter 3:8). God can even dispense with time and process altogether as apparently happened, for example, when He created light (Gen. 1:3) and when Christ instantly turned water into wine (John 2:7–9).[39]

On the other hand, the words "God made the firmament" could indicate a process leading to the completion of the expanse. There is nothing in the text to exclude that possibility. Indeed, we saw in chapter 3 above that Scripture elsewhere suggests process. For example, Isaiah said that God "stretched out the heavens" (Isa. 44:24). Also, as we shall see, process was certainly involved with the creation of vegetation. "Let the earth bring forth grass" (Gen. 1:11). Besides, God used a process of six days to create all things, even though he could have created everything in a moment. As Calvin noted, "We must think that God, for good reasons, while able to do everything in a single moment, followed the procedure as Moses declares it" so that "we will have no excuse not to think upon his glory in all we see when we open our eyes and enjoy the light and the benefits and conveniences we receive from it."[40]

God exercised His sovereignty and control over His creation by naming the firmament or expanse heaven. The name "heaven" (šāmayim) for the firmament provides continuity with the same word "heaven" (šāmayim) in verse 1 ("God created the heavens and the earth"). The usage of the same word to describe the heavens in verse 1 and in a more narrow sense the earth's atmosphere or sky in verse 8 underlines the fact that God is using the language of everyday experience from the vantage point of the earth. It is not scientific terminology. Chapter 7 provided justification for this position.

---

38. Sarna, *Genesis*, 8.

39. See also Allis, *God Spake by Moses*, 10–11; and Oswald T. Allis, "The Time Element in Genesis 1 and 2," *Torch and Trumpet* 8, no. 3 (1958): 16–18.

40. Calvin, *Sermons on Genesis*, 32.

God's creation work of the second day does not include the words "and God saw that it was good," which were included in the first day. As Cassuto explains, such a statement was not appropriate at this point since the work of the water had not yet been completed. Another separation was to take place on the third day.[41]

The Second Day and Science

If we envisage what it would be like to see the first appearance of light on the earth, the sight that would greet us would be an earth without form and void and covered with the waters of the deep (v. 2). God said, "Let there be a firmament in the midst of the waters, and let it divide the waters from the waters" (v. 6). This firmament was, as Cassuto puts it, "a kind of horizontal area, extending through the very heart of the mass of water and cleaving it into two layers, one above the other—the upper and lower layers of water."[42] We obviously have no idea how God did this. Douglas Kelly notes that "God by His creative activity, by His very speaking, divided out this uninhabitable mass of gasses, 'mud' and energetic elements, thus producing open breathing space or something like 'atmosphere.'"[43] Consequently, weather patterns and cycles could begin. Poythress concludes that "the separation in day two could correspond to the first establishment of a weather cycle involving the rising of clouds and the coming of rain."[44] This scenario is consistent with the clouds being the waters above the earth.

When we consider the second day and current science, we can only humbly acknowledge God's work on the second day and accept His revelation concerning it. It is beyond our ability to understand what transpired. What is clear is that God is the sole cause of what transpired. Chance development and evolution are out of the picture.

Day Three

The preparation for life on earth continued with God's creative activity on the third day. Following His separation of the light from darkness, and the waters above from those below, God separated water and land and then had the land produce vegetation.

---

41. Cassuto, *Genesis*, 34.
42. Cassuto, *Genesis*, 31.
43. Kelly, *Creation and Change*, 236.
44. Poythress, *Interpreting Eden*, 273.

Dry Land and Vegetation

"Then God said, 'Let the waters under the heavens be gathered together into one place, and let the dry land appear'; and it was so. And God called the dry land Earth, and the gathering together of the waters He called Seas. And God saw that it was good" (Gen. 1:9–10).

Once again God commanded and His word accomplished that which He purposed (Isa. 55:11), a point emphasized with the additional words "and it was so" (v. 9). Such creative speaking will continue to be the pattern for subsequent days.

God gathered the waters of the sea and put the deep in storehouses (Ps. 33:7). He "shut in the sea with doors" (Job 38:8) and "assigned to the sea its limit, so that the waters would not transgress His command" (Prov. 8:29). Genesis 1 gives no further details about how God accomplished all this, but it is possible that Psalm 104 refers to these events (as well as the Genesis flood) when the inspired poet praises God and jubilates in His mighty works.

> You covered it [the earth] with the deep as with a garment;
> the waters stood above the mountains.
> At Your rebuke they fled;
> at the voice of Your thunder they hastened away.
> They went up over the mountains; they went down into the valleys,
> to the place which You founded for them.
> You have set a boundary that they may not pass over,
> that they may not return to cover the earth. (Ps. 104:6–9)[45]

Scripture emphasizes that God's sovereign creative power on the third day should evoke fear and respect for God in our hearts. "'Do you not fear Me?' says the LORD. 'Will you not tremble at My presence, who have placed the sand as the bound of the sea, by a perpetual decree, that it cannot pass beyond it? And though its waves toss to and fro, yet they cannot prevail; though they roar, yet they cannot pass over it'" (Jer. 5:22). Peter alludes to these events when he writes that "the earth was formed out of water and through water by the word of God" (2 Peter 3:5 ESV). Peter is not suggesting that water was the raw material from which matter was made.[46] His point is that the earth came out of the water and through the water as the separation process on the third day of creation occurred by God's command.[47]

---

45. Also see the discussion of Ps. 104 in chapter 3 above.

46. As favored by some. See the overview in Sarfati, *Genesis Account*, 165–66.

47. Gene L. Green, *Jude and 2 Peter* (Grand Rapids: Baker Academic, 2008), 320; similarly, Simon J. Kistemaker, *Exposition of James, Epistles of John, Peter, and Jude* (Grand Rapids: Baker

By calling the dry land earth and the water seas, God gave this arrangement of the world permanency, formally established His dominion over them, and claimed them as His own. "The sea is His, for He made it; and His hands formed the dry land" (Ps. 95:5). In Genesis 1:1 "the earth" refers to the entire globe. In verse 10 God specifies that "earth" denotes the dry land, "the land masses, the continents whether they were originally all connected or not." The term "seas is very general, covering not only all the oceans and the rivers running into them but also inland bodies of water."[48]

Earth had been transformed from being "without form and void" to being suitable for life. The work with the water was now finished. First the water, the deep, covered the earth, with the Spirit hovering over the face of the waters. Then God created an expanse that separated the waters from the waters so that there were waters above and waters below. Now the waters below have been gathered together and dry land has appeared. With the earth as dry land, and with the completion of the division and separation of the waters, the infrastructure has been, so to speak, put in place, and "God saw that it was good" (v. 10).

Once the dry land was in place, "God said, 'Let the earth bring forth grass, the herb that yields seed, and the fruit tree that yields fruit according to its kind, whose seed is in itself, on the earth'; and it was so. And the earth brought forth grass, the herb that yields seed according to its kind, and the tree that yields fruit, whose seed is in itself according to its kind. And God saw that it was good" (vv. 11–12).

For the first time, God's creative decree is addressed to only a part of His creation. The earth is to sprout vegetation resulting in plants and trees covering the earth. Although the words "let the earth bring forth grass" may suggest a natural development of life from the earth, this is clearly not the case. The land itself is powerless to generate life. God's word of command is needed. Calvin noted that God "fructifies it [the earth] by his word," and in a sermon on this passage he stated "when the word is spoken, the thing is done forthwith.... The

---

Academic, 2002), 328. The NKJV has "the earth standing out of water [KJV: the water] and in the water." The States-General Bible (Statenvertaling) translation, which is roughly contemporary with the KJV, has a similar translation with supporting notes. R. C. H. Lenski explains that Peter described the earth as existing "'out of water (having risen out of it) and between water' (that above in the clouds, that below in the fountains of the deep)." R. C. H. Lenski, *The Interpretation of the Epistles of St. Peter, St. John and St. Jude* (Columbus, Ohio: Lutheran Book Concern, 1938), 342; similarly, Edwin A. Blum, "2 Peter," in *The Expositor's Bible Commentary: Hebrews through Revelation*, ed. Frank E. Gaebelein (Grand Rapids: Zondervan, 1981), 285.

48. Lawrenz and Jeske, *Genesis 1–11*, 57. On dry land, also see the section "The Waters Below" in chapter 7 above.

word had such power that the earth produced shoots and roots and plants."[49] It is possible that God used the means of seeds already present in the ground,[50] but the text does not say this. In any case, whatever process may have been involved, it was all completed within the third day. Such a quick appearance of mature plants yielding seed and bearing fruit reminds one of the miracle that Jonah experienced when God "prepared a plant" (Jonah 4:6) that "came up in a night" (v. 10). We need not doubt that through God's creative word the earth was able to produce vegetation in short order. It is interesting that E. J. Young comments, "The work of the third day seems to suggest that there was some process, and that what took place occurred in a period longer than twenty-four hours," but he then adds that he believes in miracles and that in Genesis 1 "there has been an intrusion of the supernatural."[51] We should not try to determine the exact length of a day, but simply accept each one as encompassing evening and morning, a day filled with the works of God, which we cannot comprehend. Also, the third day was a workday of God—a day and not eons of time. The result of God's creative work on the third day were mature plants that had the appearance of being much older than one day.

What exactly was this vegetation? God said, "Let the earth bring forth grass, the herb that yields seed, and the fruit tree that yields fruit" (Gen. 1:11). After mentioning the broad term "grass," which can best be understood here as referring to "vegetation" in general,[52] God noted two distinct types: plants and fruit trees. He had the earth sprout each "'according to its kind [mîn], whose seed is in itself, on the earth'; and it was so. And the earth brought forth grass [vegetation], the herb that yields seed according to its kind [mîn], and the tree that yields fruit, whose seed is in itself according to its kind [mîn]" (vv. 11–12). The context of these first occurrences of the term mîn ("kind") clearly indicates that it designates a category or classification within which plants reproduce.[53]

---

49. See, respectively, Calvin, *Genesis*, 1:82; and Calvin, *Sermons on Genesis*, 46; similarly Keil and Delitzsch, *Commentary on the Old Testament*, 1:34–35; Aalders, *Genesis*, 1:63.

50. Geerhardus Vos suggested that "the earth can only bring forth plant growth because seeds were already planted earlier when the Spirit was hovering." Vos, *Reformed Dogmatics*, 1:171.

51. Edward J. Young, *In the Beginning: Genesis 1–3 and the Authority of Scripture* (Edinburgh: Banner of Truth, 1984), 43–44.

52. *DCH* 2:476; *HALOT*, 234.

53. Lawrenz and Jeske, *Genesis 1–11*, 59–60; "a classification term," P. Beauchamp, "mîn," *TDOT* 8:289. Schafer's denial of mîn as a term of classification linked to reproduction, which she argues on the basis of the term not being used in the blessing (Gen. 1:22), is not convincing since the context clearly implies this limitation. A. Rahel Davidson Schafer, "The 'Kinds' of Genesis 1: What Is the Meaning of Mîn?," *Journal of the Adventist Theological Society* 14 (2003): 90–92. Neville suggests to translate "in all their varieties" or "all kinds of." He rejects as misleading

God organized what He had made in clearly distinguishable categories or kinds. The term "kind" should not be equated with the technical term "species" of modern-day science since it uses different criteria for organizing plant and animal life. For example, while modern science separates birds and bees into different classifications, Scripture includes both as "winged creatures" (v. 20) belonging in the same category.[54]

With the greening of the earth, the Creator took yet another step in making the earth a place for the crown of His creation to dwell in. "And God saw that it was good. So the evening and the morning were the third day" (v. 12).

The Third Day and Science

Scripture is silent on what was involved in God's separating the waters from the land. We have no idea what sort of geologic or other processes may have been involved. Henry Morris deduced that "tremendous chemical reactions got under way, as dissolved elements precipitated and combined with others to form the vast complex of minerals and rocks making up the solid earth—its crust, its mantle and its core."[55] This scenario appears to assume that only water constituted the initial matter. However, as John Byl observes, "the Genesis text gives no indication of such transformation. The third day relates the separation of water and dry land, but no mention is made of the creation of land. Both water and the elements of the earth seem to have been created from the start, in Day One."[56] The theory most consistent with Scripture is probably the one articulated by Carl Lawrenz, who writes that "many of the basic geological formations which do not involve imbedded organic matter and animal fossils were undoubtedly formed on the third day of creation."[57] Herman Bavinck mentions "colossal mechanical and chemical processes" that "were aroused by

---

the translation "according to their kinds" and asserts that the expression "does not indicate *how* God created (kind by kind by kind) but *what* God created (all kinds of)." However, his thesis that "the expression conveys variety in order to establish the comprehensiveness of God's creative work" is not persuasive, especially considering the context of Gen. 1. The quotes (italics in the original) are from Richard Neville, "Differentiation in Genesis 1: An Exegetical Creation *Ex Nihilo*," *JBL* 130 (2011): 226. The translation "according to their kinds" is justifiably still given in the most recent standard Hebrew lexicon, *DCH* 5:262, and is also reflected in the LXX. The sense of this translation is "(with its) seed begetting according to kind and according to likeness." John William Wevers, *Notes on the Greek Text of Genesis* (Atlanta: Scholars Press, 1993), 6.

54. NKJV has "birds," which is literally "flying things" or "winged creatures." *DCH* 6:312; *HALOT*, 801; see further Mark D. Futato, "*mîn*, Kind, Variety," in *NIDOTTE* 2:934–35.

55. Morris, *Genesis Record*, 61.

56. Byl, *God and the Cosmos*, 161.

57. Lawrenz and Jeske, *Genesis 1–11*, 57.

the divine word of power and the animation of the Spirit and have given the earth its cosmic shape and appearance."[58] Obviously, all of this is according to our human reasoning as we try to understand what led to the present, basic configuration of the earth. Simply expressed, as Poythress puts it, "day 3 corresponds to the origins of continents and earlier forms of life."[59]

With respect to plant life, Genesis 1 makes it very clear that the earth itself cannot produce life. Only the creative word of God could cause the earth to produce all kinds of vegetation. This fact contradicts the theory of abiogenesis, whereby living organisms spontaneously originate from lifeless matter.[60] Living things cannot function without having received the necessary information. It is essential to life. Information scientist Werner Gitt has noted that evolutionary views cannot account for the origin of information in living beings. "It has never been shown that a coding system and semantic information could originate by itself in a material medium, and the information theorems predict that this will never be possible. A purely material origin of life is thus precluded."[61] God's creative word imparted the necessary information and is the origin of life.

The creation account also stresses that the seed of each plant was "according to its kind" (v. 12). God's creation of different kinds calls to mind the notion of separation that characterizes God's work of creation (vv. 4, 6–7, 14, 18). Not only plants, but also animals, were created "according to their kind" (v. 21). God set clear boundaries that placed His creation into different categories that could not be transgressed. This basic divine ordinance or law contradicts a basic premise of evolutionary theory, namely, that life is to have evolved from a lower to a higher form, ignoring the boundaries of the "kinds" God created. Al Wolters has therefore correctly noted that "the separation theme is a significant datum for the question of the relationship between Scripture and theorizing" and "a recognition of the created separateness of things can function as a biblical antidote to the kind of historicism according to which any kind of thing can, over time, turn into any other kind of thing."[62]

The fact that each plant was "according to its kind" means that each seed was able to reproduce a plant like the one it came from. As Andrew Snelling

---

58. Bavinck, *Reformed Dogmatics*, 2:481.

59. Poythress, *Interpreting Eden*, 273.

60. See for a discussion of this theory, Kelly, *Creation and Change*, 241–53.

61. Gitt, *In the Beginning*, 124; on the origin of information, also see Lennox, *God's Undertaker*, 174–92.

62. Al Wolters, "Creation as Separation: A Proposed Link between Bible and Theory," in *Facets of Faith and Science*, ed. Jitse van der Meer, vol. 4, *Interpreting God's Action in the World* (Lanham, Md.: University Press of America, 1996), 350–51.

comments, "In terms of modern scientific understanding of heredity and genetics, a seed having its own uniquely structured, extremely complex DNA can only specify the reproduction of that same plant type." The expression "according to its kind" "does emphatically place limitations on the tremendous amount of variational potential with each type of kind of organism God created." Consequently, "this would not allow interrelation of all living things by common ancestry and descent as modern evolutionary dogma insists,"[63] and so science needs to take heed to this biblical teaching. The matter is important, as indicated by the fact that the phrase "according to its kind" is repeated several times in Genesis 1 (vv. 11, 12, 21, 25). Jonathan Sarfati comments that "because of the inadequacies of man-made classification systems, creationists have devised a biblically-based system called *baraminology*, the study of the boundaries of the created kinds."[64] The kinds that God created in the various types of organisms endure up to the present. The apostle Paul noted that "God gives it [what you sow] a body as He pleases, and to each seed its own body. All flesh is not the same flesh, but there is one kind of flesh of men, another flesh of animals, another of fish, and another of birds" (1 Cor. 15:38–39).

God created plant life before animals, thus ensuring that food was available for them. "However, this totally contradicts the accepted evolutionary progression of life forms that has marine animals, both invertebrates and vertebrates, evolving hundreds of millions of years before the appearance of fruit trees and other complex plants."[65]

Although we have difficulty imagining it, God created the plant life before he made the sun. There was light, of course, but not sunlight. Again, we need to respect and be in awe of God's inscrutable wisdom in deciding on this sequence of events. As Calvin noted, this order did not happen by chance. "But in order that we might learn to refer all things to him, he did not then make use of the sun" for the sustenance of the plants. It is God who makes plants grow.[66]

---

63. Snelling, *Earth's Catastrophic Past*, 1:215; similarly Edward J. Young, *Studies in Genesis One*, 92n96.

64. Sarfati, *Genesis Account*, 180; for more on this issue and related matters, see Wayne Frair, "Baraminology—Classification of Created Organisms," *CRSQ* 37 (2000): 82–91; Wise, *Faith, Form, and Time*, 99–139.

65. Snelling, *Earth's Catastrophic Past*, 1:216.

66. See Calvin, *Genesis*, 1:82–83.

Day Four

"Then God said, 'Let there be lights in the firmament of the heavens to divide the day from the night; and let them be for signs and seasons, and for days and years; and let them be for lights [lit. luminaries] in the firmament of the heavens to give light on the earth'; and it was so. Then God made two great lights: the greater light to rule the day, and the lesser light to rule the night. He made the stars also. God set them in the firmament of the heavens to give light on the earth, and to rule over the day and over the night, and to divide the light from the darkness. And God saw that it was good. So the evening and the morning were the fourth day" (Gen. 1:14–19).

With the word of His command, God placed lights in the expanse of the heavens. This is the same firmament or expanse that separated the waters on the second day of creation. We saw in an earlier discussion (chapter 7) that this expanse is the sky or heaven that we see. Depending on the context it could refer to the immediate atmosphere where the clouds are or to what is beyond our atmosphere, outer space, where the sun, moon, and stars are found.

The Luminaries

The placing of these lights or luminaries in the expanse or firmament of heaven means that God created them or called them into being on the fourth day ("let there be lights"). Some would deny that this is the case and assert that God only gave existing entities a certain function. Interestingly, such thinking is found in the Dutch Reformed tradition of the late nineteenth and early twentieth century. G. Ch. Aalders, for example, considered that when the heavens were created at the very beginning (v. 1), they must have included the heavenly bodies. In his view, "although these bodies did exist, as far as their substance was concerned, they were now established as 'lights' to 'give light on the earth.' The emphasis is placed on the *function* of certain heavenly bodies to give light on the earth."[67]

But this view fails to explain why heaven or the heavens could not exist without the planets and objects that now populate its space. Furthermore, and

---

67. Aalders, *Genesis*, 1:63–64 (italics in the original); also Aalders, *De Goddelijke openbaring*, 275–76. His contemporaries Geerhardus Vos and Herman Bavinck held similar views: "These [the lights] are the substantial objects, but the material for them will have been present earlier" (Vos, *Reformed Dogmatics*, 1:171). "This [the creation of sun and moon] does not imply that the masses of matter of which the planets are composed were only then called into being, but only that all these planets would on this day become what they would henceforth be to the earth" (Bavinck, *Reformed Dogmatics*, 2:481). Similarly, others, such as Leupold, *Exposition of Genesis*, 1:70–71, and more recently, Sailhamer, *Genesis Unbound*, ch. 13, Kindle.

more tellingly, the biblical text uses the same terminology ("let there be") with the creation of the luminaries—the sun, moon, and stars—as was used for the creation of light and the firmament or expanse (vv. 3, 6). Also, it is clearly stated that on the fourth day "God made two great lights…. He made the stars also. God set them in the firmament of the heavens" (vv. 16–17). There is no indication that this making was from preexisting material. Given the context, the verb translated "made" in the expression "God made two great lights" (v. 16) means "to create." This usage of the verb rendered "to make," meaning in the context (of "let there be") "to create," is found earlier in the narrative (vv. 6–7) and elsewhere, as the parallelism in the Isaiah passages indicates (Isa. 41:20; 43:7; 45:7, 12).

Another consideration is that if God had simply made the luminaries visible on the fourth day by giving them the function of light-bearers, one would have expected the text to say that they appeared, as the dry land is described as appearing on the third day (Gen. 1:9). It is very difficult to escape the notion that Genesis 1 teaches that the heavenly bodies that give light were created on the fourth day, and the earliest interpretations and translations of the Old Testament support this. Furthermore, this is the historic Reformation understanding, and the vast majority of scholars today also agree that this is the plain message of the text.[68]

It is noteworthy that the light created on the first day is distinct from the sun and moon, which are identified as light-bearers (*məʾôrôt*). They are not the origin of the light, but only instruments to diffuse the light.[69] With the creation of light-bearers, God instituted, as Calvin noted, "a new order in nature, that the sun should be the dispenser of diurnal light, and the moon and stars should shine by night…. God ordained certain instruments to diffuse through the earth, by reciprocal changes, that light which had been previously created. The only difference is this, that the light was before dispersed, but now proceeds from lucid bodies; which, in serving this purpose, obey the command

---

68. See translations in McNamara, *Targum Neofiti 1: Genesis*, 54; Mahler, *Targum Pseudo-Jonathan: Genesis*, 18; Grossfeld, *The Targum Onqelos to Genesis*, 42; NETS, 6; Luther, *Works*, 1:41; Calvin, *Genesis*, 1:83; Turretin, *Institutes*, 1:451; for modern views from a variety of backgrounds, see Westermann, *Genesis 1–11*, 129; Adele Berlin, Marc Zvi Brettler, and Michael Fishbane, eds., *The Jewish Study Bible* (New York: Oxford University Press, 2004), 13; Van Selms, *Genesis*, 1:31; Mathews, *Genesis 1–11:26*, 153. For a critique of Sailhamer (see previous note), see Kulikovsky, *Creation, Fall, Restoration*, 114–15.

69. Martin J. Selman, "ʾwr," *NIDOTTE* 1:326, 328. One could render Gen. 1:15 literally: "and let them be for light-bearers in the firmament of the heavens to give light on the earth."

of God."[70] As instruments to spread the light, the light-bearers are servants of God. This characterization contrasts with, and may polemize against, pagan mythological and astrological beliefs that the sun, moon, and stars are deities that rule the earth. Indeed, it is noteworthy that Genesis 1 avoids using the names "sun" and "moon." Israel's neighbors considered these to be gods.[71]

The Task of the Luminaries

As servants of God, the luminaries have the God-given task "to divide the day from the night," and therefore they also determined "days and years" (v. 14). The fact that the days and years are mentioned together as entities known to us again underlines the fact that the creation days, in terms of their approximate length, are days as we know them. The days as God created them in the beginning are the days we can still use today to calculate the span of a day and the length of a year. Although day and night had already been a reality for three days, the sun and moon were henceforth to rule over and demarcate the periods of light and darkness (v. 16). Their rule is evident from their dominance of the day and night skies, respectively. Although they have the task of separating light from darkness, making day and night, they can only do so according to the will of the sovereign Creator. As the psalmist praised God, "The day is Yours, the night also is Yours; You have prepared the light and the sun" (Ps. 74:16). Calvin notes, "God governs the days and nights by the ministry of the sun and moon."[72]

These luminaries are also to be "for signs and seasons, and for days and years" (Gen. 1:14). This passage can also be rendered "as signs to mark seasons and days and years" (NIV 1984). Both translations are possible. With the second one, the luminaries have the task of indicating the seasons, days, and years. The word translated "sign" is therefore descriptive of the function the luminaries have. The first rendering is, however, also possible. Then the luminaries themselves are to be for signs, apart from their duty to indicate days and years. This rendition therefore enlarges the task of the luminaries.[73]

How can the luminaries be for signs? What are signs? Geerhardus Vos aptly noted that they are "a kind of writing, written by God in the sky with His fingers. These signs indicate the climate, the weather and its changes, and

---

70. Calvin, *Genesis*, 1:83.

71. Gerhard F. Hasel, "The Significance of the Cosmology in Genesis 1 in Relation to Ancient Near Eastern Parallels," *AUSS* 10 (1972): 12–14. See also Mathews, *Genesis 1–11:26*, 154–55.

72. Calvin, *Genesis*, 1:87–88.

73. A good discussion on the purpose of the luminaries can be found in Gispen, *Genesis*, 1:59–61; also see Lawrenz and Jeske, *Genesis 1–11*, 61–64.

sometimes by their constellations or by their sudden appearances proclaim important events in advance."[74] Indeed, at times during the history of salvation the LORD used the heavenly bodies to convey a message, for both the present and the future. The light of the rainbow was set in the heavens as a sign that God remembers His covenant between Noah and every living creature that "the waters shall never again become a flood to destroy all flesh" (Gen. 9:15). Abraham was assured that his descendants would be as plentiful as the stars in the heavens (15:5). Joel prophesied that God would "show wonders in the heavens and in the earth: blood and fire and pillars of smoke. The sun shall be turned into darkness, and the moon into blood, before the coming of the great and awesome day of the LORD" (Joel 2:30–31). Christ taught that at His second coming "the sun will be darkened, and the moon will not give its light; the stars will fall from heaven, and the powers of the heavens will be shaken" (Matt. 24:29). God could even use a star as a sign to guide the wise men to Christ's cradle (Matt. 2:1–12).

However, apart from such special divinely ordained signs, the heavenly luminaries also function as signs in more common ways. They show God's glory as creator (Ps. 8:1–3; 19:1–6). They help forecast weather. When the sun sets red, fair weather will come; when it rises red, foul weather is in store (Matt. 16:2–3). Seafarers have for millennia used the stars to guide their ships. One purpose for which God did not create the luminaries is that they serve as astrological signs, that is, that we would use the heavenly bodies for the purpose of divining their supposed influence on human affairs and events on earth. The LORD warned against worshiping the heavenly bodies and looking to them for guidance (Deut. 4:19; Isa. 47:13; Jer. 10:2; Dan. 2:27).

The luminaries are also to be for "seasons." The word used here in the original language (*mô'ēd*) means an appointed time or fixed time. The moon has a decisive role to play in determining such times and seasons and in so doing also sets the dates for Israel's festivals. Indeed, one can justify the translation that the luminaries are "for festivals" since these festivals could also be in view here. When Scripture says elsewhere (Ps. 104:19) that God "appointed the moon for seasons" (the same word for "seasons" is used here as in Gen. 1:14), Calvin comments, "This is to be understood of the ordinary and appointed feasts."[75] The fact that the task of the moon can be understood to include setting the times

---

74. Vos, *Reformed Dogmatics*, 1:172.
75. Calvin, *Commentary on the Book of Psalms*, 4:161; for a full discussion of the translation "festivals," see David J. Rudolph, "Festivals in Genesis 1:14," *TynBul* 54, no. 2 (2003): 23–40.

for the feasts is another indication that the creation work of God is preparing the world for human habitation.

It is not until Genesis 1:16 that God identifies the lights He has set in the heavens. "Then God made two great lights: the greater light to rule the day, and the lesser light to rule the night. He made the stars also." Although the stars are in fact a greater light than the moon, Scripture here uses the language of human observation and so accurately describes the luminaries.

At the end of the day, "God saw that it was good. So the evening and the morning were the fourth day" (v. 19). We today can also testify to how good God's creation of the heavens is and how it reflects His glory (Ps. 8:3–4; 19:1–2). Who can look up at the night sky and see the innumerable stars and not be completely in awe at the immense grandeur of God's work? "Lift up your eyes on high, and see who has created these things, who brings out their host by number; He calls them all by name, by the greatness of His might and the strength of His power; not one is missing" (Isa. 40:26). God determined their number and indeed "calls them all by name" (Ps. 147:4). This is an astounding fact. According to Jonathan Sarfati, the number of stars "is so vast that even using a computer that could count a trillion of these every second, it would take over 300 years to count this high." Indeed, "the host of heaven cannot be numbered" (Jer. 33:22).[76]

The Fourth Day and Science

Some would say that Scripture errs when it speaks of a greater and lesser light, referring to the sun and moon. After all, the moon has no light of itself and only gives reflected light. Calvin correctly and sensibly responds to such thoughts by remarking that although Moses realized that the moon's light was not its own, "he deemed it enough to declare what we all may plainly perceive, that the moon is a dispenser of light to us." In other words, the heavens are described from humanity's vantage point: "Moses here addresses himself to our senses."[77] Calvin makes similar comments when discussing the fact that God "made two great lights" in the expanse of the heavens (Gen. 1:16), referring to the sun and moon. Calvin notes that scientifically speaking this is not accurate, since Saturn is larger than the moon. However, "Moses wrote in a popular style things which, without instruction all ordinary persons, endued with common sense, are able to understand; but astronomers investigate with great labour whatever the sagacity of the human mind can comprehend." Calvin expresses

---

76. Sarfati, *Genesis Account*, 207.
77. Calvin, *Genesis*, 1:85–86.

appreciation for the scientific endeavor and also comments that to quibble about Saturn being larger than the moon is "something abstruse, for to the sight it appears differently. Moses, therefore, rather adapts his discourse to common usage."[78] In other words, Scripture speaks from our vantage point as we perceive the heavens.

Francis Watson has noted that Calvin's approach shows that we need to distinguish between the concerns and perspectives of Scripture and science. In any discussion of the Bible and science, each case needs to be considered on its merits. If there is a difference between Scripture and science on a given topic, "a scientific finding or hypothesis may simply represent a different perspective from that of the scriptural text rather than the assertion of one truth claim in opposition to another." Since Scripture views creation from our human vantage point, "the scriptural account should have precedence over the scientific one at points where the two come in contact." But "the scientific account is not to be neglected" since it speaks of God's own creation and "provokes a more insightful reading of the scriptural text that is not content merely to note and paraphrase its fact-like assertions, but seeks to uncover their significance and rationale." Furthermore, "since the scientific account operates within a different frame of reference from the scriptural one, the interpreter should seek to *explain* the difference rather than *deny* it." An important consequence of recognizing this difference is that "where one attempts to show that scripture is confirmed by science or science by scripture, the integrity of both discourses may be compromised."[79]

Calvin's distinguishing between the concerns and perspectives of the scientist and those of the reader of Scripture is indeed a helpful reminder that we should neither distill scientific data from the plain reading of the biblical text in an unwarranted way nor impose scientific theory on the biblical text in an unjustifiable manner. This does not mean that we cannot see agreements and points of convergence with what Scripture and scientific fact or theory tell us, but the integrity of both Scripture and science must be respected. This includes the fact that in principle Scripture is not falsifiable by science.[80] The creation

---

78. Calvin, *Genesis*, 1:86–87; similarly, 79 (on Gen. 1:6); cf. the sixteenth-century discussion described in Howell, *God's Two Books*, 100–102, 141–43, 221–22.

79. Francis Watson, "Genesis Before Darwin," 27–28 (italics in the original); also see Poythress, *Interpreting Eden*, 231–36.

80. In the attempts to harmonize Scripture with current scientific insights, "the shared assumption was that scripture is in principle *falsifiable* by science." Francis Watson, "Genesis Before Darwin," 28 (italics in the original). Calvin did not seek harmonization if matters were not clear. For example, he interpreted Gen. 1:20 as indicating that birds were created from the

events recorded in Scripture as factual cannot be disproved because scientists have no empirical access to these events and reconstructing them unavoidably depends on assumptions that cannot be verified. These observations need to be kept in mind when we consider the next issue provoked by the Genesis account of the fourth day.

Scientists have balked at the notion that light was created before the luminaries. Physicist Howard J. Van Till asks, "How is it possible to have light before lights?" and indicates that this is a nonsense question because there is no chronological order in Genesis 1.[81] We might ask whether exegetes such as Aalders, who held that the substance of the luminaries was already in existence on the first day and that God only gave them a function on the fourth day, struggled with the same scientific question. In any case, there are currently exegetes who hold this position because of the difficulty of scientifically envisaging the appearance of light before light-bearers.[82] But as Meredith Kline notes, if the luminaries were not created on the fourth day, then in fact this was the only day on which God did not create anything, making this day unjustifiably unique.[83]

Scientists who want to honor the clear message of Genesis 1 have suggested scenarios to try to think through what was involved. As a physicist, Humphreys has put forth theories as to what may have been involved, but as Douglas Kelly notes, although further research may confirm some of Humphreys's ideas, "in the meantime it seems best to admit our ignorance of 'the mechanics' of light on the first and fourth days."[84] The same can be said of other theories.[85]

What is clear is that within the space of a day, within the evening and the morning of the fourth day, God called all the luminaries into existence! We cannot comprehend this. This is totally counter to what science is theorizing today with its evolutionary models to explain how the cosmos came into existence over billions of years. But as Snelling notes, if we accept God's Word as true, then we need to question the uniformitarian, naturalistic assumptions underpinning modern astronomy. He admits that in spite of current theories by scientists who respect the authority of Scripture, the final explanation may not

---

waters. Yet, he accepted this seemingly unreasonable fact because one should submit to God's Word. Calvin, *Genesis*, 1:88–89.

81. Howard J. Van Till, *The Fourth Day* (Grand Rapids: Eerdmans, 1986), 90.

82. See for a brief overview, Kulikovsky, *Creation, Fall, Restoration*, 133–35.

83. Kline, "Space and Time," 8.

84. Humphreys, *Starlight and Time*, ch. 2, Kindle; the quote is from Kelly, *Creation and Change*, 264.

85. See, e.g., Sarfati, *Genesis Account*, 216–18.

yet have been discovered. But "our allegiance should be, without question, first and foremost to the Scriptures and not to the interpretations made by finite, fallible men who do not acknowledge either God or His work in creation."[86]

Day Five

God has established firm boundaries between land and water and between the firmament and the waters. Vegetation flourished and the luminaries are separated and rule day and night. Everything was now ready for creation's first inhabitants to begin populating the earth, water, and sky. On the fifth day God created the fish and the birds. "Then God said, 'Let the waters abound with an abundance of living creatures, and let birds fly above the earth across the face of the firmament of the heavens.' So God created great sea creatures and every living thing that moves, with which the waters abounded, according to their kind, and every winged bird according to its kind. And God saw that it was good. And God blessed them, saying, 'Be fruitful and multiply, and fill the waters in the seas, and let birds multiply on the earth.' So the evening and the morning were the fifth day" (Gen. 1:20–23).

The Creation of Fish and Birds

God's creation work on the fifth day resulted in living creatures. For the first time living beings moved about! There was conscious life and motion according to the wishes of the creatures in the waters and the sky. The waters did not bring forth the fish; God called them into existence.[87] This point is underlined with the words "so God created great sea creatures and every living thing that moves" (v. 21). This first use of the term "create" since verse 1 indicates that God's creation work reaches a new stage with the calling into existence of animate beings. In the next chapter of Genesis we read something of God's method of creating the birds. He had formed them out of the ground or soil (2:19).

The living creatures that swarmed through the waters included all types of life—not only fish but all variations of life inhabiting the waters ("every living thing that moves") including "the great sea creatures," such as whales and the like (1:21). The separate, specific mention of "great sea creatures" underlines God's almighty creative power. Even the largest beings on earth are under His sovereign control (cf. Ps. 148:7)—a message possibly also directed against pagan

---

86. Snelling, *Earth's Catastrophic Past*, 1:223.

87. Regrettably, the KJV mistranslates with "let the waters bring forth" following the ancient Greek translation. See the discussion in Lawrenz and Jeske, *Genesis 1–11*, 66–67; and Gispen, *Genesis*, 1:64.

mythological notions of divine, big monsters that need to be conquered.[88] The description of what flew through the air is, like what was created in the waters, equally comprehensive ("every winged bird according to its kind") (Gen. 1:21). Although the translation "every winged bird" is not inaccurate, the original term is more comprehensive and here, considering the context, includes all winged creatures. Dictionaries therefore correctly define the basic sense of the term as "everything that flies," "flying things," and "flying creatures, fowl, insects."[89]

There was a veritable explosion of life. The text gives the impression that large numbers were immediately created. The waters swarmed with life and every kind of winged creature—every imaginable kind of birds and insects— was flying around. Each was made "according to its kind" (v. 21). As noted with the third day, the criteria of what belongs to a biblical "kind" are different from those used by modern science to define different classifications of life.

For the first time during the events of creation, God addresses His creation and speaks words of blessing. Blessing implies endowing with power; it is not a mere wish. When God blessed the life He had created, He gave His creation the ability to regenerate, and so His blessing was articulated as a command: "Be fruitful and multiply!" It is because of that blessing and command that we today can still witness the seas and sky full of living creatures, each according to its kind. God's blessing at creation works through and is effective right up to the present time.

The Fifth Day and Science

Contrary to evolutionary theory, there was no gradual chance development of animate life from lower forms of life to higher forms. Rather, God commanded and there was abundant life with enormous variety in the waters and in the sky! This included every type of living entity inhabiting earth's waters and atmo- sphere. God created the sea animals and the birds simultaneously, a fact also contradicting the theory of evolution.

Andrew Snelling helpfully contrasts what happened on the fifth day with what evolutionary theory holds. According to the theory, "marine invertebrate organisms evolved first, followed by marine vertebrates, then land plants, later

---

88. In favor of seeing the reference to pagan mythological beasts are, e.g., Sarna, *Genesis*, 10; Cassuto, *Genesis*, 49–51; Currid, *Against the Gods*, 44–45; expressing doubt is, e.g., Gispen, *Genesis*, 1:65–66; also see Douglas Frayne, "The Fifth Day of Creation in Ancient Syrian and Neo-Hittite Art," in *Creation and Chaos: A Reconsideration of Hermann Gunkel's Chaoskampf Hypothesis*, ed. John Scurlock and Richard H. Beal (Winona Lake, Ind.: Eisenbrauns, 2013), 63–97.

89. Respectively, *HALOT*, 801; *DCH* 6:312; BDB, 733.

still land animals, then birds, and finally, mammals." Genesis, however, states that plants came on the third day followed on the fifth day by the simultaneous appearance of all life in the waters and atmosphere. Large and small were all created together. Snelling then notes that it is therefore

> impossible to equate the biblical order with the evolutionary scheme, which is unfortunately what many well-meaning Christians have suggested in their efforts to somehow reconcile the claims of modern science with the Genesis record. Such compromises, whether labeled theistic evolution, day-age creation, or progressive creation, all utterly fail because the evolutionary order simply does not match the God-given record of creation.[90]

God created the creatures of the fifth day "according to their kinds" (v. 21). These "kinds" are not the same as what we call "species."[91] Scientifically, "according to its kind" means, in the words of Snelling, that "God had programmed the actual biochemical reproductive systems of these animals to assure the fixity of the different 'kinds.' Thus, the DNA molecule of heredity for each kind allows for wide individual variations only within these boundaries and not beyond the structures of the kinds themselves." This is consistent with the science of genetics.[92] In other words, God designed all the forms of living things to have and preserve their distinctiveness within clear boundaries. A "kind" can only beget the same "kind," or "like begets like." O. T. Allis writes that evolutionists try to prove that like begets *un*like, and so attempt "to bridge all the gaps which separate the different forms of existence, one from the other, in order that all may be evolved ultimately from 'protoplasm.'"[93] Such an understanding contradicts Scripture.

Day Six

A lot happened on this climactic sixth day. Three times we read "God said," resulting in the creation of all the living creatures that make earth their home, the creation of the first human beings, and the divine blessing on them. The events of this day conclude God's work of creation. His handiwork is now finished.

---

90. Snelling, *Earth's Catastrophic Past*, 1:227.
91. See further Wise, *Faith, Form, and Time*, 99–139; also see above in the discussion of the third day on this issue.
92. Snelling, *Earth's Catastrophic Past*, 1:225.
93. Allis, *God Spake by Moses*, 12.

The Creation of Animals

"Then God said, 'Let the earth bring forth the living creature according to its kind: cattle and creeping thing and beast of the earth each according to its kind'; and it was so. And God made the beast of the earth according to its kind, cattle according to its kind, and everything that creeps on the earth according to its kind. And God saw that it was good" (Gen. 1:24–25).

"Let the earth bring forth." As with the creation of plants on the third day (v. 11), God's creative decree is again addressed to the earth. However, also now the earth does not make the living creatures or bring them forth in their own creative power as in Egyptian myth.[94] "God made the beast of the earth" (v. 25), using the ground or soil as material. "Out of the ground the LORD God formed every beast of the field and every bird of the air" (Gen. 2:19; cf. Ps. 104:29).

The terrestial animals or "living creatures," that is, those that have the "breath of life," are categorized into three kinds: "cattle" or "livestock," that is, those animals that human beings would find most useful and would domesticate; "the creeping things," that is, "everything that creeps on the earth" (Gen. 1:25), all those creatures that move along the face of the earth from small mammals and reptiles to creeping and crawling insects; and "beast of the earth," that is, all those animals neither desirable nor suitable for domestication. It is noteworthy that there is an emphasis on "according to its kind." Once again, God stresses that these creatures can only reproduce within their "kind."[95]

Although no special blessing for the animals is recorded, in contrast to what was recorded in the case of the fish and fowl on the fifth day, yet such a blessing of being fruitful is explicitly mentioned after the Noachian flood (8:17) and is clearly implied in this chapter, since the text informs us that "God saw that it was good" (1:25). This statement of the goodness of creation, coming after the creation of animals, clearly separates this work of God from the creation of man which takes place on the same day.

With the creation of the animals, the earth is now ready to receive the first humans, the crown of God's work of creation. The great moment has come!

The Creation of Man: Male and Female

The importance of the creation of man is evident from the fact that prior to his creation, God took counsel with Himself. Instead of simply speaking the command, such as "let there be," we now read, "God said, 'Let Us make man'" (1:26).

---

94. Clifford, *Creation Accounts*, 105–6; Gispen, *Genesis*, 1:68.
95. For more detail on the Hebrew terms used for the different kinds of animals, see Lawrenz and Jeske, *Genesis 1–11*, 70–71.

This is an astounding revelation from God Himself given to us in clear historical prose. He takes counsel with Himself; He deliberates with Himself as He
considers His next creative and climactic work. The fullness of what the phrase
"let Us make" can imply only becomes evident in the New Testament revelation of the Holy Trinity—Father, Son, and Spirit.[96] The notion that God is here
addressing angels is not possible since God says, "Let Us make man in Our
image," and God "created man in His own image" (vv. 26, 27). Nowhere does
Scripture suggest that man is created in the image of angels.[97]

Created as God's image. In beautiful poetic parallelism, the high point of God's
creative activity is described.

> So God created man in His own image;
> in the image of God He created him;
> male and female He created them. (v. 27)

The great significance of this final handiwork of God's creation is also evident from the fact that man will be made, as God put it, "in Our image, according
to Our likeness" (v. 26). This is not the place for an extended discussion on the
meaning of these phrases,[98] but this description obviously does not refer to any
corporeal resemblance to God since He does not have a physical body. "God is
Spirit" (John 4:24). However, in creating male and female, God considered the
human body to be the most apt form for Him to show His image in creation.
After all, man was created in His image—yes, to be *God's* image. How are we to
understand the phrase "in Our image, according to Our likeness"? The answer
to that question will be found by carefully comparing Scripture with Scripture.
Although interesting studies have been done on ancient Near Eastern notions
of the relation of images to gods and the possible relevance of these notions for

---

96. For the plural of self-deliberation, see GKC §124g n2; Arnold, *Genesis*, 44; Van Selms,
Genesis, 1:35. The so-called "royal we" is not known in the Old Testament. Joüon §114e; cf.
§§114d–e. For a survey of the different views, see Randall W. Garr, *In His Own Image and Likeness: Humanity, Divinity, and Monotheism* (Leiden: Brill, 2003), 17–21.

97. Lawrenz and Jeske, *Genesis 1–11*, 73; Cassuto, *Genesis*, 55. It is interesting that although
Gispen favored the Trinitarian view, he was also attracted to the notion of angels being involved.
Gispen, *Genesis*, 1:71–73.

98. The literature on Gen. 1:26–27 is enormous. Besides the standard commentaries, one
can also consult, e.g., Bavinck, *Reformed Dogmatics*, 2:530–62; John Murray, "Man in the Image
of God," in *Collected Writings of John Murray*, vol. 2 (Edinburgh: Banner of Truth, 1977), 34–46;
J. Richard Middleton, *The Liberating Image: The Imago Dei in Genesis 1* (Grand Rapids: Brazos,
2005); Ryan S. Peterson, *The* Imago Dei *as Human Identity: A Theological Interpretation* (Winona
Lake, Ind.: Eisenbrauns, 2016), 66–83.

understanding Genesis, we need to turn to Scripture's own authoritative explanation of what being the image of God entails.[99]

Paying close attention to the larger context of Genesis and comparing Scripture with Scripture, we notice that in chapter 5 the same terms "image" and "likeness" refer to the relationship between father and son. Adam was made "in the likeness of God" (Gen. 5:1), and as such was "son of God" (Luke 3:38); Adam's son Seth was in turn made "in his own likeness, after his image" (Gen. 5:3). All of this emphasizes that when God created humans, He created them as His image, as His children, so to speak—a reality that makes human beings unique in creation and a completely different class of living beings from all others. Their identity as created in God's own image, both male and female (1:27), was special; their identity was bound in a very specific way to the Creator. This identity also meant that they were endowed with characteristics reflecting His image: true knowledge, righteousness, and holiness (Eph. 4:24; Col. 3:10). These gifts and attributes enabled Adam and Eve to pursue their God-given calling.[100]

As image of God, man was equipped to represent God's interests on earth and to act as His viceroy or vice-regent and have dominion on His behalf over creation. Indeed, the fact that this was to be his office or task as image of God is made especially clear when the Hebrew text of Genesis is translated to include a purpose clause, which is grammatically justifiable. The text then reads: "Let Us make man in Our image, after Our likeness so that they may have dominion" (Gen. 1:26).[101] To be God's image is to be His ruling representative on earth. The rule and dominion that the Creator delegated to the crown of His creation is very comprehensive and includes the blessing and responsibility to "be fruitful and multiply; fill the earth and subdue it" (v. 28). Furthermore, God gave to both man and every creature all the plants and their fruits for food (vv. 29–30). It should be noted that man's task as ruler and subduer of creation as God's representative implies that he should be the faithful and caring steward

---

99. For an attempt to find concepts of humankind as image of God in ancient Near Eastern rituals for the creation, animation, and consecration of images, see Catherine L. McDowell, *The Image of God in the Garden of Eden* (Winona Lake, Ind.: Eisenbrauns, 2015), 117–77. Also for a general survey on a possible ancient Near Eastern background for understanding the notion of image of God, see Middleton, *Liberating Image*, 93–145. For the need to determine the meaning of the image of God from Scripture rather than approaching the subject from ancient Near Eastern data, see Gispen, *Genesis*, 1:75.

100. For the image as child of the Creator, also see Meredith G. Kline, *Kingdom Prologue: Genesis Foundations for a Covenantal Worldview* (Overland Park, Kans.: Two Age, 2000), 45–46.

101. Similarly, NIV (2011) and NET; see also Arnold, *Genesis*, 45; Averbeck, "A Literary Day," 24–26.

of creation, which God made to be "very good" (v. 31). Man does not hold absolute ownership over creation (Ps. 24:1). The Creator did not give man license to
destroy or plunder it.

Man's awesome task as given by his Maker underlines and emphasizes
that when God made male and female in His image and after His likeness, He
bestowed them with a dignity and status that no other part of His creation has.
As David put it,

> What is man that You are mindful of him,
> and the son of man that You visit him?
> For You have made him a little lower than the angels,
> and You have crowned him with glory and honor.
> You have made him to have dominion over the works of Your hands;
> You have put all things under his feet. (Ps. 8:4–6)

Humans were created as a totally different class from any other living
being. This special status is also made abundantly clear from the unique way
in which God made male and female. Scripture provides more information on
their creation in the next chapter of Genesis. Although we will be returning to
Genesis 2 in the next chapter, it seems most profitable to discuss both passages
dealing with the creation of the first humans together.

The process of creation. In Genesis 1 God informs us that He took counsel with
Himself to "make" man, and He subsequently "created" him (vv. 26–27). More
detail is given in the following chapter where we read that "the LORD God formed
man ['ādām] of the dust of the ground ['adāmâ], and breathed into his nostrils
the breath of life; and man became a living being" (2:7).[102] The verb used for
forming the man from the dust (*yāṣar*) reminds us of the work of a potter. The
same verb is used of such an artisan shaping the clay into a vessel (Isa. 29:16).
It is interesting that it is also used in parallel with the verb "to create"
to describe the forming of the earth (Isa. 45:18).

To form the first human body, God used the dust of the ground. This "dust"
is "the natural earthen material which may vary from solid (even packed) earth

---

102. Walton's attempt to deny that this passage speaks of the LORD God forming man of
dust from the ground is misguided and ignores the context and Hebrew grammar. Walton, *Lost
World of Adam and Eve*, 72–74. For the translation, see standard grammars like *IBHS*, 174; Joüon,
§125v. For a critique of Walton, see Wayne Grudem, "Theistic Evolution Undermines Twelve
Creation Events and Several Crucial Christian Doctrines," in Moreland et al., *Theistic Evolution*,
800–801; and Steve Ham, "What's Lost in John Walton's *The Lost World of Adam and Eve*?," in
Mortenson, *Searching for Adam*, 165–93.

to dry, coarsely crumbled soil, to very find dust or sand."[103] "Dust" can also be used synonymously with "clay." Job addressed God, "Remember, I pray, that You have made me like clay. And will You turn me into dust again?" (Job 10:9; cf. Rom. 9:20–21). Indeed, Eliphaz pictured human bodies as "houses of clay" whose foundation or origin is dust (Job 4:19). With the fall into sin, God told Adam that he would "return to the ground, for out of it you were taken; for dust you are, and to dust you shall return" (Gen. 3:19). Yet, in spite of man's lowly origins, God set him above creation as His representative to have dominion over it![104]

Underlining the high position of man as image of God, the LORD God "breathed into his nostrils the breath of life; and man became a living being" (2:7). Elsewhere, the "spirit in man" is called "the breath of the Almighty" (Job 32:8). It is this "breath of the Almighty" that gives life to man (Job 33:4). So the LORD God personally animated and gave life to the human form that He had made from the dust of the ground and "man became a living being" (Gen. 2:7). The gift of life was given to man in a unique way compared to the rest of creation. God Himself personally imparted the breath of life and so clearly separated the being of man from the animals.[105]

Can this breath of life be equated with the Holy Spirit? From the passages just mentioned and from the fact that the Spirit re-creates the crown of creation in the renewal of all things (Ezek. 37; John 6:63; Rom. 8:10–11), we may infer that the Holy Spirit was involved in giving Adam life. But to equate the "breath of life" with the Holy Spirit says more than the biblical text makes explicit, considering that animals also have the "breath of life" (Gen. 7:22 ESV).[106] However, it is also clear that man was created for fellowship with God, and such fellowship is only

---

103. James A. Swanson, *Dictionary of Biblical Languages with Semantic Domains: Hebrew (Old Testament)* (Oak Harbor, Wash.: Logos Research Systems, 1997), no. 6760.

104. It is interesting to note that this true account of God's making man is apparently reflected in a corrupted form in ancient Near Eastern myths, both Egyptian and Mesopotamian, which picture the gods making humans from clay. See the examples in John M. Soden, "From the Dust: Creating Adam in Historical Context," *BSac* 172 (2015): 52–59, 62–66; Tikva Frymer-Kensky, "The Planting of Man: A Study in Biblical Imagery," in *Love & Death in the Ancient Near East: Essays in Honor of Marvin H. Pope*, ed. John H. Marks and Robert M. Good (Guilford, Conn.: Four Quarters, 1987), 129–31.

105. A point also made and emphasized by John Murray, "The Origin of Man," in *Collected Writings of John Murray*, vol. 2 (Edinburgh: Banner of Truth, 1977), 4–9.

106. See on these points Poythress, *Redeeming Science*, 242–44. It is interesting that it has been argued "the breath of the spirit of life" refers only to man in Gen. 7:22. T. C. Mitchell, "The Old Testament Usage of nᵉšāmâ," *VT* 11 (1961): 181; but this is not convincing considering the context, and Mitchell himself admits that his interpretation "cannot be pressed." For more on man's identity as image of God, also in light of Gen. 2:7, see Bavinck, *Reformed Dogmatics*, 2:554–62.

possible with the Holy Spirit. As a perfect human being and child of God, Adam was endowed with the Holy Spirit.[107] Indeed, the death Adam and Eve died on the day they sinned was the immediate loss of communion with God, a spiritual death (cf. Prov. 12:28; Eph. 2:1) that led to an eventual physical death (Rom. 5:12). The immediate spiritual death could only be reversed by God graciously seeking and reestablishing fellowship with them. He promised eventual victory over the serpent, Satan (Gen. 3:8–21; John 8:44; Rev. 12).[108]

The creation of the woman is mentioned later in Genesis 2. Because no helper fit for Adam was found among the animals he had named, "the LORD God caused a deep sleep to fall on Adam, and he slept; and He took one of his ribs, and closed up the flesh in its place. Then the rib which the LORD God had taken from man He made into a woman, and He brought her to the man" (Gen. 2:21–22). Consequently, the man rejoiced: "This is now bone of my bones and flesh of my flesh; she shall be called Woman, because she was taken out of Man" (v. 23).

For this divine operation, the LORD God graciously caused the man to go into a deep sleep, which functioned as an anesthetic when God removed one of his ribs, closed up the wound, and fashioned the rib into a woman. This manner of creating the woman underlined the complete unity of the human race as having only one common progenitor, namely Adam. Furthermore, it also showed beyond any shadow of a doubt that the woman is not inferior to her male counterpart, but on the same level as a creation of God. The Hebrew verb translated "made" literally means "build" and thus arouses associations, as Cassuto noted, that "just as a builder builds, with the raw materials of stones and dust, an edifice of grace and perfection, so from an ordinary piece of bone and flesh the Lord God fashioned the most comely of his creatures."[109] The fact that God also took flesh from the man along with the rib is clear from the fact that Adam could rejoice that the woman was not only "bone of my bones" but also "flesh of my flesh" (v. 23).

Is it real history? The question has been repeatedly raised whether we need to take the account of the creation of man, male and female, as recounted in Genesis 1 and 2 as true history. Did it really happen this way? Although the matter

---

107. On the indwelling Holy Spirit in Adam before the fall, see Bavinck, *Reformed Dogmatics*, 2:558–59.

108. On the reference to spiritual death, see Calvin, *Genesis*, 1:127–28; Collins, *Genesis 1–4*, 116–18; Allis, *God Spake by Moses*, 19; S. Greijdanus, *Schriftoverdenkingen* (Kampen: Kok, n.d.), 41–45.

109. Cassuto, *Genesis*, 135.

of historicity of Genesis 2 will also be addressed in the next chapter, the issue here is whether God literally took soil and made a human being from it. Did He actually breathe into the new nostrils the breath of life? There is considerable resistance to taking this account as truly relating historical events.

It is, for example, fairly common for scholars to stress that the passages about the creation of man should be understood in a figurative manner. Tremper Longman, for example, states that "the intention of the inspired author is not to inform the reader how God made the first human being but rather to tell us about the nature of humanity and important features of God's relationship with humans." Similarly, with respect to the creation of Eve, he says, "the text does not intend to tell us how God created the first woman but something about women and their relationship to men."[110] One problem with this approach is that the account itself assumes historicity, for it wants to explain the reason for a man leaving the parental home and being attracted to a woman for marriage. As the text puts it after describing the creation of the woman, "Therefore a man shall leave his father and mother and be joined to his wife, and they shall become one flesh" (2:24). It would make little sense to give such a rationale for marriage if in fact the creation of woman had not taken place from the rib of Adam so that she was of his bone and flesh.[111] But more needs to be said about determining the historicity of the accounts of the creation of male and female.

We need to recognize that when God communicates to us events of the past, He does so in such a manner that we as mere creatures can understand what the Creator is revealing about the origin of human beings. He is not conveying the events to us in terms of scientific formulae describing exactly what all took place chemically or otherwise as the body of man was created. The account was written for our human level of understanding. Furthermore, since God also elsewhere in Scripture speaks of human beginnings, we must take that information into consideration as well and accept what God reveals as true. His word is truth (John 17:17). It then becomes clear that we need to be careful not to hide behind the notion that God's accommodating to our understanding means or implies that He gives us only a figurative or symbolic and less than truthful account.

---

110. Longman, "What Genesis 1–2 Teaches," 106; for the trend and other examples, see Eugene H. Merrill, "'Where Are You, Adam?' The Disappearance of Adam and the Death of Truth," in Mortenson, *Searching for Adam*, 117–18.

111. See, e.g., Robert B. Chisholm Jr., "'For This Reason': Etiology and Its Implications for the Historicity of Adam," *Criswell Theological Review* 10, no. 2 (2013): 27–51.

With respect to Adam being created from the dust, other Scripture affirms that this is what happened. The LORD God Himself confirmed this fact when He confronted Adam with his sin and said, "In the sweat of your face you shall eat bread till you return to the ground, for out of it you were taken; for dust you are, and to dust you shall return" (Gen. 3:19). The author of Ecclesiastes describes human death in several ways and clearly alludes to the account of Adam's creation when he writes, "Then the dust will return to the earth as it was, and the spirit will return to God who gave it" (Eccl. 12:7). The apostle Paul assumes the historicity of Genesis 2:7 when he almost literally quotes the last part of this passage in the ancient Greek translation of the Old Testament: "the first man Adam became a living being" (1 Cor. 15:45). The apostle cites this passage to indicate that if there is a natural body, there is a spiritual one (v. 44), and then he also notes that "the first man was of the earth, made of dust; the second Man is from heaven" (v. 47 ESV), referring to Adam's creation from the dust and the second Adam, Christ, coming from heaven.[112] In light of the above, E. J. Young was fully justified in asserting with respect to Adam's creation that "the man was real, the dust was real, the ground was real as was also the breath of life."[113] This does not mean that we can understand it or picture the process that led to Adam's creation, but we have no choice but to accept what God Himself conveys in His Word.

Also, the historicity of Eve being created from the side of Adam is attested elsewhere in Scripture. Adam himself realized that Eve was made from his side when he rejoiced, "She shall be called Woman, because she was taken out of Man" (Gen. 2:23). The apostle Paul alludes to Genesis 2 when he writes, "Man is not from woman, but woman from man" (1 Cor. 11:8). From this passage it is clear that the apostle accepted the plain meaning of the account of God taking a rib from Adam to make Eve. This is what actually took place. It is possible that when Paul enjoins husbands to "love their own wives as their own bodies" (Eph. 5:28) he is also indirectly referring to Eve's creation. The apostle

---

112. For a summary treatment of the New Testament evidence, see David A. Croteau and Michael P. Naylor, "The Question of a Historical Adam: A New Testament Perspective," in Mortenson, *Searching for Adam*, 53–72.

113. Edward J. Young, *Studies in Genesis One*, 57. Young writes these words in the context of his discussion of anthropomorphism. See chapter 5 above under the heading "Anthropomorphic days?" Similarly, Reformed New Testament scholar S. Greijdanus, "In Edens Hof," *GTT* 17 (1916): 239–41. For a denial of the historicity and uniqueness of Adam's creation from the dust, see Walton, *Lost World of Adam and Eve*, 74–77; for a rebuttal, John D. Currid, "Theistic Evolution Is Incompatible with the Teachings of the Old Testament," in Moreland et al., *Theistic Evolution*, 859–60; and Grudem, "Theistic Evolution," 799–802.

also reaffirmed the historical order of events when he stated that "Adam was formed first, then Eve" (1 Tim. 2:13).[114]

Scripture also affirms the historicity of Adam by including him in historical genealogies (Gen. 5:1–32; 1 Chron. 1:1–27; Luke 3:23–38) and by making it clear that if there is no first Adam, then the work of the second Adam, Christ, loses its meaning. The integrity and coherence of redemptive history depends on the contrast between the first and last Adam—the first Adam being a type of the one to come (Rom. 5:12–19; 1 Cor. 15:21–22, 45–49).[115] Other indicators of the historicity of Adam and Eve include Christ's affirmation that God "who made them at the beginning 'made them male and female'" (Matt. 19:4), and the apostle Paul, in an obvious reference to Adam, asserted that God "made from one man every nation" (Acts 17:26 ESV)[116] and called him "the first man" (1 Cor. 15:45).

The Sixth Day and Science

It is interesting to note that the animals are listed twice, but the order is not the same. The first order is livestock, creeping things, beasts (Gen. 1:24); the second is beasts, livestock, creeping things (v. 25). This lack of adherence to a certain order suggests that these lists do not indicate the sequence in which the animals were created. Indeed, as Snelling notes, one can conclude that it is possible God created the land animals simultaneously. "This rules out any correlation with an evolution-based order for the development of life (that is, insects, then amphibians, then reptiles, and finally all mammals). In any case, the fact that Genesis records the birds being created the day before the land reptiles immediately makes comparison [with evolution] impossible."[117]

Another indication against evolutionary theory is that God created each class of living creatures "according to its kind." This is most emphatically stated since the phrase "according to its kind" is repeated after every category mentioned: beasts of the earth, livestock, and everything that creeps on the earth. As we detailed earlier under the third and fifth days, a "kind" can only beget the same "kind." This fact does not allow for progressive evolution of lower to

---

114. On the historicity of the creation of Eve, also see Poythress, *Redeeming Science*, 249–51.

115. Merrill, "Where Are You, Adam?," 126–36; Richard B. Gaffin Jr., *No Adam, No Gospel: Adam and the History of Redemption* (Philadelphia: Westminster Seminary Press; Phillipsburg, N.J.: P&R, 2015).

116. For the Greek text behind the NKJV's "from one blood" (instead of "from one," with "man" being understood), and for the preference of the Greek text behind virtually all translations like the ESV, see C. K. Barrett, *A Critical and Exegetical Commentary on the Acts of the Apostles* (Edinburgh: T&T Clark, 2004), 842.

117. Snelling, *Earth's Catastrophic Past*, 1:230; cf. Poythress, *Interpreting Eden*, 273.

higher forms of life. Creatures within a certain kind category, for example, a "dog kind," can, however, diversify into a wide assortment of descendants. As Sarfati notes, "Noah didn't need to take wolves, foxes, coyotes, dingoes, chihuahuas, great danes, spaniels, dachshunds, etc. on the Ark, because it was sufficient to take a pair of wolf-like creatures with all the potential for diversifying into different varieties."[118] This is not an evolution according to the theory of evolution as generally understood, but a very limited microevolution, if one wishes to use the term, since such development is restricted to within a single "kind."

It is striking and important to note that when it comes to the creation of man, no mention is made of the term "kind" (*mîn*). It is only used with plants and animals. As Rahel Davidson Schafer observes, this indicates "that humans are not capable of larger microevolution. We are God's crowning creation, made in His image. The animals can change in small or even large ways to adapt to their surroundings, but humans were created as God's perfect climax to all that had thus far been created."[119]

Under the pressures of the evolutionary theory of human origins, Reformed Old Testament scholar N. H. Ridderbos more than fifty years ago already maintained that we cannot exclude the possibility that there was a genetic continuity among all living organisms and that Adam came from an animal.[120] As one who maintained the framework hypothesis discussed in chapter 5, he gave himself this exegetical room. If the theory of evolution is accepted and Adam is considered to have evolved from a hominid or two-footed primate mammal, then he was probably not the only one around with humanlike intelligence, since others would be moving up the evolutionary path as well. So scholars have imagined that Adam would have been part of an existing population of which he may have been chieftain. Such a scenario of an existing hominid population

---

118. For a discussion of created kinds for the sixth day, see Sarfati, *Genesis Account*, 237–38; also see Kulikovsky, *Creation, Fall, Restoration*, 138.

119. Schafer, "The 'Kinds' of Genesis 1," 100. In light of the fact that the human being is unique and not part of a "kind" grouping, it is not helpful to compare animal reproduction "after their kind" with human reproduction "after his image" as done in Poythress, *Redeeming Science*, 237–38.

120. Nic. H. Ridderbos, *Beschouwingen over Genesis I*, 112–13. For a history of the theory of evolution in the Reformed Churches in the Netherlands, see Hittjo Kruyswijk, *Baas in eigen boek? Evolutietheorie en Schriftgezag bij de Gereformeerde Kerken in Nederland (1881–1981)* (Hilversum: Verloren, 2011); also Rob P. W. Visser, "Dutch Calvinists and Darwinism, 1900–1960," in *Nature and Scripture in the Abrahamic Religions: 1700–Present*, ed. Jitse M. van der Meer and Scott Mandelbrote (Leiden: Brill, 2008), 293–315.

would explain how Cain was able to get married and why he would be afraid of someone killing him for his murder of Abel (Gen. 4:14, 17).[121]

Once the theory of evolution and the possibility of pre-Adamite human-like creatures became widely accepted, many scholars generally identified as conservative have embraced views consistent with some form of the theory of evolution, and they have questioned the need to accept the literal meaning of the biblical text. This approach is often justified with the argument that Genesis does not address the issue of how Adam was created. Rather, it sets forth theological truths pertaining to the nature of humanity and its relationship to God.[122] Once this premise is accepted, various views of the origin of Adam and Eve are possible, such as that the dust the LORD God used to form Adam was actually the body of a hominid or ape that God then transformed into His image.[123] However, such a scenario contradicts the clear teaching of Scripture, and the supporting rationale remains an unproven scientific hypothesis.

Scripture clearly teaches that God did not create some intermediate, pre-human form of life before the first human being appeared. God said, "Let Us make man" (Gen. 1:26) and "the LORD God formed man of the dust of the ground" (2:7). The form of a human being was there when God breathed into him the breath of life and he became a living being (v. 27). A similar order is found elsewhere. "The first man Adam became a living being" (1 Cor. 15:45). Also, Eve is clearly distinguished from the animal world. No one suitable for Adam was found among the animals after he had become acquainted with and named all of them (Gen. 2:19–20). That reality led to God's creation of Eve.

Furthermore, with respect to the issue of the earth's population subsequent to Adam's creation, we need to remember that Adam and Eve were created as adults and they had a long life span. Adam lived to be 930 years old (5:5).

---

121. See, e.g., Kidner, *Genesis*, 28–30. For possible ways to interpret Adam's creation in the context of pre-Adamite hominids, a possibility Collins is willing to accept, see C. John Collins, "Adam as Federal Head of Humankind," in *Finding Ourselves after Darwin: Conversations on the Image of God, Original Sin, and the Problem of Evil*, ed. Stanley P. Rosenberg (Grand Rapids: Baker Academic, 2018), 157–58; C. John Collins, *Did Adam and Eve Really Exist? Who They Were and Why You Should Care* (Wheaton, Ill.: Crossway, 2011), 111–31. The pre-Adamite theory in its many different forms has a long history. David N. Livingstone, *Adam's Ancestors: Race, Religion, and the Politics of Human Origins* (Baltimore: Johns Hopkins University Press, 2011).

122. See, e.g., Walton, *Lost World of Adam and Eve*, 70–81, 103; Longman, "What Genesis 1–2 Teaches," 104–6, 120–21; also, e.g., Enns, *Evolution of Adam*, 122, 138.

123. E.g., Kidner, *Genesis*, 26–31. Collins refers to the possibility that the dust was the body of an ape or hominid but, although he could commend the view in a certain way, does not agree with it. Collins, *Science and Faith*, 268–69. For a survey of varying attempts to integrate the theory of evolution with the creation of Adam, see VanDoodewaard, *Quest*, 282–84.

Since Scripture's purpose is to give us the history of redemption, it only notes the birth of key individuals. The births of Cain and Abel are mentioned. Cain's descendants became the genealogy of unbelievers. After Cain's murder of godly Abel, the line of believers continued with the birth of Seth when Adam was 130. In the meantime, Adam and Eve undoubtedly had many other children about which Scripture makes no specific reference since it did not serve the purpose of Genesis in presenting God's work of creation and redemption. There is, however, the telling general note that Adam "had sons and daughters" (5:4). It therefore makes sense to assume that Cain married a sister and the other siblings also married each other or someone from the next generation. In any case, Eve "was the mother of all living" (3:20) and all peoples and nations descended from Adam (Acts 17:26). Consequently, marriages between next of kin must have taken place because there was no other way for Adam and Eve to be the origin of every subsequent human being.[124] Later God would ban the marriages between siblings (Lev. 18:9, 11; 20:17; Deut. 27:22), but at this time in history God made it possible for humanity to increase in this way without ill biological effects.[125]

It also needs to be noted that the evolutionary hypothesis in support of pre-Adamite creatures is unproven. Charles Darwin asserted that "all the organic beings which have ever lived on this earth have descended from some one primordial form."[126] This theory of a universal common ancestor is convincing, it is often said, because of the congruence of multiple lines of evidence from genetics, anatomy, embryology, and fossils. Scientifically speaking, however, the evidence for an evolution of human beings from some remote common ancestor is such that it remains an unproven hypothesis even though one often gets the impression that such an evolution is a settled fact. As noted in chapter 2,

---

124. Ancient Jewish tradition holds that Cain married his sister Awan. Jubilees 4:9 (2nd c. BC). See further on Jewish tradition and the fact that marriage to a sister was known in antiquity, especially in Egypt, Van Selms, *Genesis Deel*, 1:85. The view that Adam came from an existing human or near-human population is incompatible with Gen. 2:7. Such a view has been suggested by conservative scholars, e.g., Kidner, *Genesis*, 28–30; Collins, *Did Adam and Eve Really Exist?*, 121. It is remarkable that Collins gives no actual exegesis of Gen. 2:7, but does warn against "applying too firm a literalism" to this passage (154).

125. It can be noted that Abraham married his half-sister, Sarah, and God blessed this marriage (Gen. 20:12; 21:1–3). Since Adam and Eve were perfect, they had no mutant genes. The fall into sin changed that and eventually God forbade marriage of close relatives likely in part to protect humanity from defective offspring due to the large number of accumulated mutant genes by this time. See, e.g., on this issue Sarfati, *Genesis Account*, 424–28.

126. Cited from Darwin's *The Origin of Species* by Günter Bechly and Stephen C. Meyer, "The Fossil Record and Universal Common Ancestry," in Moreland et al., *Theistic Evolution*, 332n1.

the scientific enterprise has clear limitations and due to the nature of the case cannot unravel and explain how the world and human beings came into existence. We need to briefly consider the views of scientists who evaluate these so-called converging lines of evidence for a universal common ancestor.

Much has been made of advances in genetics and the apparent similarity of human and chimpanzee DNA.[127] The claim is often made that there is 99 percent identity between human DNA and that of the chimp. Interpreted through a Darwinian lens, this seems to indicate that through a random process of evolution man descended from apes. However, the reality of the data and its interpretation is far more complicated than that. By using different criteria, studies have indicated that the percentage of agreement between human and chimpanzee DNA is considerably lower. Indeed, the genetic differences are far greater than is usually reported.[128] Underlying presuppositions determine the criteria for selecting how the DNA should be compared and how the resulting statistics are interpreted. When considering all this, the question arises, why can God not use similar DNA for similar functions?[129] Or, as Norman Nevin, emeritus professor of medical genetics, puts it, "Similar structures does not mean that the organisms had a common ancestor."[130] Scripture acknowledges that there is an underlying unity in God's work of creating life. As Vern Poythress observes, "The Bible does give hints concerning similarities between human beings and the animal world. Genesis 2:7 says that, when God made man, 'the man became a living creature.' The expression 'living creature' is the same as the expression used in Gen 1:20, 21, and 24 to describe animals."[131] Seeing a certain

---

127. For what follows, see Vern S. Poythress, "Adam Versus Claims from Genetics," *WTJ* 75 (2013): 65–82. For an introduction to DNA's amazing ability to carry information, see Casey Luskin, "DNA," in *DCS*, 189–90.

128. Ann K. Gauger, Ola Hössjer, and Colin R. Reeves, "Evidence for Human Uniqueness," in Moreland et al., *Theistic Evolution*, 475–502.

129. This notion was well put by Ransom H. Poythress, a professor of biology, in his critical review of Dennis R. Venema and Scot McKnight, *Adam and the Genome: Reading Scripture after Genetic Science* (2017): "existing genetic similarity could be explained by common design to meet common functions displaying the same elegance in simplicity and symmetry we also find in the governing laws of physics and math" (*WTJ* 80 [2018]: 190).

130. Norman C. Nevin, "Homology," in Nevin, *Should Christians Embrace Evolution?*, 139 (Nevin's chapter also provides supporting evidence); further, Nathaniel Jeanson and Jeffrey Tomkins, "Genetics Confirms the Recent Supernatural Creation of Adam and Eve," in Mortenson, *Searching for Adam*, 287–330; also see Geoff Barnard, "Does the Genome Provide Evidence for Common Ancestry?," in Nevin, *Should Christians Embrace Evolution?*, 166–86.

131. Poythress, "Adam," 71; similarly, Murray, "Origin of Man," 7, 13; also see Ola Hössjer, Ann K. Gauger, and Colin R. Reeves, "An Alternative Population Genetics Model," in Moreland et al., *Theistic Evolution*, 503–21.

commonality in physical structure and design between humans and animals is therefore not unexpected.

Another aspect of the genome research that needs to be noted is that the more scientists know of the genetic system underlying the human genome, the more scientists realize its enormous complexity. Geneticist John C. Sanford demonstrated that the genetic evidence indicates that an impersonal evolutionary process could never account for the enormous irreducible complexity of the fifty thousand parts comprising a single gene. "*A single gene is just a microscopic speck of irreducible complexity within the universe of irreducible complexity comprising a single cell. Life itself is the very essence of irreducible complexity, which is why we cannot even begin to think of creating life from scratch....* If we cannot do this, why would we think that random mutations, combined with a very limited amount of reproductive sieving, could accomplish this?"[132] Furthermore, "the near-neutral nature of beneficial mutations is strong evidence that every gene had to be designed, and there is no conceivable way to build a gene one nucleotide at a time via selection."[133] Sanford concluded that "the genome, and each of its genes, must have been designed and could not have evolved." What Sanford called the primary axiom of modern Darwinism—namely, "that man is merely the product of *random mutations* plus *natural selection*"—is "false."[134]

Biological studies in the supposed evolutionary history of a kind of organism (phylogeny and phylogenetic trees) and embryology also cast doubt on the theory of evolution and the Darwinian "tree of life."[135] Anatomical studies of apes and humans also show differences that no evidence can explain as having occurred by evolution.[136] There is some scientific biological evidence that does not prove but is in agreement with what Scripture teaches. For example, with respect to the creation of Eve from Adam's rib, it is interesting to note that, according to Christopher Shaw, professor at Queen's University, Belfast, "a rib is one of the few bones in the human body that can be removed without

---

132. John C. Sanford, *Genetic Entropy*, 4th ed. (N.p.: FMS, 2014), ch. 9, under point 8, Kindle (italics in the original); also see Michael J. Behe, "Irreducible Complexity," in *DCS*, 390–91.

133. Sanford, *Genetic Entropy*, ch. 9, under point 9, Kindle.

134. Sanford, *Genetic Entropy*, ch. 9, under point 10.d, and prologue, Kindle (italics in the original); see also the detailed work of a specialist in biology and bioinformatics, Nathaniel T. Jeanson, *Replacing Darwin: The New Origin of Species* (Green Forest, Ariz.: Master, 2017).

135. Casey Luskin, "Universal Common Descent: A Comprehensive Critique," in Moreland et al., *Theistic Evolution*, 376–401; Paul Nelson, "Five Questions Everyone Should Ask about Common Descent," in Moreland et al., *Theistic Evolution*, 403–30.

136. David Menton, "Did Humans Really Evolve from Ape-Like Creatures?," in Mortenson, *Searching for Adam*, 229–62; Stuart Burgess, "Human Anatomy: Unique Upright Design," in Mortenson, *Searching for Adam*, 331–74.

significant loss of function." Furthermore, Italian scientists Francesco Callea and Michele Callea observed in connection with Eve's creation that "the rib, in particular, represents an anatomic type of long bone with a wide, spongious component rich in hematopoietic bone marrow, containing multipotent, pluripotent, and unipotent stem cells."[137]

Another area said to prove Darwinian theory is the fossil record. However, on close examination, it does not prove that all living organisms ultimately came from a single common ancestor. Reasons include the fact that the fossil record has been interpreted in different ways, earlier factual claims have evaporated, and there are many gaps and discontinuities. Such considerations have fueled skepticism about the strength and value of the fossil record for the theory of universal common descent.[138]

Conclusion

God's work of creation is truly awesome! We cannot fathom all that was involved when God in those momentous six days created all things. The words of Psalm 8 come to mind where David exclaimed:

O LORD, our Lord, how excellent is Your name in all the earth…!
When I consider Your heavens, the work of Your fingers,
The moon and the stars, which You have ordained,
What is man that You are mindful of him,
And the son of man that You visit him?…
You have made him to have dominion over the works of Your hands;
You have put all things under his feet. (Ps. 8:1, 3–4, 6)

The fact that God has subjected creation to His earthly representative, humanity, means that the scientific enterprise in seeking to think God's thoughts after Him is a most noble undertaking. It allows those with eyes to see to perceive something of the Creator's glory and greatness in His handiwork. However, when it comes to origins, the ability of science to explain how this world and life came to be must be recognized as being quite limited. The long and short of it is that the creature cannot experimentally redo creation or figure out exactly how the Creator made life in all its forms come into existence. Going through

---

137. The Shaw quotation is from Wayne Grudem, "Theistic Evolution," 802n36, in which Grudem also refers to Francesco Callea and Michelle Callea, "Adam's Rib and the Origin of Stem Cells," *American Journal of Hematology* 86, no. 6 (2011): 529.

138. Bechly and Meyer, "The Fossil Record," 331–61; Luskin, "Universal Common Descent," 372–76; Casey Luskin, "Missing Transitions: Human Origins and the Fossil Record," in Moreland et al., *Theistic Evolution*, 437–73. On the fossil record, also see the next chapter below.

each day of creation, we have seen that the biblical account leaves no room for the theory of evolution. Hard evidence from science also does not prove evolutionary theories on the origin of the cosmos, the earth, plants, animals, and humans. We can accept in faith God's clear revelation as given in Scripture. Such an acceptance does not disparage the role of science. It simply recognizes that when it comes to the origin of the world and life, science is simply not equipped to figure out how exactly the Creator did what He did. These are one-time, inaccessible events that are beyond human ability to unravel.

After God finished His creation work, He "saw everything He had made, and indeed it was very good" (Gen. 1:31). Exactly what that statement entails will be discussed in the next chapter.

9

The Completed Creation
and the Seventh Day

With His work of creation completed, "God saw everything that He had made, and indeed it was very good" (Gen. 1:31). God then "rested on the seventh day from all His work which He had done" (2:2). What does all this mean and imply? What was the state of the world when God was finished? What is the meaning of God's rest on the seventh day? Why does this day not have the ending "so evening and morning were the seventh day"? These and related issues are the focus of this chapter.

Creation after Six Days

The Work Was Finished

After the six days of creation, Scripture informs us that "on the seventh day God ended His work which he had done" (Gen. 2:2 NKJV; similarly, ESV and RSV). This is a possible literal translation of the original Hebrew. However, such a rendering suggests that God still did some creation work on the seventh day, which is clearly not the case (Ex. 20:11). To prevent misunderstanding as to when God actually finished, it is better to opt for a translation that is more accurate in this context and render: "By the seventh day God had finished his work he had been doing" (NIV; similarly, NASB, NET).[1] In agreement with this translation, Umberto Cassuto has also shown that the sense of the Hebrew text can be formulated this way: "Since God was on the seventh day in the position of one who had already finished His work, consequently He abstained from work on the seventh day."[2]

---

1. Sarna, *Genesis*, 15, 354.
2. Cassuto, *Genesis*, 62. For an interesting overview of Jewish interpretation on these issues, see Michael Carasik, ed. and trans., *The Commentator's Bible: The Rubin JPS Miqra'ot Gedolot: Genesis* (Philadelphia: Jewish Publication Society of America, 2018), 24.

It is also worthy of note how the biblical text underscores the fact that God had indeed completed His work of creating. Three times in Genesis 2:2–3 His creating activity of the first six days is described as a single work. By the seventh day "God ended His work which He had done, and He rested on the seventh day from all His work which He had done. Then God blessed the seventh day and…rested from all His work." This emphasis on God's finishing all His creation work by the end of the sixth day stresses that God left His work of creation and moved solely to His work of providence, that is, "upholding all things by the word of His power" (Heb. 1:3). While theistic evolutionists would appeal to God's creating by using providential processes, the emphatic discontinuity that Genesis 2:2–3 makes between God's finished work of creation and the history that follows argues strongly against such evolutionary reasoning.[3]

"Very Good"

After God had seen in succession that each of His acts of creation were "good," now on the sixth day we read that "God saw everything that He had made, and indeed it was very good" (Gen. 1:31). What does "very" signify? It means, of course, as Scripture continues to inform us, that "the heavens and the earth, and all the host of them, were finished" (2:1). The "host" likely refers to the sun, moon, and stars, as well as all the living creatures found in the heavens and on earth (cf. Deut. 4:19).[4] Angels could also be included (1 Kings 22:19), and their creation will be discussed in the appendix to this book. Since Genesis 1 focuses on God's work of creation with a view to preparing the world for humanity, the point to note at the completion of His work is that everything was now ready for the crown of creation, and so God's work was "very good." Everything that God had made conformed to His will and fulfilled the purpose for which He had made it. Human history can begin and bring glory to God.

In opposition to evolutionary theory, which maintains that the world began in an imperfect state and gradually improved, Scripture tells us that God's creation was good right from its very beginnings and "very good" as a completed whole.[5] There is therefore absolutely no basis for suggesting that God is the source of evil or of any imperfection. Sin, as Herman Bavinck put it, "is a power that does not belong to the essential being of the creation, a power

---

3. The same basic point is made by Lawrenz and Jeske, *Genesis 1–11*, 83. This topic has been dealt with in more detail in chapter 6.

4. Cassuto, *Genesis*, 61.

5. Gispen, *Genesis*, 1:83; Lawrenz and Jeske, *Genesis 1–11*, 80.

that originally did not exist, but that came by way of disobedience and transgression, that is, entered the creation unlawfully and did not belong there."[6]

At the same time it is difficult for us, from our vantage point in a sin-filled world, to imagine the world in its pristine condition. Accordingly, it is easy to ask all sorts of questions that Scripture does not directly answer, such as, was there any sort of death in the natural realm before the fall? Would such a death be necessarily evil? These questions have been answered differently because they require speculation.[7] According to Romans 5:12 the first sin caused death to come for all humans ("as through one man sin entered the world, and death through sin, and thus death spread to all men"). There is no mention of animal death. "The bondage of corruption" of which Romans 8:21 speaks describes our fallen world but says nothing about whether animals or sea creatures preyed on one another prior to the fall. What we do know is that the catastrophic, large-scale death and destruction of life pictured in the fossil record is consistent with "the bondage of corruption" and a world that has fallen into sin. The fossil record must therefore reflect conditions subsequent to Adam's fall. We will be returning to the issue of fossils later in this chapter.[8]

How Old Was the Earth on the Sixth Day?

Mainstream science considers the earth to be about 4.5 billion years old within a universe estimated at nearly 14 billion years. Such enormous and difficult-to-conceptualize time spans have been called deep time, an important concept for evolutionary theories.

The notion of deep time arose in the field of geology during the nineteenth century. The acceptance of this theory as a virtual fact was facilitated by ignoring or denying the biblical data that was relevant for geological research

---

6. Bavinck, *Reformed Dogmatics*, 3:74.

7. See, e.g., for an acknowledgment of plant death and of being unable to conclude that animals were originally immortal, Vos, *Reformed Dogmatics*, 1:175; similarly, Poythress, *Redeeming Science*, 120–22; arguing for animal death before the fall, Ingrid Faro, "The Question of Evil and Animal Death Before the Fall," *TJ* 36 (2015): 193–213. On the question of whether all pain and death in the natural realm is evil, see William Edgar, review of *The End of Christianity: Finding a Good God in an Evil World*, by William A. Dembski, *Themelios* 35 (2010): 140. Asserting that no animal died prior to the fall: Lisle, *Understanding Genesis*, 275–77; Jacques B. Doukhan, "'When Death Was Not Yet': The Testimony of Biblical Creation," in Gerald A. Klingbeil, *Genesis Creation Account*, 329–42.

8. For an overview of some of the issues respecting the fossil record, see Gregg Davidson, "Fossil Record (Evolutionary-Creation View)," in *DCS*, 287–90; and Marcus R. Ross, "Fossil Record (Young Earth–Creation View)," in *DCS*, 290–94.

and pointed to a young earth. The fact that leading Christian theologians also embraced the notion of deep time as truth also contributed to its acceptance.[9]

The scientific acceptance of deep time meant that it was the mechanism that theoretically enabled and gave credence to the theory of evolution. Many evolutionary problems are supposedly solved with incredibly long periods of time. But, as Old Testament professor O. T. Allis (1880–1973) noted, science is concerned with processes. The creation account "does not deny process; it ignores it. It speaks in terms of a divine fiat, which can both use and dispense with process." Allis observed that it is absurd for Christians to postulate deep time of billions of years since God is omnipotent and created time and finished his creation work in six days. Then, using the example of Christ's miracle of turning water into wine (John 2:6–11), Allis wrote, "to 'evolve' water into wine could not be done any more successfully in a million years or in a thousand million than in a 'day.' Natural processes could not accomplish it at all."[10]

Since the concept of deep time is used to solve all manner of evolutionary problems, deep time has enormous power! Indeed, astrophysicist Jason Lisle has ably defended the idea that deep time functions as a god. It has divine characteristics. It "has the power of creation." This god "has made stars, planets, and galaxies. He has made canyons, and mountains. Deep Time separated the continents and oceans. He has made all living creatures through his servant—evolution." Lisle quoted the famous words of George Wadd, "Time is the hero of the plot…. Given so much time, the impossible becomes possible, the possible becomes probable, the probable becomes virtually certain. One only has to wait; time itself performs the miracles." Like any god, deep time is also worshiped. Science textbooks pay homage to him. "Deep Time must not be questioned. That would be sacrilege!"[11]

Deep time is a false god. As we have seen, Genesis 1 gives no basis for it.[12] Biblical scholars need to be more sensitive to the unproven nature of current scientific speculation on deep time and not let it influence their exegesis of Genesis 1.[13] However, since scientific theory routinely assigns a multibillion-year

---

9. For an overview see Terry Mortenson, "'Deep Time' and the Church's Compromise: Historical Background," in Mortenson and Ury, *Coming to Grips with Genesis*, 79–104.

10. Oswald T. Allis, *God Spake by Moses* (Nutley, N.J.: Presbyterian and Reformed, 1958), 10–11.

11. Jason Lisle, "Deep Time—the God of Our Age," November 9, 2012, http://www.jasonlisle.com/2012/11/09/deep-time-the-god-of-our-age/.

12. See also Trevor Craigen, "Can Deep Time Be Embedded in Genesis?," in *Coming to Grips with Genesis*, 193–210.

13. For an informative overview see Mortenson, "Deep Time," 79–104.

age to our planet as if it is a scientifically verifiable fact, we need to take a further look at this dating from the perspective of God's finishing His work by the end of the sixth day. We will consider the biblical evidence and also briefly the scientific, and close with some additional observations.

The Events of the Sixth Day

One argument raised against the notion that each day actually consisted of a nighttime and daytime is that the events of the sixth day could not possibly fit into such a time frame. It is said that too many things happened. Genesis 1 and 2 inform us that on this day God created the terrestial creatures and Adam. He planted a garden and instructed Adam not to eat from the tree of the knowledge of good and evil. The Creator brought the animals to Adam so he could name them and come to the realization that there was no helper suitable for him. God consequently caused a deep sleep to fall on Adam, removed one of his ribs, closed up the flesh, made a woman from the rib, and presented her to Adam. God then blessed them and gave them their mandate. Some scholars have difficulty seeing how this could all take place in one day.[14] In Bavinck's view, "It may be possible for all these things to have taken place with the span of a few hours, but it is not likely." He elaborated by saying that "much more took place in each day of creation than the sober words of Genesis would lead us to suspect," and "each day's work of creation must certainly have been much grander and more richly textured than Genesis summarily reports in its sublime narrative.... The creation days are workdays of God."[15] But Bavinck nevertheless affirmed that they were days, workdays of God as defined by Scripture, that is, each having an evening and morning.

When reflecting on all the events of the sixth day, we should note that God is of course able to do as He pleases and that the time frame of a single day is more than sufficient for Him to do all that Scripture says He did on the sixth day. Furthermore, while realizing our creaturely limitations, there are indications in the text that Adam's task was humanly possible. He did not have to go looking for the animals. God brought them to him. Also, he did not have to name sea creatures or creeping things. One of reasons for the naming was

---

14. E.g., Gleason L. Archer, "A Response to the Trustworthiness of Scripture in Areas Relating to Natural Science," in *Hermeneutics, Inerrancy, and the Bible*, ed. Earl D. Radmacher and Robert D. Preus (Grand Rapids: Zondervan, 1984), 325–29; Hugh Ross and Gleason L. Archer, "The Day-Age View," in *The Genesis Debate: Three Views on the Days of Creation*, ed. David G. Hagopian (Mission Viejo, Calif.: Crux, 2001), 143–44; and for more detail, Archer, "A Response," 325–29.

15. Bavinck, *Reformed Dogmatics*, 2:500.

that God would make clear to Adam that he had no counterpart in any of the living beings God had created thus far, and so the number of creatures he had to name was limited (Gen. 2:18–20). In addition, as we noted in the previous chapter, the Hebrew word for "kind" does not denote "species." It has been estimated that Adam only had to name a couple thousand of these "kinds" or proto-species, a manageable God-given task for the perfect man whom the LORD God had created with intelligence and insight.[16]

We could entertain and consider all sorts of proposals about how the events of the sixth day transpired in order to show that these events were possible within the time frame given. But it makes little sense to go in this direction. We need to accept the biblical account in faith, knowing that the Creator is all-powerful and sovereign. He was also able to equip the perfect man He created to do the task He had assigned to him.

Apart from the fact that Scripture tells us that God created all things in six days, another piece of biblical evidence that undermines the notion that the earth is billions of years old is that what God created had all the characteristics of maturity.

A Mature Creation

God created Adam, the very first human being, as a mature person on the sixth day of creation. Furthermore, the fact that his son Seth was born when Adam was 130 years old (Gen. 5:3) implies that the sixth day was indeed a relatively short period of time. The sixth day did not take up thousands or millions of years. In any case, Adam's maturity and his full functionality right from the outset of his existence is evident from his ability to name the animals, which necessitated mature insight, from his receiving the responsibility not to eat from the tree of the knowledge of good and evil, and from his praise and understanding when he received Eve from the hand of God as his wife. The maturity of earth's first human couple immediately after their creation is also obvious from God's blessing and mandate "be fruitful and multiply" (1:28). Although chronologically merely hours old, Adam and Eve were adults.

The rest of creation also had the appearance of a certain maturity. The trees in the garden already had fruit (2:16), although they only came into existence three days prior to Adam's appearance. We can assume that creation as a whole appeared older than a few days. The landscape and any visible rocks would have had the appearance of age. The stars, which were created on the fourth

---

16. For more detail on such a scenario, see Kulikovsky, *Creation, Fall, Restoration*, 167–69; and Russell M. Grigg, "Naming the Animals," *Creation* 18, no. 4 (September 1996): 46–49.

day, were presumably visible to Adam and Eve, although mainstream science holds that the stars are so far away that it takes many light years for them to become visible on earth. More examples could be given. The six-day-old creation appeared to be much older.[17]

This state of affairs raises a question. Was God being deceptive by creating everything to appear as though it had been around for many years? The answer must be no. God, after all, has told us in His Word that He made the world in six days and that by the end of that period there were mature animals, vegetation, and human beings. We cannot impose our assumptions about how the earth should have looked after six days if God has told us otherwise. All of this of course brings us back to the issue of whether the scientific, data-based conclusion that the earth is billions of years old is accurate or whether the plain meaning of God's Word should be accepted as true, namely, that the earth is relatively young, having an age measured in thousands, not millions, of years. In dealing with this problem, it may be beneficial to consider some of the factors involved. We will consider more closely two examples of contentious issues related to dating: the evidence of the stars and fossils and how scholars who have accepted the biblical narrative of a young earth have handled the scientific evidence in these areas. Since this book is primarily a study of the biblical text, the discussion of scientific evidence will be necessarily brief, but those interested in further discussion can consult the resources mentioned in the footnotes.

Stars. According to mainstream science, the stars we see today must have originated some billions of years ago because it takes that long for light to travel the enormous distance from the stars to the earth. So God would be lying to us, so to speak, if His creation contradicts His written Word, which speaks of a world merely thousands of years old.

In response, it should be noted, however, that the laws of nature, such as the speed of light, are not autonomous unchangeable laws. As we saw in chapter 2, they are the result of creation obeying God's commands. God is free to make exceptions to what is "normal," and He informed us that He did indeed make exceptions in the first six days of creation. Those were unique events. We may therefore assume that just as the earth brought forth trees at an amazing rate so that they had a mature age on the same day, so too the stars and galaxies could have undergone a miraculously fast development so that their light was transmitted to earth and visible to Adam and Eve.

---

17. On the creation of Adam and Eve and the world having the appearance of maturity, also see Bavinck, *Reformed Dogmatics*, 2:537; Snelling, *Earth's Catastrophic Past*, 647–52.

Scientists who accept the Genesis account of a young earth and reject an evolutionary model of origins have come up with various theories as to how one could scientifically defend a young age of the universe with respect to the creation of the stars. While these theories are completely outside my field of expertise, it may be useful to mention a few for the benefit of those who may wish to follow up.[18] Australian scientist Barry Setterfield has proposed a decay in the speed of light, which close to the origin of the universe was extremely fast. American physicist D. Russell Humphreys has proposed a solution using the fact that gravity affects time, which is known as gravitational time dilation. Fellow physicist John G. Hartnett has built on this work. Astrophysicist Jason Lisle argues that the one-way speed of light is not a natural constant but a human convention. In his view, one-way speed of light to earth is essentially instantaneous, and so stars would have been visible on earth almost immediately. None of these theories is without problems, but then evolutionary paradigms are also plagued by problems. It belongs to science to keep striving to find coherence in the data it uncovers.

At the same time it is good to realize our limitations and to take seriously God's revelation in His Word. In response to the charge that God would be acting deceptively by creating stars with an apparent age of billions of years when they are only thousands of years old, John Frame aptly comments that "God has never told us that the methods scientists use to calculate the age of stars are absolutely and universally valid.... What scientists may learn from Genesis is that these methods do not work for objects that have been specially created." Frame then notes that "anyone who admits to any special creations at all must grant the reality of apparent age."[19] Similarly, Jason Lisle observed that "age is a concept of history, and is not a substance that can be measured by scientific analysis (observation and experimentation)." Scientists can "measure present rates and processes and then make an educated guess about the object's age. But that guess will be influenced by the person's view of history, and will only

---

18. What follows is from a general overview of these theories (with further references) as given in Kelly, *Creation and Change*, 192–206; a similar beneficial overview is found in Byl, *God and the Cosmos*, 189–94. More recently, John Byl, "Light-speed, Convention, and Creation," *Bylogos* (blog), February 9, 2019, http://bylogos.blogspot.com/2019/02/light-speed-convention-and-creation.html, in which Byl discusses T. G. Tenev, J. Baumgardner, and M. F. Horstemeyer, "A Solution for the Distant Starlight Problem Using Creation Time Coordinates," in *Proceedings of the Eighth International Conference on Creationism*, ed. J. H. Whitmore (Pittsburgh: Creation Science Fellowship, 2018), 82–94. Byl's solution is a rapidly matured creation; see John Byl, "Rapidly Matured Creation," *Bylogos* (blog), February 6, 2019, http://bylogos.blogspot.com/2019/02/rapidly-matured-creation.html.

19. John M. Frame, *The Doctrine of God* (Phillipsburg, N.J.: P&R, 2002), 308.

be as good as the assumptions that went into it."[20] Consequently, those holding to a young earth will consider and analyze the data differently from those with evolutionary presuppositions. At the end of the day, we say in faith with E. J. Young, "Why could not God in the twinkling of an eye have formed the stars so that their light could be seen from earth? We cannot limit the creative power of God by what we today have learned from his providential working."[21]

Fossils. Another major point of contention with respect to the age of the earth concerns fossils. If God created the earth in a mature form, does that mean that the fossils were already in place by the sixth day? If so, does that mean that large-scale death was a fact of life before the fall into sin? Is this consistent with God's pronouncing His creation "very good" (Gen. 1:31)? Furthermore, if creation was mature from the outset, how can one possibly do science and seek to measure the age of rock layers and other geological features? Answering such questions adequately is of course beyond the scope of this chapter, but a few comments can be made.

First, it should be noted that the fossil record as understood by mainline science does not provide the required proof for an evolutionary narrative in spite of protestations to the contrary. Indeed, as geologist Emil Silvestru writes, "The fossil record is as much an Achilles' heel of evolutionary theory today as it was in Darwin's time."[22] However, if Scripture is taken seriously and the effects of the devastating worldwide flood in the days of Noah (Gen. 6–9; 2 Peter 3:5–7) are factored into scientific theorizing on fossils and other geological features of our planet, then the fossil record is plausible as a consequence of that flood.[23] There is no justification for the view that God created the earth with preformed fossils in place.[24]

---

20. Lisle, *Understanding Genesis*, 291.

21. Edward J. Young, *Studies in Genesis One*, 101.

22. Emil Silvestru, "The Fossil Record," in *Evolution's Achilles' Heels*, ed. Robert Carter (Powder Springs, Ga.: Creation Ministries International, 2014), ch. 4, Kindle.

23. For more on the Noachian flood, see chapter 10 on the geography of Eden. The fossil record is used to argue for macroevolution, but the evidence from that source simply is not there; see W. R. Bird, *The Origin of Species Revisited: The Theories of Evolution and of Abrupt Appearance*, vol. 1, *Science* (New York: Philosophical Library, 1989), 178–86. For features of the strata and the fossilized life in them as consistent with a catastrophic worldwide flood, see Snelling, *Earth's Catastrophic Past*, 723–61; Wise, *Faith, Form, and Time*, 170–76.

24. Such was the view of Philip Henry Gosse, *Omphalos: An Attempt to Untie the Geological Knot* (London: John Van Voorst, 1857), 344–47; for further reasons to reject Gosse's thesis, see Terry Mortenson, "Were Fossils Created *Ex Nihilo* During Creation Week?," *Answers in Genesis*, October 6, 2006, https://answersingenesis.org/fossils/fossil-record/fossils-ex-nihilo-creation

Second, the appearance of a mature creation on day six does not make current scientific work of no avail. But again one must recognize that the work of creation was unique, which is a fact that needs to be factored into current scientific theorizing. As we saw in chapter 2, the competence of science does not extend to determining precisely how creation came to be, but science can certainly study God's world and discover the laws of nature operative today and theorize on that basis. However, if clear and relevant facts that Scripture presents are not taken into consideration in formulating scientific hypotheses, scientists will not be making use of all the available evidence and thus undermine the credibility of their theories. This fact takes us to the next consideration.

Third, new scientific evidence also needs to be taken into account even if such data is awkward and does not fit the current evolutionary paradigm. One needs to honestly confront and follow through on such evidence. For example, American paleontologist Mary H. Schweitzer made the widely reported and unexpected discovery of soft tissue in a dinosaur fossil dated according to the evolutionary framework at 67 million years ago. Since such soft tissue, including blood cells, has no known way of surviving such a time span, one would think scientists might consider dating the fossil in question to a younger age, especially since this is not the only evidence of soft tissue and remains of blood in fossils. But no, the discovery had to be fitted into the reigning scientific models, and so the issue became how such soft tissue could survive for so many millions of years.[25]

Other scientific discoveries have also prompted legitimate concerns about the reliability of methods used to date rocks and fossils. For instance, the 1980 eruption of Mount St. Helens in Washington State has raised many questions. In a single afternoon, this eruption deposited eight meters of finely layered sediment, a deposit which, according to standard geologic thinking, should have taken long periods of time. Indeed, such layered sediments are typically used to confirm a vast age for the earth. Furthermore, conventional methods of dating the new lava dome of this mountain yielded ages from 350,000 to 2.8

-week/; also John Rendle-Short, *Green Eye of the Storm* (Edinburgh: Banner of Truth, 1998), 34–37.

25. Mary H. Schweitzer, "Blood from Stone," *Scientific American* 303, no. 6 (December 2010): 62–69; also see, e.g., Mary H. Schweitzer et al., "A Role for Iron and Oxygen Chemistry in Preserving Soft Tissues, Cells and Molecules from Deep Time," *Proceedings of the Royal Society: Biological Sciences* 281, no. 1775 (January 2014): 1–10. For more examples and young-earth responses, see Sarfati, *Genesis Account*, 241–45; Philip Robinson, "Soft Tissue Preservation in a 'Jurassic' Ichthyosaur," *Creation* 42, no. 1 (2020): 36–37.

million years while in fact the dome was less than ten years old.[26] There are also indications that carbon-14 dating is not reliable. Indeed, the BBC reported that scientists discovered that "carbon dates were wrong by thousands of years and that the further back in time they went, the more out-of-date they were." Consequently, "a complete rewrite of the history of modern humans could be needed."[27] Other dating methods have also been shown to be unreliable.[28]

An evolutionary approach to fossils and geology in general has been dominant, but new hard scientific data, such as the proven unreliability of conventional dating methods and the discovery of soft tissue in fossils, does not fit the evolutionary paradigm but rather contradicts it. In light of the above, one can maintain that there had been no massive upheaval in creation resulting in countless catastrophic deaths prior to Adam and Eve's creation, and thus we may assume that there were no fossils in Eden when the first humans were placed on this earth.

Conclusion. Douglas Kelly has correctly observed that a lot of emerging scientific evidence indicates that we may be in need of a major paradigm shift in the interpretation of origins and the age of the earth.[29] Theological liberals and evangelical evolutionists are still operating within an old evolutionary model in spite of the many challenges and indicators that the model is outdated and does not fit with a lot of the scientific evidence, some of which we just noted. The importance of the presuppositional lens through which scientific evidence is filtered and theoretically organized cannot be overestimated.

Professor John Byl has emphasized the importance of giving attention to the underlying philosophical questions in the construction of scientific theory. He rightly noted that defending the faith is better done by exposing the limitations of scientific theorizing, especially with respect to origins, than by trying to demonstrate "how well the Bible fits in with human theories and standards."[30]

---

26. For the sediments, see Tasman Walker, "The Geologic Record," in *Evolution's Achilles' Heels*, ed. Robert Carter (Powder Springs, Ga.: Creation Ministries International, 2014), ch. 5, Kindle. For the dating of the lava dome, see Snelling, *Earth's Catastrophic Past*, 804. For a detailed critical review of geologic dating methods, see Snelling, *Earth's Catastrophic Past*, 797–864.

27. Cited in Terry Mortenson, "When Was Adam Created?," in *Searching for Adam: Genesis and the Truth About Man's Origin*, ed. Terry Mortenson (Green Forest, Ariz.: Master, 2016), 161.

28. See the overview of the evidence in Kelly, *Creation and Change*, 213–34.

29. For what follows, see Kelly, *Creation and Change*, 189–91; also see Kelly's chapter 9 for an overview of new, hard scientific data demonstrating a relatively young earth.

30. Byl, *God and the Cosmos*, 213; also see Byl, "Scripture and Geologists," 143–52.

In view of the clear testimony of Scripture and the limitations of science, as well as the problems with the evolutionary paradigm, there is every reason to accept the plain and obvious meaning of Genesis 1 and 2 that the earth and its inhabitants were created in six days with an appearance we today would consider old and mature. On the sixth day creation was six days old. There is no biblical warrant for an earth billions of years old but every reason to accept one merely thousands of years old. This understanding was almost universally accepted throughout the history of the church until the rise of modern science, especially geology, in the eighteenth century.[31] The overwhelming dominance of the view that the earth was relatively young is not surprising, for it is also in complete accord with the teaching of the New Testament.[32]

Additional Biblical Testimony

The Lord Jesus and His apostles Peter and Paul touched on the issue of the time of creation when dealing with a question about divorce. Christ referred to God's norm for marriage and said that "from [or "at" NIV] the beginning of the creation, God 'made them male and female'" (Mark 10:6), obviously referring to Genesis 1 and 2. Similarly, the apostle Peter used the phrase "from the beginning of creation" (2 Peter 3:4) to mean "since the world began" (NEB) or "from the time God created the world."[33] Because this is the way the phrase is used, when Christ spoke of God's creation of Adam and Eve being dated "from the beginning of creation" or "at the beginning of creation" the Savior "believed and taught that man existed essentially as long as the entire cosmos has."[34] In other words, it is impossible to place "the beginning of creation" billions of years prior to the creation of humans as evolutionary theory would have it. Humans were there right from the beginning when God created the world and all it contained.

---

31. Young and Stearley, *The Bible, Rocks and Time*, 27–46; subsequent chapters of Young and Stearley's book deal with the rise of geology as a scientific discipline and the questioning of a young earth. For a history of this development and the emerging debate on the age of the earth, see also Mortenson, *The Great Turning Point*.

32. For much more detail on the material that follows in the next section, see Terry Mortenson, "Jesus' View of the Age of the Earth," in Mortenson and Ury, *Coming to Grips with Genesis*, 315–46.

33. Daniel C. Arichea and Howard Hatton, *A Handbook on the Letter from Jude and the Second Letter from Peter* (New York: United Bible Societies, 1993), 146.

34. Mortenson, "Jesus' View," 325. Mortenson is answering Collins, who concluded that Mark 10:6 does not refer to the time since creation and thus has no bearing on the age of the earth. See, respectively, Collins, *Science and Faith*, 105–7; Mortenson, "Jesus' View," 337–39.

The apostolic testimony likewise attests to a young earth.[35] The apostle Paul indicates that humans are basically as old as creation because from the time the world was created they could see God's invisible qualities of power and divinity. As he wrote to the Roman Christians, "Since the creation of the world His invisible attributes are clearly seen, being understood by the things that are made, even His eternal power and Godhead, so that they are without excuse" (Rom. 1:20). As New Testament scholar C. E. B. Cranfield noted, "The point made is that the self-revelation of God here referred to has been continuous ever since the creation" or "since the creation of the world."[36] From the beginning ("since the creation of the world") humans saw this revelation—it was "clearly seen"—so that humankind is without excuse. Consequently, the beginning of humankind coincides with the beginning of the world, and the human race is basically (since the sixth day) just as old as the world.[37]

In sum, the biblical testimony counters the mainstream geologic understanding of rock strata of enormous ages and the reigning evolutionary theory. There is also no basis for arguing that God made use of evolution to make His creation come about. Scripture gives no justification for theistic evolution. There is also no basis for old-earth creationism, which accepts much of the evolutionary model.

As a final note on the subject of the earth and its maturity at creation, we need to remember that the six-day creation is not the only example of God making something that had the appearance of age. When the LORD reaffirmed the legitimacy of Aaron's priesthood, he had twelve rods representing all the tribes of Israel placed in the tent of meeting. The next day, when the rods were retrieved, the one of Levi, with Aaron's name on it, had sprouted, produced buds and blossoms, and had even yielded almonds. What one would have expected to take months, had now taken place within a matter of hours (Num. 17:1–9). One can be sure that these were real blossoms and real almonds, as though they had matured normally. Another example of miraculous growth is the plant "which came up in a night" to shade Jonah (Jonah 4:10). A further example of sudden maturity is the miracle in the days of Elijah when the widow's jar of flour and the jug of oil could be repeatedly used to prepare food without the jar and jug becoming empty until the day that the LORD sent rain on the land (1 Kings

---

35. For what follows, see especially Ron Minton, "Apostolic Witness to Genesis Creation and the Flood," in Mortenson and Ury, *Coming to Grips with Genesis*, 347–71.

36. C. E. B. Cranfield, *A Critical and Exegetical Commentary on the Epistle to the Romans* (repr., London: T&T Clark, 2004), 1:114.

37. See further Minton, "Apostolic Witness," 355–58.

17:8–16). The flour and oil appeared to be the result of harvesting and process-
ing, but that was not the case. A similar miracle of producing something that
appeared much older than it actually was took place when the Lord Jesus turned
water into wine in a matter of seconds. The wine was experienced as being of
top quality, as one would expect of expertly aged wine that had gone through
a long fermentation process (John 2:1–11). Likewise, the bread and fish that
were miraculously multiplied appeared as if they had gone through a process of
growing and maturation before being available for consumption (John 6:9–13).

Examples like these should make us realize that God can sovereignly bring
into existence something that appears to be older than it actually is. There is
no reason to question that God could do the same during the creation week.
We do not know, and do not need to know, how God did this. Indeed, what is
the creature to demand of the Creator and question Him (cf. Isa. 55:8–9; 1 Cor.
2:14)? But as surely as the Son of God did His miracles on earth, so through
Him the entire universe was called into being within six days (Col. 1:16). We
can accept this in faith.

Summary

When the LORD God finished His work of creation by the end of the sixth day,
His handiwork looked much older than the number of days involved in their
making would suggest. After all, these days were defined by an evening and a
morning and not by eons of time. But in spite of the relatively short time span
the Creator took to bring it all about, a mature-looking world greeted Adam
and Eve. The first humans were also full-grown adults who were given the mandate to be fruitful and multiply. The trees bore fruit for their sustenance, and
mature animals, insects, and sea creatures populated His world in abundance.
We need to accept this young age of a mature earth in faith.

Attempting to calculate the exact age of the relatively young earth is not
necessary. Since this book is a study of Genesis 1 and 2, it is also beyond its
scope to delve into the question of the precise age of the world and to discuss all
sorts of chronological issues, such as, for example, the genealogies of Genesis 5
and 11. Suffice it to say that the consensus among those who honor Scripture as
reliable is that the earth is roughly between six and ten thousand years old—a
biblically defensible position, whether you hold to gaps in the genealogies or
not.[38] The important takeaway is that maintaining that the earth is young is in

---

38. For a recent summarizing study on this point, see Mortenson, "When Was Adam
Created?," 139–63. Mortenson mentions an age of six to seven thousand years; for six to ten thousand years, see Todd S. Beall, "Age of the Universe and Earth," in *DCS*, 33. The issue of possible

full accord with Scripture and is not disproven by current scientific data and theories. The factual scientific information available can be explained in more than one way, and at the end of the day it needs to be underlined that it is beyond the competence of science to understand the origin of the universe and to determine when exactly it came into being.

When God had finished His work, He rested on the seventh day. What was the nature of the seventh day, and what constituted His rest?

The Nature of the Seventh Day

Scripture informs us that after God had finished His six-day work of creation, "He rested on the seventh day from all His work which He had done. Then God blessed the seventh day and sanctified it, because in it He rested from all His work which God had created and made" (Gen. 2:2–3).

Remarkably, this day does not end with the formula that characterized all other days, as for example, "so the evening and the morning were the sixth day" (1:31). This fact has led some to conclude that the seventh day was and is unending.[39] To sort out the different arguments we will first consider the material strictly from the point of view of its immediate context and of the Hebrew text and style. Subsequently, we will deal with specific arguments for its unending character and with the wider context of the rest of Scripture.

The Context of Genesis 2

Was the seventh day without end? To answer that question, the text and context of Genesis 2 are of prime importance. As a first observation, it can be noted that in and of itself, the omission of the refrain ("so the evening and the morning were") is no justification for negating the apparent meaning of the passage in its context. After six unique days of creation, each characterized by the phrase "evening and morning," a climactic seventh day follows in which no creative activity takes place. Since that day is not like the preceding

---

genealogical gaps disrupting the chronological timeline in the Genesis genealogies continues to generate discussion. See, e.g., Andrew E. Steinmann, "Gaps in the Genealogies in Genesis 5 and 11?," *BSac* 174 (2017): 141–58; and the response of Jeremy Sexton, "Evangelicalism's Search for Chronological Gaps in Genesis 1 and 11: A Historical, Hermeneutical, and Linguistic Critique," *JETS* 61 (2018): 5–25; and the rejoinders that follow his article. Any gaps or omissions that could exist in these genealogies would not allow for millions of years of human history.

39. Collins, *Genesis 1–4*, 125; Mathews, *Genesis 1–11:26*, 181. John Murray, in an unconvincing argument, presents the seventh day as comprising all of history by contrasting the six days of creation with what followed. John Murray, *Principles of Conduct: Aspects of Biblical Ethics* (Grand Rapids: Eerdmans, 1957), 30 (see further below).

six unique days, why should the seventh day also have the designation "evening and morning"? That unique six-day period of God's awesome creation work is over. Israeli Hebrew scholar Shalom Paul has suggested that the omission of this type of refrain (in this case, "evening and morning") is a Hebrew stylistic feature also found elsewhere in Scripture after a patterned series. The omission is an "example of the breakup of a stereotypic pattern upon reaching the climactic crescendo conclusion."[40] In other words, the refrain has been intentionally left out to underline the climax of the seventh day. Consistent with this approach, Andrew Steinmann has noted that the "lack of the refrain is a literary device that sets this day apart and serves to emphasize its holiness."[41]

One can also note that just like the other days, the seventh day also is defined by a number and the term *yôm* ("day")—"the seventh day" (2:2). This feature associates the seventh day with the preceding six and is another reason not to conceive of it as never ending. It is noteworthy that the words "the seventh day" now come at the beginning and not at the end of this day. This could underline that it was the first day that God did not do any creating. He had stopped this work, and there was no need to give a "progress report" as occurred with the other days prior to the number of the day being given.

Another consideration is that God also blessed this specific day and made it holy (v. 3). God did not bless thousands of forthcoming years. No, the text says He blessed the seventh day. That also indicates that it is a day and not unending time.[42] And this day is distinct from all the other days that followed, including the day God cursed the serpent and the ground because of the fall into sin (3:14, 17). That was a day dominated by God's curse and not characterized as a day of blessing.

In answer to the question, "In what way is the seventh day different from the succeeding days, since on them, too, God did no additional work?" Cassuto responded, in part, "The difference consists in the *novel character* of the seventh day; after a series of six days on each of which some work of creation

---

40. Shalom Paul, commenting on the oracles of Amos 1 and 2, writes, "Just as the account of creation in Genesis 1 is formulated with a recurrent final refrain at the end of each of the six days, culminating with the account of the Shabbat on the seventh day, which omits this repetitive refrain, so, too, the first seven oracles (with all their internal variants) are ordered according to a preconceived pattern, which is deliberately altered when the climax of the prophecy is reached— the oracle against Israel." Shalom M. Paul and Frank Moore Cross, *Amos: A Commentary on the Book of Amos* (Minneapolis: Fortress, 1991), 76–77.

41. Steinmann, *Genesis*, 58.

42. A point also made in Terence E. Fretheim, "Were the Days of Creation Twenty-Four Hours Long?," in *The Genesis Debate: Persistent Questions about Creation and the Flood*, ed. Ronald F. Youngblood (Grand Rapids: Baker, 1990), 20.

was wrought, came a day on which God did not work or add anything to his creation; hence his abstinence from labor remained linked with the day on which this situation first arose."[43] And so God sanctified this day (and, again, not unending time) and set it apart as holy. Indeed, we have here the origin of the weekly Sabbath (Ex. 20:8–11).[44]

Perhaps an ecclesiastical study committee best sums up and puts an end to this part of the argument.

> If we assume that the absence of the morning and evening refrain means the seventh day is an unending day, we are not only guilty of a somewhat wooden method of interpretation, but also of creating a radical discontinuity between the seventh day and the other six days. We would have six days that are clearly part of the created order followed by a seventh day that is excised from the created order and still, somehow, somewhere, continuing on. Such a method would inject an element of a-historical fantasy into the most historically foundational chapter of the Bible.[45]

A completely different argument for an unending seventh day was made by John Murray. He asserted that the seventh day was "in the sphere of God's action, not the seventh day in *our* weekly cycle." He wrote of "the realm of God's activity" in which "there were six days of creative action and one day of rest. There is the strongest presumption in favour of the interpretation that this seventh day is not one that terminated at a certain point in history."[46] However, Murray gives no proof that this is so, and as Noel Weeks observes, "the text gives no indication of such a sphere distinction. The text is not concerned with God as he is in himself but with God's activity in a temporally conditioned creation. Even the seventh day refers not to God in himself but to God in relation to his creation."[47]

---

43. Cassuto, *Genesis*, 64 (italics in the original); also underlining the special character of this day as evidenced by the absence of the refrain is, e.g., Sarna, *Genesis*, 15; Arnold, *Genesis*, 49–50.

44. It is beyond the scope of this chapter to discuss issues relating to the day of rest as a creation ordinance. See further, Richard B. Gaffin Jr., "A Sabbath Rest Still Awaits the People of God," in *Pressing Toward the Mark. Essays Commemorating Fifty Years of the Orthodox Presbyterian Church*, ed. Charles G. Dennison and Richard C. Gamble (Philadelphia: Committee for the Historian of the Orthodox Presbyterian Church, 1986), 33–51.

45. "Report of the Committee to Study the Views of Creation," in *Minutes of the Seventy-First General Assembly…of the Orthodox Presbyterian Church* (Willow Grove, Pa.: Orthodox Presbyterian Church, 2004), 219.

46. Murray, *Principles of Conduct*, 30 (italics in the original).

47. Noel K. Weeks, "The Hermeneutical Problem of Genesis 1–11," *Themelios* 4 (1978): 18n17; cf. also the notion of upper registry time critiqued in chapter 5 of this book.

In light of the above, we can conclude that there is no justification from Genesis 2 for suggesting that the seventh day had no end. However, those who would defend an unending seventh day also appeal to the New Testament, to which we now turn.

John 5:17 and Hebrews 4:3–11

The main New Testament arguments have been succinctly stated by C. John Collins. As part of his justification for interpreting the days of creation as analogical days, he considers the seventh creation day to be unending not only because the closing refrain ("the evening and the morning") is not found for that day, but also because of what Jesus said when He healed a man on the Sabbath. After Jesus had restored the man's health, He met the condemnation of the Jews by answering, "My Father has been working until now, and I have been working" (John 5:17). Collins comments that God's working on His Sabbath "only makes sense if we suppose that his creation Sabbath continues."[48] Collins also finds support for this notion in Hebrews 4:3–11, which brings together Psalm 95 and Genesis 2:1–3, which both speak of God's rest. "This rest is both something into which God entered on the creation Sabbath and something into which people may enter through faith (v. 10). Of course the best way for this to make sense is if the author thought that the creation Sabbath continues into the present."[49] Collins then reasons that if the creation Sabbath, the seventh day, was not an ordinary day, the other days likewise might not have been ordinary days.[50] How does one respond to these New Testament arguments for an unending seventh day? Collins is not the only one to hold them. They are typical for this position.[51]

With respect to John 5:17, Collins reads far more into the text than what it actually says. When Christ healed on the Sabbath and said, "My Father has been working until now, and I have been working," there is nothing to suggest that the Sabbath on which God is working (e.g., in His work of providence) is

---

48. Collins, *Genesis 1–4*, 92; similarly, Collins, "Reading Genesis 1–2," 87; Collins, "Reading Genesis 1:1–2:3," 137–38.

49. Collins, *Genesis 1–4*, 93; similarly, Collins, "Reading Genesis 1–2," 87; Collins, "Reading Genesis 1:1–2:3," 137–38.

50. Collins, "Reading Genesis 1:1–2:3," 139; Collins, *Genesis 1–4*, 125; Collins, "Reading Genesis 1–2," 87–88.

51. See similar arguments in, e.g., Aalders, *Genesis*, 1:75–76; R. Laird Harris, "The Length of the Creative Days in Genesis 1," in *Did God Create in Six Days?*, ed. Joseph A. Pipa and David W. Hall (Taylors, S.C.: Southern Presbyterian Press, 1999), 109–10; Poythress, *Redeeming Science*, 133–35.

any other than the Sabbath that the Jews observe and on which the Lord Jesus did His healing. God is always at work upholding creation all the days of the week, including the Sabbath day.

The appeal to Hebrews 4:3–11 does not convince either. For one thing, this passage does not deal with the length of the seventh day after God's work of creation. Rather, it urges Christians to enter into God's rest, which He enjoyed on the seventh day. As will become clear, we need to distinguish between the duration of God's ongoing rest and the length of the seventh day. In further considering the arguments for an unending seventh day it may be helpful to do so within the context of the main message of the first half of Hebrews 4 and the quotation from Genesis 2:2.

What occasioned the rest that God enjoyed on the seventh day? Genesis 2 tells us that God "rested on the seventh day from all His work which He had done" (v. 2); this work was His work of creating. The divine rest does not mean that He became inactive. As just noted, Christ said, "My Father has been working until now" (John 5:17). God's rest means that He was no longer busy creating. "He rested from all His work which God had created and made" (Gen. 2:3).

Now, the translation "He rested" (vv. 2, 3) is fine in conveying the general meaning of the text, but to deal properly with the issue of the seventh day we should translate using the first meaning of the verb rendered "rest" (*šābat*). We then have the translation "He ceased from work" or "He abstained from work." In both cases the Hebrew text signifies completed action and translates into an English perfect. In other words, God's action on that day, the action of ceasing from work, was finished and done. The original text gives no suggestion that it continued into the indeterminate and unending future. The action of abstaining from work was completed on a specific day, the seventh day.

Of course, the result of no longer working means that one is resting, and that resting in this case continues beyond the seventh day. Using the translation "rest" rather than "cease" ("He rested") can easily lead the reader to understand the verb in question (*šābat*) to refer to God's continual rest from His creative labor so that this action on the seventh day is seen as continuing up to the present time. But that is not the meaning of the original text. It refers to a specific completed past event. God "ceased from His work." We need to distinguish that single action of stopping His creative work from the resulting and lasting divine rest that followed. The text of verses 2 and 3 speaks of a one-time completed action of abstaining from the work of creating.[52] That one-time action

---

52. For the first meaning of šābat ("to cease"), see *DCH* 8:254–55; *HALOT*, 1407; Cassuto, *Genesis*, 63. Referring to the use of the perfect in Gen. 2:2–3, E. J. Young stated, "There is no

was done on the seventh day, but the rest that followed went beyond that day. One cannot therefore say or imply that the single action of God's ceasing from His work is an ongoing action on an ongoing, unending seventh day.[53] The quotation of Genesis 2:2 in Hebrews 4:4 is consistent with the Hebrew text. Quoting the Septuagint, the verb used in Hebrews 4:4 also has as its first meaning "to cease" (*katapauō*) and should be translated as a completed past action. Again, to avoid misunderstanding, it literally translates as "and God ceased from all His works."[54]

To further support this understanding, we need to consider more closely the divine rest and the consequences of God's single, past action of stopping His creation work. God did not need to stop His work because He was tired. God does not grow weary (Isa. 40:28). The cessation of work resulted in a rest characterized by God's joy and delight in His finished creation, which He judged to be "very good" (Gen. 1:31). He was, to use human terminology, refreshed by it. Indeed, elsewhere we read that on the seventh day God "rested [*šābat*] and was refreshed [*npš*]" (Ex. 31:17). The original verb used to express this refreshment is derived from the Hebrew word for soul (*nepeš*) and, as Nahum Sarna put it, "conveys the notion of a fresh infusion of spiritual and physical vigor, reinvigoration of the totality of one's being."[55] All this is a human way of conveying the thought that God rejoiced in His creation and, as becomes clear, He wanted the crown of His creation, His children Adam and Eve, to rejoice in His creation work as well and so to participate in His rest (cf. Mark 2:27). But they fell into sin and forfeited this joy. Nevertheless, God is faithful and He still wanted them to enter into His rest and be united with Him in His joy for His creation work.

Scriptural warrant whatever (certainly not Hebrews 4:3–5) for the idea that this seventh day is eternal." Edward J. Young, *Studies in Genesis One*, 78n73; similarly, Steinmann, "A Note on the Refrain," 138n21.

53. E.g., it is unjustifiable to say on the basis of Gen. 2:3 that "since God's rest goes on forever, God's *day* of rest also goes on forever." Poythress, *Redeeming Science*, 133 (italics in the original). The verb in v. 3 translated "rested" does not express ongoing action but the completed action of ceasing from His work of creating.

54. BDAG, 524; LSJM, 904; GE, 1069. The Septuagint (Greek) of Gen. 2:2b–3 has been rendered "and he left off on the seventh day from all his works that he had made. And God blessed the seventh day and hallowed it, because on it he left off from all his works that God had begun to make." NETS, 7.

55. Nahum M. Sarna, *Exodus: The Traditional Hebrew Text with the New JPS Translation* (Philadelphia: Jewish Publication Society, 1991), 202; see also Johannes Pedersen, *Israel: Its Life and Culture* (London: Oxford University Press, 1926), 1–2:154, who characterizes the verb as implying "a fresh acquisition of strength in which manner the person in question gains more life and thus more soul."

His work will not be undone. He therefore promised to defeat Satan and renew creation (cf. Gen. 3:15).

In the context of God's ongoing promise that His people will enter His rest, we read, "There remains therefore a rest for the people of God. For he who has entered His rest has himself also ceased from his works as God did from His" (Heb. 4:9–10). Just as God completed the action of abstaining from His work of creating, so at a certain point in time His people have ceased from their works. Again, the relevant verb in verse 10 translates into a simple perfect (he "has himself also ceased from his work"), paralleling and following the example of God's one-time action of ceasing on the seventh day.[56] Once a believer has finished his pilgrimage and the task God has given him, he can enter God's rest. He has "ceased from his works" (a completed action; v. 10). Since one only enters the divine rest by faith (4:3), the author of Hebrews exhorts, "Let us therefore be diligent to enter that rest" (v. 11). The full rest spoken of is an eschatological rest, one to be realized in the future. Then one will truly enjoy the rest, refreshed and reinvigorated in the totality of one's being as a new creation. Those who enter that rest before Christ's return are blessed, for they rest from their labors (Rev. 14:13).

By quoting Genesis 2:2 in this general context of the divine rest, the writer of Hebrews shows that the Genesis passage not only describes a historical event but also indicates God's clear intention that humanity should share in His rest and rejoice in His handiwork. But this quotation also underlines that God's abstaining from His work was a completed action and not an ongoing and unending activity, just as believers need to complete their God-given task before they can enter His rest (Heb. 4:10). And just as God's abstaining from His work of creation did not mean inactivity, for the Father continues His work (John 5:17), so too the final completion of the task God has given His people in this life does not mean inactivity, but an eternity of joyous service and worship to the glory of their Creator and Redeemer. Then the rest God had intended for humanity will be fully realized.[57]

In conclusion, a careful reading of Genesis 2:2–3 and its use in Hebrews 4 teaches us that although God's rest is unending, His action of ceasing from His work of creating, and so entering that rest, was completed in the past on the seventh day. That seventh day was followed by an eighth day and so on. There

---

56. See further on this, Steinmann, "A Note on the Refrain," 138n21.

57. For the above, see Gaffin, "A Sabbath Rest," 38–41; Geerhardus Vos, *Biblical Theology: Old and New Testaments* (Grand Rapids: Eerdmans, 1954), 156–57; Philip Edgcumbe Hughes, *A Commentary on the Epistle to the Hebrews* (Grand Rapids: Eerdmans, 1977), 161–62.

is no basis for assuming that the seventh day continues until now. Believers follow the example of God. When they have ceased from their work, which is when their earthly service is completed, they too enter God's rest.

Summary and Conclusions

After six days, God finished His work of creation and pronounced His finished work to be "very good" (Gen. 2:3). Both the short time span in which creation took shape and its "very good" condition are in clear opposition to evolutionary thinking, which posits an imperfect world that gradually improved over a long period of time.

While mainstream science assigns an age of billions of years to the earth, Scripture presents us with a young earth with an age measured in mere thousands of years. Although we cannot scientifically understand the creation works of almighty God, we accept in faith the clear message of Scripture that it all took place in six days, each consisting of nighttime and daytime. By the end of that period, God's handiwork had the appearance of maturity, as clearly evidenced, for example, in a mature Adam and mature trees in the garden. Since God has informed us of earth's maturity at the outset, He was not being deceptive in making the earth look older than it actually was in real time.

Science needs to reckon with this reality and consider that the rate of current natural processes cannot necessarily be projected into the past and yield accurate dates with respect to the age of the earth. God is sovereign also over the laws of nature. One's presuppositions, whether evolutionary or young earth, are critical for how one analyzes scientific data and draws conclusions from it. Problems surrounding the methods used to date the stars and fossils illustrate this fact.

Although some would want to argue that the seventh day was unending, there is no biblical justification for such a position, either from Genesis 2 or from John 5 and Hebrews 4. God's act of ceasing His work of creation was finished by the seventh day and that single action of cessation needs to be distinguished from His rest that followed. The fact that God blessed the seventh day and made it holy only makes sense if this was a real day with nighttime and daytime. With His setting apart this special day, God established a basic rhythm of work and rest in life on earth in which He also meant Adam to participate.

What did Adam's world, the garden of Eden, look like? That question leads us to consider another aspect of Genesis 2 in the next chapter.

10

The Historicity of Genesis 2
and the Garden of Eden

Although many scholars have interpreted Genesis 2:4–25 in ways that deny or undermine its historicity,[1] the text itself indicates that this portion of Scripture also is to be accepted as relating real historical events. In this chapter we will try to listen carefully to what Scripture says. As in previous chapters, the intent is to focus on issues of historicity and not to give a running detailed commentary on the entire biblical passage. The creation of Adam and Eve as reported in Genesis 2 has already been dealt with in chapter 8. In this chapter we will consider the historicity of Genesis 2 and therefore look at its structure, the context of the biblical account of Adam's creation, the geography of the garden of Eden, the identity of the tree of the knowledge of good and evil, and the issue of whether the garden was a temple. But first we need to deal with the character and purpose of this part of Scripture.

The Character and Purpose of Genesis 2:4–25

The literary style of Genesis 2 differs markedly from that in Genesis 1. Whereas the narrative prose of Genesis 1 has a very lofty style structured according to set formulaic repetitions demarcating the days, the style of Genesis 2 is less exalted and more like the narrative that continues through the rest of Genesis. Why are the styles so different when both deal with creation?

To begin with, this part of Scripture commences with the first of the "these are the generations of [*tôlǝdôt*]" headings that provide the framework of the book of Genesis. As discussed at the beginning of chapter 3 of this study, these words can be translated as "this is the history of" and they indicate the beginning of a new narrative that relates what became of or resulted from the events recounted in the preceding section (in this case the creation narrative

---

1. See, e.g., the brief survey in Wenham, *Genesis 1–15*, 54–55.

of Genesis 1). And so we need to recognize that Genesis 2:4 is a heading that introduces the next section with the words: "This is the history [*tôlədôt*] of the heavens and the earth when they were created, in the day that the LORD God made the earth and the heavens."

As also noted in chapter 3, Genesis 2:4 is clearly a unit. It is important to honor the unity of this heading and recognize its grammatical structure as one complete sentence. Unfortunately, this characteristic is not always acknowledged, and some Bible translations place a period within verse 4 and join the rest of verse 4 to the beginning of verse 5, forming a single sentence that may be translated, "This is the account of the heavens and the earth when they were created. When the LORD God made the earth and the heavens—and no shrub of the field had yet appeared on the earth" (NIV [1984]).[2] Another possibility when verse 4 is not taken as a single separate unit is to run verse 4 and the first part of verse 5 together as a single long sentence, yielding the translation, "This is the history of the heavens and the earth when they were created, in the day that the LORD God made the earth and the heavens, before any plant of the field was in the earth" (NKJV). But the Hebrew text gives no justification for these arrangements. The Hebrew equivalent of a period is placed after verse 4 and not within that passage, and verse 5 is treated as one complete sentence. We can be grateful that many English translations acknowledge the full stop at the end of verse 4, yielding translations such as, "This is the account of the heavens and the earth when they were created, in the day that the LORD God made earth and heaven" (NASB).[3]

The fact that verse 4 introduces a new section informing the reader of what became of God's six-day work of creation makes clear that what follows in Genesis 2 cannot be called a second account of creation, as has sometimes been done. It has its own specific perspective, and its purpose is not to retell the account of creation. Indeed, the words used for creating in Genesis 1 (*bārā'* ["to create"] and *'āśâ* ["to make"]) are not even used in Genesis 2:5–25 after the heading of verse 4. We therefore need to be sensitive to the specific objective of this account when considering its contents and apparent differences with Genesis 1. Since the Holy Spirit inspired the writing of both Genesis 1 and 2, there are no contradictions between the two. Genesis 2 assumes Genesis 1 and, as we will see shortly, builds on it.

It is also good to remember that, as we saw in chapter 3, this heading has a chiastic structure, which emphasizes that the primary concern of Genesis 2

---

2. Similarly, CSB, NRSV.
3. Similarly, KJV, ESV, NET, NIV (2011).

will be the earth and what happens on it. After all, the order of the words "the heavens" and "the earth" at the beginning of verse 4 is reversed at the end of this passage so that "the earth" is mentioned first as forming the primary focus of what follows. Since "heaven" virtually always comes first in the phrase "heaven and earth," placing "earth" first ("earth and heaven") at the end of verse 4 is very emphatic and underlines the concern for what happens on the earth in the narrative that follows.[4]

And so Genesis 2:4 introduces a new account that runs to the end of Genesis 4 and relates what became of the creation events reported in Genesis 1. It tells us what developed from the original perfect creation, which was "very good" (1:31). These chapters narrate the fall into sin, the expulsion from the garden, the first offspring of Adam and Eve, and the first murder.

Indicative of the different focus of 2:4–25 is also the change in how the Creator is referred to, namely, the change from "God" in Genesis 1 to "LORD God" in chapter 2. The usage of the word *'ĕlōhîm* ("God") in Genesis 1 underlines the transcendence, greatness, and power of the Almighty who created and who is known through His creation. In Genesis 2 the shift to the designation *yhwh 'ĕlōhîm* ("LORD God") underlines the identity of God, the Creator, as the God of the covenant who revealed Himself as such to His people (cf. Ex. 3:13–15). This change in names is consistent with the main purpose of Genesis 2 of highlighting the creation of Adam, and later Eve, with whom God conversed and made a covenant (Hos. 6:7 ESV).[5] The designation "LORD God" indicates that from the beginning God related to Adam and Eve as the God of the covenant who had fellowship with them, was faithful to His work of creation, and did not abandon them even after their fall into sin. The LORD God continued to deal

---

4. According to Wenham, Ps. 148:13 is the only other place where "earth" precedes "heaven" when paired. Wenham, *Genesis 1–15*, 55.

5. "Like Adam they transgressed the covenant" (Hos. 6:7 ESV); similarly, NASB, NIV (1984). It is beyond the scope of this book to delve into the issue of whether this passage could be referring to a place named "Adam." On Hos. 6:7, see Benjamin B. Warfield, "Hosea 6.7: Adam or Man?," in *Selected Shorter Writings of Benjamin B. Warfield*, ed. John E. Meeter (Nutley, N.J.: Presbyterian and Reformed, 1970), 1:116–29; Duane A. Garrett, *Hosea, Joel* (Nashville: Broadman & Holman, 1997), 162–63; Byron G. Curtis, "Hosea 6:7 and Covenant-Breaking Like/at Adam," in *The Law Is Not of Faith: Essays on Works and Grace in the Mosaic Covenant*, ed. Bryan D. Estelle, J. V. Fesko, and David VanDrunen (Phillipsburg, N.J.: P&R, 2009), 170–209; and Brian C. Habig, "Hosea 6:7 Revisited," *Presb* 42 (2016): 4–20. More generally on the covenant with Adam, see, e.g., S. G. de Graaf, *From Creation to the Conquest of Canaan*, vol. 1 of *Promise and Deliverance*, trans. H. Evan Runner and Elisabeth Wichers Runner (St. Catharines, Ontario: Paideia, 1977), 36–42; Bavinck, *Reformed Dogmatics*, 2:564–71.

with the crown of His creation in the history of redemption according to His promise of salvation (Gen. 3:15).

In summary, Genesis 2:4–25 begins the narrative of what happened to the perfect world that God created in Genesis 1. To that end, the purpose of this chapter is to set the stage for the events that followed by describing how things were before the fall into sin, focusing, as we will see shortly, on what transpired on the sixth day with the climactic acts of creating Adam and Eve.[6] Indeed, we learn more of what happened on that day than is related in Genesis 1. This directed attention to the sixth day gives this chapter a special character with its key focus on the formation of man from the dust of the ground and woman from the rib of the man. To them God gave Eden and His mandate for their lives.

The Structure of Genesis 2:4–25

In order to appreciate the historicity of Genesis 2 and the context of Adam's creation, we need to understand the structure of verses 4–25 and interpret some key passages, beginning with the meaning and place of the much-discussed text of verse 5. We must also consider when God created the animals that He brought to Adam for him to name and when He planted Eden and placed Adam in it. Getting clarity on these issues will help us to understand the makeup of this part of Scripture.

No Rain and No One to Work the Ground
The narrative sets the stage with these words:

These are the generations [*tôlǝdôt*]
of the heavens and the earth when they were created,
in the day that the LORD God made the earth and the heavens.

When no bush of the field [*śîaḥ haśśādeh*] was yet in the land and no small plant of the field [*ēśeb haśśādeh*] had yet sprung up—for the LORD God

---

6. John Walton denies that Gen. 2 deals with the sixth day, and he suggests that the people created in Gen. 1 may not have been Adam and Eve. Such a denial does injustice to the heading and context of Gen. 2:4–25. Walton designates 2:5–25 as a sequel to Gen. 1 and consequently does not have "to worry about fitting Genesis 2 into day six." However, he misunderstands the nature of chapter 2 and does not sufficiently recognize that other similar *tôlǝdôt* headings introduce new material while reaching back into the previous narration before continuing the history (e.g., Gen. 5:1–2 refers back to 1:27, and Gen. 11:10–17 refers back to 10:22–25). Similarly, Gen. 2 refers back to day six in Gen. 1 in order to move the history forward. See Walton, *Lost World of Adam and Eve*, 63–69; also see the critiques of Poythress, *Interpreting Eden*, 188n3; and Currid, "Theistic Evolution Is Incompatible," 869–70.

had not caused it to rain on the land, and there was no man to work the ground, and a mist [ESV note: or *spring*] was going up from the land and was watering the whole face of the ground—then the LORD God formed the man. (Gen. 2:4–7a ESV)

What is the significance of the references to no plants and herbs being in the field because of a lack of rain and to there being no one to work the ground? How does this passage fit within the context of the first chapter of Genesis?

Meredith Kline has claimed that this passage describes a time within God's work of creating when the entire earth was without vegetation. The reference to the need for rain shows that God used ordinary providence during the days of creation. According to Kline it is clear that "the Creator did not originate plant life on earth before he had prepared an environment in which he might preserve it…. The unargued presupposition of Gen. 2:5 is clearly that the divine providence was operating during the creation period through processes which any reader would recognize as normal in the natural world of his day."[7] Consequently, the six days of creation in Genesis 1 cannot possibly describe a chronological sequence. With such an argument he supported his framework hypothesis.[8] Furthermore, Kline noted that according to the normal working of creation there would be no plants on the third day before there was sunlight on the fourth (1:11–19).[9]

What are we to make of Kline's approach? Does it do justice to the context and purpose of Genesis 2? This chapter, as just noted, is primarily concerned with what became of God's work of creation as described in Genesis 1, and its primary focus is the creation of human beings. It is not concerned with either a chronological recounting of creation or how God created the plants. Genesis 2:5 therefore does not teach that God used only providence in the six days of creation. It is clear from Genesis 1 that God created by divine fiat, including the plants on the third day.[10] As will become clear shortly, the plants mentioned in Genesis 2 are not the same as those referred to in Genesis 1. The subject matter of Genesis 2 is not the creation of plants as recorded in Genesis 1. Kline's argument that there was no sunlight has little weight since God had already created the light needed for the plants (1:3).[11]

---

7. Kline, "Because It Had Not Rained," 149–50.

8. As critically discussed in chapter 5.

9. Kline, "Because It Had Not Rained," 151–52.

10. Edward J. Young, *Studies in Genesis One*, 63–65; John D. Currid, *A Study Commentary on Genesis*, vol. 1, *Genesis 1:1–25:18* (Darlington, U.K.: Evangelical Press, 2003), 42.

11. Much more could be said on this issue. See further Kline, "Because It Had Not Rained"; Kline, "Space and Time"; and Irons and Kline, "The Framework View," 230–36, with critical

In trying to understand the reference to plants not being in the field, we need to listen very carefully to the text. As noted earlier, Genesis 2:4 is a separate unit beginning a new section of the book. "These are the generations [or history] of the heavens and the earth when they were created, in the day that the LORD God made the earth and the heavens" (ESV). What follows next is a series of circumstantial clauses (vv. 5–6) describing the conditions that existed when God created human beings (v. 7). "When no bush of the field was yet in the land and no small plant of the field had yet sprung up...then the LORD God formed the man" (Gen. 2:5–7a ESV). This was the state of affairs when God made human beings.[12]

At first glance this description of the setting for Adam's creation appears to contradict the creation account of Genesis 1, which informs us that the plants were created on the third day. First impressions, however, can be mistaken, and in this case they certainly are. God's Word does not contradict itself, and a close reading of 2:5 sheds further light on the situation.

The plants referred to in chapter 2 are not the same as those created on the third day in chapter 1. "The bush of the field [śîaḥ haśśādeh]" (2:5) is not mentioned in the account of the creation of the plants on the third day in chapter 1, and the herbs (ʿēśeb) mentioned in Genesis 1 and 2 are qualified differently. The relevant plant mentioned in 2:5 is the herb or plant (ʿēśeb) of the field, and a field suggests human cultivation. The one mentioned in chapter 1 by the same name (ʿēśeb) is "the herb that yields seed according to its kind" (v. 12). There is therefore a clear distinction between the herb mentioned as created on the third day and that referred to in Genesis 2. As Umberto Cassuto notes, Scripture stresses again and again with the repetition of the word "seed" (1:11–12) "that the world of vegetation, as it was formed on the third day, was composed of those trees and herbs that naturally reproduce themselves by *seed* alone. Those plants that needed something else, in addition to seed [such as human care and cultivation], were excluded." He further states that although single

---

responses in Hagopian, *The Genesis Debate*, 257–77. Also see Mark D. Futato, "Because It Had Rained: A Study of Gen 2:5–7 with Implications for Gen 2:4–25 and Gen 1:1–2:3," *WTJ* 60 (1998): 1–21. Some major difficulties with Futato's understanding have been pointed out by Jordan, *Creation in Six Days*, 235–45. For critiques of Kline's work, also see Edward J. Young, *Studies in Genesis One*, 58–65, 74; Jordan, *Creation in Six Days*, 51–69; Poythress, *Redeeming Science*, 341–45; Pipa, "From Chaos to Cosmos," 154–64.

12. The fact that Gen. 2:5–6 consists of circumstantial clauses is widely recognized, although interpreted variously; Hamilton, *Genesis*, 156; Wenham, *Genesis 1–15*, 57; Arnold, *Genesis*, 56; Westermann, *Genesis 1–11*, 197.

specimens of the herb ('*ēśeb*) might have been found here or there, they "were not found in the form of fields of grain until man began to till the ground."[13]

Once the above distinctions between the references to plants in Genesis 1 and 2 are recognized, we are in a better position to try to understand the significance of the fact that there was no "bush of the field" and no "herb of the field" at Adam's creation. Two interpretations of the situation can be noted.

One interpretation emphasizes that a significant part of chapter 2 is focused on Eden. Because God's preparation of a garden is in view, the earth and the field mentioned in verse 5 must refer to the future location of Eden. Alexander Heidel, for example, was of this understanding and suggested that God had apparently left this particular place desert-like with no plant life after He had separated water and land on the third day. But now God would turn this barren area into a most beautiful garden. God first caused a mist to go up, which eventually watered the land in the form of rain (cf. Job 36:27) so that the land could support vegetation. Then he created human beings, planted the garden, and charged them to tend it (Gen. 2:7–8, 15).[14] A difficulty with this view is that Eden is not even mentioned or in view until verse 8. Furthermore, once the garden is referred to, then, as Carl Lawrenz has pointed out, nothing is said about God providing Eden with these particular bushes and plants of the field. Rather, He planted trees pleasing to the eyes and good for food (v. 8).[15] Also, the text specifically says that God "had not caused it to rain on the earth." So to suggest that there was a mist that produced rain contradicts the text's statement that there was no rain.

Another, more convincing interpretation places the absence of certain plants of the field in the larger context of Genesis 2 and 3. It suggests that these plants are the plants man will struggle with as he cultivates the ground as a result of the fall into sin and as he works the land under the curse placed on his labor.[16] Three arguments support this understanding.

First, Genesis 2:5 tells us that Adam was created "before any herb of the field ['*ēśeb haśśādeh*] had grown" or "sprung up." The next time we come across the phrase "herb of the field ['*ēśeb haśśādeh*]" (NKJV), or "small plant of the

---

13. Cassuto, *Genesis*, 103 (italics in the original).

14. Alexander Heidel, "The Alleged Contradiction between Gen. 1:24–27 and 2:19," *Concordia Theological Monthly* 12 (1941): 653–54; similarly, regarding the planting of Eden, e.g., Keil and Delitzsch, *Commentary on the Old Testament*, 1:48.

15. Lawrenz and Jeske, *Genesis 1–11*, 98.

16. For what follows, see Cassuto, *Genesis*, 101–3; Lawrenz and Jeske, *Genesis 1–11*, 100; Mathews, *Genesis 1–11:26*, 192–94; Hamilton, *Genesis*, 154; Jiří Moskala, "A Fresh Look at Two Genesis Creation Accounts: Contradictions?," *AUSS* 49 (2011): 49, 59.

field" (ESV), is when God banishes Adam and Eve from the garden, curses the ground, and delivers them up to struggle and toil all their days. At that point He also says, "Both thorns and thistles it shall bring forth for you, and you shall eat the herb of the field [*ēśeb haśśādeh*]. In the sweat of your face you shall eat bread" (3:18–19). No more would Adam and Eve be able to enjoy the fruits from the trees in the garden. After the fall into sin, the LORD God sent them out of the garden "to till [*'bd*] the ground" (v. 23)—the same phrase used in 2:5 ("there was no man to till the ground"). So the reference to "the herb of the field," joined with "to till the ground," links Genesis 2:5 to the post-fall situation when sweaty, hard labor would be required in order to cultivate the herbs of the field to make bread from their grain (3:18–19). At creation God had given seed-bearing plants that reproduced themselves by seed alone as food for human beings and animals (1:29). But now hard work would be needed to provide food since, as God told Adam, "you shall eat the herb of the field [which requires cultivation]. In the sweat of your face you shall eat bread" (3:18–19). And so what was first intended to be a positive good—working (*'bd*) the garden as keeper of Eden (2:15)— became a curse of hard, unrelenting toil of working the ground outside Eden (3:23). While the original mandate to subdue the earth (1:28) remained in place, it would now become much more difficult, and human beings were now prone to abuse their God-given dominion over creation.

Second, another connection of Genesis 2:5 to the post-fall situation is the phrase "plant of the field [*śîaḥ haśśādeh*]" (NKJV) or "bush of the field" (ESV). The term *śîaḥ* is relatively rare, occurring only four times in Scripture. The plant is associated with the wilderness (21:15) and has negative connotations as, for example, providing food and shelter for the absolutely desperate, the outcasts of society (Job 30:4–7). The thorns and thistles that the earth would bring forth as a result of the curse can therefore be seen as a subcategory of the "bush" (*śîaḥ*). These bushes and grains in cultivated fields were not yet on the earth when God created human beings.

Third, when God created Adam, He "had not caused it to rain on the earth." What is the significance of there being no rain? The text goes on to explain that "a mist went up from the earth and watered the whole face of the ground" (Gen. 2:6). Although the majority of English translations use the word "mist" in translating the Hebrew word *'ēd*, this translation is far from certain and is indeed doubtful. Recent lexicons, some Bible translations, and academic studies give as first meaning of this term "stream" or "springs," which fits the context of Genesis 2.[17] As already noted, mist can only water the earth when it condenses into clouds and then falls as rain, but the text specifically states that God had not caused it to rain on the earth. Indeed, as E. J. Young notes, the translation "mist" is ruled out by the Hebrew verb (*šqh*) translated "was watering" or "watered" but literally meaning "to give to drink." How can a mist "which comes up *from* the earth, cause the earth to drink? The translation 'mist' must be abandoned."[18] The garden God had planted "eastward in Eden" (v. 8) was watered by a river that went out of Eden (v. 10).

So we have a picture of the earth being watered from an abundance of water naturally drawn up from a high water table, just as, for example, in Egypt, which has long periods of no rain and yet is fertile along the Nile. The Hebrew text indicates that this water naturally drawn up was a continuous action,[19] which again suggests an assured source from the water table. Adam would have continued to enjoy this situation had he not fallen into sin. When that happened, as Cassuto puts it, "the LORD punished him by decreeing that the soil should obtain its moisture from above, so that He might requite man according to his deeds, giving him rain in its season if he was worthy and withholding it if he was unworthy."[20] This is indeed how the LORD dealt with His people. God cursed Israel for disobedience by withholding rain (Deut. 11:17; 28:22–24).

In summary, Genesis 2:5 describes the earth as it would become after the fall into sin. It thus follows logically from the *tôlədôt* heading ("this is the history of"), which, as we saw earlier, normally introduces material describing what happened following previously recorded events, in this case God's creation work recounted in Genesis 1.

The Animals Brought to Adam

Another issue that arises when comparing Genesis 2 with Genesis 1, is whether the creation of animals mentioned in chapter 2 contradicts the order given in chapter 1. We read in chapter 1 that the animals were created before Adam and

---

17. Recent lexicons: *DCH* 1:118; *HALOT*, 11; Bible translations rendering "stream(s)," or something similar, include ancient: LXX, Vulgate, Peshitta; modern: NET, NIV, NJB, NJPS, NRSV, REB. An important and thorough study is Tsumura, *Creation and Destruction*, 85–127; cf. Max Rogland, "Interpreting אד in Genesis 2.5–6: Neglected Rabbinic and Intertextual Evidence," *JSOT* 34 (2010): 379–93.

18. Edward J. Young, *Studies in Genesis One*, 62n50.

19. GKC §107b; Joüon §113f; also see *IBHS*, 503.

20. For the above and the quote: Cassuto, *Genesis*, 104; also see Kulikovsky, *Creation, Fall, Restoration*, 181–82; Hamilton, *Genesis*, 154.

Eve (1:24–26), but some interpreters have said that chapter 2 indicates the animals were made after the creation of Adam (2:7, 19).

The crux of the matter is how one translates the verb in 2:19. In verse 18 we read that the LORD God said He would make a helper fit for Adam. Then immediately after that we read, as rendered for example in the RSV, "So out of the ground the LORD God formed every beast of the field and every bird of the air" (v. 19). On the basis of such a translation one can reason that chapter 2 contradicts chapter 1. However, there are good arguments to support translating the main verb as a pluperfect so that the passage reads, "Now out of the ground the LORD God had formed every beast of the field and every bird of the heavens" (ESV; similarly NIV). Such a rendering honors the larger context and recognizes that God had created the creatures before man, as recorded in chapter 1. Furthermore, there are grammatical considerations that support such a pluperfect translation in this instance.[21]

The situation was therefore as follows. After God had created Adam and given him the assignment to "work and keep" the garden, "the LORD God said, 'It is not good that man should be alone; I will make him a helper comparable to him'" (2:18). It is remarkable that God would share His thoughts on what He saw was still lacking in His work of creation. To prepare Adam for a suitable helper, the LORD God took steps to awaken in Adam the realization that he was all alone as a human being. To that end, God had Adam name the animals, which had already been created and which God now brought to him.[22] As Adam assigned names to the animals he realized that they were all paired—male and female—but he was without a compatible counterpart. "For Adam there was not found a helper comparable to him" (v. 20).

The Planting of Eden

When did God plant the garden of Eden? There are two possibilities. After verse 7 tells us that God made man, one can translate verse 8 as "the LORD God planted a garden eastward in Eden, and there He put the man whom He had formed," indicating that the establishing of a garden took place after man's creation. This would mean that this Edenic vegetation does not refer to the plants made on the third day (1:11–12) but rather to what God said to Adam and Eve after their creation: "See, I have given you every herb that yields seed which is

---

21. See the discussion in Lawrenz and Jeske, *Genesis 1–11*, 117–18n27; C. John Collins, "The *Wayyiqtol* as 'Pluperfect': When and Why," *TynBul* 46 (1995): 135–40; *IBHS*, 552–53.
22. See chapter 9 above on the feasibility of naming the animals.

on the face of all the earth, and every tree whose fruit yields seed; to you it shall be for food" (1:29).[23]

Another possibility is to translate Genesis 2:8 as "now the LORD God had planted a garden in the east, in Eden; and there he put the man he had formed" (NIV). This rendering places the planting of the garden prior to Adam's creation, which means it could have been included in God's work on the third day. This translation is less widely accepted but is grammatically justifiable and already evident in the ancient Latin translation, the Vulgate (late 4th–early 5th c. AD).[24]

For our purposes in understanding the structure of Genesis 2, both possibilities are consistent with honoring this part of Scripture as relating historical events. If a choice has to be made, the second possibility seems more convincing, given the context and in light of the fact that there are contextual and grammatical reasons to read a pluperfect in 2:19.[25] The first possibility means that Adam was created outside of the garden and then placed into it. H. C. Leupold notes that this order of events "serves the divine purpose of making man clearly aware at the very outset of the distinction between the garden and all the land that lay outside."[26]

Whichever translation is accepted, verse 8 ("the LORD God planted [or "had planted"] a garden eastward in Eden, and there He put the man whom He had formed") serves as a summary statement that introduces the verses that follow. These verses elaborate on this summary statement and give a description of the garden and God's placing man in it (vv. 9–15).[27] This summary character of verse 8 explains why the text twice mentions God putting Adam in Eden (vv. 8, 15).

Narrative Outline of Genesis 2:4–25

Having considered the above passages, we are now in a position to give an outline of the structure of Genesis 2:4–25.

---

23. So Wenham, *Genesis 1–15*, 61.

24. The pluperfect is therefore also in Gen. 2:8 in the Douay-Rheims Version, which is based on the Vulgate. The planting of Eden on the third day is also found in Ephrem the Syrian's commentary on Genesis (4th c. AD) (Andrew Louth with Marco Conti, eds., *Genesis 1–11*, ACCS [Downers Grove, Ill.: InterVarsity, 2001], 53–54), and in the DSV in the pluperfect translation and in its note. For the possibility of pluperfect in translating Hebrew in Gen. 2:8, see *IBHS*, 552–53.

25. It is interesting that among those who would translate as a simple past ("planted"), Lawrenz at least would still maintain that the planting took place prior to Adam's creation, with the justification that the order given in Gen. 2 is topical and not chronological. Lawrenz and Jeske, *Genesis 1–11*, 103.

26. Leupold, *Exposition of Genesis*, 1:118.

27. So also Wenham, *Genesis 1–15*, 62; Leupold, *Exposition of Genesis*, 1:118.

Verse 4 functions as a heading introducing a new narrative that relates what happened to God's good creation as described in 1:1–2:3.

Verses 5–6 are circumstantial clauses describing the situation when Adam was created. Verse 5 tells what was not present, but would become a reality after the fall into sin. Verse 6 indicates how the earth was provided with moisture at the time of Adam's creation.

Verse 7 informs us—after the background information in verses 5–6—that God made man.

Verse 8 is a summary statement introducing the next six verses.

Verses 9–14 describe the trees God caused to grow in the garden and the river that watered the garden, which became four rivers.

Verses 15–20 narrate that God placed Adam in the garden, gave him his task, and forbade him to eat of the tree of the knowledge of good and evil. To make Adam aware that he was missing a helper fit for him, the LORD God had Adam name the animals God brought to him.

Verses 21–25 describe the creation of Eve, Adam's response, and the origin of marriage.

Genesis 2 is a narrative, but should it be taken literally? We argued in chapter 8 above that there is every reason to accept the creation of Adam as a literal account, given the details of the text and the corroboration of this account elsewhere in Scripture, especially the New Testament. There are also other indicators in Genesis 2 that this chapter describes events that really happened. Aspects of Eden and of the tree of the knowledge of good and evil underline the historicity of this chapter, and so we now turn to the garden of Eden.

Eden

The garden God prepared for Adam and Eve was located in Eden. It will help us to appreciate the historicity of this place if we note the use of the name "Eden" in Genesis and Scripture as a whole. Next we will look at the physical geography of Eden and the garden, and, finally, consider whether Eden was a temple.

The Name "Eden" in Genesis and Scripture
Although the origin or etymology of the name "Eden" (*ēden*) is not certain, the meaning often attributed to the term is "delight," in accordance with the sense

of the Hebrew noun *ēden* ("delight"). The Septuagint translates the Hebrew for "the garden of Eden" (Gen. 2:15) as *paradeisos*, a Persian loanword that has been translated into English as "garden of Delight," "paradise," or "orchard."[28]

The name "Eden" as a reference to paradise is also found outside Genesis 2 and 3. Adam and Eve's son Cain "dwelt in the land of Nod on the east of Eden" (4:16). When God comforts His people, He promises that "He will make her wilderness like Eden, and her desert like the garden of the LORD" (Isa. 51:3; cf. Ezek. 36:35). This identification is also found in the phrase, "Eden, the garden of God" (Ezek. 28:13; similarly, 31:9). Since the garden is found in Eden, it is also identified as "the garden of Eden" (Gen. 2:15; 3:23, 24; Ezek. 36:35; Joel 2:3) and simply as "Eden" (Isa. 51:3) even though the garden did not actually encompass all of Eden but was found within this territory (Gen. 2:8).

It is obvious from the above that Scripture assumes the historicity of Eden and its garden. This historicity is also evident from the details given about the geography of this garden.

The Geography of Eden

> The LORD God planted a garden eastward in Eden.... Now a river went out of Eden to water the garden, and from there it parted and became four riverheads. The name of the first is Pishon; it is the one which skirts the whole land of Havilah, where there is gold. And the gold of that land is good. Bdellium and the onyx stone are there. The name of the second river is Gihon; it is the one which goes around the whole land of Cush. The name of the third river is Hiddekel; it is the one which goes toward the east of Assyria. The fourth river is the Euphrates. (Gen. 2:8, 10–14)

This description clearly indicates that Eden was a limited area within the created world. Furthermore, as noted earlier, the phrase "the garden of Eden" needs to be used in the awareness that the garden did not encompass the whole of Eden but was only found within its eastern part.

Out of Eden a river flowed to water the garden. It flowed through the garden, and at the limits of the garden it divided into four. The text is clear. "Now a river went out of Eden to water the garden, and from there it parted and became four riverheads" (v.10), that is, this stream became the source of four rivers.

---

28. *HALOT*, 792. For a discussion of the etymology, see Tsumura, *Creation and Destruction*, 112–25; also see Wevers, *Notes on the Greek Text of Genesis*, 25. For translations of *paradeisos*, see J. Lust, E. Eynikel, and K. Hauspie, comp., *A Greek-English Lexicon of the Septuagint* (Stuttgart: Deutsche Biblegesellschaft, 1992), 351; Lancelot C. L. Brenton, ed., *The Septuagint with Apocrypha: Greek and English* (repr., Grand Rapids: Zondervan, 1982), 3; and NETS.

E. A. Speiser has suggested that the four rivers flowed toward Eden and came together there, but that is not what the text says.[29] In any case, the geographical detail that is given about the rivers attests to the historicity of Eden as a real place. We are not dealing with an imaginary world, the product of someone's imagination.[30] Furthermore, the consequences of what transpired in Genesis 2-3 connect these events to our world. Adam and Eve were real people who were expelled from the garden of Eden (3:23-24). We are their descendants.

Can we today identify where Eden, and more specifically, its garden, was located? Scholars have endeavored to do just that.[31] There is little disagreement about where the third and fourth rivers are found since they are still well known today. "The name of the third river is Hiddekel; it is the one that goes toward the east of Assyria. The fourth river is the Euphrates" (2:14). Hiddekel is the Tigris River (cf. Dan. 10:4), and is so identified in Bible translations (e.g., NASB, ESV, NIV).[32] The Tigris and Euphrates are well known and have their sources in the Armenian highlands.

The first two rivers mentioned are more problematic. The Pishon River "is the one that skirts the whole land of Havilah, where there is gold. And the gold of that land is good. Bdellium and the onyx stone are there" (Gen. 2:11-12). The place where these resources are found today is Arabia, an area with which the name "Havilah" is associated in genealogical and geographical contexts (Gen. 10:7, 29; 25:18; 1 Sam. 15:7). Since this is the only place in Scripture where

---

29. E. A. Speiser, "The Rivers of Paradise," in *Festschrift Johannes Friedrich Zum 65. Geburtstag Am 27. August 1958 Gewidmet*, ed. R. von Kienle et al. (Heidelberg: Carl Winter, 1959), 477-78, most recently reprinted in Hess and Tsumura, *"I Studied Inscriptions,"* 175-82; Speiser, *Genesis*, 17, 20. Speiser is followed, e.g., by Hamilton, *Genesis*, 168. Since Speiser's view does not reflect a normal reading of the Hebrew text, not surprisingly "the majority of scholars, however, disagree with Speiser's reading of this verse"; for this quote and further evidence, see Edwin M. Yamauchi, *Africa and the Bible* (Grand Rapids: Baker Academic, 2004), 40; also, e.g., Lawrenz and Jeske, *Genesis 1-11*, 106; W. H. Gispen, "Genesis 2:10-14," in *Studia Biblica et Semitica: Theodoro Christiano Vriezen Dedicata*, ed. W. C. van Unnik and A. S. van der Woude (Wageningen: H. Veenman & Zonen, 1966), 115-16, 123.

30. See, e.g., Speiser, "Rivers of Paradise," 473-85; and Philip S. Alexander, "Geography and the Bible (Early Jewish Geography)," in *ABD* 2:979-80. For Eden as located "somewhere in the divine realm," see T. Stordalen, *Echoes of Eden: Genesis 2-3 and Symbolism of the Eden Garden in Biblical Hebrew Literature* (Leuven: Peeters, 2000), 286, also 297.

31. For an interesting brief historical overview of determining Eden's location, see Peter Harrison, *Rise of Natural Science*, 127; for an iconographical overview, Nida Stone, "The Four Rivers That Flowed from Eden," in *Beyond Eden: The Biblical Story of Paradise (Genesis 2-3) and Its Reception History*, ed. Konrad Schmid and Riedweg Christoph (Tübingen: Mohr Siebeck, 2008), 227-50.

32. Also see on the identity of the Tigris and Euphrates, *HALOT*, 293 (*ḥiddeqel*), 978-79 (*pərāt*), respectively.

the Pishon River is mentioned, it is difficult to determine its identity, but with the use of satellite imagining some scholars have suggested that the Pishon originally flowed along an ancient, newly discovered riverbed in Arabia running from the Hijaz Mountains in the vicinity of Medina to the general area where the Tigris and Euphrates empty into the Persian Gulf.[33]

The Gihon River "is the one which goes around the whole land of Cush" (Gen. 2:13). Although the name "Cush" (*kûš*) immediately reminds us of biblical references to the African land by that name (2 Kings 19:9), and is often rendered "Ethiopia" (Isa. 18:1; Jer. 46:9), in terms of Eden we need to look closer to Mesopotamia. Cush was the father of Nimrod, who built cities in Mesopotamia (Gen. 10:8–12). The name *kûš* could be related to the Akkadian *kaššû*, referring to the Kassites (or Cassites), and so gave that people its name. The Gihon River would then be identified with the Karkheh River, which flows out of the Zagros Mountains in modern Iran.[34]

These solutions for the identification of the Pishon and Gihon Rivers appear to be the best options available at the moment. If they are accepted, then, as Kenneth Kitchen put it, the "ancient author's enumeration runs counterclockwise, from southwest (Pishon) across east to the Gihon, then north and northwest to the Tigris and Euphrates, in a continuous sweep."[35] However, it is obvious that this scenario conflicts with Genesis 2, which has all the rivers originate from a single common source. Furthermore, the favored location of the Pishon River as described above is quite straight, running from west to east, but Genesis portrays this river as skirting or going around the whole land of Havilah (2:11).

Clearly, the Genesis description of the Edenic rivers does not fit current geographical realities. Since Genesis 2 is part of God's infallible Word, the geographical description is accurate. One must therefore conclude that the

---

33. Juris Zarins of Misouri State University, as articulated in Dora Jane Hamblin, "Sleuthing the Garden of Eden," *Smithsonian* 18, no. 2 (1987): 127–35, and later set forth with more advanced imaging by Boston University professor Farouk El-Baz, "A River in the Desert," *Discover* 14, no. 7 (1993): 10. The theory was accepted as likely by, e.g., James A. Sauer, "The River Runs Dry: Creation Story Preserves Historical Memory," *BAR* 22, no. 4 (1996): 52–54, 57, 64; Kitchen, *Reliability*, 429–30, 592; Hoffmeier, "Genesis 1–11," 33–34; for the technology involved, Farouk El-Baz, "Space Age Archaeology," *Scientific American* 277, no. 2 (1997): 60–65.

34. Suggested by Speiser, "Rivers of Paradise," 475, and subsequently accepted as a possibility by others, e.g., Kitchen, *Reliability*, 429; Hoffmeier, "Genesis 1–11," 34.

35. Kitchen, *Reliability*, 429.

landscape described has been lost. To put it differently, the geography has radically changed.[36]

What would have caused the geography of Eden and its surrounding territory to be so altered that the description given in Genesis 2 can no longer be discerned in the Middle East today? The most likely explanation is the physical upheavals caused by the flood in the days of Noah, which must have radically changed the landscape through the tremendous forces unleashed. All the fountains of the great deep burst forth and the floodgates of the sky were opened so that the water completely inundated the earth, covering even all the high mountains (Gen. 7:11–20). If the flood had been local, as maintained by some, there would have been no need for the ark. It was far more than a local affair. It was a "cosmic catastrophe, that is actually the undoing of creation."[37] The apostle Peter testified that "the world that then existed perished, being flooded with water" (2 Peter 3:6).[38] After that world perished, God renewed humankind's mandate in language reminiscent of that given to Adam and Eve at the dawn of creation (Gen. 9:1–3, 7; cf. 1:28–30).

The detailed geographic description of Eden indicates that this information was initially available only to eyewitnesses who had lived in the area and knew the lay of the land. In other words, we can assume that in God's providence Adam and Eve passed on the geographic information of Eden to their offspring who subsequently passed it on so that it eventually came to Noah and ultimately to Moses, who under divine inspiration included that ancient description in his account. During this process, updates from the pre-flood period, such as the inclusion of names of countries not existing at the time of creation (Havilah, Cush, and Assyria), and discoveries, such as gold, were

---

36. A factor not recognized in John C. Munday, "Eden's Geography Erodes Flood Geology," *WTJ* 58 (1996): 123–54; cf. James R. Hughes, "An Examination of the Assumptions of 'Eden's Geography Erodes Flood Geology,'" *CRSQ* 34 (1997): 154–61; also see Lita Cosner and Robert Carter, "Where Was Eden? Part 1–Examining Pre-Flood Geographical Details in the Biblical Record," *Journal of Creation* 30 (2016): 97–103; and Cosner and Carter, "Where Was Eden? Part 2–Examining Pre-Flood Geographical Details in the Biblical Record," *Journal of Creation* 30 (2016): 123–27.

37. Sarna, *Genesis*, 48.

38. For a worldwide flood, see Richard M. Davidson, "The Genesis Flood Narrative: Crucial Issues in the Current Debate," *AUSS* 42 (2004): 49–77; Lawrenz and Jeske, *Genesis 1–11*, 106–7; Gispen, *Genesis*, 1:229–32, 274; Snelling, *Earth's Catastrophic Past*, 19–72; cf. Poythress, *Redeeming Science*, 127–30. For those holding to a local flood, and in the process downplaying the clear intent of the biblical text, see Paul H. Seely, "Noah's Flood: Its Date, Extent, and Divine Accommodation," *WTJ* 66 (2004): 291–311; Carol A. Hill, "The Noachian Flood: Universal or Local?," *PSCF* 54 (2002): 170–83.

added.[39] Adam and Eve were evicted from the garden, but they and their descendants would have remembered its location. The catastrophic flood, however, would have destroyed all the evident geographic markers. As we today, so the generations who lived after the flood could therefore not locate Eden or, for that matter, other antediluvian locations like the land of Nod, which was east of Eden (Gen. 4:16).

But, one could ask, how is it that we have the Tigris and Euphrates Rivers today? Even today they almost seem to have a common source. These rivers, however, cannot be exactly the same as those mentioned in Genesis 2. But the names of these rivers have obviously been used again. That as such is not surprising. The names "Tigris" and "Euphrates" appear to be descriptive, as often happens with geographic names.[40] Etymological reasons have been given for understanding the term "Tigris" as "flowing river" and "Euphrates" as "mighty water source" or "lordly river."[41] The name "Pishon" (*pîšôn*) appears to be derived from *pûš* ("to leap, jump, scatter"), suggesting that this river moved quickly and could possibly be called "Gusher."[42] Such generic names could easily be reused for new locations. Thus the names "Tigris" and "Euphrates" could be utilized again. Also the name of the river Gihon (Gen. 2:13) reappears later in Israel's history as the identity of an important spring outside Jerusalem (1 Kings 1:33; 2 Chron. 32:30). Such a reuse is not surprising since the name "Gihon" probably relates to the verb *gîaḥ* ("to burst out"), suggesting a vigorous flow quite appropriate to describe a spring.[43]

Other names in the account of Eden have also been reused, including "Eden" itself (Ezek. 27:23). "Havilah," usually understood to mean "land of sand," resurfaces later as a geographic area (Gen. 25:18), a name probably

---

39. Although language tends to change, we may assume, given the divine inspiration of Scripture, that the meaning of the names given to the rivers as known to Adam and Eve was passed down accurately through the generations in the common language that existed before the confusion of tongues (Gen. 11) and beyond through the different languages until Moses composed Genesis in its present form. Cf. "It is generally true that geographical names preserve much older traditions than personal names." Tsumura, *Creation and Destruction*, 125; cf. T. C. Mitchell's review of an earlier edition of Tsumura's study in *EvQ* 66 (1994): 257–59. For a possible scenario for the transmission of early information to eventually form part of God's Word in Genesis, see, e.g., R. K. Harrison, *Introduction*, 543–53.

40. E.g., "Ramah" derives from *rûm* ("to be high") and suggests a high site; "Gibeah" is also the Hebrew word "hill" and so obviously refers to a place on a hill; "Kiriath-jearim" translates as "city of forests" and is thus in a wooded area.

41. Tsumura, *Creation and Destruction*, 125–27.

42. *HALOT*, 921, 926; *DCH* 6:670; Hamilton, *Genesis*, 169.

43. *HALOT*, 189; *DCH* 2:344; Hamilton, *Genesis*, 169.

related to the personal name "Havilah," which was the name of a son of Cush and a son of Joktan (10:7, 29). The names "Cush" and "Asshur," or "Assyria," were similarly reused as personal (10:6–8, 22) and geographic names (Num. 12:1; Gen. 10:11)—the personal and geographic being closely associated with each other. All these geographic names can be related to the post-flood geography.[44]

The use of names for more than one location is also found elsewhere in the Old Testament. The name "Goshen" refers both to a place in Egypt (Gen. 47:6) and to a place in the southern Negeb (Josh. 10:41); there is a "Kedesh" in the territories of both Judah (Josh. 15:23) and Naphtali (Josh. 20:7); two different places called "Zanoah" are even found within the inheritance of Judah (Josh. 15:34, 56). The use of identical names for more than one location is also common in our own fairly recent history. Places in Ontario, Canada, such as London and Stratford are reused from their very old namesakes in England. In view of the above, the reuse of antediluvian names of places recorded in Genesis 2 in subsequent history for different locales is not surprising.

Finally, with respect to the geography of Eden, it can be noted that gold, bdellium, and onyx stone are mentioned (Gen. 2:11–12). It is obvious that the gold has been found and utilized since it has been determined that "the gold of that land is good" (v. 12). Since the gold is mentioned in connection with rivers, the reference is, as Sarna notes, "not to lode or vein mining but to alluvial gold and reflects the ancient method of washing gold-bearing sands and gravel deposited by streams and rivers."[45] Bdellium is "the odoriferous yellowish transparent gum of a South Arabian tree."[46] This highly valued, translucent, and fragrant substance is compared in appearance to manna (Num. 11:7). The translation "onyx stone" is widely accepted for the Hebrew word *šōham*, but there has been considerable dispute as to its precise meaning. The term may very well relate to another similar precious stone.[47] It is noteworthy that all of these materials would fit into an antediluvian world since the formation of these substances is not dependant on a catastrophic flood. It may be possible to say the same about the pitch that Noah used for waterproofing the ark.[48] It is striking that the word used for "pitch" (*kōper*) (Gen. 6:14) is only used here

---

44. For Havilah, see *HALOT*, 297; and W. W. Müller, "Havilah (Person)," in *ABD* 3:81–82. For Asshur, see Sarna, *Genesis*, 74; for the post-flood location see, e.g., Yohanan Aharoni et al., *The Macmillan Bible Atlas*, 3rd ed. (New York: Macmillan, 1993), maps 14, 15.

45. Sarna, *Genesis*, 20; also see P. R. S. Moorey, *Ancient Mesopotamian Materials and Industries: The Archaeological Evidence* (repr., Winona Lake, Ind.: Eisenbrauns, 1999), 217.

46. *HALOT*, 110; similarly, *DCH* 2:96.

47. *HALOT*, 1424; *DCH* 8:271; see also the discussion in Hill, "Noachian Flood," 35–36.

48. Noah's use of bitumen-based pitch has been used as an argument against a worldwide

in Scripture. The normal word for "pitch" associated with petroleum bitumen in the form of tar pits is *ḥēmār* (14:10), which was also used in building the tower of Babel (11:3). It is therefore possible that the pitch Noah used was of a different type and made from pine resin mixed with charcoal, as was historically the case for European pitch-making for centuries. Noah would obviously have had access to ample supplies of wood for such a resin.[49] It is also striking that the same word used for "pitch" for Noah's ark was also used in the Gilgamesh Epic, the Mesopotamian flood story (Tablet 11:65–69). But in that account, oil is specifically mentioned along with pitch for sealing the boat, a feature lacking in the biblical account.[50]

Summary

The biblical text clearly speaks of Eden and its garden as a real geographic place that existed at the creation of the world. The description of this garden, however, does not match any current topography. The best explanation for the changed landscape is the worldwide flood of the time of Noah, which radically changed the drainage of the Middle East and the way the rivers flowed. The names of the rivers as first found after the creation of the world were, however, remembered, and two of the names, "Tigris" and "Euphrates," were again attached to rivers. Such a reuse of names is not surprising since geographic names often have a generic meaning, reflecting a certain geographic setting, and so can be used for similar landforms elsewhere.

Two Special Trees

Among the trees that the LORD God caused to grow in the garden were two trees specially identified—the tree of life and the tree of the knowledge of good and evil (Gen. 2:9). God told Adam that he could eat from any tree of the garden "but of the tree of the knowledge of good and evil you shall not eat, for in the day that you eat of it you shall surely die" (v. 17). Since this is all part of a historical narrative, these were real trees. They were among the trees that God

---

flood since, according to advocates of such a cataclysm, oil deposits are a result of this flood. See, e.g., Carol A. Hill, "The Garden of Eden: A Modern Landscape," *PSCF* 52 (2000): 43–44.

49. Sarfati, *Genesis Account*, 498–99. Safarti also notes the work of Cornell University astrophysicist Thomas Gold, who argued for a nonorganic origin of oil.

50. Heidel, *Gilgamesh Epic*, 83, 235, 265–67. Heidel understands the origin of the pitch to be from bituminous material found in Mesopotamia; similarly, *DCH* 4:457. For a more recent translation, Stephanie Dalley, ed. and trans., *Myths from Mesopotamia* (repr., Oxford: Oxford University Press, 1991), 111.

made grow (v. 9). The account in Genesis 2 and 3 would make little sense without these trees.

The Tree of Life

The tree of life was "in the midst of the garden" (2:9). Eve referred to this tree when responding to the serpent's misleading question in which he misquoted God by suggesting that God had forbidden them to eat from any tree of the garden (3:1–3). The tree of life is also mentioned after the fall into sin, when God expelled Adam and Eve from the garden lest Adam "put out his hand and take also of the tree of life, and eat, and live forever" (v. 22). Cherubim were stationed "at the east of the garden of Eden, and a flaming sword which turned every way, to guard the way to the tree of life" (v. 24).

The memory of this tree remained with God's people, and to some extent with other nations as well, although there are no direct parallels in their literature.[51] The tree of life is referenced in the book of Proverbs as a most positive and salutary image of the fullness of life, which is ultimately life with God. The fruit from such a tree of life is available through wisdom (Prov. 3:18). It is the fruit of the righteous (11:30) and a longing fulfilled (13:12). It is also the consequence of a gentle tongue (15:4). The book of Revelation also uses the image of the tree of life to express communion with God (Rev. 2:7; 22:2, 14).[52] The use of this image would not be compelling if it were not grounded in the historical reality of the actual tree of life being situated in the middle of the garden in Eden at the dawn of history.

The Tree of the Knowledge of Good and Evil

The tree of the knowledge of good and evil was the second tree singled out for special mention in Genesis 2:9 and 17.[53] Although it is referred to repeatedly in the subsequent narrative (3:3, 5, 6, 11, 12), it is not mentioned by name again. The name of the tree is literally "the knowing good and evil."[54] Exactly what

---

51. See, e.g., Howard N. Wallace, *The Eden Narrative* (Atlanta: Scholars Press, 1985), 103–15; Walton, *Lost World of Adam and Eve*, 120–25.

52. Remarkably, the single tree of life in Rev. 22:1–2 is at the same time identified with trees on both sides of the river of life (also cf. Ezek. 47:7, 12). The reference to the single tree is therefore a collective reference; see further, R. H. Charles, *A Critical and Exegetical Commentary on the Revelation of St. John* (Edinburgh: T&T Clark, 1920), 2:176; Beale, *Revelation*, 1106.

53. There is nothing similar to this tree in any of the traditions in the ancient Near East. Walton, *Lost World of Adam and Eve*, 122.

54. I.e., it is the noun "knowing" followed by two accusatives (*hadd'at ṭôb wārā'*); GKC §115d; Joüon §124d note 2.

does this name mean? The immediate context makes it clear that to know good and evil is a divine prerogative. For this reason, God responded to the sin of eating from the tree of the knowledge of good and evil by saying, "Behold, the man has become like one of Us, to know good and evil" (3:22). Also, elsewhere in Scripture, knowing good and evil belongs to God and is a divine characteristic. For example, King Solomon prayed to God for the ability to "discern between good and evil" when judging His people (1 Kings 3:9). God granted his request, and people consequently saw in Solomon's judgment in the case of the two women claiming the same son that "the wisdom of God was in him to administer justice" (v. 28).[55] Solomon had in essence spoken on behalf of God. God alone can infallibly discern between good and evil, and He gives the gift of discernment to those whom He equips with His wisdom.

Since the ability to know good and evil belongs to God, as God Himself indicated (Gen. 3:22), Adam and Eve's attempt to attain this ability by eating from the forbidden tree amounted to endeavoring to be like God. Instigated by Satan (vv. 4–5), they opposed the limitations God had set for them as creatures. Instead, they were claiming for themselves the divine privilege of knowing good and evil, that is, deciding what is right or wrong and judging what is permissible or impermissible for themselves. They refused to let God determine the norms for their life. With this sin, Adam and Eve asserted their moral autonomy.[56]

It is precisely this desire to be like God and to ignore their creatureliness that was at stake in their disobeying the probationary command not to eat from the tree of the knowledge of good and evil. When God gave this simple negative command He asserted His sovereignty as creator over His work of creation. Obedience would have brought blessing and growth in their covenantal relationship with God. But Eve and Adam did not recognize the prerogatives of the Creator, and their sin was a turning point in the history of God's work of creation. Through the sin of our first parents, Adam and Eve, death came to all (Rom. 5:12–21).[57]

As we discussed in chapter 8 above, that death was in the first place a spiritual death, for the immediate consequence of rejecting God's norms for their life was estrangement from the living God. The former fellowship with God was now in ruins (Gen. 3:8–10). Also, their relationship with each other

---

55. See for more examples and further on this issue, W. Malcolm Clark, "A Legal Background to the Yahwist's Use of 'Good and Evil' in Genesis 2–3," *JBL* 88 (1969): 266–78.

56. See on this understanding Hamilton, *Genesis*, 165–66; Bavinck, *Reformed Dogmatics*, 3:30–33; also see the survey of views in Wenham, *Genesis 1–15*, 63–64.

57. For the probationary command and the covenantal context, see, e.g., briefly, Edward J. Young, *Study of Old Testament Theology*, 65–68; and in more detail, Bavinck, *Reformed Dogmatics*, 2:565–68.

testified to their loss of innocence and sense of guilt (v. 7). Satan's promise that they would know good and evil came true in a sense, but certainly not as they had expected.[58]

Conclusion

The existence of the tree of life is recorded as part of the makeup and history of the garden of Eden. References to it elsewhere in Scripture would make little impact if this tree were not a historical reality. Furthermore, its historicity is of consequence because this tree had a certain symbolic or sacramental value, standing as it did for true life with God. Life in the garden was to be a life in communion with the Creator who walked in the garden (cf. Gen. 3:8), and eating from this tree would give eternal life (v. 22). After Adam and Eve fell into sin, God barred the way to the tree of life (v. 24), for life with God could now only be attained in Christ, who can open the way to the tree of life in the paradise of God (Rev. 2:7).[59] All this would be meaningless if no original, historical tree of life had existed in Eden.

With respect to the tree of the knowledge of good and evil, affirming its historicity is also very important. Were we to deny that it actually existed as a real tree, we would end up denying not only the reality of the probationary command not to eat of the tree but also, consequently, the fall into sin. It is interesting to note that the matter of historicity—specifically, the great importance of the historicity of this tree and the temptation—prompted a Reformed synod in the Netherlands in 1926 to declare that "the tree of the knowledge of good and evil, the snake and its speaking, and the tree of life are to be understood according to the clear intention of the biblical account of Genesis 2 and 3 in the actual or literal sense and thus were realities observable by the senses."[60]

---

58. See further, Bavinck, *Reformed Dogmatics*, 3:197–98.

59. See Vos, *Biblical Theology*, 37–39.

60. This concerned objections lodged against J. G. Geelkerken; see *Acta der buitengewone Generale Synode van De Gereformeerde Kerken in Nederland gehouden to Assen van 26 Januari tot 17 Maart, 1926* (Kampen: Kok, 1926), art. 149 (p. 53) (my translation). The synod's decision was supported by prominent Reformed scholars, such as Old Testament professors J. Ridderbos, *Het verloren paradijs: een woord met het oog op de aangaande Genesis 2 en 3 gerezen vragen* (Kampen: Kok, 1925), esp. 16–19, 35–40 (although written before the synod decision, Ridderbos clearly had the synod in view); and G. Ch. Aalders, *De exegese van Gen. 2 en 3 en de beslissing der Synode van Assen* (Kampen: Kok, [1926]), esp. 8–9; also, e.g., Klaas Schilder, characterized by Flipse as "a militant supporter of the Synod's rulings" (Abraham C. Flipse, "The Origins of Creationism in the Netherlands," *Church History* 81 [2012]: 124); Schilder, *Een Hoornstoot Tegen Assen?*; also see Schilder, *Heidelbergsche Catechismus toegelicht*, 1:322; Klaas Schilder, *Christ and Culture*, trans. William Helder et al. (Hamilton, Ontario: Lucerna, 2016), 75. Berkouwer even said that he knew

Such an affirmation is in agreement with both the plain sense of the Genesis account and the clarity of Scripture.[61]

Was Eden a Temple?

A recurring theme in current discussions on Eden is that Eden was a sanctuary. Whatever one may think of this view, the relevant point here is that when the focus and emphasis are on whether Eden was a sanctuary, the issue of historicity is easily sidestepped, ignored, or denied because Genesis 1 and 2 are seen in the first place as theologically important and full of symbols pointing beyond themselves. The discussions often include the notion that these chapters describe an ancient Near Eastern cosmology that understands the cosmos as a temple and Eden as a sanctuary.[62] If it can be demonstrated that Eden is not pictured as a temple, the case for understanding Genesis as an ancient cosmology will be seriously weakened, and it will be more difficult to sidestep the issue of the historicity of the garden. To clarify the issues it is helpful to pay some attention to John Walton's work in this regard.

Some Key Arguments for Eden as Temple

In chapter 6 we briefly considered John Walton's contention that "to create something" actually means "to give something a function." In view of the issue of Eden as a temple, we note that Walton considers Genesis 1 to be a cosmology. It is important to realize that the intent of an ancient cosmology is not so much to give a history, but, as Walton puts it, "the central intention of a cosmology is to give an explanation for the cosmos."[63] Since Genesis originated within the cognitive environment of the ancient Near East, we can expect the biblical text to reflect that environment. Because temple and cosmos were interrelated

---

of no Reformed theologian for whom the Assen decision was so determinative as it was for Schilder. G. C. Berkouwer, *Zoeken en vinden: herinneringen en ervaringen* (Kampen: Kok, 1989), 265. Although Bavinck died prior to the synod of Assen, its decision was in the line of his thinking. See van der Vaart Smit, *Bavinck's schriftbeschouwing*, esp. 18–19.

61. According to dogmatician B. Kamphuis, the key concern of the decision of the Assen synod was to maintain clarity of Scripture. B. Kamphuis, *Klare taal: de duidelijkheid van de Schrift* (Barneveld: Vuurbaak, 1988), esp. 16, 40.

62. See, e.g., John H. Walton, "Reading Genesis 1 as Ancient Cosmology," in J. Daryl Charles, *Reading Genesis 1–2*, 145; Walton, *Lost World of Adam and Eve*, 116; B. C. Hodge, *Revisiting the Days of Genesis* (Eugene, Ore.: Wipf & Stock, 2011), 35–69. Hodge concludes, in part on the basis of the seven-day structure and the cosmic temple of Gen. 1 in the light of ancient Near Eastern thought, that "Scripture is a piece of art that communicates theology" and should not be taken too literally (158–59).

63. Walton, "Reading Genesis 1 as Ancient Cosmology," 145.

in the ancient world, temple ideology can therefore, according to Walton, be expected to underlie the Genesis account. This approach of understanding Genesis 1 through the lens of ancient Near Eastern cosmology means that "the seven-day structure of Genesis 1 reflects the intention of the author to present creation of the cosmos in terms of the inauguration of a cosmic temple." After all, "the entire cosmos is viewed as a temple."[64]

Walton sees support for his views in the fact that both ancient Near Eastern texts and Genesis speak of a divine rest on the seventh day—a divine rest that involves doing the normal activities when stability has been achieved. With the temple built, an ancient Near Eastern deity could go about his work as he "rests" in his temple. Similarly, God rested on the seventh day. Consequently, "he can disengage from the set-up tasks and begin regular operations."[65]

Another important element, in Walton's view, for connecting the Genesis account to cosmic temple inauguration is the temple symbolism that he sees reflected in the garden of Eden. This garden was more than a garden. It was a type of sanctuary, key features of which are reflected later in the tabernacle and temple. If this is so, the creation account of Genesis 1 can be seen as the inauguration of a cosmic temple whose climax occurs when God takes up His rest in His Edenic sanctuary, as an ancient Near Eastern god would in its temple.[66] Walton even goes as far as suggesting that Adam and Eve were placed in the garden as priest and priestess.[67]

Considerations and Counterarguments

What are we to think of this? Is Genesis 1 presenting an ancient cosmology, described as God's cosmic temple inauguration, and should the garden in Eden in Genesis 2 be seen as God's sanctuary? If Eden is not a sanctuary, then an important argument for identifying Genesis as ancient cosmology is removed, and a historical approach to the Genesis account loses credibility. A lot could be written about this, which would take us far beyond the limitations of this chapter. Our focus is on Walton's understanding, although others before and after Walton also have understood Eden as a sanctuary.[68] In the interest of brev-

---

64. Walton, *Genesis 1 as Ancient Cosmology*, 190; also see 101–21, 178–99.

65. Walton, *Lost World of Genesis One*, 76; similarly, Walton, *Genesis 1 as Ancient Cosmology*, 190; also see 179–84.

66. Walton, *Genesis 1 as Ancient Cosmology*, 178–92.

67. Walton, *Lost World of Adam and Eve*, 104–15.

68. E.g., for the creation of the world connected with temple building, Moshe Weinfeld, "Sabbath, Temple, and the Enthronement of the Lord—the Problem of the Sitz im Leben of Genesis 1:1–2:3," in *Mélanges bibliques et orentaux en l'honneur de M. Henri Cazelles*, ed. A. Caquot

ity, the following can be noted as factors that call for caution and, ultimately, for rejection of the notion of Eden as a temple.

First, in terms of methodology, although extrabiblical literature from the ancient Near East can be helpful in elucidating the biblical text, Scripture should first of all be its own interpreter. Thus what Scripture says about creation both in Genesis and elsewhere is decisive for understanding the opening chapters of Scripture and not ancient Near Eastern texts or, as John Walton articulates it, the ancient cosmological cognitive environment of biblical times. In chapter 7 of this study we concluded that Genesis does not provide a cosmology, and therefore it also neither presents a cosmic temple nor does it narrate temple inauguration.

Second, the biblical support adduced for understanding Genesis 1 and 2 as depicting a cosmic temple and a sanctuary is not very convincing. Most importantly, nowhere do these chapters speak of a temple or sanctuary. This reality should have much greater weight in discussions on this issue than it usually does. For Walton, particularly notable in connecting temple and cosmos is Isaiah 66:1–2, "which refers to a cosmos-sized temple, a connection between temple and rest, and a connection between creation and temple."[69] This passage says,

> Heaven is My throne,
> And earth is My footstool.
> Where is the house that you will build Me?
> And where is the place of My rest?
> For all those things My hand has made,
> And all those things exist,"
> Says the LORD.

This passage underlines the greatness of God. When King Solomon dedicated the temple he acknowledged that the heavens could not contain God. "How much less this temple which I have built!" (1 Kings 8:27). Isaiah 66 takes it a step further. Rather than speaking of a throne in the heavens, we read that "heaven is My throne." In other words, the whole cosmos is God's throne and the earth is His footstool. This passage is not about the cosmos being a temple (it is God's throne), but about the greatness of God who cannot be contained in any way.[70]

---

and M. Delcor (Neukirchen-Vluyn: Neukirchener Verlag, 1981), 501–12. For the garden of Eden as the first temple, G. K. Beale, *The Temple and the Church's Mission: A Biblical Theology of the Dwelling Place of God* (Leicester, U.K.: Apollos; Downers Grove, Ill.: InterVarsity, 2004), 66–80.

69. Walton, *Genesis 1 as Ancient Cosmology*, 179.

70. See, e.g., John Goldingay, *A Critical and Exegetical Commentary on Isaiah 56–66* (London: Bloomsbury, 2014), 479–80; Block, "Eden: A Temple?," 20.

Walton justifies designating Adam and Eve as priests on the basis of Genesis 2:15. "Then the LORD God took the man and put him in the garden of Eden to tend and keep it." Walton points out that the root of the Hebrew verb translated "to tend" ('*bd*) is also used elsewhere to describe priestly activity, namely, "to do the work" of the tabernacle (Num. 3:7–8).[71] However, within the immediate context of Genesis 2, that same verb is used in an agricultural context with the comment that there was no man "to till" ('*bd*) the ground (Gen. 2:5). Walton's selective use of vocabulary, which ignores the immediate context, is far from convincing. Although no people are mentioned for whom Adam and Eve were to serve as priestly mediators, Walton suggests that "the text does not explicitly rule out the idea that there were others." Such a comment goes against the express message of the text, namely, that Adam and Eve were the first humans, a point Walton considers debatable.[72]

Third, according to Walton ancient Near Eastern literature teaches us that divine rest in a temple is not disengagement from work but freedom to rule; it is an act of engagement.[73] In response, one needs to note that in Genesis 1–2 there is no mention of God resting in His temple. The rest He experienced on the seventh day was a rest from the work He had done. It was a disengagement form of rest, for He ceased *from* His work of creation. "He rested on the seventh day from all His work which He had done.... He rested from all His work which God had created and made" (Gen. 2:2, 3); He "rested and was refreshed" (Ex. 31:17), indicating that He rested from His work of creating. This is not to suggest that God was inactive since He rested on the seventh day. Rather, He rested from His creative work and then began His work of providence (cf. John 5:17).

Fourth, although there is no mention of Eden as a sanctuary in Genesis 1–2, Walton and others have insisted that the narrative of the garden in essence describes it as such. As evidence, Walton, relying on the work of Gordon Wenham, mentions factors such as God's walking to and fro in the garden (Gen. 3:8), just as He later did in the tabernacle (Lev. 26:11–12); cherubim guarding the garden (Gen. 3:24), just as they figuratively guarded the Most Holy Place (Ex. 26:31); the entrances to the garden and the sanctuary were both on the east (Gen. 3:24; Ezek. 11:1); and the tree of life in Eden was represented in the tabernacle menorah as a stylized tree of life (Gen. 2:9; Ex. 25:31–35).[74]

---

71. Walton, *Lost World of Adam and Eve*, 105–8.
72. Walton, *Lost World of Adam and Eve*, 114–15.
73. Walton, *Genesis 1 as Ancient Cosmology*, 179–80.
74. Gordon J. Wenham, "Sanctuary Symbolism in the Garden of Eden Story," in Hess and Tsumura, "*I Studied Inscriptions*," 399–404; Walton, *Genesis 1 as Ancient Cosmology*, 184–85.

However, one can take issue with key proposed indicators that the garden of Eden was a type of sanctuary. Daniel Block, who used to think that the author of Genesis 1–3 perceived Eden as a temple, has since raised doubts whether this is so and has articulated his objections. The examples that follow rely on his work, in which he gives more examples and presents his concerns in greater detail.[75] God's walking to and fro in the garden does not match His walking in the tabernacle. The point in Leviticus 26:11–12 is not that God walks about within the tabernacle, but that the sanctuary symbolized His presence with His people. "I will set My tabernacle among you.... I will walk among you and be your God" (Lev. 26:11–12). Because God walked about the camp of Israel, it had to be holy (Deut. 23:14). The divine walking to and fro in the garden refers to the free and friendly intercourse of God with those who are in covenant with Him, a reward He promised to His people (Lev. 26:12).

The presence of cherubim does not as such establish the garden in Eden as a sanctuary. For example, in the lament over the king of Tyre in Ezekiel 28, the role of the cherub mentioned in verse 14 is fundamentally different from that of the one guarding Eden (Gen. 3:24). The cherub in Ezekiel 28 is the king of Tyre, who is in Eden, portrayed as a king dressed with the symbols of his office. He was to walk to and fro through the garden and act as its guardian and God's vice-regent, but he failed and even defiled the sanctuaries (v. 18). These sanctuaries were within Eden, the garden of God (vv. 13, 18), but the garden itself was not a sanctuary.

Genesis does not tell us that the entrance to the garden was at the east end as it was with the sanctuary (Ex. 38:13–15). It is possible that this was the case, but there is no mention of an entrance. The text only says that the garden was "eastward in Eden" (Gen. 2:8) and that God "placed the cherubim at the east of the garden of Eden" to guard the way to the tree of life (3:24). There is no mention of an entrance. Even if this had been noted, such an east gate would not have made the garden a sanctuary.

The tree of life in the garden served a completely different function from the menorah in the tabernacle or temple. The presence of the tree of life did not define the garden as a sanctuary. Only in retrospect can one possibly relate the seven-branched lampstand to the tree of life.

And finally, a sanctuary according to Old Testament usage is the place where God dwells (Ex. 40:34–35; 2 Chron. 7:1–3). Eden, however, was a place designed for Adam and Eve to live in and where they were to fulfill their

---

75. Block, "Eden: A Temple?," 5–17.

God-given mandate (Gen. 1:28–30). It was a place God visited but not in which He lived (3:8).[76]

In view of all these factors, and Daniel Block has mentioned many more, there is simply no evidence that the author of Genesis 1–3 was describing Eden as a sanctuary.

Conclusion

There is no doubt that the tabernacle and temple contain clear allusions to the Edenic garden, as seen, for example, in the images of cherubim woven into the tabernacle curtains (Ex. 26:1, 31) and in Solomon's garden motifs in the temple (1 Kings 6:18, 29, 32, 35). But the Genesis narrative as such gives no hint of the garden being designated a sanctuary. It was the place for Adam and Eve to live and work (Gen. 2:15) and where God would, as the text suggests, visit them from time to time (cf. 3:8). It is, however, never called a sanctuary. Although we can find allusions to Eden later in the tabernacle and temple, that does not warrant calling the garden of Eden itself a sanctuary or temple.

The fact that the biblical text does not present Eden as a temple removes a major argument for the view that the first chapters of Genesis are a cosmology, a view that downplays, sidesteps, or denies its historicity. Also, in this regard there is reason to consider the genre of the Genesis account as historical narrative.

Summary

The text of Genesis 2:4–25 relates historical events that demand to be taken in their plain sense. The heading of this part of Scripture, "this is the history of" (*tôladôt*), sets the tone. Similar headings are used throughout the book of Genesis to introduce a new narrative that relates what resulted from the events recounted earlier. In this case, Genesis 2:4 introduces what developed from God's perfect creation. The stage for what follows is set with a detailed description of the garden, Adam and Eve's creation, and the probationary command. A careful reading of the text with an eye to its structure indicates that there is no contradiction with Genesis 1. After the stage is set in Genesis 2, subsequent chapters relate the fall into sin, the expulsion from the garden, the first births, and the first murder.

The geographical details given for Eden and its garden indicate that a real place is in view. The location of Eden cannot be located with any certainty today due most likely to the geographical upheavals caused by the worldwide

---

76. See further Block, "Eden: A Temple?," 21–27.

catastrophic flood in the days of Noah. It is not surprising that geographic names from the pre-Noachian time would be used for different place names later.

There is every indication that the two special trees in the garden were real, historical trees. They played a critical role in the history of redemption. The tree of life is frequently referred to in subsequent Scripture, and the tree of the knowledge of good and evil is of pivotal importance for the probationary command and the subsequent fall into sin.

There is no evidence in Genesis 1–2 that the universe was a cosmic temple or that Eden was a sanctuary. This conclusion means that Genesis does not describe an ancient Near Eastern temple cosmology and thus removes an important argument for sidestepping or ignoring the historicity of Genesis 2.

In sum, Scripture presents the contents of Genesis 2 as historical material, and there is every reason for us to accept the details of this chapter as such.

11

The Work of Creation and the Gospel

The preceding chapters have shown that Genesis 1 and 2 give a true historical account of God's work of creation. In revealing this great work, the Almighty condescended to our level of understanding, but He nevertheless gives us an accurate and reliable narrative of the origin of earth and the human race. Affirming the historicity of the creation account is important. Denying its historicity can ultimately call into question the reliability of the gospel. Scripture closely relates the historicity of Genesis 1 and 2 with the history of God's work of salvation. This chapter will explore that reality.

We will first consider the close relationship of God's work of creation at the very beginning of time to His work of salvation and the new creation. Next, we will reflect on the devastating impact that acceptance of an evolutionary narrative of earth's beginnings has had on the faith of many. Finally, we will briefly address the question of how we can best defend and preserve the pure teaching about creation in a world of scientism and unbelief.

Creation and Redemption

Scripture mentions God's works of creation and salvation in close correlation with each other. This relationship suggests that if the one is historical, the other should be as well. Put differently and more personally, if God's work of re-creating us for our salvation is real and historical, then the work of creation at the beginning, with which re-creation is compared and correlated, should be as well. It makes little sense to compare a historical event with a fictitious one. After reflecting on this reality we will consider some New Testament indicators of the historicity of Genesis 1 and 2.

The Creator of Israel

God, the Creator, who brought the world into being, is virtually always identified as such when His work of delivering His people is mentioned or alluded to in one way or another. In other words, the God of creation is the God of salvation and the God of salvation is the God of creation. God's people therefore never had to doubt whether the LORD would be able to save them from their enemies. God comforted His people who would question His ability to rescue them with the reminder that "the everlasting God, the LORD, the Creator of the ends of the earth, neither faints nor is weary" (Isa. 40:28).

Other examples of the close association of God, the Creator, with His work of salvation come to mind. After Psalm 33 notes that the LORD made the heavens by His Word and "all the host of them by the breath of His mouth," the earth is called on to fear the LORD because of His creative power (vv. 6–8), and God's sovereign might is noted. "The LORD brings the counsel of the nations to nothing; He makes the plans of the peoples of no effect.... Blessed is the nation whose God is the LORD" (vv. 10, 12). He saves them from death (vv. 18–19). Another example is Psalm 136. It celebrates the LORD's steadfast love and His leading the people of Israel out of Egyptian bondage and delivering them from their enemies. But first God's work of creating the heavens and the earth is commemorated (vv. 4–9) so that His work of creation is closely associated with His work of salvation. It is noteworthy that in Psalm 136 God's steadfast love is not only praised for the LORD's delivering His people, but also for His work of creation. That work too was an act of steadfast love as God prepared a place for His people to live in. And so God's steadfast love motivated Him both to create and to save His people. Indeed, God's saving of Israel is sometimes described in terms of creation.

We see that terminology, for example, with the prophet Isaiah. He identified God as Israel's creator and redeemer. God created Israel by saving the nation. In Isaiah 43 we read,

> But now, thus says the LORD, who created you, O Jacob,
> And He who formed you, O Israel:
> "Fear not, for I have redeemed you;
> I have called you by your name;
> You are Mine....
> I am the LORD, your Holy One,
> The Creator of Israel, your King."
> Thus says the LORD, who makes a way in the sea
> And a path through the mighty waters,
> Who brings forth the chariot and horse,

The army and the power
(They shall lie down together, they shall not rise;
They are extinguished, they are quenched like a wick). (Isa. 43:1, 15–17)

It is important to note that God is identified as the creator of Israel. Israel's creation occurred when the LORD delivered His people from Egypt, an event highlighted in verses 16–17 with the references to the path through the sea and the destruction of Pharaoh's horses and chariots. In the context of God's coming judgment on His people, Isaiah is encouraging the nation destined for exile by saying that the exile will be followed by a new exodus (vv. 6–7). And as the LORD created Israel in the first exodus, He will again create for Himself a people by a new exodus out of captivity, ultimately culminating in the spiritual gathering of sinners in Christ.[1]

Other examples of the close association of God as the creator and redeemer can also be mentioned. Isaiah 44:24 identifies the LORD, Israel's redeemer, as the God who made all things. In Isaiah 51 the prophet describes God as "the LORD your Maker, who stretched out the heavens and laid the foundations of the earth" (v. 13), and in that context he refers to the exodus out of Egypt: "I am the LORD your God, who divided the sea whose waves roared—the LORD of hosts is His name" (v. 15). A final example: the creation of Israel through the exodus is celebrated in Exodus 15 in cosmic language reminiscent of Genesis 1—language that is also subtly used against pagan mythology. The watery depths (Ex. 15:5) that pagans feared and that needed to be conquered in their creation myths are mentioned in Genesis 1:2 as "the deep" that God created, and in the exodus God sovereignly used these depths to defeat Pharaoh and all his hosts (Ex. 15:5, 8–10). The result is that "the Creator of Israel" (Isa. 43:15; also Ex. 15:16)[2] can guide His people with steadfast love and mercy to the promised land (Ex. 15:13, 17).[3]

The point of all of these examples—and more could be given[4]—is that the God who created in the beginning is the same One who created for Himself a

---

1. See, e.g., Edward J. Young, *Isaiah*, 3:138–39, 144–46, 154; Motyer, *Isaiah*, 332–33, 337.

2. Ex. 15:16b, referring to Israel, can also be translated "till the people whom you created"; for the verb in question, *qānâ* with the possible meaning "create," see Peter C. Craigie, *The Book of Deuteronomy* (Grand Rapids: Eerdmans, 1976), 157n18; and the Hebrew lexicons.

3. On likely indirect references to pagan mythology in Ex. 15, see Peter C. Craigie, *Ugarit and the Old Testament* (Grand Rapids: Eerdmans, 1983), 88–89; W. J. Dumbrell, *Covenant and Creation: A Theology of Old Testament Covenants* (Nashville: Thomas Nelson, 1984), 100–104.

4. See further Dirk H. Odendaal, *The Eschatological Expectation of Isaiah 40–66 with Special Reference to Israel and the Nations* (Nutley, N.J.: Presbyterian and Reformed, 1970), 136–42, 168–69; Terrance R. Wardlaw Jr., "The Significance of Creation in the Book of Isaiah," *JETS* 59

people through the exodus from Egypt. As creator He is absolutely sovereign over everything, and so He is able to save and uphold His people and also to provide for their redemption from their sins. All this creative and redemptive activity is rooted in His steadfast love as seen in Psalm 136.

Since the creation of heaven and earth and the creation of God's people through the exodus out of Egypt are closely associated and correlated in Scripture, it is not surprising that the two reasons given for the observance of the Sabbath day are the creation of heaven and earth (Ex. 20:11) and the creation of Israel in their deliverance from Egypt (Deut. 5:15). This twofold rationale for the Sabbath celebration is not contradictory, but complementary and reflects the close association of God's work of creation (Ex. 20:11) and redemption (Deut. 5:15), which we have seen.[5]

This close connection of creation and salvation was also reflected in Israel's temple liturgy. According to ancient Jewish tradition, said to date from the time of Samuel and David, the offering of sacrifice was accompanied by reading from the creation account (Gen. 1:1–2:3), subdivided into sections to cover a full week, minus the Sabbath.[6] This practice showed that they understood the significance of creation for the redeeming work of God.

Perhaps the relationship of the Creator to His work of salvation is best summed up with the confession, "My help comes from the LORD, who made heaven and earth" (Ps. 121:2). The God of the covenant, the LORD who saves, is the Creator (cf. Ps. 148). This would be a hollow confession were it not grounded in the historical events of God's creation work as revealed by God to His people Israel in Genesis 1 and 2.

Indeed, the Creator is the only one who can make things right after the fall into sin. It was God the creator, faithful LORD of the covenant, who throughout history after the fall into sin prepared the way for *the* Savior and the new creation. For ultimately God's work of salvation climaxes in the new creation. And no one but almighty God, the Creator, can do this. To deny His work of creation is to call into question His work of renewal and re-creation. After all, His

---

(2016): 449–71; Daniel J. Estes, "Creation Theology in Psalm 148," *BSac* 171 (2014): 30–41; Elmer A. Martens, *God's Design: A Focus on Old Testament Theology*, 3rd ed. (repr., North Richland Hills, Tex.: BIBAL, 1998), 317–28.

5. See, e.g., Meredith G. Kline, *Treaty of the Great King: The Covenant Structure of Deuteronomy* (Grand Rapids: Eerdmans, 1963), 63; John M. Frame, *The Doctrine of the Christian Life* (Phillipsburg, N.J.: P&R, 2008), 513–14; see also Craigie, *Ugarit and the Old Testament*, 89–90.

6. *Mishnayoth*, trans. Philip Blackman (repr., New York: Judaica, 2000), 2:428–29 (Taanith 4:2–3); also see Alfred Edersheim, *The Temple: Its Ministry and Services as They Were at the Time of Jesus Christ* (Grand Rapids: Eerdmans, 1958), 199.

creation work extended beyond the natural world to the creation of a people for Himself, Israel (cf. Ps. 95:6–7), and ultimately the new Israel, the church (Gal. 3:29; 6:16). This grand work of re-creation, as well as its connection to God's work of creation in the very beginning, becomes increasingly clear in the New Testament.

Re-creation in Christ

The Savior who was born in Bethlehem was the Word made flesh through whom all things were made (John 1:3). The opening chapter of the gospel of John describes the coming of the Word made flesh with allusions to Genesis 1. "In Him was life, and the life was the light of men. And the light shines in the darkness, and the darkness did not comprehend it…. That was the true Light which gives light to every man coming into the world" (John 1:4–5, 9). During Christ's life on earth, He provided a clear sign that the promise of the new creation would be fulfilled when He raised the dead to new life—the son of the widow at Nain, Jairus's daughter, and Lazarus (Luke 7:13–15; Matt. 9:25; John 11:43–44). Indicative of the significance of Christ's atoning death for the new creation is also the resurrection of many saints at the time of His demise (Matt. 27:52). Christ was able to give new life even to dead bodies. The resurrection from the dead is like a new creation.[7]

The Lord made it clear that this new life and new creation begins in this life. Whoever believes in Him "has everlasting life, and shall not come into judgment, but has passed from death into life" (John 5:24). All this involves being born again through the working of the Holy Spirit (3:3–8). To believe in Christ is to be in Him. The apostle Peter can therefore address the believers as those who are "in Christ" (1 Peter 5:14; cf. Phil. 1:1). To be in Christ is to have a new existence. The transformation to being a believer and having the new life is described in terms reminiscent of God's creation work at the beginning. We read in 2 Corinthians 4:6 that "it is the God who commanded light to shine out of darkness, who has shone in our hearts to give the light of the knowledge of the glory of God in the face of Jesus Christ." In other words, as darkness was dispelled by the word of God at the beginning of creation, so in a miracle of similar magnitude, God has shone the light of the gospel into our hearts to make us a new creation. God works this re-creation through faith in Christ by

---

7. For a study on the theme of creation in the gospel of John, see Jeannine K. Brown, "Creation's Renewal in the Gospel of John," *CBQ* 72 (2010): 275–90. However, not all of her examples are convincing given the intent of the narrative. E.g., Does the setting of the garden of Gethsemane really allude to Gen. 2, and does Pilate's declaration "behold the man" actually allude to Adam?

the Word of Christ (Rom. 10:17; cf. James 1:18) through whom God has spoken in these last days and through whom He also created the world (Heb. 1:2).

The identity of a believer as a new creation is specifically affirmed by the apostle Paul. He wrote to the Corinthians: "If anyone is in Christ, he is a new creation; old things have passed away; behold, all things have become new" (2 Cor. 5:17; also Gal. 6:15). Elsewhere he writes that believers are God's "workmanship, created in Christ Jesus" (Eph. 2:10; also see 4:24). To be a new creation is to have a transformed existence. It means that when someone believes in Christ, God is re-creating him or her.

Conversion is a divine work of re-creation. As an act similar to creation, conversion is therefore far-reaching and thoroughgoing. It is like a resurrection from the dead. It shows "the exceeding greatness of His power toward us who believe, according to the working of His mighty power which He worked in Christ when He raised Him from the dead" (Eph. 1:19–20). When someone is made a new creation and raised to new life, "old things have passed away; behold, all things have become new" (2 Cor. 5:17).[8]

Those re-created by God see everything differently. The sinful attractions of the old creation are no longer the focus of their love but are cast aside. They set their vision on the new creation, the beginning of which they already experience today (cf. Heb. 4:9–11). The future renewal of all things is so sure that the apostle can say "all things have become new" (2 Cor. 5:17) in anticipation of that great day when the One seated on the throne will say, "Behold, I make all things new" (Rev. 21:5). The world in its present form is passing away and will not last (1 Cor. 7:31; 1 John 2:17), and the promise is sure that creation will be set free from its bondage to decay (Rom. 8:18–25).

Now, if we can see and accept the miracle of God raising sinners from the dead to a new creation through the agency of the Word (Rom. 10:17), and see the evidence of it in renewed and re-created lives, then how can we deny what is recorded for us in Genesis 1 and 2? Will the creature say to the Creator, "You did not do it that way" (cf. Isa. 45:9–10)?

In sum, if God's work of renewal and re-creation is historically true and evident, then the strong analogy in Scripture between God's work as re-creator and creator indicates that also His work as creator as recorded in Genesis 1–2 is historically reliable and true. Indeed, the New Testament even pictures Christ as the second Adam and in so doing reaffirms the historicity of the first Adam.

---

8. The Canons of Dort, a seventeenth-century confession, therefore rightly reminds us that conversion is "the new creation, the raising from the dead, the making alive…regeneration is not inferior in power to creation or to the raising of the dead" (III/IV, 12).

The First Adam and the Second Adam

The apostle Paul, writing to Christians in Rome, compared the first Adam with Christ as the second Adam. The Adam of Genesis is "a type of Him who was to come" (Rom. 5:14). Adam could only function as a type of the One to come if Adam actually existed as a historical person. Typology is rooted in history, the history of revelation.[9] After referring to Adam as a type, the apostle referred to his sin:

> As through one man's offense judgment came to all men, resulting in condemnation, even so through one Man's righteous act the free gift came to all men, resulting in justification of life. For as by one man's disobedience many were made sinners, so also by one Man's obedience many will be made righteous. (vv. 18–19)

In a similar vein, the Corinthians were addressed. "As in Adam all die, even so in Christ all shall be made alive" (1 Cor. 15:22). And further on, the apostle wrote, "And so it is written, 'The first man Adam became a living being.' The last Adam became a life-giving spirit" (v. 45).

By closely correlating Adam, identified as the first man (v. 45), and the real consequences of his offense as experienced today, with Christ and His saving work, which continues to impact believers, God's Word clearly treats both as historical persons. If there had not been a real act of sin by Adam in the beginning, there would have been no need for a Savior. In both Romans 5 and 1 Corinthians 15 the importance of the historicity of the first Adam and last Adam is evident from the fact that each represents those who belong to him. They are not private individuals but representative heads, and if they were not historical persons, the whole point of the argument breaks down and there is no more gospel.[10]

Adam is also presented elsewhere in the New Testament as a historical person. Timothy is reminded that "Adam was formed first, then Eve. And Adam was not deceived, but the woman being deceived, fell into transgression" (1 Tim. 2:13–14). Obviously the apostle Paul accepted the account in Genesis 2

---

9. See John VanMaaren, "The Adam-Christ Typology in Paul and Its Development in the Early Church Fathers," *TynBul* 64 (2013): 276–77; Francis Foulkes, *The Acts of God: A Study of the Basis of Typology in the Old Testament* (London: Tyndale, 1958), 34–40.

10. On Rom. 5 and 1 Cor. 15, see, in more detail, J. P. Versteeg, *Is Adam a "Teaching Model" in the New Testament?*, trans. R. B. Gaffin Jr. (Nutley, N.J.: Presbyterian and Reformed, 1978), 8–25, 33–37; Gaffin, *No Adam, No Gospel*, 9–14; Guy Prentiss Waters, "Theistic Evolution Is Incompatible with the Teachings of the New Testament," in Moreland et al., *Theistic Evolution*, 902–10; Merrill, "Where Are You, Adam?," 130–36.

and 3 literally as history. To deny this historicity and only to say, as John Walton does, that "Paul is using Adam and Eve as illustrations" lacks any justification.[11]

Adam's name also occurs in genealogical contexts. Christ's genealogy goes back all the way to "Adam, the son of God" (Luke 3:38). In Luke's genealogy, Adam's name is preceded by many names about which there is no doubt about their historicity. And true to Scripture, Adam has no earthly parents. Directly created by God, he is identified as son of God in that genealogy. John Walton's claim that Luke's genealogy does not necessarily assert that Adam was the first human being, but only that Adam was the "first significant person," is rather hollow and flatly contradicts the clear testimony of Scripture.[12] Another genealogical reference to Adam occurs when Enoch is identified as "the seventh from Adam" (Jude 14). Jude is obviously assuming the historicity of both men.[13]

Conclusion

There is no escaping the fact that Scripture teaches not only that God's work of renewal and re-creation is historically true, as witnessed in the lives of believers every day, but also that His work of creation at the very beginning of time is equally so. The tight correlation that God's Word describes between creation and re-creation, between God's work of calling into being heaven and earth and His redemptive work to save His handiwork, unmistakably shows that if the one is historical, so is the other. It is biblically indefensible to claim historicity for the one while denying it for the other.

Not surprisingly, when people hold to an evolutionary theory of creation's beginnings, it consequently leads them to deny important biblical truths. Such a denial can have terrible consequences.

The Corrosive Effects of the Theory of Evolution

We have seen throughout this study that to accept the theory of evolution is to deny the clear teaching of the opening chapters of Scripture. At every

---

11. Walton, *Lost World of Adam and Eve*, 94–95; also see the detailed critique in Waters, "Theistic Evolution Is Incompatible," 888–91.

12. Walton, *Lost World of Adam and Eve*, 188–89; also see the critique of Waters, "Theistic Evolution Is Incompatible," 882–84. Peter Enns denies the historicity of Adam due to its conflict with the theory of evolution. Enns, *Evolution of Adam*, xv–xviii, 119–35; cf. Hans Madueme, "Some Reflections on Enns and *The Evolution of Adam*," *Themelios* 37 (2012): 275–86; and chapter 2 above on the nature and limitations of science.

13. John Walton distinguishes in Jude 14–15 between literary factuality and historical factuality and denies that Jude is making a historical claim. Walton, *Lost World of Adam and Eve*, 100. For a detailed critique see Waters, "Theistic Evolution Is Incompatible," 891–93.

step of the way, the biblical account of creation counters the prevailing evolutionary paradigm.

We have also seen in the preceding chapters how Old Testament scholars who, according to their own testimony, wish to honor Scripture as the trustworthy Word of God have nevertheless tried to make room in their exegesis of Genesis 1–2 for the theory of evolution. But as has become evident in this study, such an approach usually entails muting or doing injustice to the clear message of Scripture. The only way that the Bible and the theory of evolution can be reconciled with each other is to put aside the clear teaching of Scripture and to reinterpret the historic narrative of the creation account in such a way that the demands of the theory of evolution are satisfied. This theory denies biblical truth and is in complete antithesis to the biblical teaching of creation. Study after study has shown this.[14]

Unbiblical teaching has consequences, and so we must now consider the consequences of accepting evolutionary theory instead of the plain sense of Genesis. After all, Christ said that you will know a tree by its fruit (Luke 6:43–46). Two fruits, or results, can be mentioned here. First, Christians who accept this theory are more likely to be in danger of denying the gospel and losing their faith. A second outcome is that this theory continues to contribute significantly to the erosion of biblical morals in society as a whole.

It Undermines the Christian Faith

We have seen earlier in this chapter that if one denies the reality of the first Adam as a historical person, the first member of the human race, then one must logically deny the reality of the second Adam. Now, many Christians who have embraced the theory of evolution resist this consequence, but logically their position is untenable and creates tension between the clear biblical teaching of the historical Adam and the evolutionary notion of human descent from apes. In chapter 8 we saw how some scholars try to rationalize the problem away by holding that the intention of Scripture is not to inform us how God made the first human, but rather to tell us the nature of humanity and its relationship to God. Others conjecture that there was a pre-Adamite population of human-like creatures and that Adam's appearance in Scripture should be interpreted in that light. Common to all such attempts to wed evolutionary theory of human origins with Scripture is that the plain truth of the Bible is denied. This reality

---

14. To give a few examples: Moreland et al., *Theistic Evolution*; Nevin, *Should Christians Embrace Evolution?*; Wise, *Faith, Form, and Time*; and Gerard Berghoef and Lester DeKoster, *The Great Divide: Christianity or Evolution* (Edinburgh: Banner of Truth, 1989).

results in far too many instances of Christians choosing for the scientific theory and denying the truth of God's Word.

If one denies a doctrine that is so clearly taught in Scripture, as the doctrine of creation is, one's confidence in other biblical teachings can be eroded as well, and one can become skeptical of key doctrines such as the historical fall into sin by Eve and Adam and the need for atonement through the blood of Christ. Indeed, by breaking the biblical connection between a historical first Adam and Christ as the second Adam, one can also end up denying the resurrection. Scripture clearly links the two. "For since by man came death, by Man also came the resurrection of the dead. For as in Adam all die, even so in Christ all shall be made alive" (1 Cor. 15:21–22). Christians may stubbornly refuse to draw such logical consequences when they accept the theory of evolution, but the tension between accepting Scripture and believing the theory of evolution has often led people to deny the faith. The theory of evolution is incompatible with the teachings of Scripture and undermines key Christian doctrines.

Not surprisingly, the sad consequences of Christians losing their faith as a result of the theory of evolution are easy to enumerate.

Some examples. Charles Darwin himself lost faith in the God of Scripture. In an 1879 letter he wrote, "I have never been an Atheist in denying the existence of God. I think that generally…that an Agnostic would be the more correct description of my state of mind."[15] It was in his reflections on his scientific findings that he lost faith in Scripture. "I had gradually come by this time, i.e. 1836 to 1839, to see that the Old Testament was no more to be trusted than the sacred books of the Hindoos." And, "the more we know of the fixed laws of nature the more incredible do miracles become…. By such reflections as these…I gradually came to disbelieve in Christianity as a divine revelation."[16] Warfield summarized Darwin's developments: "The doctrine of evolution once heartily adopted by him gradually undermined his faith, until he cast off the whole of Christianity as an unproved delusion."[17] Warfield's article on Darwin's religious life serves as a warning about the corrosive effects of the theory of evolution on faith in the God of Scripture. Darwin could not reconcile the logical consequences of

---

15. Charles Darwin, *The Life and Letters of Charles Darwin*, ed. Francis Darwin (New York: D. Appleton, 1898), 1:274.

16. Darwin, *Life and Letters*, 1:277–78.

17. Benjamin B. Warfield, "Charles Darwin's Religious Life: A Sketch in Spiritual Biography," *The Presbyterian Review* 9 (1888): 575; this article is reprinted in Benjamin B. Warfield, *Studies in Theology* (repr., Edinburgh: Banner of Truth, 1988), 541–82; and in Warfield, *B. B. Warfield—Evolution, Science, and Scripture*, 68–111.

a theory that opposed the clear teaching of Scripture and consequently lost the faith. What Charles Hodge said in his day about the theory of evolution and its denial that God designed and brought into existence all things is still true today: "The denial of design in nature is virtually the denial of God. Mr. Darwin's theory does deny all design in nature; therefore, his theory is virtually atheistical."[18] The fact that many have, sadly, experienced a similar abandonment of the Christian faith as Darwin did confirms Hodge's observation.

Only one of the following can be true: the plain teaching of the Genesis account or the current scientific theory of evolution. Acceptance of the theory logically leads to denial of the Genesis account. The destructive power of the theory of evolution is difficult to underestimate. Indeed, Darwin's personal journey to unbelief is symptomatic of many who followed him. As the late Fuller Seminary professor Colin Brown put it, "By far the most potent single factor to undermine popular belief in the existence of God in modern times is the evolutionary theory of Charles Darwin."[19] These words are corroborated by a few examples of high-profile individuals who either lost the faith or denied the existence of God due largely to their embrace of the theory of evolution.

Recent instances include Howard Van Till, Professor Emeritus of Physics and Astronomy at Calvin University and a promoter of theistic evolution. In 2006 he gave a presentation "From Calvinism to Freethought" in which he described his journey from orthodox Calvinism to uncertainty. He articulated that his goal "is to craft my new Portrait of Reality as consciously and intentionally as I am able. In order to do so I must often admit that I don't 'know' nearly as much as I once did."[20] Since then, according to an internet exchange with a clergyman, "his reflections on evolution and theodicy led him to renounce belief in a supernatural God altogether."[21] William B. Provine, late professor at Cornell University, drew the implications of accepting the theory of evolution very forthrightly when he said, "Belief in modern evolution makes atheists of

---

18. Charles Hodge, *What is Darwinism?*, ed. Mark A. Noll and David N. Livingstone (Grand Rapids: Baker, 1994), 155.

19. Colin Brown, *Philosophy and the Christian Faith: A Historical Sketch from the Middle Ages to the Present Day* (London: Tyndale, 1969), 147.

20. Howard Van Till, "From Calvinism to Freethought: The Road Less Traveled" (lecture, Center for Inquiry, Grand Rapids, Mich., May 24, 2006), 10, https://cfimichigan.org/event /from-calvinism-to-freethought-the-road-less-traveled/ (accessed January 7, 2020; the text of the lecture has since been removed from the website).

21. Colin R. Reeves, "Bringing Home the Bacon: The Interaction of Science and Scripture Today," in Moreland et al., *Theistic Evolution*, 724.

people" and "one can have a religious view that is compatible with evolution only if the religious view is indistinguishable from atheism."[22]

Another example is Nicolaas A. Rupke, who began his career as a geologist but is now Johnson Professor of History at Washington and Lee University. Although he grew up believing the biblical account of creation, "he had come to accept organic evolution and had forsaken the faith of his family."[23]

As a final example there is Richard Dawkins. He was confirmed in the Anglican faith at age thirteen. In his memoir he wrote, "I became intensely religious around the time I was confirmed…I prayed every night." But eventually a friend "persuaded me of the full force of Darwin's brilliant idea and I shed my last vestige of theistic credulity, probably at the age of about sixteen. It wasn't long then before I became strongly and militantly atheistic."[24] As an evolutionary biologist he famously declared that "Darwin made it possible to be an intellectually fulfilled atheist."[25] This statement must, however, be read in the light of Dawkins's own implied admission that embracing the theory of evolution is ultimately a matter of faith and not intellect. According to him, "The theory of evolution by cumulative natural selection is the only theory we know of that is in principle *capable* of explaining the existence of organized complexity. Even if the evidence did not favour it, it would *still* be the best theory available! In fact the evidence does favour it. But that is another story."[26] This admission reveals something of the dogmatism underlying Dawkins's championing of the theory of evolution. "Even if the evidence did not favour it [the theory of evolution], it would *still* be the best theory available!" With such a statement Dawkins refuses to acknowledge the possibility that the Creator made all things. With no creator, the theory of evolution will have to do.

These examples prompt the question whether involving God somehow in the evolutionary process would solve the problem of atheism associated with the theory and enable a person to maintain both Genesis and the theory of evolution.

Theistic evolution? American philosopher and theologian J. P. Moreland has helpfully described what theistic evolutionists affirm. They "are theists who believe that, when it comes to scientifically detectable empirical evidence, the

---

22. "William Provine, RIP: Noble in His Honesty," Evolution News and Science Today (website), September 3, 2015, https://evolutionnews.org/2015/09/william_provine/.

23. Numbers, *The Creationists*, 308.

24. Richard Dawkins, *An Appetite for Wonder: The Making of a Scientist, a Memoir* (New York: HarperCollins, 2013), 103, 142.

25. Richard Dawkins, *The Blind Watchmaker*, 30th anniv. ed. (London: Penguin, 2006), 6.

26. Dawkins, *Blind Watchmaker*, 316.

processes by which evolution occurred are blind, purposeless, naturalistic processes with no goal-directed activity or supernatural intervention, but that, in some fairly unclear sense, God 'guided' the process—but that this involvement by God is not detectable." Moreland goes on to note that theistic evolutionists reject philosophical naturalism and hold that there is more to reality than the material world. They believe in the existence of God. However, "while doing science, they are willing to lay their theism aside."[27]

Defenders of theistic evolution, such as those associated with BioLogos, reject the atheistic worldview of evolutionism, but they nevertheless maintain all the key hallmarks of the theory of evolution. A key feature is, of course, maintaining that all species, including humans, are descended from a common ancestor over many generations. Accordingly, today's human population could not have derived from Adam and Eve. Evolutionary theory asserts that an effective ancestral population size for *Homo sapiens* was in the range of eight to ten thousand individuals.[28] Furthermore, theistic evolution denies that human death originated with the original sin recorded in Genesis 3 (cf. Rom. 5:12). After all, in the long evolutionary time scale, death was everywhere among prehuman ancestors before humans finally emerged.[29] More examples could be given, but the point is that theistic evolution contradicts Scripture, and when Christians try to make it agree with the Word of God they are attempting to make two completely incompatible accounts of human origins agree. One must make a choice. When one chooses for theistic evolution it is difficult not to embrace some form of evolutionism—a worldview that denies the biblical notion of God the creator. And if one is consistent with the underlying

---

27. J. P. Moreland, *Scientism and Secularism* (Wheaton, Ill.: Crossway, 2018), 160–61.

28. Dennis R. Venema, "Genesis and the Genome: Genomics Evidence for Human-Ape Common Ancestry and Ancestral Hominid Population Sizes," *PSCF* 62 (2010): 173–74. See also, e.g., "Were Adam and Eve Historical Figures?," BioLogos, February 18, 2020, https://biologos .org/common-questions/were-adam-and-eve-historical-figures, and other articles on the BioLogos website.

29. For the rejection of original sin by theistic evolution, see, e.g., Denis O. Lamoureux, "Beyond Original Sin: Is a Theological Paradigm Shift Inevitable?," *PSCF* 67 (2015): 35–49; for an (unsuccessful) attempt at reconciliation with Scripture, Gijsbert Van den Brink, "Questions, Challenges, and Concerns for Original Sin," in *Finding Ourselves After Darwin: Conversations on the Image of God, Original Sin, and the Problem of Evil*, ed. Stanely P. Rosenberg (Grand Rapids: Baker Academic, 2018), 117–29. Van den Brink's attempt is unsuccessful because he contradicts Scripture when asserting, e.g., "humans emerged from prehuman ancestors in times immemorial as a group rather than as a couple" (126); similarly, Cornelis van der Kooi and Gijsbert van den Brink, *Christian Dogmatics: An Introduction*, trans. Reinder Bruinsma with James D. Bratt (Grand Rapids: Eerdmans, 2017), 302.

materialistic presuppositions of evolutionism, one can even end up denying the existence of God.[30]

It is consequently not surprising that the theory of evolution, which in both its secular and theistic form blatantly contradicts the clear testimony of Scripture, has had a devastating impact on the faith of many. A 2016 Discovery Institute nationwide survey of a representative sample of 3,664 American adults sought to ascertain the impact of evolutionary ideas on those who had lost their religious faith. It showed that "unguided chemical evolution and the Darwinian mutation/selection mechanism are the most significant drivers of science-related erosion in faith in God."[31] American philosopher Daniel Dennett rightly called Darwin's notions a universal acid that is so corrosive that "it eats through just about every traditional concept" including, therefore, biblical beliefs. "Faith, like a species, must evolve or go extinct when the environment changes."[32]

Impact on churches. With the growing acceptance of the theory of evolution, even in conservative churches, and with the theory's corrosive effects on Christian faith, it is small wonder that the impact on churches is significant. Although the decline of Christianity in the West is due to many factors, history has shown that the acceptance of the theory of evolution plays a significant role because it called into question the truthfulness of God's Word regarding creation. Once doubt is expressed about the reliability or authority of Scripture in one area of life, such distrust can extend to other areas as well. One is then left with a Bible that is lessened in authority and no longer normative for every aspect of the Christian life. Two ecclesiastical examples, one in the Netherlands and the other in the United States, illustrate how the theory of evolution played a significant role in undermining the authority of Scripture within these churches.[33]

The Reformed Churches in the Netherlands (GKN) initially upheld the plain sense of the opening chapters of Genesis by defending the historicity

---

30. There are continuing attempts to reconcile theistic evolution with Scripture; a recent example is Stanely P. Rosenberg, ed., *Finding Ourselves After Darwin: Conversations on the Image of God, Original Sin, and the Problem of Evil* (Grand Rapids: Baker Academic, 2018); cf. the critique by Hans Madueme, "Adam and Sin as a Bane of Evolution? A Review of *Finding Ourselves After Darwin," Themelios* 44 (2019): 466–76.

31. John G. West, *Darwin's Corrosive Idea: The Impact of Evolution on Attitudes about Faith, Ethics, and Human Uniqueness* (Seattle: Discovery Institute, 2016), 6.

32. Daniel C. Dennett, *Darwin's Dangerous Idea: Evolution and the Meanings of Life* (New York: Touchstone, 1996), 63, 516.

33. A detailed survey of scholars and churches from the nineteenth century to the present shows that when they made room for the theory of evolution they abandoned a literal interpretation of Genesis. See VanDoodewaard, *Quest*, 133–312.

of the tree of the knowledge of good and evil in the 1926 Geelkerken case.[34] Eventually, however, the acceptance of the hypothesis of evolution by leading scholars in these churches meant that their 1967 Synod revoked the 1926 decision and new unbiblical interpretations of the Genesis creation account were tolerated. Eventually these churches abandoned the classic understanding of the inspiration and authority of Scripture and became more and more liberal.[35]

The issue of biological evolution created enormous debate and conflict in the United States during the early twentieth century. Within this larger context, the struggle for maintaining the historic Christian faith in the Presbyterian Church in the United States of America (PCUSA) came to a head in 1924 when nearly thirteen hundred ministers accepted the Auburn Affirmation, which denied, among other teachings, the inerrancy of Scripture—a denial that would also make room for the acceptance of the theory of evolution. The wide acceptance of the Auburn Affirmation in the PCUSA was one factor that led to the founding of the Orthodox Presbyterian Church (OPC) under the leadership of J. Gresham Machen, who fought for the traditional orthodox teachings of the church. Although B. B. Warfield had been less than clear in his interaction with the theory of evolution, Machen was more forthright, although very careful, in engaging the subject. But, as his student, colleague, and biographer, Ned Stonehouse put it, Machen was "by no means indifferent to the issue. And to the extent that evolution involved a philosophy of materialism, and contradicted the plain teaching of the Bible, he was quite opposed to it as a matter of course." As a New Testament scholar, Machen did not concentrate on Old Testament issues but focused on defending the historicity of new covenant events such as the virgin birth and the resurrection of the Lord Jesus. But even then he used his research to assert that Adam was not a product of evolution, but that God created him.[36] True to this early history, the OPC has reaffirmed its opposition

---

34. See chapter 10, note 61.

35. For detailed accounts of this development, Kruyswijk, *Baas in eigen boek?*, 198, 207–93; A. M. Lindeboom, *De theologen gingen voorop: eenvoudig verhaal van de ontmateling van de Gereformeerde Kerken* (Kampen: Kok, 1987), 20–100; this book subsequently shows the destructive effects in the church of abandoning the clear teaching of Scripture; also see Flipse, "The Origins of Creationism in the Netherlands," 104–47; Flipse, *Christelijke wetenschap*, passim; Visser, "Dutch Calvinists and Darwinism," 293–315; Marinus J. Arntzen, "Inspiration and Trustworthiness of Scripture," in *Interpreting God's Word Today*, ed. Simon Kistemaker (Nutley, N.J.: Presbyterian and Reformed, 1970), 198–201.

36. Ned B. Stonehouse, *J. Gresham Machen: A Biographical Memoir* (Grand Rapids: Eerdmans, 1954), 402; also see J. Gresham Machen, "What Fundamentalism Stands for Now," in Machen, *Selected Shorter Writings*, ed. D. G. Hart (Phillipsburg, N.J.: P&R, 2004), 116–22, esp. 118, 120; for a clear rejection of the view that Adam was the result of evolution, in the context

to the theory of evolution. The 1996 General Assembly judged as contrary to God's Word and the doctrinal standards of the church the view that Adam had primate ancestors.[37] After the ecclesiastical conflicts of the 1920s and 1930s, the PCUSA became increasingly liberal and, having merged with other Presbyterian denominations in the twentieth century, continues today in the mainline Presbyterian Church (USA).

Besides the corrosive effects of the theory of evolution in undermining the Christian faith, with devastating results for Christians and churches that accept it, this theory has also contributed significantly to the eroding of biblical morals in the Western world.

It Erodes Biblical Morals in Society

Charles Colson and Nancy Pearcey have perceptively noted that "our view of origins shapes our understanding of ethics, law, education—and yes, even sexuality."[38] If God created us for a purpose, then we need to ask how He wants us to live to fulfill His purpose. The answer is found in His Word where He reveals His will for all of life. Christian morals are not based on personal feelings but are founded on the objective norms of God's revealed law. The theory of evolution, however, claims that we are the products of a mindless process, evolution. According to evolutionism, we created the notion of God, and our moral direction should come from our scientific knowledge. In other words, there is no ultimate objective moral standard, no final authoritative basis for law, and so we must make our own. "Since the only objective reality that exists is the natural world, and it is in constant evolutionary flux, our ideas about right and wrong are constantly changing as well. The result is radical ethical relativism."[39]

Since Darwin considered humans to have gradually evolved from lower forms of life, human morals also developed gradually due to changing circumstances. The evolving morals depended on the situation and were completely variable. Darwin therefore opined that

---

of a discussion of the virgin birth of Christ, see J. Gresham Machen, *The Christian View of Man* (London: Banner of Truth, 1967), 114–24; cf. D. G. Hart, *Defending the Faith: J. Gresham Machen and the Crisis of Conservative Protestantism in Modern America* (Baltimore: Johns Hopkins University Press, 1994), 84–107, esp. 98–99.

37. *Minutes of the Sixty-Third General Assembly…and Yearbook of the Orthodox Presbyterian Church* (Philadelphia: Orthodox Presbyterian Church, 1996), §§137, 158.

38. Charles Colson and Nancy Pearcey, *How Now Shall We Live?* (Carol Stream, Ill.: Tyndale House, 2004), 92; what follows in this paragraph is also dependent on 92–93.

39. Colson and Pearcey, *How Now Shall We Live?*, 93; a 2016 poll confirmed this point: West, *Darwin's Corrosive Idea*, 10.

if, for instance, to take an extreme case, men were reared under precisely the same conditions as hive-bees, there can hardly be a doubt that our unmarried females would, like the worker-bees, think it a sacred duty to kill their brothers, and mothers would strive to kill their fertile daughters; and no one would think of interfering. Nevertheless, the bee, or any other social animal, would gain in our supposed case, as it appears to me, some feeling of right or wrong, or a conscience…. In this case an inward monitor would tell the animal that it would have been better to have followed the one impulse rather than the other.[40]

For Darwin, "the difference in mind between man and the higher animals, great as it is, certainly is one of degree and not of kind."[41] So, just as animals, humans adjust their sense of right and wrong solely to the circumstances in which they find themselves, even though Darwin acknowledged that "the moral sense perhaps affords the best and highest distinction between man and the lower animals."[42] But the underlying principle that humans are in the same category as the animal kingdom is determinative and means that morals are a by-product of evolution.

With the current great impact of the theory of evolution, it is small wonder that the ethics of our society are evolving, or rather collapsing, at an alarming rate. The fruits of many years of naturalistic thinking are becoming evident in the moral decline, which reflects the notion that humans are simply part of the animal kingdom and as such are nothing special. Western culture is embracing ethical lows unthinkable fifty years ago as attested by the denial of God-given creational norms through the legalization of same-sex marriage, abortion, and euthanasia. There is also the denial of God-given gender in the transgender phenomenon. This is not the place to enter into a discussion on these issues, but the point is simply to note that the ethical slide in the West has been helped by and is consistent with the embrace of the theory of evolution and its atheistic view that morals need to evolve according to changing circumstances.[43]

---

40. Charles Darwin, *The Descent of Man and Selection in Relation to Sex*, new ed. (London: John Murray, 1901), 151–52.

41. Darwin, *Descent of Man*, 193.

42. Darwin, *Descent of Man*, 194.

43. See further Benjamin Wiker, *Moral Darwinism: How We Became Hedonists* (Downers Grove, Ill.: InterVarsity, 2002); John G. West, *Darwin Day in America: How Our Politics and Culture Have Been Dehumanized in the Name of Science* (Wilmington, Del.: Intercollegiate Studies Institute, 2014); James Rachels, *Created from Animals: The Moral Implications of Darwinism* (Oxford: Oxford University Press, 1990); Margaret Helder, *No Christian Silence on Science: Science from a Christian Perspective* (Edmonton: Creation Science Association of Alberta, 2016), 63–79. For a historical study of the devastating consequences of the theory of evolution, see

Defending the Truth of Genesis 1 and 2

Western culture is hostile to the biblical teaching of creation. The theory of evolution has transformed our society's worldview to such an extent that every aspect of life is affected by it. How are we to defend and promote in an effective manner the truth of Scripture? It is beyond the focus of this book to explore the many ways that people and organizations can and do promote biblical teaching on creation. For our purposes, two areas merit special consideration: the education of the next generation and the need for churches faithfully to maintain the biblical teaching on creation.

Education

It is critically important that each new generation is taught the biblical view of creation and the place of science in relation to Scripture. It goes without saying that parents have the first responsibility to train their children in the fear of the Lord and in the truth of His Word. But that first responsibility is here assumed and is not our focus. For our purposes we want to direct our attention to especially one institution of primary importance, the church.

The church as "the pillar and ground of the truth" (1 Tim. 3:15) has great educational responsibility. Christian educational institutions from elementary schools to universities obviously also have an important task in this regard. But, unfortunately, it appears that this responsibility is far too often not honored since theistic evolution is for many Christian schools the accepted norm. Those who are qualified should teach the mainstream theory of evolution, critique it, point out the limitations of scientific inquiry into origins, and uphold the unique authority of God's Word. It should of course be made clear that Christianity is not against science. Indeed, being a scientist and studying God's creation is an immense privilege and an awesome calling.

But as just noted, the church should be the first to assume responsibility in preparing the next generation with a biblical view of creation. After all, only a minority of Christians go to Christian schools, and so we need to underline the task of the church in equipping the congregation, including the young people, to withstand the onslaught of the dominant mainstream evolutionary theory.

It is often said that young people lose the faith once they go to college. According to some polls, the truth appears to be somewhat different. The young people in these polls lost their faith long before they went to college—they lost

---

Richard Weikart, *From Darwin to Hitler: Evolutionary Ethics, Eugenics, and Racism in Germany* (New York: Palgrave Macmillan, 2004).

it while being good members of a church! A major reason was unresolved questions and conflicts that students wrestled with regarding what Scripture says and what the theory of evolution affirms.[44] This reality underlines the need for the church to be up front about this issue and to address it before young people get inundated with evolutionist science and its worldview. And that happens very early on. Science textbooks and classes in public elementary schools subject students to evolutionism years before they enter high school. Unless there is a strong biblical counterforce in the home and church against the theory of evolution—and that seems to be less and less the case—the minds of children and teens going through a secular education system are being molded to accept as a given that the evolutionary view of reality is the only correct one. Consequently, the authority of scientific theory is promoted at the expense of Scripture's authority. It is not surprising that this elevation of the teaching of current science above the clear teaching of Genesis leads children and teens to become confused, question their faith, and even abandon it.

There are at least two excellent ways to prepare young people to meet the challenge of the theory of evolution. First, preaching the gospel of creation is of utmost importance. The pulpit cannot be silent on this issue. We have noted how Scripture's teaching on creation is closely related to its instruction on redemption. The two cannot be separated. We must believe either Scripture or mainstream evolutionary science. It is impossible to consistently believe both. At bottom it is a matter of the presupposition of faith either in science as the essence of truth or in Scripture as the very Word of God. In this connection a congregation can also be reminded of the limitations of science in the case of origins and the first humans.

Second, special attention should also be given to these issues in Sunday school, catechetical classes, young adult groups, or wherever an occasion for discussing these matters can be arranged. In such contexts, the wonder of God's world, which reveals His glory, and the high calling of being a scientist can also

---

44. Research commissioned from America's Research Group has shown that already in elementary school, students from conservative churches had doubts and questions about the Bible that were not being answered. The inconsistency between what they were taught in science classes and what they read in the Bible was an important factor that led to skepticism and doubt about Genesis and, for many, unbelief. For the report, see Ken Ham and Britt Beemer with Todd Hillard, *Already Gone: Why Your Kids Will Quit Church and What You Can Do to Stop It* (Green Forest, Ariz.: Master, 2009); other studies came to similar conclusions: David Kinnaman, "Six Reasons Young Christians Leave Church," Barna Group, September 27, 2011, https://www.barna .com/research/six-reasons-young-christians-leave-church/; John G. West, "Are Young People Losing Their Faith Because of Science?" (Discovery Institute, 2013), https://www.discovery .org/m/2019/04/AreYoungPeopleLosingTheirFaith.pdf.

be emphasized. The church is not antiscience. At the same time the inability of science to deal with origins and past events that cannot be duplicated needs to be addressed but also, and perhaps especially, the philosophical framework within which current science operates. Many people assume that science is neutral and not affected by religious presuppositions. The opposite is the case.

This fact is evident from the writings of evolutionists themselves. Three examples come to mind. Professor William Provine has insisted that a conflict between science and religion is unavoidable. According to him, if you do wish to retain your Christian religious beliefs you will "have to check [your] brains at the church-house door." He further states that modern science directly implies that "there are no purposive principles whatsoever in nature. There are no gods and no designing forces that are rationally detectable."[45] Provine's materialistic presuppositions are clearly evident here, and they are at bottom religious because science cannot determine the presence of gods. His materialistic beliefs lead him to this conclusion.

Another well-known scientist, Harvard research professor Richard Lewontin, admitted that his belief in materialism determined his understanding of the nature of science. In a 1997 book review he wrote,

> Our willingness to accept scientific claims that are against common sense is the key to an understanding of the real struggle between science and the supernatural. We take the side of science...because we have a prior commitment...to materialism. It is not that the methods and institutions of science somehow compel us to accept a material explanation of the phenomenal world but on the contrary, that we are forced by our *a priori* adherence to material causes to create an apparatus of investigation and a set of concepts that produce material explanations, no matter how counter-intuitive, no matter how mystifying to the uninitiated. Moreover that materialism is absolute, for we cannot allow a Divine foot in the door.[46]

And so the real battle, as John Lennox put it when commenting on the above quote, "is not so much between science and faith in God, but rather between a materialistic, or more broadly, a naturalistic worldview and a supernaturalistic, or theistic, worldview. After all, Lewontin's faith commitment to materialism is self-confessedly *not* rooted in his science" but in his desire to exclude God from science.[47]

---

45. Quoted in Phillip E. Johnson, *Darwin on Trial* (Downers Grove, Ill.: InterVarsity, 1991), 124.

46. Quoted in Lennox, *God's Undertaker*, 35–36.

47. Lennox, *God's Undertaker*, 36 (italics in the original).

The all-embracing faith system of evolution was starkly described by the evolutionist, paleontologist, and theologian Pierre Teilhard de Chardin. "Is evolution a theory, a system, or a hypothesis? It is much more: it is a general condition to which all theories, all hypotheses, all systems must bow and which they must satisfy henceforth if they are to be thinkable and true. Evolution is a light illuminating all facts, a curve that all lines must follow."[48] In view of these words, the late Phillip Johnson, well-known critic of evolution, aptly noted, "Evolution is, in short, the God we must worship. It is taking us to heaven."[49] If one denies the God of Scripture, the Creator, by not believing His account of creation, then one must create another god to try to explain how all things came to be.

It is a responsibility of the church to make its members realize that a faith commitment to a materialistic worldview drives the thinking of mainstream, atheistic evolutionism. This will enable God's people to ask the appropriate questions when they are confronted with theories that undermine their faith in God the creator. It is good to remember the words of Herman Bavinck that were quoted earlier in this book:

> When Scripture...comes in contact with other sciences and also sheds its light on them, it does not all at once cease to be the Word of God but remains that Word. Even when it speaks about the genesis of heaven and earth, it does not present saga or myth or poetic fantasy but offers, in accordance with its own clear intent, history, the history that deserves credence and trust. And for that reason Christian theology, with only a few exceptions, continued to hold onto the literal historical view of the creation story.[50]

Scientific theories change, but God's Word remains true and trustworthy. Old Testament scholar E. J. Young once pointed out that although the Bible is not a textbook of science, yet "on whatever subject the Bible speaks, whether it be creation, the making of the sun, the fall, the flood, man's redemption, it is authoritative and true. We are to think God's thoughts after him and his thoughts are expressed in the words of Scripture." He also remarked, "Read what it says and understand what you read"![51]

It is the responsibility of the church to make its members fully aware of this state of affairs and to encourage the flock to accept the Word as true and faithful.

---

48. Pierre Teilhard de Chardin, *The Phenomenon of Man* (London: Collins, 1970), 241.
49. Johnson, *Darwin on Trial*, 130.
50. Bavinck, *Reformed Dogmatics*, 2:495.
51. See, respectively, Edward J. Young, *Studies in Genesis One*, 54 and 53n31.

The church and its members, young and old, do not need to be intimidated by evolutionary science that denies the veracity of Scripture. The materialistic presuppositions of mainstream science are religious, and the utmost devotion is given to the god of the theory of evolution. The church should also encourage Christian scientists to take up the challenge to present alternative interpretations of available scientific data to counter the reigning mainstream theories that oppose the Word of God. Such scientists and like-minded organizations deserve our support.

Ecclesiastical Faithfulness

In order for the church to fulfill its teaching ministry with respect to Genesis 1 and 2, it must remain faithful to the Word, and that includes upholding the historicity of what is narrated in the opening chapters of Scripture. Confessional Reformed and Presbyterian churches are well equipped to maintain what has been the historic position of the church throughout the ages. After all, their confessions clearly and faithfully reflect Scripture in affirming the historicity of God's creation work as recorded in Scripture.

The Three Forms of Unity attest to the historicity of Genesis 1 and 2, as is evident from the following quotes. The Belgic Confession confesses in article 12 that the triune God "created out of nothing the heaven, the earth and all creatures" and in article 14 that "God created man of dust from the ground." The Heidelberg Catechism affirms that God the Father "out of nothing created heaven and earth" (Q. 26) and that "God created man good and in his image" (Q. 6). The Canons of Dort affirm that "in the beginning man was created in the image of God" (III/IV, 1). In even greater detail the Westminster Standards uphold biblical teaching. It pleased the triune God "in the beginning, to create, or make of nothing, the world, and all things therein whether visible or invisible in the space of six days," and "he created man, male and female, with reasonable and immortal souls, endued with knowledge, righteousness, and true holiness, after his own image" (WCF 4.1, 2). Similar formulations are found in the Westminster Shorter Catechism (Q. 9, 10). The Larger Catechism similarly notes that creation took place "within the space of six days" (Q. 15).

On occasion there are calls for a new confessional formulation to meet the dangers of evolutionism. However, such is not really necessary for Reformed and Presbyterian churches. Scripture is clear and their confessions faithfully reflect that testimony. A difficulty with preparing a new formulation asserting the historicity of Genesis 1 and 2 is the temptation to go beyond what Scripture says, in other words, to provide specifics about that which Scripture gives no additional detail. An example would be to define precisely what constituted a day of creation by specifying that each day was twenty-four hours. Now, Scripture indicates that these days were like our days, literal days, consisting of evening and morning, periods of darkness and light—days obviously measured in hours not years. And that should be enough. There is no need to go further than Scripture. These were days unique in world history, witnessed by God alone, and who are we to add details to that which God has adequately revealed to us in Scripture?

If new confessional formulations were to add more information than Scripture specifically provides, then we would face the related danger of infringing on the freedom of exegesis. Inquisitive theologians and scientists may sometimes wish God had told us more than He has actually revealed in Genesis 1 and 2. But God in His wisdom only told us so much. At the same time, we have a complete Scripture, and scholars can attempt to elucidate details in Genesis 1 and 2 from the entire Word of God. As long as the integrity of Scripture is honored, the church should allow such work of interpretation even if different scholars come to different conclusions. Discussion within the church on exegetical details can be most refreshing when carried out in acknowledgment of the supreme authority of Scripture and in confessional faithfulness. Should an exegesis of a biblical passage that is being pushed and promoted raise questions and confusion in a church community about whether it is biblical, such a matter can be dealt with on a case-by-case basis by the church community or federation affected.

Churches should be wary of going beyond the clear text of Scripture and should augment their confessional formulations only when they clearly need elaboration.[52] It is incumbent upon the church to protect its members by forbidding in its midst the promotion of the theory of evolution and its implied worldview since that theory is clearly opposed to Scripture.[53] This theory is also motivating many well-meaning evangelical interpreters of Scripture to try to develop an understanding of Genesis that is consistent with current

---

52. Sixteenth-century Lutheran confessional formulations, for instance, do not specifically deal with creation. To meet the challenge of evolutionism, the Lutheran Church–Missouri Synod affirmed six-day creation at their sixty-seventh Regular Convention on July 23, 2019, reinforcing their 1932 *Brief Statement of the Doctrinal Position of the Missouri Synod*, which teaches creation in six days; also see Louis Lavallee, "Creeds and the Six Creation Days," *Acts and Facts* 22, no. 1 (1993): n.p., https://www.icr.org/article/creeds-six-creation-days.

53. It is outside the scope of this study to give an overview of how conservative churches and institutions during and after the twentieth century have responded to the threat of the theory of evolution. See, e.g., VanDoodewaard, *Quest*, 193–280.

mainstream science. Although apparently motivated by a desire to save the faith of those struggling with how to relate Genesis 1 and 2 to evolutionary science, the effort has borne mixed fruits. And no wonder, for one must still come to terms with the biblical text, which testifies to the historicity of a six-day creation. One must ultimately choose either for the biblical account of the earth's beginnings or for the theory of evolution.

We do not know the future of scientific theory or the way it will relate to the book of Genesis. One thing is certain. Although many may deny it, the simple fact remains that science is not and will never be competent to explain the events of God's work of creation. These are incomprehensible to human minds and out of the reach of science. No scientific endeavor can make demonstrable truth claims about what exactly happened during the first six days of the history of our planet. Those who uphold the full authority of Scripture on creation have nothing to fear from the theory of evolution and the science that endeavors to prove it. This theory cannot be empirically proven, but it has become a revered idol, and academics in the sciences who challenge it often do so at their own peril. Christians should reject this god and trust God's Word. It is only by faith that we can understand that the world and the universe were formed at God's command (Heb. 11:3).

The famed Dutch theologian and politician Abraham Kuyper gave an address on evolution at the Free University in Amsterdam in 1899. Near the end of his speech he clearly delineated what was at stake. "Evolution," he said, "is a newly conceived system, a newly established theory, a newly formed dogma, a newly emerged faith, which embracing and dominating all of life, is diametrically opposed to the Christian faith, and can erect its temple only upon the ruins of our Christian Confessions."[54]

Christians need to choose between a current idol and the true God, and that can cause grief. Indeed, British theologian R. T. Kendall plausibly suggested that "every generation of Christianity has its own stigma by which the believer's faith is severely tested."[55] Our generation's trial is the theory of evolution and all that comes with it. Our burden and stigma is "to believe God's account of creation *without* the empirical evidence.... We must be willing to be unvindicated and laughed at; and not rush to make our belief in the Bible

---

54. Abraham Kuyper, "Evolution," *CTJ* 31 (1996): 49–50. The address can also be found in James D. Bratt, ed., *Abraham Kuyper: A Centennial Reader* (Grand Rapids: Eerdmans; Carlisle, U.K.: Paternoster, 1998), 405–40.

55. R. T. Kendall, "Faith and Creation," in Nevin, *Should Christians Embrace Evolution?*, 109 (italics removed).

credible to others…. It often means to be scoffed at and made to look like a fool or an obscurantist."[56] In other words, we must be prepared to bear this cross and live by faith, as faithful believers before us have done (cf. Heb. 11). But Christians should not be defeatist, for it is at bottom a matter of faith either in the fallible human theory of evolution or in God's inspired Word. And believers can be encouraged by the fact that the entire creation witnesses to God's glory (Rom. 1:20)!

Summary

The first part of this chapter showed that Scripture closely correlates God's work of creation at the beginning of time with His work of salvation in both Old and New Testament times. Israel's redeemer is frequently described as the maker of heaven and earth and also as the creator of Israel. Such descriptions of God's person and work would have little meaning and impact if they were not historically grounded, both at the beginning of time and throughout the history of Israel. Similarly, in New Testament times salvation in Christ is described in terms of God's work of creation. To be saved is to be a new creation in Christ; it is to be God's workmanship created in Christ Jesus, God's Son, by whom God made the heavens and the earth. Conversion is a divine act of creation; it is like a resurrection from the dead. Every Christian today who has true faith can rest assured that as surely as God has raised him or her to a new life as a new creation, so God was able to call into being all things at the beginning of time. God's present miraculous work of salvation and re-creation attests to the truth of His creation account.

God further tightens the historical correlation between Genesis 1–2 and His work of salvation by making it clear in His Word that the first Adam was a type of the second Adam, Christ—the first Adam being the representative head of the human race lost in sin and Christ being the head of the new, redeemed human race. Such typology of representative heads would be completely meaningless were it not grounded in the historical reality of both the first Adam and the second Adam.

The theory of evolution destroys the correlation between God's work of creation and salvation for it denies that God created all things and brought the enormous diversity of life into being. Also those who wish to somehow involve God by way of what is called theistic evolution deny the plain sense of the opening chapters of Scripture. The theory of evolution, in whatever dress

---

56. Kendall, "Faith and Creation," 110, 112, 116 (italics in the original).

it is presented, clearly denies Genesis 1 and 2 and thus works corrosively and undermines the Christian faith. This chapter has shown examples of that both personally and ecclesiastically. Not surprisingly, the theory of evolution has also contributed to the erosion of societal morals.

The church as pillar and ground of truth has a very important role to play, by means of the pulpit and its educational ministry, in challenging the hegemony of mainstream evolutionary theory. The church should not deride or attack science. The pursuit of scientific endeavor is to be applauded and encouraged. Christians need to enter this field and challenge evolutionary theory with scientific facts that show that creation displays God's handiwork. But the church is duty bound to point out that we are at bottom involved in a spiritual battle. Evolutionist scientists themselves admit that their materialistic presuppositions exclude any involvement of God in their scientific theorizing. As noted earlier, in a real sense the struggle is between faith in the theory of evolution and faith in the Word of God.

In this spiritual warfare Christians can take courage by accepting with childlike faith the Word of God for what it is, the truth, even when it speaks of earth's beginnings.

Doxology

As we conclude this study it is fitting to praise God for His incredible work of creation. The natural sciences have the glorious task of investigating the world and all its wonders, which the Almighty has entrusted to us. In the process, scientists with eyes to see will behold something of the glory of the Creator. Indeed, so clearly has God shown His power in the work of His hands, and so obvious is His greatness revealed in creation, that there is absolutely no excuse for those who refuse to see His splendor (Rom. 1:19–20). As human minds try to make sense of what they discover and formulate theories and hypotheses of how everything fits together and works, those who acknowledge the Creator will humbly recognize their human limitations and praise Him for what they are allowed to see and discover. Such scientists will also thank God for His infallible Word and accept as true the historical account of His six days of creative activity.

How great and awesome is the Creator! The heavens declare His glory and the skies proclaim the work of His hands (Ps. 19:1)! Who cannot but exclaim,

> Oh, the depth of the riches both of the wisdom and knowledge of God!
> How unsearchable are His judgments and His ways past finding out!

"For who has known the mind of the LORD?
Or who has become His counselor?"
"Or who has first given to Him
And it shall be repaid to him?"

For of Him and through Him and to Him are all things, to whom be glory forever. Amen. (Rom. 11:33–36)

And we may echo the song of the elders who worship before the heavenly throne:

You are worthy, O Lord,
To receive glory and honor and power;
For You created all things,
And by Your will they exist and were created. (Rev. 4:11)

APPENDIX

The Creation of Heaven and the Angels

Since Genesis 1 and 2 focus on God preparing the earth as the dwelling place for humans, these chapters say very little about heaven as the dwelling place of God and the creation of the angels. This appendix will very briefly consider what God has revealed to us about these topics.[1]

Heaven as God's Dwelling Place

"In the beginning God created the heavens and the earth" (Gen. 1:1). This comprehensive statement includes not only the sky or firmament that we see, but also heaven as the dwelling place of God. In other words, the terms "heavens" (*šāmayîm*) and "earth" (*'ereṣ*) together encompass all of creation. God made everything, including heaven as His dwelling place. As the narrative in Genesis 1 continues, the Hebrew term for "heavens" is used in a more restrictive sense to refer to the sky and outer space as perceived and experienced from earth (vv. 7–8, 14–18).

Elsewhere in Scripture, however, the term "heavens" or "heaven" (*šāmayîm*) is also used as the dwelling place of God. We find both uses in Psalm 33.

> By the word of the LORD the heavens [*šāmayîm*] were made,…
> The LORD looks from heaven [*šāmayîm*];
> He sees all the sons of men.
> From the place of His dwelling He looks
> On all the inhabitants of the earth. (Ps. 33:6, 13–14)

This passage tells us that heaven is both part of creation and God's home. In his prayer to God, King Solomon recognized where God was when he

---

1. For detailed treatments, see Joel Beeke and Paul M. Smalley, *Revelation and God* (Wheaton, Ill.: Crossway, 2019), 1109–57; Klaas Schilder, *Heaven: What Is It?*, trans. Marian M. Schoolland (Grand Rapids: Eerdmans, 1950); Bavinck, *Reformed Dogmatics*, 2:443–72; Turretin, *Institutes*, 1:539–67.

addressed Him and said: "Hear in heaven Your dwelling place" (1 Kings 8:39). Indeed, "the heaven, even the heavens, are the LORD's; but the earth He has given to the children of men" (Ps. 115:16; also cf. Eccl. 5:2). One can say, as Klaas Schilder put it, "though God's dwelling place is distinct from that of man, both live within the one 'house' of creation." To be sure, "God and His creation are *forever distinct*," but on the other hand "God and man are never *divorced*."[2]

God is omnipresent. His Spirit is everywhere (Ps. 139:5–10). He fills heaven and earth (Jer. 23:24) and, as King Solomon confessed, "heaven and the heaven of heavens cannot contain" Him (1 Kings 8:27). God is not a created being, and He is therefore not bound to created realities such as space.[3] But it pleased God to localize His presence (I am using human terminology here) and to make for Himself a heavenly habitation that is "holy and glorious" (Isa. 63:15). Since heaven is God's dwelling place, it is not surprising that "the LORD has established His throne in heaven" (Ps. 103:19) where He sits and holds rebellious nations in derision (Ps. 2:4). Heaven as part of creation is a real place. But where is heaven?

Where Is Heaven?

For earthbound creatures the heavens with their clouds and stars are high overhead. Scripture similarly pictures heaven as God's dwelling place above us. God dwells on high. He is "up there." "The LORD Himself is God in heaven above" (Deut. 4:39). "The LORD is exalted, for He dwells on high" (Isa. 33:5; similarly, Ps. 113:5). And therefore "every good gift and every perfect gift is from above, and comes down from the Father of lights, with whom there is no variation or shadow of turning" (James 1:17).

When God wants to know what is happening on earth, so to speak, Scripture describes very concretely in terms we can understand how He does that. In the Psalms we read, "The LORD looks down from heaven upon the children of men" (Ps. 14:2). "He looked down from the height of His sanctuary; from heaven the LORD viewed the earth" (102:19). Accordingly, God's people were encouraged to pray and ask God: "Look down from Your holy habitation, from heaven, and bless Your people Israel" (Deut. 26:15). Small wonder that when Solomon prayed to God, "he spread out his hands toward heaven"

---

2. Schilder, *Heaven*, 43 (italics in the original); for the unabridged in the original Dutch and in a subsequent revised edition, see Klaas Schilder, *Wat is de hemel?*, 2nd ed. (Kampen: Kok, 1954), 89.

3. Space "is a mode of existence of creation. Space is an aspect of the structure of created reality." Van Genderen and Velema, *Concise Reformed Dogmatics*, 180.

(1 Kings 8:22). God is in heaven; His people are on earth, and they reach out to God in prayer, knowing God sees them from heaven. "Unto You I lift up my eyes, O You who dwell in the heavens" (Ps. 123:1).

Sometimes Scripture tells us that God came down to take a closer look. He did so to check out the building of the Tower of Babel. "The LORD came down to see the city and the tower which the sons of men had built" (Gen. 11:5, also 7). Another example of God coming down from heaven is found in connection with God's intent to deliver His people from Egypt. He told Moses that He had heard the cry of His people and seen their oppression and "so I have come down to deliver them out of the hand of the Egyptians" (Ex. 3:8). The LORD also came down to meet His people at Mount Sinai (19:11, 18, 20). The Son of God also came "from heaven" (e.g., John 3:13; 6:32–33, 38), that is, "from above" (3:31; 8:23), when He came to this world.

We also read of going up into heaven. The LORD took His prophet Elijah up into heaven by a whirlwind. While talking to his fellow prophet Elisha, it happened. "Suddenly a chariot of fire appeared with horses of fire, and separated the two of them; and Elijah went up by a whirlwind into heaven" (2 Kings 2:11; cf. Gen. 5:24). The Lord Jesus Christ of course also went up into heaven. In Luke's gospel account we read that while Christ blessed His disciples "He was parted from them and carried up into heaven" (Luke 24:51). Luke gave more detail in Acts. After the Lord had finished giving His disciples instructions, while "they watched, He was taken up, and a cloud received Him out of their sight. And while they looked steadfastly toward heaven as He went up, behold, two men stood by them in white apparel, who also said, 'Men of Galilee, why do you stand gazing up into heaven? This same Jesus, who was taken up from you into heaven, will so come in like manner as you saw Him go into heaven'" (Acts 1:9–11). The fact that a cloud took the Lord Jesus out of the sight of the disciples reminds us that heaven is normally invisible to human eyes on earth.

Sometimes God opened heaven and allowed people to see something of its glory. Jacob, during his flight to Haran, had a dream one night "and behold, a ladder was set up on the earth, and its top reached to heaven; and there the angels of God were ascending and descending on it. And behold, the LORD stood above it" and renewed the covenant promises (Gen. 28:12–13). When Jacob awoke, he said, among other things, "How awesome is this place! This is none other than the house of God, and this is the gate of heaven!" (v. 17). The prophet Isaiah received a vision in which he saw heavenly realities. He writes, "I saw the Lord sitting on a throne, high and lifted up, and the train of His robe filled the temple." Above the throne were seraphim who cried, "Holy, holy, holy is the LORD of hosts; the whole earth is full of His glory!" (Isa. 6:1, 3).

The prophets Ezekiel and Daniel were also privileged to see visions of God in heaven (Ezek. 1:1; Dan. 7:9–10).

In New Testament times, the shepherds tending their flock outside Bethlehem saw something of heaven's splendor. After an angel of the Lord told them of the birth of the Savior, "suddenly there was with the angel a multitude of the heavenly host praising God and saying: 'Glory to God in the highest, and on earth peace, goodwill toward men!'" (Luke 2:13–14). After John had baptized Christ, "the heavens were opened to Him, and He saw the Spirit of God descending like a dove and alighting upon Him. And suddenly a voice came from heaven, saying, 'This is My beloved Son, in whom I am well pleased'" (Matt. 3:16–17). A similar heavenly message came from the cloud on the mountain where Christ was transfigured before His disciples (17:5). The apostle Paul experienced heaven in a vision and recounted that he "was caught up to the third heaven…caught up into Paradise" (2 Cor. 12:2–4), clearly referring to heaven where God dwells, since that is the significance of the reference to Paradise in this regard (Luke 23:43; Rev. 2:7).[4] The first Christian martyr, Stephen, was allowed to see inside heaven after he had addressed the Jewish council before whom he had been accused of blasphemy. Then Stephen, "being full of the Holy Spirit, gazed into heaven and saw the glory of God, and Jesus standing at the right hand of God, and said, 'Look! I see the heavens opened and the Son of Man standing at the right hand of God!'" (Acts 7:55–56; cf. 10:11). And finally there are of course the visions of heaven in the final book of Scripture. The apostle John was privileged to behold, in the Spirit, God's throne in heaven—a scene he conveys to his readers in symbolic language in accordance with the genre of Revelation (Rev. 4–5; cf. 19:11).

It is clear from the above that heaven, which is a created entity, is "up there" but invisible. Scripture clearly articulates this reality when it states that by the Son "all things were created that are in heaven and that are on earth, visible and invisible" (Col. 1:16). How are we to conceive of heaven's location when we, for example, pray "Our Father in heaven"? It is obvious that we cannot pinpoint a physical place. The Hubble Space Telescope has not been able to find God's dwelling place and never will.

At the same time, heaven is a real place of which believers in the past have had a glimpse. It thus seems that invisible heaven is close to physical earth. In other words, our present world is not isolated from the spiritual world of

---

4. One can interpret the first heaven to be where we find the clouds, the second heaven contains the stars, and the third is the dwelling place of God. See Simon J. Kistemaker, *Exposition of the Second Epistle to the Corinthians* (Grand Rapids: Baker, 1997), 408.

heaven and angels. You could perhaps say that heaven is in a dimension beyond our three-dimensional physical space—possibly close by but invisible.[5] Hints of such a situation could conceivably be seen in Christ's resurrection body, which is now in heaven. Before His ascension, while still on earth, Christ could appear and disappear at will in His resurrection body (Luke 24:31, 36; John 20:19). We have no idea how this functions spatially, but these instances make us realize that the spiritual world is not isolated from ours. Indeed, Christ's ascension has, so to speak, brought earth and heaven into a close conjunction with each other. After all, He is in heaven with a real, physical human body; that means, as the Heidelberg Catechism puts it: "We have our flesh in heaven" (Q. 49). In this general context Schilder correctly noted that Christ's ascension "reveals anew that the history of heaven is closely bound up with that of the earth."[6]

This history involves not only the event of the ascension of Christ, but also the ongoing reality that because of Christ's atoning sacrifice and ascension believers have close proximity to heaven. Although Christians cannot as yet literally enter heaven while on this current earth, they nevertheless have access to its threshold and can perceive in faith the heavenly realities of the Most Holy Place. The author of Hebrews therefore exhorted, "Seeing then that we have a great High Priest who has passed through the heavens, Jesus the Son of God, let us hold fast our confession.... Let us therefore come boldly to the throne of grace" (Heb. 4:14, 16). "Therefore, brethren, having boldness to enter the Holiest by the blood of Jesus…let us draw near with a true heart in full assurance of faith" (10:19, 22). "You have come to Mount Zion and to the city of the living God, the heavenly Jerusalem, to an innumerable company of angels, to the general assembly and church of the firstborn who are registered in heaven, to God the Judge of all, to the spirits of just men made perfect, to Jesus the Mediator of the new covenant" (12:22–24). These exhortations underline that earth and heaven are separate entities. There is a clear distinction between them, a boundary that cannot be ignored. At the same time, due to Christ's work and ascension, earth and heaven are close for believers who in faith see and hear their Savior in heaven through His Word and Spirit.[7] Indeed, believers are now already citizens of heaven (Phil. 3:20–21). Also, because they are "in Christ" (Eph. 1:3) and Christ is in heaven, "God, who is rich in mercy," made Christians

---

5. E.g., Byl, God and the Cosmos, 169–70.

6. Schilder, Heaven, 56; cf. Schilder, Wat is de hemel?, 110.

7. For the above, see further Nicholas J. Moore, "Heaven's Revolving Door? Cosmology, Entrance, and Approach in Hebrews," Bulletin for Biblical Research 29 (2019): 187–207.

"sit together in the heavenly places in Christ Jesus" (2:4, 6). This is a spiritual reality. After all, Christians continue on this earth to live the new life in Christ (v. 10), while seeking "those things which are above, where Christ is, sitting at the right hand of God" (Col. 3:1). In Christ heaven has come close for Christians. The Savior has brought them to its threshold, but it can only be perceived in faith.

Heaven is part of God's invisible creation, hidden from our physical eyes. Yet there is a materiality to heaven. It *is* part of creation where Christ's physical body is found. Our inquisitive human minds can ask and wonder how exactly the spiritual world of heaven relates to our visible realities. But it is futile to enter into a detailed discussion on this matter for God has not revealed such particulars to us. Schilder has soberly and realistically noted that "we must not attempt to classify the heavens or to locate heaven in the cosmos from our standpoint."[8] Such an exercise is a fertile ground for questions and speculation. Such inquiry can be done in a believing manner, but at the end of the day we acknowledge our limitations as part of creation.[9]

Renewal of Heaven and Earth

Because heaven is part of creation, it, like the earth we live on, will one day be renewed. God already made this promise when He spoke through His prophet Isaiah: "Behold, I create new heavens and a new earth; and the former shall not be remembered or come to mind" (Isa. 65:17). The apostle Peter could therefore write, "We, according to His promise, look for new heavens and a new earth in which righteousness dwells" (2 Peter 3:13). Although at first glance these passages may appear to suggest that the current heaven and earth will be completely destroyed, Scripture teaches that such is not the case. Certainly this present world in its present form will pass away (1 John 2:17; Rev. 21:1), but that means that "the creation itself...will be delivered from the bondage of corruption into the glorious liberty of the children of God" who eagerly wait for the redemption of their body (Rom. 8:21, 23). The new heaven and earth will not be a second heaven and earth but the present heaven and earth restored from the corruption and pollution of sin, just as the bodies of Christians will be not annihilated but restored. "The body is sown in corruption, it is raised in incorruption. It is sown in dishonor, it is raised in glory. It is sown in weakness, it is raised in power. It is sown a natural body, it is raised a spiritual body" (1 Cor.

---

8. Schilder, *Heaven*, 38; cf. Schilder, *Wat is de hemel?*, 84.
9. For an example of such an inquiry, see Byl, *God and the Cosmos*, 206–14.

15:42–44). Just as a Christian is a new creation and the old has passed away and all is made new (2 Cor. 5:17), so too this present world will be a new creation and the old will pass away (1 John 2:17; Rev. 21:1).[10]

God's renewed dwelling place, heaven, will one day come down to earth (Rev. 21:1). The apostle John "saw the holy city, New Jerusalem, coming down out of heaven from God.... Behold, the tabernacle of God is with men, and He will dwell with them, and they shall be His people" (vv. 2, 3). Since heaven is characterized as God's dwelling place, God's living on earth means that heaven and earth will no longer be apart from each other, the one invisible and the other visible. Rather, heaven and earth will come together and merge into one. It will be heaven on earth, and all sorrow and brokenness of life due to sin will be a thing of the past. "God will wipe away every tear from their eyes; there shall be no more death, nor sorrow, nor crying. There shall be no more pain, for the former things have passed away" (v. 4). God's people will even "see His face, and His name shall be on their foreheads" (22:4). Fellowship with God will be perfect and complete.[11]

The Creation of Angels

Angels are part of God's work of creation. Psalm 148 enjoins the angels, the sun, the moon, and other created entities to praise the LORD. Why? Because God had created all of them. "Let them praise the name of the LORD, for He commanded and they were created" (Ps. 148:5). Angels are referred to as "the host of heaven" (1 Kings 22:19; Neh. 9:6). Although the expression can also describe the stars and planets (Deut. 4:19), its use in Genesis 2:1 could certainly include the angels. We read there that "the heavens and the earth, and all the host of them, were finished." Another indication that angels are created beings is the apostle Paul's comment that by the Son "all things were created that are in heaven and that are on the earth, visible and invisible, whether thrones or dominions or principalities or powers. All things were created through Him and for Him" (Col. 1:16). Such a sweeping description of creation includes the angels. Indeed, the angel who showed the apostle John what must soon take place himself acknowledged his status as part of creation. When John fell down

---

10. See further on this renewal, R. C. H. Lenski, *The Interpretation of St. John's Revelation* (Columbus, Ohio: Lutheran Book Concern, 1935), 614–15; Bavinck, *Reformed Dogmatics*, 4:716–20; Anthony A. Hoekema, *The Bible and the Future* (repr., Grand Rapids: Eerdmans, 1994), 280–81.

11. For the meaning of seeing God, see further Cornelis P. Venema, *The Promise of the Future* (Edinburgh: Banner of Truth, 2000), 482–88.

to worship the angel, he said, "See that you do not do that! I am your fellow servant.... Worship God!" (Rev. 19:10; 22:9; also Col. 2:18). The Belgic Confession is therefore fully in accord with Scripture when it states that God also created the angels (art. 12).

Angels are spiritual beings (Heb. 1:14) and therefore normally invisible. God needs to make them visible to human eyes (e.g., 2 Kings 6:15–17; Luke 2:9–15). Angels are finite beings; they cannot be everywhere at once. They come and go (e.g., Gen. 19:1; 28:12).

When were the angels created? Scripture does not directly inform us, but the available evidence makes it plausible that they were created on the first day. Angels are referred to as the sons of God who present themselves before the LORD as described in the book of Job (1:6; 2:1). Later the LORD challenges Job out of the whirlwind and asks, "Where were you when I laid the foundations of the earth?... When the morning stars sang together, and all the sons of God shouted for joy?" (38:4, 7). From the parallelism, it is evident that angels, the sons of God, are also referred to as the morning stars. This passage suggests that the angels had already been called into being when God created the earth. The laying of earth's foundations would refer to God's work on the first day of creation. "In the beginning God created the heavens and the earth." Similar terminology of laying foundations, as well as allusion to Genesis 1:1, is found elsewhere. The psalmist said, "Of old You laid the foundation of the earth, and the heavens are the work of Your hands" (Ps. 102:25; similarly, Isa. 48:13). So, the angels, the morning stars as they are also called in Job 38, apparently witnessed God's work of calling the earth into existence, and they applauded it with joy. If this understanding is correct, then angels were among the very first of God's creation work when heaven was made (Gen. 1:1).[12]

Where Are the Angels?

Angels are in heaven in great numbers, under the command of God, who is therefore called "the LORD of hosts" (e.g., 1 Sam. 1:3; Isa. 6:3, 5). Indeed, He is surrounded by innumerable angels (Dan. 7:10; Heb. 12:22; Rev. 5:11). The prophet Micaiah reported, "I saw the LORD sitting on His throne, and all the host of heaven standing by, on His right hand and on His left" (1 Kings 22:19). They are there to serve their master. As David exulted,

---

12. This understanding is found, e.g., in Turretin, *Institutes*, 1:448; Bavinck, *Our Reasonable Faith*, 171 (cf. Bavinck, *Reformed Dogmatics*, 2:454–55); Beeke and Smalley, *Revelation and God*, 1120. Calvin warned against making too much of when the angels were created. *Institutes*, 1.14.4. Also see chapter 3 above, under the heading "Job 38:4–11."

The LORD has established His throne in heaven,
And His kingdom rules over all.
Bless the LORD, you His angels,
Who excel in strength, who do His word,
Heeding the voice of His word.
Bless the LORD, all you His hosts,
You ministers of His, who do His pleasure. (Ps. 103:19–21)

In New Testament times, the shepherds at Bethlehem saw "a multitude of the heavenly host praising God" (Luke 2:13). The Lord Jesus told Peter on the night of His betrayal to put away his sword and then said, "Do you think that I cannot now pray to My Father, and He will provide Me with more than twelve legions of angels?" (Matt. 26:53). The angels in heaven are also referred to elsewhere, for example, in Christ's saying to Nathanael, "You shall see heaven open, and the angels of God ascending and descending upon the Son of Man" (John 1:51), and in the vision of heaven witnessed by the apostle John, who heard a loud voice of a great multitude in heaven praising God (Rev. 19:1, 6).

At a certain point some angels fell into sin, and one of them, Satan, tempted Adam and Eve in Eden. The apostle Peter informs us that "God did not spare the angels who sinned, but cast them down to hell and delivered them into chains of darkness, to be reserved for judgment" (2 Peter 2:4; also see Jude 6). During Old Testament times, Satan, a high-ranking fallen angel (cf. Jude 9), nevertheless had access to heaven. He was among the sons of God (angels) when he accused Job of false motives in fearing the LORD (Job 1:6–11). The prophet Zechariah witnessed, in a vision, Satan opposing Joshua the high priest, who was standing before the angel of the LORD (Zech. 3:1). However, after Christ's death, resurrection, and ascension, the Savior's atoning work was finished. He triumphed over Satan, who can no longer bring any accusation against God's people. God's justice has been satisfied. Christ has fulfilled the requirements of the law and thereby undid any attempt by Satan and his hosts to bring charges against those who believe in Christ. Indeed, with His work, Christ therefore disarmed all the principalities and powers arranged against God's people (Col. 2:12–15; Rom. 8:33–34), and Satan and all his angels were cast out of heaven and to the earth (Rev. 12:7–10).

Satan and other fallen angels no longer have access to heaven, the dwelling place of God. They are restricted to the earth and the lower heavens (Eph. 2:2; 6:11–12).[13] They hate God's people and therefore present an ongoing danger to

---

13. The reference to "heavenly places" (Eph. 6:12) needs to be understood as somewhere

them. Christians must be on their guard. As the apostle Paul exhorts, "Put on the whole armor of God, that you may be able to stand against the wiles of the devil. For we do not wrestle against flesh and blood, but against principalities, against powers, against the rulers of the darkness of this age, against spiritual hosts of wickedness in the heavenly places" (6:11–12; cf. 2:2). Indeed, the battle is real, for Satan is real even though he cannot be seen, and he has great power. He is called "the ruler of this world" (John 12:31; 14:30; 16:11) and "the god of this age" (2 Cor. 4:4). Peter warned, "Be sober, be vigilant; because your adversary the devil walks about like a roaring lion, seeking whom he may devour" (1 Peter 5:8).[14]

Christians may, however, be assured of God's help against the demons and the powers of darkness. God is sovereign and He has curtailed the power of demons and evil angels and kept them "in everlasting chains under darkness for the judgment of the great day" (Jude 6). Although they used to be, as John Calvin noted, "not only free spirits but celestial powers; they are now held bound by perpetual chains.... Wherever they go, they drag with them their own chains."[15] Chained to God's judgment, their doom is sure. They will not escape it. Christ has triumphed over them, and He will also be victorious in the lives of those who belong to Him. Neither angels nor principalities nor powers can separate them from the love of God that is in Christ Jesus (Rom. 8:38–39).

Furthermore, God's angels are in the service of His children. "Are they not all ministering spirits sent forth to minister for those who will inherit salvation?" (Heb. 1:14). According to His promise, God will give His angels charge of those who make the LORD their refuge. They will not be hurt but be victorious over the enemy (Ps. 91:9–13). Angels are invisible spirits, but in faith Christians know that they are at their service as God's children (cf. Matt. 18:10). The angels are intensely interested in the salvation of God's people (1 Peter 1:12), and they rejoice in heaven when a sinner repents (Luke 15:7, 10). They will accompany the Lord at His second coming with blessings for the faithful and judgment for the ungodly (Matt. 16:27; 2 Thess. 1:7–8).

Where are the angels? They are in heaven and they are on earth according to the needs of God's children. They are ministering spirits. They cannot be

---

outside heaven as the dwelling place of God; see William Hendriksen, *Exposition of Ephesians* (Grand Rapids: Baker, 1967), 273.

14. For the casting of the sinful angels into hell, the activity of the evil one in heaven and subsequent casting out, and the activity of the evil angels after Christ's victory, see Bavinck, *Reformed Dogmatics*, 3:186.

15. John Calvin, *The Catholic Epistles*, trans. John Owen (Edinburgh: Calvin Translation Society, 1855), 436.

seen, but their presence according to God's promise is real. And their presence is necessary because the fallen angels also are active on earth. But their doom is sure.

Conclusion

The dominant worldview today is materialistic. Only what we can see with our physical eyes is real. Astronomer Carl Sagan succinctly expressed this outlook when he opened his television series *Cosmos* with the words: "The cosmos is all there is, or was, or ever shall be." In other words, what we see around us in nature and elsewhere is "a closed system of cause and effect. There is no realm of the transcendent or supernatural. There is no 'outside.'"[16]

But the Bible teaches that there is much more than meets the human eye. Close to our world there is a real but invisible realm, heaven, where God dwells. There are untold numbers of angels, spiritual beings, both in the service of God and in the service of Satan. The angels, both good and bad, are operative on earth. They are part of an immense unseen world that impacts our lives daily.

But this invisible reality can only be accepted and realized in faith. And so, Christians need to live by faith, also in this respect. Scripture tells us that faith is the assurance of things hoped for, "the evidence of things not seen" (Heb. 11:1). Christians hope for that which they do not see, or rather, for that which they do not *yet* see. Believers live in anticipation of more to come. "If we hope for what we do not see, we eagerly wait for it with perseverance" (Rom. 8:25). That hope will be realized. A time will come when the invisible will become visible. The apostle John was assured that this will certainly take place when he saw the vision of a new heaven coming down to a new earth and God's heavenly dwelling coming to be with His people. The invisible realm will become visible, and God's people will even be privileged to see Him (1 John 3:2; Rev. 21:1–3).

---

16. The Sagan quote and the description of naturalism and materialism are from Lennox, *God's Undertaker*, 30.

Bibliography

Aalders, G. Ch. *De exegese van Gen. 2 en 3 en de beslissing der Synode van Assen.* Kampen: Kok, [1926].

———. *De Goddelijke openbaring in de eerste drie hoofdstukken van Genesis.* Kampen: Kok, 1932.

———. *Genesis.* Translated by William Heynen. 2 vols. Bible Student's Commentary. Grand Rapids: Zondervan, 1981.

Acta der buitengewone Generale Synode van De Gereformeerde Kerken in Nederland gehouden to Assen van 26 Januari tot 17 Maart, 1926. Kampen: Kok, 1926.

Adamthwaite, Murray R. "Is Genesis 1 Just Reworked Babylonian Myth?" *Journal of Creation* 27 (2013): 99–104.

Aharoni, Yohanan, Michael Avi-Yonah, Anson F. Rainey, and Ze'ev Safrai, eds. *The Macmillan Bible Atlas.* 3rd ed. New York: Macmillan, 1993.

Alexander, Denis R. *Creation or Evolution: Do We Have to Choose?* 2nd ed. Oxford: Monarch, 2014.

Alexander, Philip S. "Geography and the Bible (Early Jewish Geography)." In *ABD* 2:977–88.

Allis, Oswald T. *God Spake by Moses.* Nutley, N.J.: Presbyterian and Reformed, 1958.

———. "Old Testament Emphases and Modern Thought." *Princeton Theological Review* 23 (1925): 432–64.

———. "The Time Element in Genesis 1 and 2." *Torch and Trumpet* 8, no. 3 (1958): 16–18.

Anderson, Gary A. "The Interpretation of Genesis 1:1 in the Targums." *Catholic Biblical Quarterly* 52 (1990): 21–29.

Anderson, Gary A., and Markus Bockmuehl, eds. *Creation* ex nihilo: *Origins, Development, Contemporary Challenges.* Notre Dame: University of Notre Dame Press, 2018.

Anselm. *Proslogium; Monologium; an Appendix in Behalf of the Fool by Gaunilon; and Cur Deus Homo*. Translated by Sidney Norton Deane. Chicago: Open Court, 1903.

Applegate, Kathryn, and J. B. Stump, eds. *How I Changed My Mind About Evolution: Evangelicals Reflect on Faith and Science*. Downers Grove, Ill.: IVP Academic, 2016.

Archer, Gleason L. "A Response to the Trustworthiness of Scripture in Areas Relating to Natural Science." In *Hermeneutics, Inerrancy, and the Bible*, edited by Earl D. Radmacher and Robert D. Preus, 321–34. Grand Rapids: Zondervan, 1984.

Arichea, Daniel C., and Howard Hatton. *A Handbook on the Letter from Jude and the Second Letter from Peter*. UBS Handbook Series. New York: United Bible Societies, 1993.

Arnold, Bill T. *Genesis*. The New Cambridge Bible Commentary. Cambridge: Cambridge University Press, 2009.

Arntzen, Marinus J. "Inspiration and Trustworthiness of Scripture." In *Interpreting God's Word Today*, edited by Simon Kistemaker, 179–212. Nutley, N.J.: Presbyterian and Reformed, 1970.

Atwell, James E. "An Egyptian Source for Genesis 1." *Journal of Theological Studies* 51 (2000): 441–77.

Augustine. *The Literal Meaning of Genesis*. Translated and edited by John Hammond Taylor. Ancient Christian Writers. New York: Paulist Press, 1982.

Averbeck, Richard E. "A Literary Day, Inter-Textual, and Contextual Reading of Genesis 1–2." In J. Daryl Charles, *Reading Genesis 1–2*, 7–34.

Axe, Douglas. *Undeniable: How Biology Confirms Our Intuition That Life is Designed*. San Francisco: HarperOne, 2016.

Bahnsen, Greg L. *Van Til's Apologetic: Readings and Analysis*. Phillipsburg, N.J.: P&R, 1998.

Barker, Kenneth, ed. *The NIV Study Bible. New International Version*. Grand Rapids: Zondervan, 1985.

Barker, William S. "The Westminster Assembly on the Days of Creation: A Reply to David W. Hall." *Westminster Theological Journal* 62 (2000): 113–20.

Barnard, Geoff. "Does the Genome Provide Evidence for Common Ancestry?" In Nevin, *Should Christians Embrace Evolution?*, 166–86.

Barr, James. *Fundamentalism*. London: SCM, 1977.

———. *The Semantics of Biblical Language*. London: Oxford University Press, 1961.

———. "Story and History in Biblical Theology." *Journal of Religion* 1 (1976): 1–17.

Barrett, C. K. *A Critical and Exegetical Commentary on the Acts of the Apostles.* International Critical Commentary. 2 vols. Reprint, Edinburgh: T&T Clark, 2004.

Bartelmus, G. "*šāmayim.*" In *TDOT* 15:204–36.

Battles, Ford Lewis. "God Was Accommodating Himself to Human Capacity." *Interpretation* 31 (1977): 19–38.

Batto, Bernard F. "The Combat Myth in Israelite Tradition Revisited." In *Creation and Chaos: A Reconsideration of Hermann Gunkel's* Chaoskampf *Hypothesis,* edited by John Scurlock and Richard H. Beal, 217–36. Winona Lake, Ind.: Eisenbrauns, 2013.

———. *In the Beginning: Essays on Creation Motifs in the Ancient Near East and the Bible.* Siphrut. Winona Lake, Ind.: Eisenbrauns, 2013.

Bavinck, Herman. *Essays on Religion, Science, and Society.* Edited by John Bolt. Translated by Harry Boonstra and Gerrit Sheeres. Grand Rapids: Baker Academic, 2008.

———. *Our Reasonable Faith.* Translated by Henry Zylstra. 1956. Reprint, Grand Rapids: Baker, 1977.

———. *Reformed Dogmatics.* Edited by John Bolt. Translated by John Vriend. 4 vols. Grand Rapids: Baker Academic, 2003–2008.

Beale, G. K. *The Book of Revelation: A Commentary on the Greek Text.* New International Greek Testament Commentary. Grand Rapids: Eerdmans, 1999.

———. *The Erosion of Inerrancy in Evangelicalism: Responding to New Challenges to Biblical Authority.* Wheaton, Ill.: Crossway, 2008.

———. *The Temple and the Church's Mission: A Biblical Theology of the Dwelling Place of God.* New Studies in Biblical Theology. Leicester, U.K.: Apollos; Downers Grove, Ill.: InterVarsity, 2004.

Beale, G. K., and Mitchell Kim. *God Dwells Among Us: Expanding Eden to the Ends of the Earth.* Downers Grove, Ill.: InterVarsity, 2014.

Beall, Todd S. "Age of the Universe and Earth." In *DCS,* 32–36.

———. "Reading Genesis 1–2: A Literal Approach." In J. Daryl Charles, *Reading Genesis 1–2,* 45–59.

Beauchamp, P. "*mîn.*" In *TDOT* 8:288–90.

Bechly, Günter, and Stephen C. Meyer. "The Fossil Record and Universal Common Ancestry." In Moreland et al., *Theistic Evolution,* 331–61.

Becking, Bob, and Marjo C. A. Korpel. "To Create, to Separate or to Construct." *Journal of Hebrew Scriptures* 10, no. 3 (2010): 1–21.

Bédard, Paulin. *In Six Days God Created.* N.p.: Xulon, 2013.

Bediako, Daniel. *Genesis 1:1–2:3: A Textlinguistic Analysis.* Saarbrücken, Germany: VDM, 2011.

Beeke, Joel R., ed. *The Reformation Heritage KJV Study Bible*. Grand Rapids: Reformation Heritage Books, 2014.

Beeke, Joel, and Paul M. Smalley. *Revelation and God*. Reformed Systematic Theology. Wheaton, Ill.: Crossway, 2019.

Behe, Michael J. *Darwin Devolves: The New Science about DNA that Challenges Evolution*. New York: HarperOne, 2019.

————. "Irreducible Complexity." In *DCS*, 390–91.

Berghoef, Gerard, and Lester DeKoster. *The Great Divide: Christianity or Evolution*. Edinburgh: Banner of Truth, 1989.

Berkouwer, G. C. *General Revelation*. Studies in Dogmatics. Grand Rapids: Eerdmans, 1955.

————. *Zoeken en vinden: herinneringen en ervaringen*. Kampen: Kok, 1989.

Berlin, Adele. "The Wisdom of Creation in Psalm 104." In *Seeking Out the Ancients. Essays Offered to Honor Michael V. Fox on the Occasion of His Sixty-Fifth Birthday*, edited by Ronald L. Troxel, Kelvin G. Friebel, and Dennis R. Magary, 71–83. Winona Lake, Ind.: Eisenbrauns, 2005.

Berlin, Adele, Marc Zvi Brettler, and Michael Fishbane, eds. *The Jewish Study Bible*. New York: Oxford University Press, 2004.

Bernhardt, Karl-Heinz. "*bārāʾ*." In *TDOT* 2:246–48.

Betteridge, Maurice S. "The Bitter Notes: The Geneva Bible and Its Annotations." *Sixteenth Century Journal* 14 (1983): 41–62.

The Bible and Holy Scriptures Conteyned in the Olde and Newe Testament. Translated According to the Ebrue and Greke, and Conferred with the Best Translations in Divers Langages with Moste Profitable Annotations.... Geneva: Rovland Hall, 1560.

Bijbel, dat is de gansche heilige Schrift, bevattende al de canonieke boeken des Ouden en Nieuwen Testaments, door last van de hoog-mog. heeren Staten-Generaal der Vereenigde Nederlanden [= de Staten-vertaling]. Kampen: Kok, 1913.

Bird, W. R. *The Origin of Species Revisited: The Theories of Evolution and of Abrupt Appearance*. 2 vols. New York: Philosophical Library, 1989.

Birkett, Kirsten. "Science and Scripture." In *The Enduring Authority of the Christian Scriptures*, edited by D. A. Carson, 948–86. Grand Rapids: Eerdmans, 2016.

Blaising, Craig A., and Carmen S. Hardin, eds. *Psalms 1–50*. Ancient Christian Commentary on Scripture. Downers Grove, Ill.: InterVarsity, 2008.

Blocher, Henri A. G. "God and the Scripture Writers: The Question of Double Authorship." In *The Enduring Authority of the Christian Scriptures*, edited by D. A. Carson, 497–541. Grand Rapids: Eerdmans, 2016.

Block, Daniel I. "Eden: A Temple? A Reassessment of the Biblical Evidence." In *From Creation to the New Creation: Biblical Theology and Exegesis. Essays in Honor of G. K. Beale*, edited by Daniel M. Gurtner and Benjamin L. Gladd, 3–29. Peabody, Mass.: Hendrickson, 2013.

Blum, Edwin A. "2 Peter." In *The Expositor's Bible Commentary: Hebrews through Revelation*, edited by Frank E. Gaebelein, 255–89. Grand Rapids: Zondervan, 1981.

Bolt, John. "Getting the 'Two Books' Straight: With a Little Help from Herman Bavinck and John Calvin." *Calvin Theological Journal* 46 (2011): 315–32.

Bouw, Gerardus D. *Geocentricity*. Cleveland: Association for Biblical Astronomy, 1992.

Boyd, Steven W. "The Genre of Genesis 1:1–2:3: What Means This Text?" In Mortenson and Ury, *Coming to Grips with Genesis*, 163–92.

Bratt, James D., ed. *Abraham Kuyper: A Centennial Reader*. Grand Rapids: Eerdmans; Carlisle, U.K.: Paternoster, 1998.

Brenton, Lancelot C. L., ed. *The Septuagint with Apocrypha: Greek and English*. 1851. Reprint, Grand Rapids: Zondervan, 1982.

Briggs, Richard S. "Speech-Act Theory." In *Dictionary for the Theological Interpretation of the Bible*, edited by Kevin J. Vanhoozer, 763–66. Grand Rapids: Baker Academic, 2005.

Brooke, John Hedley. *Science and Religion: Some Historical Perspectives*. Cambridge History of Science. Cambridge: Cambridge University Press, 1991.

Brown, Andrew J. *The Days of Creation: A History of Christian Interpretation of Genesis 1:1–2:3*. History of Biblical Interpretation Series. Blandford Forum, U.K.: Deo, 2014.

Brown, Colin. *Philosophy and the Christian Faith: A Historical Sketch from the Middle Ages to the Present Day*. London: Tyndale, 1969.

Brown, Jeannine K. "Creation's Renewal in the Gospel of John." *Catholic Biblical Quarterly* 72 (2010): 275–90.

Brush, Nigel. *The Limitations of Scientific Truth*. Grand Rapids: Kregel Academic and Professional, 2005.

Bullard, Roger A., and Howard A. Hatton. *A Handbook on Sirach*. United Bible Societies' Handbooks. New York: United Bible Societies, 2008.

Burgess, Stuart. "Human Anatomy: Unique Upright Design." In Mortenson, *Searching for Adam*, 331–74.

Byl, John. "General Revelation and Evangelicalism." *Mid-America Journal of Theology* 5 (1989): 1–13.

———. *God and the Cosmos: A Christian View of Time, Space, and the Universe*. Edinburgh: Banner of Truth, 2001.

———. "Light-speed, Convention, and Creation." *Bylogos* (blog). February 9, 2019. http://bylogos.blogspot.com/2019/02/light-speed-convention-and-creation.html.

———. "A Moving Earth?" *Bylogos* (blog). July 18, 2011. http://bylogos.blogspot.com/2011/07/moving-earth.html.

———. "Rapidly Matured Creation." *Bylogos* (blog). February 6, 2019. http://bylogos.blogspot.com/2019/02/rapidly-matured-creation.html.

———. "The Role of Belief in Modern Cosmology." In *Facets of Faith and Science*, edited by Jitse M. van der Meer, vol. 3, *The Role of Beliefs in the Natural Sciences*, 47–62. Lanham, Md.: University Press of America, 1996.

———. "Scripture and Geologists." *Westminster Theological Journal* 51 (1989): 143–52.

Callea, Francesco, and Michelle Callea. "Adam's Rib and the Origin of Stem Cells." *American Journal of Hematology* 86, no. 6 (2011): 529.

Calvin, John. *The Catholic Epistles*. Translated by John Owen. Edinburgh: Calvin Translation Society, 1855.

———. *Commentaries on the First Book of Moses, Called Genesis*. Translated by John King. 2 vols. Grand Rapids: Eerdmans, 1948.

———. *Commentary on the Book of Psalms*. Translated by James Anderson. 5 vols. 1845–1849. Reprint, Grand Rapids: Eerdmans, 1963.

———. *The Epistles of Paul the Apostle to the Galatians, Ephesians, Philippians and Colossians*. Edited by D. W. Torrance and T. F. Torrance. Translated by T. H. L. Parker. Calvin's Commentaries. Grand Rapids: Eerdmans, 1965.

———. *The Epistles of Paul the Apostle to the Romans and to the Thessalonians*. Translated by Ross MacKenzie. Calvin's Commentaries. Grand Rapids: Eerdmans, 1960.

———. *Institutes of the Christian Religion*. Edited by John T. McNeill. Translated by Ford Lewis Battles. 2 vols. Library of Christian Classics. Philadelphia: Westminster, 1960.

———. *The Second Epistle of Paul the Apostle to the Corinthians and the Epistles to Timothy, Titus and Philemon*. Edited by D. W. Torrance and T. F. Torrance. Translated by T. A. Smail. Calvin's Commentaries. Grand Rapids: Eerdmans, 1964.

———. *Sermons on Genesis, Chapters 1:1–11:4*. Translated by Rob Roy McGregor. Edinburgh: Banner of Truth, 2009.

Cameron, Nigel M. de S. *Evolution and the Authority of the Bible*. Greenwood, S.C.: Attic, 1983.

Canadian Reformed Churches. *Book of Praise: Anglo-Genevan Psalter*. Winnipeg: Premier, 2014.

Carasik, Michael, ed. and trans. *The Commentator's Bible: The Rubin JPS Miqra'ot Gedolot: Genesis.* Philadelphia: Jewish Publication Society of America, 2018.

Carson, D. A. "Is the Doctrine of *Claritas Scripturae* Still Relevant Today?" In D. A. Carson, *Collected Writings on Scripture,* 179–93. Wheaton, Ill.: Crossway, 2010.

———. "Recent Developments in the Doctrine of Scripture." In *Hermeneutics, Authority, and Canon,* edited by D. A. Carson and John D. Woodbridge, 5–48. Grand Rapids: Zondervan, 1986.

Cassuto, U. *A Commentary on the Book of Genesis: Part I from Adam to Noah.* Israel Abrahams. Jerusalem: Magnes, 1989.

Chambers, Nathan. "Genesis 1.1 as the First Act of Creation." *Journal for the Study of the Old Testament* 43 (2019): 385–94.

Charles, Elizabeth Rundle. *Chronicles of the Schönberg-cotta Family.* New York: T. Nelson; Philadelphia: Lippincott, 1864.

Charles, J. Daryl, ed. *Reading Genesis 1–2: An Evangelical Conversation.* Peabody, Mass.: Hendrickson, 2013.

Charles, R. H. *A Critical and Exegetical Commentary on the Revelation of St. John.* International Critical Commentary. Edinburgh: T&T Clark, 1920.

Childs, Brevard S. *Myth and Reality in the Old Testament.* 2nd ed. Studies in Biblical Theology 27. London: SCM, 1962.

Chilton, Bruce D., trans. and ed. *The Isaiah Targum: Introduction, Translation, Apparatus and Notes.* The Aramaic Bible. Collegeville, Minn.: Liturgical Press, 1987.

Chisholm, Robert B., Jr. "'For This Reason': Etiology and Its Implications for the Historicity of Adam." *Criswell Theological Review* 10, no. 2 (2013): 27–51.

Clark, Gordon H. "Cosmic Time: A Critique of the Concept in Herman Dooyeweerd." *The Gordon Review* 2, no. 3 (September 1956): 94–99.

Clark, W. Malcolm. "A Legal Background to the Yahwist's Use of 'Good and Evil' in Genesis 2–3." *Journal of Biblical Literature* 88 (1969): 266–78.

Clifford, Richard J. *Creation Accounts in the Ancient Near East and in the Bible.* The Catholic Biblical Quarterly Monograph Series. Washington, D.C.: Catholic Biblical Association of America, 1994.

Clines, David J. A. *Job 38–42.* Word Biblical Commentary. Nashville: Thomas Nelson, 2011.

Clouser, Roy. "Is Theism Compatible with Evolution?" In *Intelligent Design, Creationism, and Its Critics: Philosophical, Theological, and Scientific Perspectives,* edited by Robert T. Pennock, 513–36. Cambridge, Mass.: MIT Press, 2001.

Cochrane, Arthur C., ed. *Reformed Confessions of the 16th Century*. Philadelphia: Westminster, 1966.

Collins, C. John. "Adam as Federal Head of Humankind." In *Finding Ourselves After Darwin: Conversations on the Image of God, Original Sin, and the Problem of Evil*, edited by Stanley P. Rosenberg, 143–59. Grand Rapids: Baker Academic, 2018.

———. *Did Adam and Eve Really Exist? Who They Were and Why You Should Care*. Wheaton, Ill.: Crossway, 2011.

———. *Genesis 1–4: A Linguistic, Literary, and Theological Commentary*. Phillipsburg, N.J.: P&R, 2006.

———. "How Old is the Earth? Anthropomorphic Days in Genesis 1:1–2:3." *Presbyterion* 20 (1994): 109–30.

———. "Reading Genesis 1:1–2:3 as an Act of Communication: Discourse Analysis and Literal Interpretation." In *Did God Create in Six Days?*, edited by Joseph A. Pipa and David W. Hall, 131–51. Taylors, S.C.: Southern Presbyterian Press, 1999.

———. "Reading Genesis 1–2 with the Grain: Analogical Days." In J. Daryl Charles, *Reading Genesis 1–2*, 73–92. Peabody, Mass.: Hendrickson, 2013.

———. *Reading Genesis Well: Navigating History, Poetry, Science, and Truth in Genesis 1–11*. Grand Rapids: Zondervan, 2018.

———. "The Refrain of Genesis 1: A Critical Review of Its Rendering in the English Bible." *The Bible Translator* 60 (2009): 121–31.

———. *Science and Faith: Friends or Foes?* Wheaton, Ill.: Crossway, 2003.

———. "The *Wayyiqtol* as 'Pluperfect': When and Why." *Tyndale Bulletin* 46 (1995): 117–40.

Colson, Charles, and Nancy Pearcey. *How Now Shall We Live?* Carol Stream, Ill.: Tyndale House, 2004.

Copan, Paul, and William Lane Craig. *Creation Out of Nothing: A Biblical, Philosophical, and Scientific Exploration*. Grand Rapids: Baker Academic, 2004.

Cosner, Lita, and Robert Carter. "Where Was Eden? Part 1–Examining Pre-Flood Geographical Details in the Biblical Record." *Journal of Creation* 30 (2016): 97–103.

———. "Where Was Eden? Part 2–Examining Pre-Flood Geographical Details in the Biblical Record." *Journal of Creation* 30 (2016): 123–27.

Craigen, Trevor. "Can Deep Time Be Embedded in Genesis?" In Mortenson and Ury, *Coming to Grips with Genesis*, 193–210.

Craigie, Peter C. *The Book of Deuteronomy*. New International Commentary on the Old Testament. Grand Rapids: Eerdmans, 1976.

———. "The Conquest and Early Hebrew Poetry." *Tyndale Bulletin* 20 (1969): 76–94.

———. *Psalms 1–50*. Word Biblical Commentary. Waco, Tex.: Word, 1983.

———. *Ugarit and the Old Testament*. Grand Rapids: Eerdmans, 1983.

Cranfield, C. E. B. *A Critical and Exegetical Commentary on the Epistle to the Romans*. 2 vols. International Critical Commentary. Reprint, London: T&T Clark, 2004.

Croteau, David A., and Michael P. Naylor. "The Question of a Historical Adam: A New Testament Perspective." In Mortenson, *Searching for Adam*, 53–72.

Currid, John D. *Against the Gods: The Polemical Theology of the Old Testament*. Wheaton, Ill.: Crossway, 2013.

———. *Ancient Egypt and the Old Testament*. Grand Rapids: Baker, 1997.

———. "The Hebrew World-and-Life View." In *Revolutions in Worldview*, edited by W. Andrew Hoffecker, 37–70. Phillipsburg, N.J.: P&R, 2007.

———. *A Study Commentary on Genesis*. Vol. 1, *Genesis 1:1–25:18*. Darlington, U.K.: Evangelical Press, 2003.

———. "Theistic Evolution Is Incompatible with the Teachings of the Old Testament." In Moreland et al., *Theistic Evolution*, 839–78.

Curtis, A. H. W. "Genesis." In *A Dictionary of Biblical Interpretation*, edited by R. J. Coggins and J. L. Houlden, 251–55. London: SCM, 1990.

Curtis, Byron G. "Hosea 6:7 and Covenant-Breaking Like/at Adam." In *The Law Is Not of Faith: Essays on Works and Grace in the Mosaic Covenant*, edited by Bryan D. Estelle, J. V. Fesko, and David VanDrunen, 170–209. Phillipsburg, N.J.: P&R, 2009.

Custance, Arthur C. *Without Form and Void: A Study of the Meaning of Genesis 1.2*. Brockville, Ontario: Custance, 1970.

Dalley, Stephanie, ed. and trans. *Myths from Mesopotamia*. 1989. Reprint, Oxford: Oxford University Press, 1991.

Darwin, Charles. *The Descent of Man and Selection in Relation to Sex*. New ed. London: John Murray, 1901.

———. *The Life and Letters of Charles Darwin*. Edited by Francis Darwin. 2 vols. New York: D. Appleton, 1898.

d'Assonville, Victor E. "'Monumentum aere perennius' – Discussions and Decisions by the Synod of Dort on the Translation of the Bible." *KOERS – Bulletin for Christian Scholarship* 84 (2019): 1–14.

Davidson, Gregg. "Fossil Record (Evolutionary-Creation View)." In *DCS*, 287–90.

Davidson, Richard M. "The Creation Theme in Psalm 104." In Gerald A. Klingbeil, *Genesis Creation Account*, 149–88.

————. "The Genesis Account of Origins." In Gerald A. Klingbeil, *Genesis Creation Account*, 59–130.

————. "The Genesis Flood Narrative: Crucial Issues in the Current Debate." *Andrews University Seminary Studies* 42 (2004): 49–77.

Dawkins, Richard. *An Appetite for Wonder: The Making of a Scientist, a Memoir.* New York: HarperCollins, 2013.

————. *The Blind Watchmaker.* 30th anniversary ed. London: Penguin, 2006.

Day, John. *God's Conflict with the Dragon and the Sea. Echoes of a Canaanite Myth in the Old Testament.* Cambridge: Cambridge University Press, 1985.

————. Review of *Revisiting the Days of Genesis,* by B. C. Hodge. *Journal of Theological Studies* 66 (2015): 692–94.

de Graaf, S. G. *From Creation to the Conquest of Canaan.* Vol. 1 of *Promise and Deliverance.* Translated by H. Evan Runner and Elisabeth Wichers Runner. St. Catharines, Ontario: Paideia, 1977.

Delitzsch, Franz. *A New Commentary on Genesis.* Translated by Sophia Taylor. 2 vols. 1888. Reprint, Minneapolis: Klock & Klock, 1978.

Dembski, William A., Wayne J. Downs, and Justin B. A. Frederick, eds. *The Patristic Understanding of Creation: An Anthology of Writings from the Church Fathers on Creation and Design.* Riesel, Tex.: Erasmus, 2008.

Dennett, Daniel C. *Darwin's Dangerous Idea: Evolution and the Meanings of Life.* New York: Touchstone, 1996.

Dennis, Lane T., and Wayne Grudem, et al., eds. *The ESV Study Bible, English Standard Version.* Wheaton, Ill.: Crossway, 2007.

Denton, Michael. *Evolution: Still a Theory in Crisis.* Seattle: Discovery Institute, 2016.

Diehl, David W. "Evangelicalism and General Revelation: An Unfinished Agenda." *Journal of the Evangelical Theological Society* 30 (1987): 441–55.

Dillow, Joseph C. *The Waters Above: Earth's Pre-Flood Vapor Canopy.* 2nd ed. Chicago: Moody, 1982.

Doedens, J. J. T. "Taal en teken van trouw: Over vorm en functie van Genesis 1." In *Woord op Schrift. Theologische reflecties over het gezag van de Bijbel,* edited by C. Trimp, 71–108. Kampen: Kok, 2002.

Dooyeweerd, Herman. "Cornelius Van Til and the Transcendental Critique of Theoretical Thought." With a response by Cornelius Van Til. In *Jerusalem and Athens: Critical Discussions on the Theology and Apologetics of Cornelius Van Til,* edited by E. R. Geehan, 74–127. N.p.: Presbyterian and Reformed, 1971.

―――. "De leer van de mensch in de Wijsbegeerte der Wetsidee." *Correspondentie-Bladen* 7 (December 1942): 134–44. English text available at http://www.members.shaw.ca/aevum/32Propositions.html.

―――. "De tussen wijsbegeerte en theologie en de strijd der faculteiten - II." *Philosophia Reformata* 23 (1958): 49–84.

―――. *In the Twilight of Western Thought. Studies in the Pretended Autonomy of Philosophical Thought*. Nutley, N.J.: Craig, 1968.

―――. *A New Critique of Theoretical Thought*. Translated by David H. Freeman and William S. Young. 4 vols. Amsterdam: H. J. Paris; Philadelphia: Presbyterian and Reformed, 1953–1958.

Dorsey, David A. *The Literary Structure of the Old Testament: A Commentary on Genesis–Malachi*. Grand Rapids: Baker, 1999.

Doukhan, Jacques B. *The Genesis Creation Story: Its Literary Structure*. Andrews University Seminary Doctoral Dissertation Series. Berrien Springs, Mich.: Andrews University Press, 1978.

―――. "'When Death Was Not Yet': The Testimony of Biblical Creation." In Gerald A. Klingbeil, *Genesis Creation Account*, 329–42.

Douma, Jochem. *Another Look at Dooyeweerd*. Translated by J. M. Batteau. Winnipeg: Premier, n.d.

―――. *Genesis*. Gaan in het spoor van het Oude Testament. Kampen: Kok, 2005.

Dumbrell, W. J. *Covenant and Creation: A Theology of Old Testament Covenants*. Nashville: Thomas Nelson, 1984.

Duncan, J. Ligon, III, and David W. Hall. "The 24-Hour View." In *The Genesis Debate: Three Views on the Days of Creation*, edited by David G. Hagopian, 21–66, 95–119. Mission Viejo, Calif.: Crux, 2001.

Edersheim, Alfred. *The Temple: Its Ministry and Services as They Were at the Time of Jesus Christ*. Grand Rapids: Eerdmans, 1958.

Edgar, William. Review of *The End of Christianity: Finding a Good God in an Evil World*, by William A. Dembski. *Themelios* 35 (2010): 137–41.

El-Baz, Farouk. "A River in the Desert." *Discover* 14, no. 7 (July 1993): 10.

―――. "Space Age Archaeology." *Scientific American* 277, no. 2 (August 1997): 60–65.

Enns, Peter. *The Evolution of Adam: What the Bible Does and Doesn't Say About Human Origins*. Grand Rapids: Brazos, 2012.

―――. *Inspiration and Incarnation: Evangelicals and the Problem of the Old Testament*. Grand Rapids: Baker Academic, 2005.

Estes, Daniel J. "Creation Theology in Psalm 148." *Bibliotheca Sacra* 171 (2014): 30–41.

Faro, Ingrid. "The Question of Evil and Animal Death Before the Fall." *Trinity Journal*, n.s., 36 (2015): 193–213.

Faulkner, Danny R. "Geocentrism and Creation." *Journal of Creation* 15, no. 2 (2001): 110–21.

Fesko, J. V. "The Days of Creation and Confession Subscription in the OPC." *Westminster Theological Journal* 63 (2001): 235–49.

———. *The Theology of the Westminster Standards: Historical Context and Theological Insights*. Wheaton, Ill.: Crossway, 2014.

Fields, Weston W. *Unformed and Unfilled*. Nutley, N.J.: Presbyterian and Reformed, 1976.

Flipse, Abraham C. *Christelijke wetenschap. Nederlandse rooms-katholieken en gereformeerden over de natuurwetenschap, 1880–1940*. Hilversum: Verloren, 2014.

———. "The Origins of Creationism in the Netherlands." *Church History* 81 (2012): 104–47.

Foulkes, Francis. *The Acts of God: A Study of the Basis of Typology in the Old Testament*. The Tyndale Old Testament Lecture for 1955. London: Tyndale, 1958.

Frair, Wayne. "Barminology—Classification of Created Organisms." *Creation Research Society Quarterly* 37 (2000): 82–91.

Frame, John M. *The Doctrine of God*. A Theology of Lordship. Phillipsburg, N.J.: P&R, 2002.

———. *The Doctrine of the Christian Life*. A Theology of Lordship. Phillipsburg, N.J.: P&R, 2008.

———. *The Doctrine of the Knowledge of God*. A Theology of Lordship. Phillipsburg, N.J.: P&R, 1987.

———. *A History of Western Philosophy and Theology*. Phillipsburg, N.J.: P&R, 2015.

———. *Systematic Theology: An Introduction to Christian Belief*. Phillipsburg, N.J.: P&R, 2013.

Frayne, Douglas. "The Fifth Day of Creation in Ancient Syrian and Neo-Hittite Art." In *Creation and Chaos: A Reconsideration of Hermann Gunkel's Chaoskampf Hypothesis*, edited by John Scurlock and Richard H. Beal, 63–97. Winona Lake, Ind.: Eisenbrauns, 2013.

Freedman, David Noel. "Early Israelite Poetry and Historical Reconstructions." In *Symposia Celebrating the Seventy-Fifth Anniversary of the Founding of the American Schools of Oriental Research (1900–1975)*, edited by Frank Moore Cross, 85–96. Zion Research Foundation Occasional Publications 1–2. Cambridge, Mass.: American Schools of Oriental Research, 1979.

————, ed. *The Leningrad Codex: A Facsimile Edition*. Grand Rapids: Eerdmans; Leiden: Brill, 1998.

Freitheim, Terence E. "Were the Days of Creation Twenty-Four Hours Long? Yes." In *The Genesis Debate: Persistent Questions about Creation and the Flood*, edited by Ronald F. Youngblood, 12–35. Grand Rapids: Baker, 1990.

Friesen, J. Glenn. "95 Theses of Herman Dooyeweerd." *Philosophia Reformata* 74 (2009): 78–104.

Frymer-Kensky, Tikva. "The Planting of Man: A Study in Biblical Imagery." In *Love & Death in the Ancient Near East: Essays in Honor of Marvin H. Pope*, edited by John H. Marks and Robert M. Good, 129–42. Guilford, Conn.: Four Quarters, 1987.

Futato, Mark D. "Because It Had Rained: A Study of Gen 2:5–7 with Implications for Gen 2:4–25 and Gen 1:1–2:3." *Westminster Theological Journal* 60 (1998): 1–21.

————. "*mîn*, Kind, Variety." In *NIDOTTE* 2:934–35.

Gaffin, Richard B., Jr. *God's Word in Servant-Form: Abraham Kuyper and Herman Bavinck on the Doctrine of Scripture*. Jackson, Miss.: Reformed Academic Press, 2008.

————. *No Adam, No Gospel: Adam and the History of Redemption*. Philadelphia: Westminster Seminary Press; Phillipsburg, N.J.: P&R, 2015.

————. "A Sabbath Rest Still Awaits the People of God." In *Pressing Toward the Mark. Essays Commemorating Fifty Years of the Orthodox Presbyterian Church*, edited by C. G. Dennison and R. C. Gamble, 33–51. Philadelphia: Committee for the Historian of the Orthodox Presbyterian Church, 1986.

Garner, Paul A. *The New Creationism: Building Scientific Theories on a Biblical Basis*. Welwyn Garden City, U.K.: EP Books, 2009.

Garr, Randall W. *In His Own Image and Likeness: Humanity, Divinity, and Monotheism*. Culture and History of the Ancient Near East. Leiden: Brill, 2003.

Garrett, Duane A. *Hosea, Joel*. New American Commentary. Nashville: Broadman & Holman, 1997.

————. *Rethinking Genesis: The Sources and Authorship of the First Book of the Pentateuch*. Grand Rapids: Baker, 1991.

Gauger, Ann K., Ola Hössjer, and Colin R. Reeves. "Evidence for Human Uniqueness." In Moreland et al., *Theistic Evolution*, 475–502.

Gelernter, David. "Giving Up Darwin." *Claremont Review of Books* 19, no. 2 (2019): 104–9.

Gispen, W. H. *De Spreuken van Salomo*. 2 vols. Korte verklaring der Heilige Schrift. Kampen: Kok, 1952.

———. "Genesis 2:10–14." In *Studia Biblica et Semitica: Theodoro Christiano Vriezen Dedicata*, edited by W. C. van Unnik and A. S. van der Woude, 115–24. Wageningen: H. Veenman, 1966.

———. *Genesis*. 3 vols. Commentaar op het Oude Testament. Kampen: Kok, 1974–1983.

———. *Schepping en paradijs: Verklaring van Genesis 1–3*. Kampen: Kok, 1966.

Gitt, Werner. *In the Beginning Was Information*. Bielefeld, Germany: CLV, 2000.

Goheen, Michael. "Scriptural Revelation, Creational Revelation and Natural Science: The Issue." In *Facets of Faith and Science*, edited by Jitse van der Meer, vol. 4, *Interpreting God's Action in the World*, 331–45. Lanham, Md.: University Press of America, 1996.

Goldingay, John. *A Critical and Exegetical Commentary on Isaiah 56–66*. International Critical Commentary. London: Bloomsbury, 2014.

———. *The Message of Isaiah 40–55: A Literary-Theological Commentary*. London: T&T Clark, 2005.

Goldingay, John, and David Payne. *A Critical and Exegetical Commentary on Isaiah 40–55*. 2 vols. International Critical Commentary. London: T&T Clark, 2006.

Gootjes, Nicolaas H. "Farming According to General Revelation? The Meaning of Isaiah 28:22–29." In *Teaching and Preaching the Word: Studies in Dogmatics and Homiletics*, edited and compiled by Cornelis Van Dam, 23–32. Winnipeg: Premier, 2010.

———. "General Revelation and Science: Reflections on a Remark in Report 28." *Calvin Theological Journal* 30 (1995): 94–107.

———. "Is Creation the Same as Providence?" In *Teaching and Preaching the Word: Studies in Dogmatics and Homiletics*, edited and compiled by Cornelis Van Dam, 229–47. Winnipeg: Premier, 2010.

———. "What Does God Reveal in the Grand Canyon?" In *Teaching and Preaching the Word: Studies in Dogmatics and Homiletics*, edited and compiled by Cornelis Van Dam, 3–21. Winnipeg: Premier, 2010.

Gordis, Robert. *The Book of Job: Commentary, New Translation, and Special Studies*. Moreshet Series. New York: Jewish Theological Seminary of America, 1978.

Gosse, Philip Henry. *Omphalos: An Attempt to Untie the Geological Knot*. London: John Van Voorst, 1857.

Green, Gene L. *Jude and 2 Peter*. Baker Exegetical Commentary on the New Testament. Grand Rapids: Baker Academic, 2008.

Green, James Benjamin, ed. *A Harmony of the Westminster Presbyterian Standards*. N.p.: Collins-World, 1976.

Greene-McCreight, K. E. *Ad Litteram: How Augustine, Calvin, and Barth Read the "Plain Sense" of Genesis 1–3*. Issues in Systematic Theology. New York: Peter Lang, 1999.

Greenwood, Kyle. *Scripture and Cosmology: Reading the Bible Between the Ancient World and Modern Science*. Downers Grove, Ill.: IVP Academic, 2015.

Greijdanus, S. "In Edens Hof." *Gereformeerd Theologisch Tijdschrift* 17 (1916): 237–54.

———. *Schriftoverdenkingen*. Kampen: Kok, n.d.

Grigg, Russell M. "Naming the Animals." *Creation* 18, no. 4 (September 1996): 46–49.

Grogan, Geoffrey W. "Isaiah." In *The Expositor's Bible Commentary*, vol. 6, *Isaiah, Jeremiah, Lamentations, Ezekiel*, edited by Frank E. Gaebelein, 1–354. Grand Rapids: Zondervan, 1986.

Grosheide, F. W. "Kan van een bijbelsch wereldbeeld worden gesproken?" *Gereformeerd Theologisch Tijdschrift* 28 (1927–1928): 17–34.

Grossfeld, Bernard, trans. and ed. *The Targum Onqelos to Genesis*. The Aramaic Bible 6. Collegeville, Minn: Liturgical Press, 1988.

Grudem, Wayne A. "Scripture's Self-Attestation and the Problem of Formulating a Doctrine of Scripture." In *Scripture and Truth*, edited by D. A. Carson and John D. Woodbridge, 19–59. 1983. Reprint, Grand Rapids: Baker, 1992.

———. "Theistic Evolution Undermines Twelve Creation Events and Several Crucial Christian Doctrines." In Moreland et al., *Theistic Evolution*, 783–837.

Gundlach, Bradley J. *Process and Providence: The Evolution Question at Princeton, 1845–1929*. Grand Rapids: Eerdmans, 2013.

Gunkel, Hermann. *The Legends of Genesis*. Chicago: Open Court, 1901.

Habig, Brian C. "Hosea 6:7 Revisited." *Presbyterion* 42 (2016): 4–20.

Hall, David W. "The Evolution of Mythology: Classic Creation Survives as the Fittest Among Its Critics and Revisers." In *Did God Create in Six Days?*, edited by Joseph A. Pipa and David W. Hall, 267–305. Taylors, S.C.: Southern Presbyterian Press, 1999.

———. *Lux Supra Tenebrae: Essays on Calvin and Calvinism*. Vol. 3. Powder Springs, Ga.: The Covenant Foundation, 2015.

———. "What Was the View of the Westminster Assembly Divines on Creation Days?" In *Did God Create in Six Days?*, edited by Joseph A. Pipa and David W. Hall, 41–52. Taylors, S.C.: Southern Presbyterian Press, 1999.

Ham, Ken, Britt Beemer, with Todd Hillard. *Already Gone: Why Your Kids Will Quit Church and What You Can Do to Stop It*. Green Forest, Ariz.: Master, 2009.

Ham, Steve. "What's Lost in John Walton's *The Lost World of Adam and Eve?*" In Mortenson, *Searching for Adam*, 165–93.

Hamblin, Dora Jane. "Sleuthing the Garden of Eden." *Smithsonian* 18, no. 2 (1987): 127–35.

Hamilton, Victor P. *The Book of Genesis: Chapters 1–17.* New International Commentary on the Old Testament. Grand Rapids: Eerdmans, 1990.

Harinck, G., C. van der Kooi, and J. Vree, eds. *"Als Bavinck nu eens kleur bekende."* Amsterdam: VU Uitgeverij, 1994.

Harris, R. Laird. "The Bible and Questions of Cosmology." *Presbyterion* 7 (1981): 195–202.

———. "The Length of the Creative Days in Genesis 1." In *Did God Create in Six Days?*, edited by Joseph A. Pipa and David W. Hall, 101–11. Taylors, S.C.: Southern Presbyterian Press, 1999.

Harrison, Peter. "The Bible, Protestantism and the Rise of Natural Science: A Rejoinder." *Science and Christian Belief* 21 (2009): 155–62.

———. *The Bible, Protestantism, and the Rise of Natural Science.* Cambridge: Cambridge University Press, 2001.

———. "Hermeneutics and Natural Knowledge in the Reformers." In *Nature and Scripture in the Abrahamic Religions: Up to 1700*, edited by Jitse M. van der Meer and Scott Mandelbrote, 341–62. Brill's Series in Church History 37.2. Leiden: Brill, 2008.

———. "Subduing the Earth: Genesis 1, Early Modern Science, and the Exploitation of Nature." *Journal of Religion* 79 (1999): 86–109.

Harrison, R. K. *Introduction to the Old Testament.* Grand Rapids: Eerdmans, 1969.

Hart, D. G. *Defending the Faith: J. Gresham Machen and the Crisis of Conservative Protestantism in Modern America.* Baltimore: Johns Hopkins University Press, 1994.

Hartley, John E. *The Book of Job.* New International Commentary on the Old Testament. Grand Rapids: Eerdmans, 1988.

Hartnett, John. "Does the Bible Really Describe Expansion of the Universe?" *Journal of Creation* 25 (2011): 125–27.

Hasel, Gerhard F. "The 'Days' of Creation in Genesis 1: Literal 'Days' or Figurative 'Periods/Epochs' of Time?" *Origins* 21 (1994): 5–38.

———. *Old Testament Theology: Basic Issues in the Current Debate.* 4th ed. Grand Rapids: Eerdmans, 1991.

———. "The Polemic Nature of the Genesis Cosmology." *Evangelical Quarterly* 46 (1974): 81–102.

———. "The Significance of the Cosmology in Genesis 1 in Relation to Ancient Near Eastern Parallels." *Andrews University Seminary Studies* 10 (1972): 1–20.

Hasel, Gerhard F., and Michael G. Hasel. "The Unique Cosmology of Genesis 1 against Ancient Near Eastern and Egyptian Parallels." In Gerald A. Klingbeil, *Genesis Creation Account*, 9–29.

Heidel, Alexander. "The Alleged Contradiction between Gen. 1:24–27 and 2:19." *Concordia Theological Monthly* 12 (1941): 652–57.

———. *The Babylonian Genesis: The Story of Creation.* 2nd ed. Chicago: University of Chicago Press, 1963.

———. *The Gilgamesh Epic and Old Testament Parallels.* 2nd ed. Chicago: University of Chicago Press, 1963.

Helder, Margaret. *No Christian Silence on Science: Science from a Christian Perspective.* Edmonton: Creation Science Association of Alberta, 2016.

Hendel, Ronald. Review of *Genesis 1 as Ancient Cosmology*, by John H. Walton. *Journal of Semitic Studies* 58 (2013): 221–22.

Hendriksen, William. *Exposition of Ephesians.* New Testament Commentary. Grand Rapids: Baker, 1967.

Hertz, J. H., ed. *The Soncino Edition of the Pentateuch and Haftorahs.* 2nd ed. 1936. Reprint, London: Soncino, 1961.

Hess, Richard S., and David Toshio Tsumura, eds. *"I Studied Inscriptions from Before the Flood": Ancient Near Eastern, Literary, and Linguistic Approaches to Genesis 1–11.* Sources for Biblical and Theological Study 4. Winona Lake, Ind.: Eisenbrauns, 1994.

Hill, Carol A. "The Garden of Eden: A Modern Landscape." *Perspectives on Science and Christian Faith* 52 (2000): 31–46.

———. "The Noachian Flood: Universal or Local?" *Perspectives on Science and Christian Faith* 54 (2002): 170–83.

Hodge, B. C. *Revisiting the Days of Genesis.* Eugene, Ore.: Wipf & Stock, 2011.

Hodge, Charles. *What is Darwinism?* Edited by Mark A. Noll and David N. Livingstone. Grand Rapids: Baker, 1994.

Hoekema, Anthony A. *The Bible and the Future.* 1979. Reprint, Grand Rapids: Eerdmans, 1994.

Hoffmeier, James K. "Genesis 1–11 as History and Theology." In *Genesis: History, Fiction, or Neither? Three Views on the Bible's Earliest Chapters*, by James K. Hoffmeier, Gordon J. Wenham, and Kenton L. Sparks, 21–58. Counterpoints: Bible and Theology. Grand Rapids: Zondervan, 2015.

———. "'The Heavens Declare the Glory of God': The Limits of General Revelation." *Trinity Journal*, n.s., 21 (2000): 17–24.

———. "Response to Kenton L. Sparks." In *Genesis: History, Fiction, or Neither? Three Views on the Bible's Earliest Chapters*, by James K. Hoffmeier, Gordon J. Wenham, and Kenton L. Sparks, 140–49. Counterpoints: Bible and Theology. Grand Rapids: Zondervan, 2015.

———. "Some Thoughts on Genesis 1 & 2 and Egyptian Cosmology." *Journal of the Ancient Near Eastern Society of Columbia University* 15 (1983): 39–49.

Holding, James Patrick. "Is the 'Erets (Earth) Flat?" *Journal of Creation* 14, no. 3 (2000): 51–54.

Honey, Charles. "Adamant on Adam." *Christianity Today* 54, no. 6 (June 2010): 14.

Hooykaas, R. *Religion and the Rise of Modern Science*. Grand Rapids: Eerdmans, 1972.

Horowitz, Wayne. *Mesopotamian Cosmic Geography*. Mesopotamian Civilizations. Winona Lake, Ind.: Eisenbrauns, 1998.

Hössjer, Ola, Ann K. Gauger, and Colin R. Reeves. "An Alternative Population Genetics Model." In Moreland et al., *Theistic Evolution*, 503–21.

Houtman, C. *De hemel in het Oude Testament: een onderzoek naar de voorstellingen van het oude Israël omtrent de kosmos*. ThD diss. Franeker: Wever, 1974.

Howell, Kenneth J. *God's Two Books: Copernican Cosmology and Biblical Interpretation in Early Modern Science*. Notre Dame: University of Notre Dame Press, 2002.

Hughes, James R. "An Examination of the Assumptions of 'Eden's Geography Erodes Flood Geology.'" *Creation Research Society Quarterly* 34 (1997): 154–61.

Hughes, Philip Edgcumbe. *A Commentary on the Epistle to the Hebrews*. Grand Rapids: Eerdmans, 1977.

Huijgen, Arnold. *Divine Accommodation in John Calvin's Theology: Analysis and Assessment*. Reformed Historical Theology. Göttingen: Vandenhoeck & Ruprecht, 2011.

Humphreys, D. Russell. "A Biblical Basis for Creationist Cosmology." In *Proceedings of the Third International Conference on Creationism*, edited by R. E. Walsh, 255–66. Pittsburgh: Creation Science Fellowship, 1994.

———. *Starlight and Time*. Green Forest, Ariz.: Master, 1994.

Irons, Lee, and Meredith G. Kline. "The Framework View." In *The Genesis Debate: Three Views on the Days of Creation*, edited by David G. Hagopian, 217–56. Mission Viejo, Calif.: Crux, 2001.

Jacob, Benno. *The First Book of the Bible: Genesis*. Abridged, edited, and translated by Ernest I. Jacob and Walter Jacob. New York: Ktav, 1974.

———. *The Second Book of the Bible: Exodus*. Hoboken, N.J.: Ktav, 1992.

Jaki, Stanley L. *Genesis 1 through the Ages.* 2nd ed. Royal Oak, Mich.: Real View; Edinburgh: Scottish Academic Press, 1998.

Jeanson, Nathaniel T. *Replacing Darwin: The New Origin of Species.* Green Forest, Ariz.: Master, 2017.

Jeanson, Nathaniel T., and Jeffrey Tomkins. "Genetics Confirms the Recent Supernatural Creation of Adam and Eve." In Mortenson, *Searching for Adam,* 287–330.

Jenni, E. "*yôm* Day." In *TLOT,* 526–39.

Johnson, Alan F. "The Historical-Critical Method: Egyptian Gold or Pagan Precipice?" In Quo Vadis, *Evangelicalism? Perspectives on the Past, Direction for the Future,* edited by Andreas J. Köstenberger, 91–108. Wheaton, Ill.: Crossway, 2007.

Johnson, Phillip E. *Darwin on Trial.* 20th anniversary ed. Downers Grove, Ill.: InterVarsity, 2010.

———. *Darwin on Trial.* Downers Grove, Ill.: InterVarsity, 1991.

Johnston, Gordon H. "Genesis 1 and Ancient Egyptian Creation Myths." *Bibliotheca Sacra* 165 (2008): 178–94.

Jordan, James B. *Creation in Six Days: A Defense of the Traditional Reading of Genesis One.* Moscow, Idaho: Canon, 1999.

Kaiser, Walter C., Jr. "The Literary Form of Genesis 1–11." In *New Perspectives on the Old Testament,* edited by J. Barton Payne, 48–65. Waco, Tex.: Word, 1970.

Kalsbeek, L. *Contours of a Christian Philosophy: An Introduction to Herman Dooyeweerd's Thought.* Translated and edited by Bernard Zylstra and Josina Zylstra. Toronto: Wedge, 1975.

Kamphuis, B. *Klare taal: de duidelijkheid van de Schrift.* Kampen bijdragen 29. Barneveld: Vuurbaak, 1988.

Keel, Othmar. *The Symbolism of the Biblical World: Ancient Near Eastern Iconography and the Book of Psalms.* Translated by Timothy J. Hallett. Winona Lake, Ind.: Eisenbrauns, 1997.

Keel, Othmar, and Silvia Schroer. *Creation: Biblical Theologies in the Context of the Ancient Near East.* Translated by Peter T. Daniels. Winona Lake, Ind.: Eisenbrauns, 2015.

Keil, C. F., and F. Delitzsch. *Commentary on the Old Testament.* 1866–1891. Reprint, Peabody, Mass.: Hendrickson, 1996.

Keller, Timothy. "Creation, Evolution and Christian Laypeople." The BioLogos Foundation, 2009. https://biologos.org/uploads/projects/Keller_white_paper.pdf.

———. *The Reason for God: Belief in an Age of Skepticism.* New York: Riverhead, 2008.

Kelly, Douglas F. *Creation and Change: Genesis 1.1–2.4 in the Light of Changing Scientific Paradigms*. Rev. ed. Fearn, U.K.: Mentor, 2017.

Kendall, R. T. "Faith and Creation." In Nevin, *Should Christians Embrace Evolution?*, 108–16.

Kidner, Derek. *Genesis*. Tyndale Old Testament Commentaries. Downers Grove, Ill.: InterVarsity, 1967.

———. *Proverbs*. Tyndale Old Testament Commentaries. Downers Grove, Ill.: InterVarsity, 1964.

———. *Psalms 73–150*. Tyndale Old Testament Commentaries. Downers Grove, Ill.: InterVarsity, 1975.

Kinnaman, David. "Six Reasons Young Christians Leave Church." Barna Group. September 27, 2011. https://www.barna.com/research/six-reasons-young-christians-leave-church/.

Kistemaker, Simon J. *Exposition of James, Epistles of John, Peter, and Jude*. New Testament Commentary. Grand Rapids: Baker Academic, 2002.

———. *Exposition of the Second Epistle to the Corinthians*. New Testament Commentary. Grand Rapids: Baker, 1997.

Kitchen, K. A. *Ancient Orient and Old Testament*. London: Tyndale, 1966.

———. *The Bible in Its World: The Bible & Archaeology Today*. Downers Grove, Ill.: InterVarsity, 1978.

———. "The Old Testament in Its Context: 1 from the Origins to the Eve of the Exodus." *Theological Students' Fellowship Bulletin* 59 (1971): 2–10.

———. *On the Reliability of the Old Testament*. Grand Rapids: Eerdmans, 2003.

Klein, Ralph W. *1 Samuel*. Word Biblical Commentary. Waco, Tex.: Word, 1983.

Kline, Meredith G. "Because It Had Not Rained." *Westminster Theological Journal* 20 (1958): 146–57.

———. *Kingdom Prologue: Genesis Foundations for a Covenantal Worldview*. Overland Park, Kans.: Two Age, 2000.

———. "Space and Time in the Genesis Cosmogony." *Perspectives on Science and Christian Faith* 48 (1996): 2–15.

———. *Treaty of the Great King: The Covenant Structure of Deuteronomy*. Grand Rapids: Eerdmans, 1963.

Klingbeil, Gerald A., ed. *The Genesis Creation Account and Its Reverberations in the Old Testament*. Berrien Springs, Mich.: Andrews University Press, 2015.

Klingbeil, Martin G. "Creation in the Prophetic Literature of the Old Testament: An Intertextual Approach." In Gerald A. Klingbeil, *Genesis Creation Account*, 257–89.

Klooster, Fred H. "The Role of the Holy Spirit in the Hermeneutic Process: The Relationship of the Spirit's Illumination to Biblical Interpretation." In

Hermeneutics, Inerrancy, and the Bible, edited by Earl D. Radmacher and Robert D. Preus, 451–72. Grand Rapids: Zondervan, 1984.

Knafl, Anne K. *Forming God: Divine Anthropomorphism in the Pentateuch*. Siphrut. Winona Lake, Ind.: Eisenbrauns, 2014.

Kraus, Hans-Joachim. *Psalms 1–59: A Commentary*. Translated by Hilton C. Oswald. 1978. Reprint, Minneapolis: Augsburg, 1988.

Kruyswijk, Hittjo. *Baas in eigen boek? Evolutietheorie en Schriftgezag bij de Gereformeerde Kerken in Nederland (1881–1981)*. Hilversum: Verloren, 2011.

Kuhn, Thomas S. *The Structure of Scientific Revolutions*. 4th ed. Chicago: University of Chicago Press, 2012.

Kulikovsky, Andrew S. *Creation, Fall, Restoration: A Biblical Theology of Creation*. Geanies House, U.K.: Mentor, 2009.

———. "Scripture and General Revelation." *Journal of Creation* 19, no. 2 (2005): 23–28.

Kuyper, Abraham. "Evolution." *Calvin Theological Journal* 31 (1996): 11–50.

———. *Locus de sacra scriptura, creatione, creaturis: college-dictaat van een der studenten*. 6 parts. Dictaten dogmatiek 2. Kampen: Kok, 1910.

Kwakkel, Gert. "Er is meer dan Genesis 1. Andere outtestamentische teksten over de schepping." In *In den beginne en verder: een bijbels-theologische reflectie op de schepping*, edited by G. Kwakkel and P. H. R. van Houwelingen, 25–54. TU-Bezinningsreeks 8. Barneveld: Vuurbaak, 2011.

Lamoureux, Denis O. "Beyond Original Sin: Is a Theological Paradigm Shift Inevitable?" *Perspectives on Science and Christian Faith* 67 (2015): 35–49.

———. "No Historical Adam: Evolutionary Creation View." In *Four Views on the Historical Adam*, edited by Matthew Barrett and Ardel B. Caneday, 37–65. Counterpoints. Grand Rapids: Zondervan, 2013.

Landes, George M. "Creation Tradition in Proverbs 8:22–31 and Genesis 1." In *A Light Unto My Path: Old Testament Studies in Honor of Jacob M. Myers*, edited by Howard N. Bream, Ralph D. Heim, and Carey A. Moore, 279–93. Gettysburg Theological Studies 4. Philadelphia: Temple University Press, 1974.

Lavallee, Louis. "Augustine on the Creation Days." *Journal of the Evangelical Theological Society* 32 (1989): 457–64.

———. "Creeds and the Six Creation Days." *Acts and Facts* 22, no. 1 (1993): n.p.. https://www.icr.org/article/creeds-six-creation-days.

Lawrenz, Carl J., and John C. Jeske. *A Commentary on Genesis 1–11*. Milwaukee: Northwestern Publishing House, 2004.

Lee, Hoon J. "Accommodation—Orthodox, Socinian, and Contemporary." *Westminster Theological Journal* 75 (2013): 335–48.

Lennox, John C. *God's Undertaker: Has Science Buried God?* Oxford: Lion, 2009.

———. *Seven Days That Divide the World. The Beginning According to Genesis and Science.* Grand Rapids: Zondervan, 2011.

Lenski, R. C. H. *The Interpretation of St. John's Revelation.* Columbus, Ohio: Lutheran Book Concern, 1935.

———. *The Interpretation of the Epistles of St. Peter, St. John and St. Jude.* Columbus, Ohio: Lutheran Book Concern, 1938.

Letham, Robert. "'In the Space of Six Days': The Days of Creation from Origen to the Westminster Assembly." *Westminster Theological Journal* 61 (1999): 149–74.

Leupold, H. C. *Exposition of Genesis.* 2 vols. Grand Rapids: Baker, 1950–53.

Lewis, Jack P. "The Days of Creation: An Historical Survey of Interpretation." *Journal of the Evangelical Theological Society* 32 (1989): 433–55.

Lillback, Peter A. "'The Infallible Rule of Interpretation of Scripture': The Hermeneutical Crisis and the Westminster Standards." In *Resurrection and Eschatology: Theology in Service of the Church. Essays in Honor of Richard B. Gaffin Jr.,* edited by Lane G. Tipton and Jeffrey C. Waddington, 283–339. Phillipsburg, N.J.: P&R, 2008.

Lindeboom, A. M. *De theologen gingen voorop: eenvoudig verhaal van de ontmateling van de Gereformeerde Kerken.* Kampen: Kok, 1987.

Lipiński, E. "*qānâ; miqneh, miqnâ; qinyān.*" In *TDOT* 13:58–65.

Lisle, Jason. "Deep Time—the God of Our Age." November 9, 2012. http://www.jasonlisle.com/2012/11/09/deep-time-the-god-of-our-age/.

———. *Taking Back Astronomy.* Green Forest, Ariz.: Master, 2006.

———. *Understanding Genesis: How to Analyze, Interpret, and Defend Scripture.* Green Forest, Ariz.: Master, 2015.

Livingstone, David N. *Adam's Ancestors: Race, Religion, and the Politics of Human Origins.* Baltimore: Johns Hopkins University Press, 2011.

———. *Darwin's Forgotten Defenders: The Encounter Between Evangelical Theology and Evolutionary Thought.* Grand Rapids: Eerdmans; Edinburgh: Scottish Academic Press, 1987.

Livingstone, David N., and Mark A. Noll. "B. B. Warfield (1851–1921): A Biblical Inerrantist as Evolutionist." *Journal of Presbyterian History* 80 (2002): 153–71.

Loewenstamm, S. E. "The Seven Day-Unit in Ugaritic Epic Literature." *Israel Exploration Journal* 15 (1965): 121–33.

Longman, Tremper, III. "Biblical Narrative." In *A Complete Literary Guide to the Bible,* edited by Leland Ryken and Tremper Longman III, 69–79. Grand Rapids: Zondervan, 1993.

————. "Tremper Longman Responds to Justin Taylor on the Historicity of Adam." *The Logos Academic Blog.* March 25, 2014. https://academic.logos.com /tremper-longman-responds-to-justin-taylor-on-the-historicity-of-adam/.

————. "What Genesis 1–2 Teaches (and What It Doesn't)." In J. Daryl Charles, *Reading Genesis 1–2*, 103–28.

Longman, Tremper, III, and John H. Walton. *The Lost World of the Flood: Mythology, Theology, and the Deluge Debate.* Downers Grove, Ill.: IVP Academic, 2018.

Louth, Andrew, and Marco Conti, eds. *Genesis 1–11.* Ancient Christian Commentary on Scripture. Downers Grove, Ill.: InterVarsity, 2001.

Luskin, Casey. "DNA." In *DCS*, 189–90.

————. "Missing Transitions: Human Origins and the Fossil Record." In Moreland et al., *Theistic Evolution*, 437–73.

————. "Universal Common Descent: A Comprehensive Critique." In Moreland et al., *Theistic Evolution*, 363–401.

Lust, J., E. Eynikel, and K. Hauspie, eds. *A Greek-English Lexicon of the Septuagint.* Stuttgart: Deutsche Bibelgesellschaft, 1992.

Luther, Martin. *D. Martin Luthers Werke: Kritische Gesamtausgabe: Briefwechsel, Vol. 3.* Edited by Ulrich Köpf. 1933. Reprint, Weimar: Böhlau, 2002.

————. *Luther's Works.* Vol. 1, *Lectures on Genesis: Chapters 1–5.* Edited by Jaroslav Pelikan. Translated by George V. Schick. St. Louis, Mo.: Concordia, 1999.

Lyon, Jeremy D. "Gen 1:1–3 and the Literary Boundary of Day One." *Journal of the Evangelical Theological Society* 62 (2019): 269–85.

Machen, J. Gresham. *The Christian View of Man.* London: Banner of Truth, 1967.

————. "What Fundamentalism Stands for Now." In J. Gresham Machen, *Selected Shorter Writings*, edited by D. G. Hart, 116–22. Phillipsburg, N.J.: P&R, 2004.

Madueme, Hans. "Adam and Sin as a Bane of Evolution? A Review of *Finding Ourselves After Darwin*." *Themelios* 44 (2019): 466–76.

————. "Some Reflections on Enns and *The Evolution of Adam*." *Themelios* 37 (2012): 275–86.

Mahler, Michael, trans. and ed. *Targum Pseudo-Jonathan: Genesis.* The Aramaic Bible 1B. Collegeville, Minn.: Liturgical Press, 1992.

Mangalwadi, Vishal. *The Book That Made Your World. How the Bible Created the Soul of Western Civilization.* Nashville: Thomas Nelson, 2011.

Marsden, George M. *Understanding Fundamentalism and Evangelicalism.* Grand Rapids: Eerdmans, 1991.

Martens, Elmer A. *God's Design: A Focus on Old Testament Theology.* 3rd ed. 1981. Reprint, North Richland Hills, Tex.: BIBAL, 1998.

Mathews, Kenneth A. *Genesis 1–11:26.* New American Commentary. Nashville: Broadman & Holman, 1996.

McBride, S. Dean, Jr. "Divine Protocol: Genesis 1:1–2:3 as Prologue to the Pentateuch." In *God Who Creates: Essays in Honor of W. Sibley Towner,* edited by William P. Brown and S. Dean McBride Jr., 3–41. Grand Rapids: Eerdmans, 2000.

McCabe, Robert V. "A Defense of Literal Days in the Creation Week." *Detroit Baptist Seminary Journal* 5 (2000): 97–124.

McDowell, Catherine L. *The Image of God in the Garden of Eden.* Siphrut. Winona Lake, Ind.: Eisenbrauns, 2015.

McGovern, John J. "The Waters of Death." *Catholic Biblical Quarterly* 21 (1959): 350–58.

McGrath, Alister E. *The Foundations of Dialogue in Science and Religion.* Malden, Mass.: Blackwell, 1998.

———. *A Life of John Calvin: A Study in the Shaping of Western Culture.* Oxford: Blackwell, 1990.

McGuire, J. Amanda. "Evening or Morning: When Does the Biblical Day Begin?" *Andrews University Seminary Studies* 46 (2008): 201–14.

McIntire, C. T. "Herman Dooyeweerd in North America." In *Dutch Reformed Theology,* edited by David F. Wells, 55–70. Grand Rapids: Baker, 1989.

McNamara, Martin, trans. and ed. *Targum Neofiti 1: Genesis.* The Aramaic Bible 1A. Collegeville, Minn.: Liturgical Press, 1992.

Medawar, Peter. *The Limits of Science.* Oxford: Oxford University Press, 1987.

Menton, David. "Did Humans Really Evolve from Ape-Like Creatures?" In Mortenson, *Searching for Adam,* 229–62.

Merrill, Eugene H. "'Where Are You, Adam?' The Disappearance of Adam and the Death of Truth." In Mortenson, *Searching for Adam,* 113–38.

Meyer, Stephen C. "Scientific and Philosophical Introduction: Defining Theistic Evolution." In Moreland et al., *Theistic Evolution,* 33–60.

Miano, David. *Shadow on the Steps: Time Measurement in Ancient Israel.* Resources for Biblical Study / Society of Biblical Literature. Atlanta: Society of Biblical Literature, 2010.

Middleton, J. Richard. *The Liberating Image: The Imago Dei in Genesis 1.* Grand Rapids: Brazos, 2005.

Millard, Alan. "From Weal to Woe: Completing a Pattern in the Bible and the Ancient Near East." In *Let Us Go up to Zion: Essays in Honour of H. G. M. Williamson on the Occasion of His Sixty-Fifth Birthday,* edited by Iain Provan and Mark J. Boda, 193–201. Supplements to Vetus Testamentum 153. Leiden: Brill, 2012.

Miller, Patrick D. *The Way of the Lord: Essays in Old Testament Theology*. Grand Rapids: Eerdmans, 2007.

Minton, Ron. "Apostolic Witness to Genesis Creation and the Flood." In Mortenson and Ury, *Coming to Grips with Genesis*, 347–71.

Mishnayoth. Translated and annotated by Philip Blackman. 7 vols. 1963. New York: Judaica, 2000.

Mitchell, T. C. "The Old Testament Usage of nᵉšāmâ." *Vetus Testamentum* 11 (1961): 177–87.

————. Review of *The Earth and the Waters in Genesis 1 and 2: A Linguistic Investigation*, by David Toshio Tsumura. *Evangelical Quarterly* 66 (1994): 257–59.

Möller, Karl. "Images of God and Creation in Genesis 1–2." In *A God of Faithfulness: Essays in Honour of J. Gordon McConville on His 60th Birthday*, edited by Jamie A. Grant, Alison Lo, and Gordon J. Wenham, 3–29. New York: T&T Clark International, 2011.

Moo, Douglas J. *The Letters to the Colossians and to Philemon*. The Pillar New Testament Commentary. Grand Rapids: Eerdmans, 2008.

Moore, Nicholas J. "Heaven's Revolving Door? Cosmology, Entrance, and Approach in Hebrews." *Bulletin for Biblical Research* 29 (2019): 187–207.

Moorey, P. R. S. *Ancient Mesopotamian Materials and Industries: The Archaeological Evidence*. 1994. Reprint, Winona Lake, Ind.: Eisenbrauns, 1999.

Moreland, J. P. *Christianity and the Nature of Science*. Grand Rapids: Baker, 1989.

————. *Scientism and Secularism*. Wheaton, Ill.: Crossway, 2018.

Moreland, J. P., Stephen C. Meyer, Christopher Shaw, Ann K. Gauger, and Wayne Grudem, eds. *Theistic Evolution: A Scientific, Philosophical, and Theological Critique*. Wheaton, Ill.: Crossway, 2017.

Morris, Henry M. *The Genesis Record: A Scientific and Devotional Commentary on the Book of Beginnings*. Grand Rapids: Baker, 1976.

————. *Studies in the Bible and Science; or, Christ and Creation*. Philadelphia: Presbyterian and Reformed, 1966.

Mortenson, Terry. "Adam, Morality, the Gospel, and the Authority of Scripture." In Mortenson, *Searching for Adam*, 459–501.

————. "'Deep Time' and the Church's Compromise: Historical Background." In Mortenson and Ury, *Coming to Grips with Genesis*, 79–104.

————. *The Great Turning Point: The Church's Catastrophic Mistake on Geology—Before Darwin*. Green Forest, Ariz.: Master, 2004.

————. "Jesus' View of the Age of the Earth." In Mortenson and Ury, *Coming to Grips with Genesis*, 315–46.

————, ed. *Searching for Adam: Genesis and the Truth about Man's Origin*. Green Forest, Ariz.: Master, 2016.

———. "Were Fossils Created *Ex Nihilo* During Creation Week?" *Answers in Genesis*. October 6, 2006. https://answersingenesis.org/fossils/fossil-record/fossils-ex-nihilo-creation-week/.

———. "When Was Adam Created?" In Mortenson, *Searching for Adam*, 139–63.

Mortenson, Terry, and Thane H. Ury, eds. *Coming to Grips with Genesis: Biblical Authority and the Age of the Earth*. Green Forest, Ariz.: Master, 2008.

Moskala, Jiří. "A Fresh Look at Two Genesis Creation Accounts: Contradictions?" *Andrews University Seminary Studies* 49 (2011): 45–65.

Motyer, J. Alec. *The Prophecy of Isaiah*. Downers Grove, Ill.: InterVarsity, 1993.

Munday, John C. "Eden's Geography Erodes Flood Geology." *Westminster Theological Journal* 58 (1996): 123–54.

Murán, Alexej. "The Creation Theme in Selected Psalms." In Gerald A. Klingbeil, *Genesis Creation Account*, 189–223.

Murray, John. *The Epistle to the Romans*. 2 vols. New International Commentary on the New Testament. Reprint, Grand Rapids: Eerdmans, 1968.

———. "Man in the Image of God." In *Collected Writings of John Murray*, 2:34–46. Edinburgh: Banner of Truth, 1977.

———. "The Origin of Man." In *Collected Writings of John Murray*, 2:3–13. Edinburgh: Banner of Truth, 1977.

———. *Principles of Conduct: Aspects of Biblical Ethics*. Grand Rapids: Eerdmans, 1957.

Müller, H.-P. "*rō'š* Head." In *TLOT*, 1184–94.

Müller, W. W. "Havilah (Person)." In *ABD* 3:81–82.

Nelson, Paul. "Five Questions Everyone Should Ask About Common Descent." In Moreland et al., *Theistic Evolution*, 403–30.

Neusner, Jacob. *Genesis Rabbah. The Judaic Commentary to the Book of Genesis: A New American Translation*. Brown Judaic Studies. Atlanta: Scholars Press, 1985.

Neville, Richard. "Differentiation in Genesis 1: An Exegetical Creation *Ex Nihilo*." *Journal of Biblical Literature* 130 (2011): 209–26.

Nevin, Norman C. "Homology." In Nevin, *Should Christians Embrace Evolution?*, 137–42.

———. ed. *Should Christians Embrace Evolution? Biblical and Scientific Responses*. Nottingham, U.K.: Inter-Varsity, 2009.

Newman, Robert C. "Are the Events in the Genesis Creation Account Set Forth in Chronological Order? Yes." In *The Genesis Debate: Persistent Questions about Creation and the Flood*, edited by Ronald F. Youngblood, 36–55. Grand Rapids: Baker, 1990.

Niehr, H. "'ereb." In *TDOT* 11:335–41.

Noll, Mark A. "The Evangelical Mind Today." *First Things*, no. 146 (October 2004): 34–39.

———. *The Scandal of the Evangelical Mind*. 1994. Reprint, Grand Rapids: Eerdmans; Leicester, U.K.: Inter-Varsity, 1995.

Noordtzij, A. *Gods Woord en der eeuwen getuigenis: het Oude Testament in het licht der oostersche opgravingen*. 2nd ed. Kampen: Kok, 1931.

Numbers, Ronald L. *The Creationists: From Scientific Creationism to Intelligent Design*. Expanded ed. Cambridge, Mass.: Harvard University Press, 2006.

Odendaal, Dirk H. *The Eschatological Expectation of Isaiah 40–66 with Special Reference to Israel and the Nations*. Nutley, N.J.: Presbyterian and Reformed, 1970.

Ollenburger, Ben C. "Isaiah's Creation Theology." *Ex Auditu* 3 (1987): 54–71.

Orthodox Presbyterian Church. *The Confession of Faith and Catechisms*. Willow Grove, Pa.: Orthodox Presbyterian Church, 2005.

———. *Minutes of the Sixty-Third General Assembly…and Yearbook of the Orthodox Presbyterian Church*. Philadelphia: Orthodox Presbyterian Church, 1996.

———. "Report of the Committee to Study the Views of Creation." In *Minutes of the Seventy-First General Assembly…of the Orthodox Presbyterian Church*, 193–350. Willow Grove, Pa.: Orthodox Presbyterian Church, 2004.

Osborne, Grant R. *Revelation*. Baker Exegetical Commentary on the New Testament. Grand Rapids: Baker Academic, 2002.

Oswalt, John N. *The Bible among the Myths*. Grand Rapids: Zondervan, 2009.

———. *The Book of Isaiah, Chapters 1–39*. New International Commentary on the Old Testament. Grand Rapids: Eerdmans, 1986.

———. *The Book of Isaiah, Chapters 40–66*. New International Commentary on the Old Testament. Grand Rapids: Eerdmans, 1998.

———. "*Creatio Ex Nihilo*: Is It Biblical and Does It Matter?" *Trinity Journal*, n.s., 39 (2018): 165–80.

Ouweneel, Willem J. *Wisdom for Thinkers: An Introduction to Christian Philosophy*. Jordan Station, Ontario: Paideia, 2014.

Parker, T. H. L. *Calvin's New Testament Commentaries*. Grand Rapids: Eerdmans, 1971.

Paul, M. J. *Oorspronkelijk: overwegingen bij schepping en evolutie*. Apeldoorn: Labarum Academic, 2017.

Paul, Shalom M., and Frank Moore Cross. *Amos: A Commentary on the Book of Amos*. Hermeneia. Minneapolis: Fortress, 1991.

Pearcey, Nancy. *Total Truth: Liberating Christianity from Its Cultural Captivity*. Study guide ed. Wheaton, Ill.: Crossway, 2005.

Pedersen, Johannes. *Israel: Its Life and Culture.* 4 vols. London: Oxford University Press, 1926.

Peterson, Ryan S. *The* Imago Dei *as Human Identity: A Theological Interpretation.* Journal of Theological Interpretation Supplement. Winona Lake, Ind.: Eisenbrauns, 2016.

Phillips, Richard D. *Revelation.* Reformed Expository Commentary. Phillipsburg, N.J.: P&R, 2017.

Pipa, Joseph A., Jr. "From Chaos to Cosmos: A Critique of the Non-Literal Interpretations of Genesis 1:1–2:3." In *Did God Create in Six Days?*, edited by Joseph A. Pipa and David W. Hall, 153–98. Taylors, S.C.: Southern Presbyterian Press, 1999.

Plantinga, Alvin. "Evolution, Neutrality, and Antecedent Probability." In *Intelligent Design, Creationism, and Its Critics: Philosophical, Theological, and Scientific Perspectives*, edited by Robert T. Pennock, 196–236. Cambridge, Mass.: MIT Press, 2001.

——. "When Faith and Reason Clash: Evolution and the Bible." In *Intelligent Design, Creationism, and Its Critics: Philosophical, Theological, and Scientific Perspectives*, edited by Robert T. Pennock, 113–45. Cambridge, Mass.: MIT Press, 2001.

——. *Where the Conflict Really Lies: Science, Religion, and Naturalism.* New York: Oxford University Press, 2011.

Porter, J. R. "Old Testament Historiography." In *Tradition and Interpretation: Essays by Members of the Society for Old Testament Study*, edited by G. W. Anderson, 125–62. Oxford: Clarendon, 1979.

Poythress, Vern S. "Adam Versus Claims from Genetics." *Westminster Theological Journal* 75 (2013): 65–82.

——. "Canon and Speech Act: Limitations in Speech-Act Theory, with Implications for a Putative Theory of Canonical Speech Acts." *Westminster Theological Journal* 70 (2008): 337–54.

——. "Correlations with Providence in Genesis 1." *Westminster Theological Journal* 77 (2015): 71–99.

——. "Dealing with the Genre of Genesis and Its Opening Chapters." *Westminster Theological Journal* 78 (2016): 217–30.

——. "Genesis 1:1 is the First Event, not a Summary." *Westminster Theological Journal* 79 (2017): 97–121.

——. *Interpreting Eden: A Guide to Faithfully Reading and Understanding Genesis 1–3.* Wheaton, Ill.: Crossway, 2019.

————. "A Misunderstanding of Calvin's Interpretation of Genesis 1:6–8 and 1:5 and Its Implications for Ideas of Accommodation." *Westminster Theological Journal* 76 (2014): 157–66.

————. "Rain Water Versus a Heavenly Sea in Genesis 1:6–8." *Westminster Theological Journal* 77 (2015): 181–91.

————. *Redeeming Science: A God-Centered Approach.* Wheaton, Ill.: Crossway, 2006.

————. "Reforming Ontology and Logic in the Light of the Trinity: An Application of Van Til's Idea of Analogy." *Westminster Theological Journal* 57 (1995): 187–219.

————. "Rethinking Accommodation in Revelation." *Westminster Theological Journal* 76 (2014): 143–56.

————. "Time in Genesis 1." *Westminster Theological Journal* 79 (2017): 213–41.

Price, Ira Maurice. *The Monuments and the Old Testament.* Philadelphia: American Baptist Publication Society, 1909.

Provan, Iain, V. Philips Long, and Tremper Longman III. *A Biblical History of Israel.* Louisville, Ky.: Westminster John Knox, 2003.

Rachels, James. *Created from Animals: The Moral Implications of Darwinism.* Oxford: Oxford University Press, 1990.

Rae, Murray A. "Anthropomorphism." In *Dictionary for the Theological Interpretation of the Bible*, edited by Kevin J. Vanhoozer, 48–49. Grand Rapids: Baker Academic; London: SPCK, 2005.

Rashi [Shelomoh ben Yitsḥak]. *The Metsudah Chumash.* Translated and edited by Avrohom Davis. 5 vols. New York: Ktav, 1997–1998.

Reeves, Colin R. "Bringing Home the Bacon: The Interaction of Science and Scripture Today." In Moreland et al., *Theistic Evolution*, 705–29. Wheaton, Ill.: Crossway, 2017.

Rendle-Short, John. *Green Eye of the Storm.* Edinburgh: Banner of Truth, 1998.

Ridderbos, J. *De Psalmen.* Commentaar op het Oude Testament. Kampen: Kok, 1955.

————. *Het verloren paradijs: een woord met het oog op de aangaande Genesis 2 en 3 gerezen vragen.* Kampen: Kok, 1925.

Ridderbos, Nic. H. *Beschouwingen over Genesis I.* 2nd ed. Kampen: Kok, 1963.

————. *De Psalmen.* 2 vols. Korte verklaring. Kampen: Kok, 1962.

————. *Die Psalmen. Stilistische Verfahren und Aufbau met besonderer Berücksichtigung von Ps 1–41.* Beihefte zur Zeitschrift für die alttestamentliche Wissenschaft. Berlin: De Gruyter, 1972.

————. *Is There a Conflict between Genesis 1 and Natural Science?* Translated by John Vriend. Grand Rapids: Eerdmans, 1957.

Ringgren, Helmer. "*bārāʾ*." In *TDOT* 2:242–49.

Ringgren, Helmer, and L. A. Mitchel. "*ḥāšak, ḥōšek*." In *TDOT* 5:245–59.

Robinson, Philip. "Soft Tissue Preservation in a 'Jurassic' Ichthyosaur." *Creation* 42, no. 1 (2020): 36–37.

Rodríguez, Ángel M. "Biblical Creationism and Ancient Near Eastern Evolutionary Ideas." In Gerald A. Klingbeil, *Genesis Creation Account*, 293–328.

———. "Genesis and Creation in the Wisdom Literature." In Gerald A. Klingbeil, *Genesis Creation Account*, 225–56.

Rogers, Cleon L., III. "The Meaning and Significance of the Hebrew Word אָמוֹן in Proverbs 8:30." *Zeitschrift für die alttestamentliche Wissenschaft* 109 (1997): 208–21.

Rogers, Jack B. *The Authority and Interpretation of the Bible: An Historical Approach.* San Francisco: Harper & Row, 1979.

Rogland, Max. "*Ad Litteram*: Some Dutch Reformed Theologians on the Creation Days." *Westminster Theological Journal* 63 (2001): 211–33.

———. "Interpreting אֵד in Genesis 2.5–6: Neglected Rabbinic and Intertextual Evidence." *Journal for the Study of the Old Testament* 34 (2010): 379–93.

Rooker, Mark F. "Genesis 1:1–3: Creation or Recreation? Part 2." *Bibliotheca Sacra* 149 (1992): 411–27.

Ross, Hugh, and Gleason L. Archer. "The Day-Age View." In *The Genesis Debate: Three Views on the Days of Creation*, edited by David G. Hagopian, 123–63. Mission Viejo, Calif.: Crux, 2001.

Ross, Marcus R. "Fossil Record (Young Earth–Creation View)." In *DCS*, 290–94.

Routledge, Robin. *Old Testament Theology: A Thematic Approach.* Downers Grove, Ill.: IVP Academic, 2008.

Rudolph, David J. "Festivals in Genesis 1:14." *Tyndale Bulletin* 54, no. 2 (2003): 23–40.

Sailhamer, John H. *Genesis Unbound: A Provocative New Look.* 2nd ed. Colorado Springs: Dawson Media, 2011.

Sanford, John C. *Genetic Entropy.* 4th ed. N.p.: FMS, 2014.

Sarfati, Jonathan D. *The Genesis Account: A Theological, Historical, and Scientific Commentary on Genesis 1–11.* Powder Springs, Ga.: Creation Book Publishers, 2015.

Sarna, Nahum M. *Exodus: The Traditional Hebrew Text with the New JPS Translation.* The JPS Torah Commentary. Philadelphia: Jewish Publication Society, 1991.

———. *Genesis: The Traditional Hebrew Text with the New JPS Translation.* The JPS Torah Commentary. Philadelphia: Jewish Publication Society, 1989.

———. *Understanding Genesis.* New York: Schocken, 1966.

Sauer, James A. "The River Runs Dry: Creation Story Preserves Historical Memory." *Biblical Archaeology Review* 22, no. 4 (July-August 1996): 52–54, 57, 64.

Schaeffer, Francis A. *The Great Evangelical Disaster.* Wheaton, Ill.: Crossway, 1984.

Schafer, A. Rahel Davidson. "The 'Kinds' of Genesis 1: What Is the Meaning of *Mîn?*" *Journal of the Adventist Theological Society* 14 (2003): 86–100.

Schilder, Klaas. *Christ and Culture.* Translated by William Helder and Albert H. Oosterhoff. Annotated by Jochem Douma. Hamilton, Ontario: Lucerna, 2016.

———. *Een hoornstoot tegen Assen? (Antwoord op een 'conscientiekreet').* 2nd ed. Kampen: Kok, 1929.

———. *Heaven: What Is It?* Translated and condensed by Marian M. Schoolland. Grand Rapids: Eerdmans, 1950.

———. *Heidelbergsche Catechismus toegelicht.* 4 vols. Goes: Oosterbaan & Le Cointre, 1947–1951.

———. *Schriftoverdenkingen.* Edited by L. Doekes, P. A. C. Schilder, C. Veenhof, and W. G. de Vries. 3 vols. Goes: Oosterbaan & Le Cointre, 1956–1958.

———. *Wat is de hemel?* 2nd ed. Kampen: Kok, 1954.

Schmidt, W. H. "*br'* to create." In *TLOT* 1:253–56.

Schreiner, Thomas R. *Romans.* Baker Exegetical Commentary on the New Testament. Grand Rapids: Baker, 1998.

Schwartz, Sarah. "Narrative *Toledot* Formulae in Genesis: The Case of Heaven and Earth, Noah, and Isaac." *Journal of Hebrew Scriptures* 16 (2016): 1–37.

Schweitzer, Mary H. "Blood from Stone." *Scientific American* 303, no. 6 (December 2010): 62–69.

Schweitzer, Mary H., Wenxia Zheng, Timothy P. Cleland, Mark B. Goodwin, Elizabeth Boatman, Elizabeth Theil, Matthew A. Marcus, and Sirine C. Fakra. "A Role for Iron and Oxygen Chemistry in Preserving Soft Tissues, Cells and Molecules from Deep Time." *Proceedings of the Royal Society: Biological Sciences* 281, no. 1775 (January 2014): 1–10.

Scofield, C. I., ed. *The Scofield Reference Bible. The Holy Bible, Containing the Old and New Testaments. Authorized King James Version, with a New System of Connected Topical References to All the Greater Themes of Scripture.* New York: Oxford University Press, 1917.

Scurlock, JoAnn. "Searching for Meaning in Genesis 1:2." In *Creation and Chaos: A Reconsideration of Hermann Gunkel's* Chaoskampf *Hypothesis*, edited by John Scurlock and Richard H. Beal, 48–61. Winona Lake, Ind.: Eisenbrauns, 2013.

Seely, Paul H. "Creation Science Takes Psalm 104:6–9 Out of Context." *Perspectives on Science and Christian Faith* 51 (1999): 170–74.

———. "The Firmament and the Water Above: Part 1." *Westminster Theological Journal* 53 (1991): 227–40.

———. "The Firmament and the Water Above: Part 2." *Westminster Theological Journal* 54 (1992): 31–46.

———. "The First Four Days of Genesis in Concordist Theory and in Biblical Context." *Perspectives on Science and Christian Faith* 49 (1997): 85–95.

———. "The Geographical Meaning of 'Earth' and 'Seas' in Genesis 1:10." *Westminster Theological Journal* 59 (1997): 231–55.

———. "Noah's Flood: Its Date, Extent, and Divine Accommodation." *Westminster Theological Journal* 66 (2004): 291–311.

Selman, Martin J. " 'wr." In *NIDOTTE* 1:324–29.

Sexton, Jeremy. "Evangelicalism's Search for Chronological Gaps in Genesis 1 and 11: A Historical, Hermeneutical, and Linguistic Critique." *Journal of the Evangelical Theological Society* 61 (2018): 5–25.

Silvestru, Emil. "The Fossil Record." In *Evolution's Achilles' Heels*, edited by Robert Carter, chapter 4. Powder Springs, Ga.: Creation Ministries International, 2014. Kindle.

Skinner, John. *A Critical and Exegetical Commentary on Genesis.* 2nd ed. International Critical Commentary. 1910. Reprint, Edinburgh: T&T Clark, 1930.

Smith, Mark S. "Light in Genesis 1:3—Created or Uncreated: A Question of Priestly Mysticism?" In *Birkat Shalom: Studies in the Bible, Ancient Near Eastern Literature, and Postbiblical Judaism Presented to Shalom M. Paul on the Occasion of His Seventieth Birthday*, edited by Chaim Cohen, Victor Avigdor Hurowitz, Avi M. Hurvitz, Yochanan Muffs, Baruch J. Schwartz, and Jeffrey H. Tigay, 125–34. Winona Lake, Ind.: Eisenbrauns, 2008.

Snelling, Andrew A. *Earth's Catastrophic Past: Geology, Creation, and the Flood.* Green Forest, Ariz.: Master; Petersburg, Ky.: Answers in Genesis, 2014.

Snow, Robert E. "A Critique of the Creation Science Movement." In *Portraits of Creation: Biblical and Scientific Perspectives on the World's Formation*, by Howard J. Van Till, Robert E. Snow, John H. Stek, and Davis A. Young, 166–202. Grand Rapids: Eerdmans, 1990.

Soden, John M. "From the Dust: Creating Adam in Historical Context." *Bibliotheca Sacra* 172 (2015): 45–66.

Sparks, Kenton L. *God's Word in Human Words: An Evangelical Appropriation of Critical Biblical Scholarship.* Grand Rapids: Baker Academic, 2008.

Speiser, E. A. *Genesis.* Anchor Bible 1. New York: Doubleday, 1964.

———. "The Rivers of Paradise." In *Festschrift Johannes Friedrich Zum 65. Geburtstag Am 27. August 1958 Gewidmet*, edited by R. von Kienle, A. Moortgat, H. Otten, E. von Schuler, and W. Zamseil, 473–85. Heidelberg: Carl Winter, 1959.

Spier, J. M. *An Introduction to Christian Philosophy*. Translated by David Hugh Freeman. 2nd ed. Nutley, N.J.: Craig, 1966.

Sproul, R. C., ed. *New Geneva Study Bible: Bringing the Light of the Reformation to Scripture*. Nashville: Thomas Nelson, 1995.

———, ed. *The Reformation Study Bible: English Standard Version*. Orlando: Reformation Trust, 2015.

Spykman, Gordon J. *Reformational Theology: A New Paradigm for Doing Dogmatics*. Grand Rapids: Eerdmans, 1992.

Stadler, Rob. *The Scientific Approach to Evolution*. Self-published, CreateSpace, 2016.

Steinmann, Andrew E. "Gaps in the Genealogies in Genesis 5 and 11?" *Bibliotheca Sacra* 174 (2017): 141–58.

———. *Genesis: An Introduction and Commentary*. Tyndale Old Testament Commentaries. Downers Grove, Ill.: IVP Academic, 2019.

———. "Night and Day, Evening and Morning." *The Bible Translator* 62 (2011): 145–50.

———. "A Note on the Refrain in Genesis 1: Evening, Morning, and Day as a Chronological Summary." *Journal for the Evangelical Study of the Old Testament* 5 (2016–2017): 125–40.

———. "אחד as an Ordinal Number and the Meaning of Genesis 1:5." *Journal of the Evangelical Theological Society* 45 (2002): 577–84.

Stek, John H. "What Says the Scripture?" In *Portraits of Creation: Biblical and Scientific Perspectives on the World's Formation*, by Howard J. Van Till, Robert E. Snow, John H. Stek, and Davis A. Young, 203–65. Grand Rapids: Eerdmans, 1990.

Sterchi, David A. "Does Genesis 1 Provide a Chronological Sequence?" *Journal of the Evangelical Theological Society* 39 (1996): 529–36.

Stone, Nida. "The Four Rivers That Flowed from Eden." In *Beyond Eden: The Biblical Story of Paradise (Genesis 2–3) and Its Reception History*, edited by Konrad Schmid and Riedweg Christoph, 227–50. Tübingen: Mohr Siebeck, 2008.

Stonehouse, Ned B. *J. Gresham Machen: A Biographical Memoir*. Grand Rapids: Eerdmans, 1954.

Stordalen, Terje. *Echoes of Eden: Genesis 2–3 and Symbolism of the Eden Garden in Biblical Hebrew Literature*. Contributions to Biblical Exegesis and Theology. Leuven: Peeters, 2000.

———. "Genesis 2,4: Restudying a *Locus Classicus*." *Zeitschrift für die alttestamentliche Wissenschaft* 104 (1992): 163–77.

Stroes, H. R. "Does the Day Begin in the Evening or in the Morning?" *Vetus Testamentum* 16 (1966): 460–75.

Swanson, James A. *Dictionary of Biblical Languages with Semantic Domains: Hebrew (Old Testament)*. Oak Harbor, Wash.: Logos Research Systems, 1997.

Tate, Marvin E. *Psalms 51–100*. Word Biblical Commentary. Waco, Tex.: Word, 1990.

Teilhard de Chardin, Pierre. *The Phenomenon of Man*. London: Collins, 1970.

Tenev, T. G., J. Baumgardner, and M. F. Horstemeyer. "A Solution for the Distant Starlight Problem Using Creation Time Coordinates." In *Proceedings of the Eighth International Conference on Creationism*, edited by J. H. Whitmore, 82–94. Pittsburgh: Creation Science Fellowship, 2018.

te Velde, Dolf, ed. *Synopsis Purioris Theologiae. Synopsis of a Purer Theology. Latin Text and English Translation*. Translated by Riemer A. Faber. Vol. 1. Studies in Medieval and Reformation Traditions. Leiden: Brill, 2015.

Thompson, Mark D. "Biblical Interpretation in the Works of Martin Luther." In *A History of Biblical Interpretation*, vol. 2, *The Medieval through the Reformation Periods*, edited by Alan J. Hauser and Duane F. Watson, 299–318. Grand Rapids: Eerdmans, 2009.

———. "The Generous Gift of a Gracious Father: Toward a Theological Account of the Clarity of Scripture." In *The Enduring Authority of the Christian Scriptures*, edited by D. A. Carson, 615–43. Grand Rapids: Eerdmans, 2016.

Thomson, Keith Stewart. "Marginalia: The Meanings of Evolution." *American Scientist* 70 (1982): 529–31.

Throntveit, Mark A. "Are the Events in the Genesis Creation Account Set Forth in Chronological Order? No." In *The Genesis Debate: Persistent Questions about Creation and the Flood*, edited by Ronald F. Youngblood, 36–55. Grand Rapids: Baker, 1990.

Timmer, Daniel C. *Creation, Tabernacle, and Sabbath*. Forschungen zur Religion und Literatur des Alten und Neuen Testaments. Göttingen: Vandenhoeck & Ruprecht, 2009.

Töyräänvuori, Joanna. "The Northwest Semitic Conflict Myth and Egyptian Sources from the Middle and New Kingdoms." In *Creation and Chaos: A Reconsideration of Hermann Gunkel's Chaoskampf Hypothesis*, edited by John Scurlock and Richard H. Beal, 112–26. Winona Lake, Ind.: Eisenbrauns, 2013.

Troost, Andree. *What Is Reformational Philosophy? An Introduction to the Cosmonomic Philosophy of Herman Dooyeweerd*. Edited by Harry Van Dyke. Translated by Antony Runia. N.p.: Paideia, 2012.

Tsumura, David Toshio. *Creation and Destruction: A Reappraisal of the Chaoskampf Theory in the Old Testament*. Winona Lake, Ind.: Eisenbrauns, 2005.

———. *The First Book of Samuel*. New International Commentary on the Old Testament. Grand Rapids: Eerdmans, 2007.

———. "Genesis and Ancient Near Eastern Stories of Creation and Flood: An Introduction." In Hess and Tsumura, *"I Studied Inscriptions,"* 27–57.

———. Review of *Genesis 1 as Ancient Cosmology*, by John H. Walton. *Journal of the American Oriental Society* 135 (2015): 353–55.

Turretin, Francis. *Institutes of Elenctic Theology*. Edited by James T. Dennison Jr. Translated by George Musgrave Giger. 3 vols. Phillipsburg, N.J.: P&R, 1992.

Unger, Merrill F. *Archaeology and the Old Testament*. Grand Rapids: Zondervan, 1954.

Van Bemmelen, Peter M. "Divine Accommodation and Biblical Creation: Calvin vs. McGrath." *Andrews University Seminary Studies* 39 (2001): 109–16.

Van Dam, Cornelis. "Duidelijke taal. De boodschap van de hemelen volgens Psalm 19:5a." In *Een sprekend begin: opstellen aangeboden aan Prof. Drs. H. M. Ohmann*, edited by R. ter Beek, E. Brink, C. van Dam, and G. Kwakkel, 86–93. Kampen: Van den Berg, 1993.

———. "How Does God Reveal Himself in His Works and Word?" *Clarion* 41 (1992): 154–56, 179–81, 201–2.

———. "Interpreting Historical Narrative: Truth Claim, Truth Value, and Historicity." In *Correctly Handling the Word of Truth: Reformed Hermeneutics Today*, edited by Mees te Veld and Gerhard H. Visscher, 83–115. Eugene, Ore.: Wipf & Stock, 2014.

———. "A Lesson from Galileo's Trial." *Clarion* 65 (2016): 90–92.

van Delden, J. A. *Schepping en Wetenschap*. Amsterdam: Buijten & Schipperheijn, 1977.

van den Belt, Henk. "Lessons from the Reformation for Hermeneutics Today." *Unio Cum Christo* 4, no. 2 (2018): 95–109.

VandenBerg, Mary L. "What General Revelation Does (and Does Not) Tell Us." *Perspectives on Science and Christian Faith* 62 (2010): 16–24.

van den Brink, Gijsbert. "Questions, Challenges, and Concerns for Original Sin." In *Finding Ourselves After Darwin: Conversations on the Image of God, Original Sin, and the Problem of Evil*, edited by Stanley P. Rosenberg, 117–29. Grand Rapids: Baker Academic, 2018.

van der Kooi, Cornelis, and Gijsbert van den Brink. *Christian Dogmatics: An Introduction*. Translated by Reinder Bruinsma with James D. Bratt. Grand Rapids: Eerdmans, 2017.

van der Meer, Jitse M., and Richard J. Oosterhoff. "The Bible, Protestantism and the Rise of Natural Science: A Response to Harrison's Thesis." *Science and Christian Belief* 21 (2009): 133–53.

———. "God, Scripture, and the Rise of Modern Science." In *Nature and Scripture in the Abrahamic Religions: Up to 1700*, edited by Jitse M. van der Meer and Scott Mandelbrote, 363–96. Brill's Series in Church History 37.2. Leiden: Brill, 2008.

van der Vaart Smit, H. W. *Bavinck's schriftbeschouwing in verband met de eerste hoofdstukken van Genesis*. Wageningen: H. Veenman, 1933.

VanDoodewaard, William. *The Quest for the Historical Adam: Genesis, Hermeneutics, and Human Origins*. Grand Rapids: Reformation Heritage Books, 2015.

van Driel, C. M. *Gewantrouwd gereformeerd: het omstreden leiderschap van neocalvinist Arie Noordtzij (1871–1944)*. ADChartasreeks. Barneveld: Vuurbaak, 2010.

VanGemeren, Willem A. "Psalms." In *The Expositor's Bible Commentary*, vol. 5, *Psalms, Proverbs, Ecclesiastes, Song of Songs*, edited by Frank E. Gaebelein, 1–880. Grand Rapids: Zondervan, 1991.

van Genderen, J., and W. H. Velema. *Concise Reformed Dogmatics*. Translated by Gerrit Bilkes and Ed M. van der Maas. Phillipsburg, N.J.: P&R, 2008.

Van Leeuwen, Raymond C. "*br'* I." In *NIDOTTE* 1:728–35.

VanMaaren, John. "The Adam-Christ Typology in Paul and Its Development in the Early Church Fathers." *Tyndale Bulletin* 64 (2013): 275–97.

Vannoy, J. Robert. "Divine Revelation and History in the Old Testament." In *Interpretation and History: Essays in Honour of Allan A. MacRae*, edited by R. Laird Harris, Swee-Hwa Quek, and J. Robert Vannoy, 67–74. Singapore: Christian Life, 1986.

Van Raalte, Theodore G. "Another Wax Nose? Accommodation in Divine Revelation." In *Correctly Handling the Word of Truth: Reformed Hermeneutics Today*, edited by Mees te Velde and Gerhard H. Visscher, 226–51. Eugene, Ore.: Wipf & Stock, 2014.

van Selms, A. *Genesis*. 2 vols. 5th ed. De prediking van het Oude Testament. Nijkerk: Callenbach, 1989.

Van Til, Cornelius. "Bavinck the Theologian: A Review Article." *Westminster Theological Journal* 24 (1961): 48–65.

———. *Christian-Theistic Evidences*. Phillipsburg, N.J.: Presbyterian and Reformed, 1978.

Van Til, Nick. "Dooyeweerd's 'History' and the Historian." *Pro Rege* 2, no. 2 (December 1973): 7–15.

Van Till, Howard J. *The Fourth Day*. Grand Rapids: Eerdmans, 1986.

———. "From Calvinism to Freethought: The Road Less Traveled." Lecture presented at the Center for Inquiry, Grand Rapids, Mich., May 24, 2006. https://cfimichigan.org/event/from-calvinism-to-freethought-the-road -less-traveled/.

Van Vliet, Jason. "The Two Books Debate. What If Scripture and Science Seem to Say Different Things?" In *Correctly Handling the Word of Truth: Reformed Hermeneutics Today*, edited by Mees te Velde and Gerhard H. Visscher, 1–16. Eugene, Ore.: Wipf & Stock, 2014.

van Wolde, Ellen. "Semantics and the Semantics of ברא: A Rejoinder to the Arguments Advanced by B. Becking and M. Korpel." *Journal of Hebrew Scriptures* 11, no. 9 (2011): 1–39.

———. "Separation and Creation in Genesis 1 and Psalm 104, a Continuation of the Discussion of the Verb ברא." *Vetus Testamentum* 67 (2017): 611–47.

———. "Why the Verb ברא Does Not Mean 'to Create' in Genesis 1.1–2.4a." *Journal for the Study of the Old Testament* 34 (2009): 3–23.

Vaughan, Curtis, ed. *The Old Testament Books of Poetry from 26 Translations*. Grand Rapids: Zondervan, 1973.

Venema, Cornelis P. *The Promise of the Future*. Edinburgh: Banner of Truth, 2000.

Venema, Dennis R. "Evolution, Biological." In *DCS*, 226–28.

———. "Genesis and the Genome: Genomics Evidence for Human-Ape Common Ancestry and Ancestral Hominid Population Sizes." *Perspectives on Science and Christian Faith* 62 (2010): 166–78.

Versteeg, J. P. *Is Adam a "Teaching Model" in the New Testament?* Translated by R. B. Gaffin Jr. Nutley, N.J.: Presbyterian and Reformed, 1978.

Visee, G. *Onderwezen in het koninkrijk der hemelen*. Kampen: Van den Berg, 1979.

Visscher, James. "Bavinck on Creation." In *Living Waters from Ancient Springs: Essays in Honor of Cornelis Van Dam*, edited by Jason Van Vliet, 135–51. Eugene, Ore.: Pickwick, 2011.

Visser, Rob P. W. "Dutch Calvinists and Darwinism, 1900–1960." In *Nature and Scripture in the Abrahamic Religions: 1700–Present*, edited by Jitse M. van der Meer and Scott Mandelbrote, 293–315. Brill's Series in Church History 37.2. Leiden: Brill, 2008.

von Soden, Wolfram. *The Ancient Orient: An Introduction to the Study of the Ancient Near East*. Translated by Donald G. Schley. Grand Rapids: Eerdmans, 1994.

Vos, Geerhardus. *Biblical Theology: Old and New Testaments*. Grand Rapids: Eerdmans, 1954.

———. *Reformed Dogmatics*. Translated and edited by Richard B. Gaffin Jr. Associate editors Kim Batteau and John R. de Witt, with Daan van der Kraan, Harry Boonstra, Annemie Godbehere, Roelof van Lijken, Jonathan Pater, and Allan Janssen. 5 vols. Bellingham, Wash.: Lexham, 2012–2016.

Walker, Tasman. "The Geologic Record." In *Evolution's Achilles' Heels*, edited by Robert Carter, chapter 5. Powder Springs, Ga.: Creation Ministries International, 2014. Kindle.

Wallace, Howard N. *The Eden Narrative*. Harvard Semitic Monographs 32. Atlanta: Scholars Press, 1985.

Waltke, Bruce K. *The Book of Proverbs: Chapters 1–15*. New International Commentary on the Old Testament. Grand Rapids: Eerdmans, 2004.

———. "The Creation Account in Genesis 1:1–3. Part I: Introduction to Biblical Cosmology." *Bibliotheca Sacra* 132 (1975): 25–36.

———. "The Creation Account in Genesis 1:1–3. Part II: The Restitution Theory." *Bibliotheca Sacra* 132 (1975): 136–44.

———. "The Creation Account in Genesis 1:1–3. Part III: The Initial Chaos Theory and the Precreation Chaos Theory." *Bibliotheca Sacra* 132 (1975): 216–28.

———. "The Creation Account in Genesis 1:1–3. Part IV: The Theology of Genesis 1." *Bibliotheca Sacra* 132 (1975): 327–34.

———. "The Literary Genre of Genesis, Chapter One." *Crux* 27, no. 4 (1991): 2–10.

———. "Myth, History, and the Bible." In *The Enduring Authority of the Christian Scriptures*, edited by D. A. Carson, 542–76. Grand Rapids: Eerdmans, 2016.

Waltke, Bruce K., with Cathi J. Fredricks. *Genesis: A Commentary*. Grand Rapids: Zondervan, 2001.

Waltke, Bruce K., with Charles Yu. *An Old Testament Theology: An Exegetical, Canonical, and Thematic Approach*. Grand Rapids: Zondervan, 2007.

Walton, John H. *Genesis 1 as Ancient Cosmology*. Winona Lake, Ind.: Eisenbrauns, 2011.

———. *The Lost World of Adam and Eve: Genesis 2–3 and the Human Origins Debate*. With a contribution by N. T. Wright. Downers Grove, Ill.: IVP Academic, 2015.

———. *The Lost World of Genesis One: Ancient Cosmology and the Origins Debate*. Downers Grove, Ill.: IVP Academic, 2009.

———. "Reading Genesis 1 as Ancient Cosmology." In J. Daryl Charles, *Reading Genesis 1–2*, 141–69.

Walton, John H., and D. Brent Sandy. *The Lost World of Scripture*. Downers Grove, Ill.: IVP Academic, 2013.

Ward, Rowland. Review of *The Bible, Protestantism, and the Rise of Natural Science*, by Peter Harrison. *Reformed Theological Review* 58, no. 3 (1999): 168–69.

Wardlaw, Terrance Randall, Jr. "The Meaning of בָּרָא in Genesis 1:1–2:3." *Vetus Testamentum* 64 (2014): 502–13.

———. "The Significance of Creation in the Book of Isaiah." *Journal of the Evangelical Theological Society* 59 (2016): 449–71.

Warfield, Benjamin B. *B. B. Warfield—Evolution, Science, and Scripture: Selected Writings*. Edited by Mark A. Noll and David N. Livingstone. Grand Rapids: Baker Books, 2000.

———. "Calvin's Doctrine of the Creation." *Princeton Theological Review* 13 (1915): 190–255.

———. "Charles Darwin's Religious Life: A Sketch in Spiritual Biography." *The Presbyterian Review* 9 (1888): 569–601.

———. "Hosea 6.7: Adam or Man?" In *Selected Shorter Writings of Benjamin B. Warfield*, edited by John E. Meeter, 1:116–29. Nutley, N.J.: Presbyterian and Reformed, 1970.

———. *Studies in Theology*. 1932. Reprint, Edinburgh: Banner of Truth, 1988.

Waters, Guy Prentiss. "Theistic Evolution Is Incompatible with the Teachings of the New Testament." In Moreland et al., *Theistic Evolution*, 879–926.

Watson, Francis. "Genesis Before Darwin: Why Scripture Needed Liberation from Science." In *Reading Genesis After Darwin*, edited by Stephen C. Barton and David Wilkinson, 23–37. New York: Oxford University Press, 2009.

Watson, Rebecca S. *Chaos Uncreated: A Reassessment of the Theme of "Chaos" in the Hebrew Bible*. Beihefte zur Zeitschrift für die alttestamentliche Wissenschaft. Berlin: De Gruyter, 2005.

Weeks, Noel K. "The Ambiguity of Biblical 'Background.'" *Westminster Theological Journal* 72 (2010): 219–36.

———. "The Bible and the 'Universal' Ancient World: A Critique of John Walton." *Westminster Theological Journal* 78 (2016): 1–28.

———. "Cosmology in Historical Context." *Westminster Theological Journal* 68 (2006): 283–93.

———. "The Hermeneutical Problem of Genesis 1–11." *Themelios* 4 (1978): 12–19.

———. *The Sufficiency of Scripture*. Edinburgh: Banner of Truth, 1988.

Weikart, Richard. *From Darwin to Hitler: Evolutionary Ethics, Eugenics, and Racism in Germany*. New York: Palgrave Macmillan, 2004.

Weinfeld, Moshe. "Sabbath, Temple, and the Enthronement of the Lord—the Problem of the Sitz im Leben of Genesis 1:1–2:3." In *Mélanges bibliques et orentaux en l'honneur de M. Henri Cazelles*, edited by A. Caquot and M. Delcor, 501–12. Alter Orient und Altest Testament 212. Neukirchen-Vluyn: Neukirchener, 1981.

Weiser, Artur. *The Psalms*. Old Testament Library. Philadelphia: Westminster, 1962.

Wenham, Gordon J. *Genesis 1–15*. Word Biblical Commentary. Waco, Tex.: Word, 1987.

———. "Sanctuary Symbolism in the Garden of Eden Story." In *"I Studied Inscriptions,"* 399–404.

West, John G. "Are Young People Losing Their Faith Because of Science?" Discovery Institute, 2013. https://www.discovery.org/m/2019/04/AreYoungPeopleLosingTheirFaith.pdf.

———. *Darwin Day in America: How Our Politics and Culture Have Been Dehumanized in the Name of Science*. Wilmington, Del.: Intercollegiate Studies Institute, 2014.

———. *Darwin's Corrosive Idea: The Impact of Evolution on Attitudes about Faith, Ethics, and Human Uniqueness*. Seattle: Discovery Institute, 2016.

Westermann, Claus. *Genesis 1–11*. Translated by John J. Scullion. Minneapolis: Augsburg, 1984.

———. *Isaiah 40–66*. Translated by David M. G. Stalker. Old Testament Library. Philadelphia: Westminster, 1969.

Wevers, John William. *Notes on the Greek Text of Genesis*. Septuagint and Cognate Studies 35. Atlanta: Scholars Press, 1993.

Whitcomb, John C., Jr. "Biblical Inerrancy and the Double-Revelation Theory." *Grace Journal* 4, no. 1 (1963): 4–17.

———. "The Science of Historical Geology in the Light of the Biblical Doctrine of Mature Creation." *Westminster Theological Journal* 36 (1973): 65–77.

Whitehouse, Owen C. "Cosmogony." In *A Dictionary of the Bible*, edited by James Hastings, 1:501–7. New York: Charles Scribner's, 1908.

Wieland, Carl. "Editorial: 'But the Bible's Not a Science Textbook, Is It?'" *Creation* 22, no. 2 (March-May 2000): 4.

Wiker, Benjamin. *Moral Darwinism: How We Became Hedonists*. Downers Grove, Ill.: InterVarsity, 2002.

"William Provine, RIP: Noble in His Honesty." *Evolution News and Science Today*. September 3, 2015. https://evolutionnews.org/2015/09/william_provine/.

Williams, Robert Charles. "Scientific Creationism: An Exegesis for a Religious Doctrine." *American Anthropologist* 85 (1983): 92–102.

Williams, Ronald J. *Hebrew Syntax: An Outline*. 3rd ed. Revised and expanded by John C. Beckman. Toronto: University of Toronto Press, 2007.

Williamson, G. I. "Some Thoughts on Creation." *Ordained Servant* 9 (2000): 24–26.

Wise, Kurt P. *Faith, Form, and Time: What the Bible Teaches and Science Confirms about Creation and the Age of the Universe*. Nashville: B&H, 2002.

Wiseman, P. J. *Clues to Creation in Genesis*. Edited by Donald J. Wiseman. 1936–48. Reprint, London: Marshall, Morgan & Scott, 1977.

Wolfson, H. A. "The Veracity of Scripture in Philo, Halevi, Maimonides and Spinoza." In *Alexander Marx Jubilee Volume*, edited by Saul Lieberman, 603–30. New York: Jewish Theological Seminary of America, 1950.

Wolters, Albert M. "Creation as Separation: A Proposed Link Between Bible and Theory." In *Facets of Faith and Science*, edited by Jitse van der Meer, vol. 4, *Interpreting God's Action in the World*, 347–52. Lanham, Md.: University Press of America, 1996.

———. *Creation Regained: Biblical Basics for a Reformational Worldview*. 2nd ed. Grand Rapids: Eerdmans, 2005.

———. "What is to Be Done...Toward a Neocalvinist Agenda?" *Comment*, December 2005, 36–43.

Wolters, A., D. Holwerda, D. Ratzsch, J. DeKoning, A. Dragt, R. Maatman, G. Spykman, and R. C. Van Leeuwen. "Report 28 Committee on Creation and Science." In *Agenda for Synod 1991*, 367–433. Grand Rapids: Christian Reformed Church in North America, 1991.

Wright, G. Ernest. *The Old Testament Against Its Environment*. Studies in Biblical Theology 2. London: SCM, 1950.

Yamauchi, Edwin M. *Africa and the Bible*. Grand Rapids: Baker Academic, 2004.

Young, Davis A. *John Calvin and the Natural World*. Lanham, Md.: University Press of America, 2007.

———. "The Reception of Geology in the Dutch Reformed Tradition: The Case of Herman Bavinck (1854–1921)." In *Geology and Religion: A History of Harmony and Hostility*, edited by Martina Kölbl-Ebert, 289–300. London: The Geological Society, 2009.

———. "Where Are We?" In *Portraits of Creation: Biblical and Scientific Perspectives on the World's Formation*, by Howard J. Van Till, Robert E. Snow, John H. Stek, and Davis A. Young, 1–12. Grand Rapids: Eerdmans, 1990.

Young, Davis A., and Ralph F. Stearley. *The Bible, Rocks and Time: Geological Evidence for the Age of the Earth*. Downers Grove, Ill.: IVP Academic, 2008.

Young, Edward J. *The Book of Isaiah*. 3 vols. New International Commentary on the Old Testament. Grand Rapids: Eerdmans, 1965–1972.

———. "Creation." In *The Encyclopedia of Christianity*, edited by Philip E. Hughes, 3:238–45. Marshallton, Del.: National Foundation for Christian Education, 1964–1972.

———. *In the Beginning: Genesis 1–3 and the Authority of Scripture*. Edinburgh: Banner of Truth, 1984.

———. *An Introduction to the Old Testament*. Rev. ed. Grand Rapids: Eerdmans, 1964.

———. *The Prophecy of Daniel*. Grand Rapids: Eerdmans, 1949.

———. *Studies in Genesis One*. Philadelphia: Presbyterian and Reformed, 1964.

———. *The Study of Old Testament Theology Today*. London: James Clarke, 1958.

Younker, Randall W., and Richard M. Davidson. "The Myth of the Solid Heavenly Dome." In Gerald A. Klingbeil, *Genesis Creation Account*, 31–56.

Zaspel, Fred G. "Additional Note: B. B. Warfield Did Not Endorse Theistic Evolution as It Is Understood Today." In Moreland et al., *Theistic Evolution*, 953–72.

———. "B. B. Warfield on Creation and Evolution." *Themelios* 35 (2010): 198–211.

———. "Princeton and Evolution." *The Confessional Presbyterian* 8 (2012): 91–98.

Subject Index